MW00779479

A Genealogy of Terrorism

Using India as a case study, Joseph McQuade demonstrates how the modern concept of terrorism was shaped by colonial emergency laws dating back into the nineteenth and early twentieth centuries. Beginning with the 'thugs', 'pirates', and 'fanatics' of the nineteenth century, McQuade traces the emerging and novel legal category of 'the terrorist' in early twentieth-century colonial law, ending with an examination of the first international law to target global terrorism in the 1930s. Drawing on a wide range of archival research and a detailed empirical study of evolving emergency laws in British India, he argues that the idea of terrorism emerged as a deliberate strategy by officials seeking to depoliticize the actions of anti-colonial revolutionaries, and that many of the ideas embedded in this colonial legislation continue to shape contemporary understandings of terrorism today.

Joseph McQuade is the RCL Postdoctoral Fellow at the University of Toronto's Asian Institute.

A Genealogy of Terrorism

Colonial Law and the Origins of an Idea

Joseph McQuade
University of Toronto

CAMBRIDGE
UNIVERSITY PRESS

University Printing House, Cambridge CB2 8BS, United Kingdom

One Liberty Plaza, 20th Floor, New York, NY 10006, USA

477 Williamstown Road, Port Melbourne, VIC 3207, Australia

314–321, 3rd Floor, Plot 3, Splendor Forum, Jasola District Centre,
New Delhi – 110025, India

79 Anson Road, #06-04/06, Singapore 079906

Cambridge University Press is part of the University of Cambridge.

It furthers the University's mission by disseminating knowledge in the pursuit of education, learning, and research at the highest international levels of excellence.

www.cambridge.org
Information on this title: www.cambridge.org/9781108842150
DOI: 10.1017/9781108896238

First published 2021

A catalogue record for this publication is available from the British Library.

ISBN 978-1-108-84215-0 Hardback

For Emily

It is a principle of the law of nations, recognized I believe by every civilized people, that assassins by profession shall find in no country a sanctuary, but shall every where be delivered up to the Sovereign who reclaims them and in whose dominions they have perpetrated their crimes; and as the crimes of these assassins are never confined to the country in which they reside, and as every country in India must now be considered as under the protection of the Supreme Government in some relation or other, that Government very properly undertook the duty which seemed to be imposed upon it by the laws of humanity and of nations, and determined to reclaim them from every State in which they might seek shelter.

– W. H. Sleeman, *Ramaseeana; or A vocabulary of the peculiar language used by the thugs* (Calcutta: G. H. Huttman, Military Orphan Press, 1836), pp. 48–9.

Authority is, it seems, at one all the world over, and we must recognize that there is now no longer the least illogical loophole of escape for a fleeing man on this earth or in its waters; it is merely a question of which uniform shall arrest him. In old days there was always some leakage, some chunk for escape between the machineries of different nationalities. ... But the nets are drawn closer now ... daily the elaborate international system for maintaining the status quo becomes more perfect, and from it there is no appeal. The fugitive – 'assassin', or 'patriot', 'avatar' or that weird monster the 'anarchist' of the newspapers, whatever he may be ... can find no corner of the globe to shelter him, and the only doubt is under which precise code of regulations he shall be judged, punished, and put away.

– Josiah Wedgwood, *Essays and Adventures of a Labour M.P.* (London: George Allen & Unwin Ltd, 1924), p. 153

The search is underway for those who are behind these evil acts. I've directed the full resources of our intelligence and law enforcement communities to find those responsible and to bring them to justice. We will make no distinction between the terrorists who committed these acts and those who harbor them. ... America and our friends and allies join with all those who want peace and security in the world, and we stand together to win the war against terrorism.

– George W. Bush, Statement by the President in his address to the nation, 11 September 2001

Contents

Figures

Acknowledgements

Throughout the process of researching and writing this book, I have accumulated a wide range of debts, both intellectual and personal. This project has evolved over the better part of a tumultuous decade, and it would be impossible to credit everyone who helped shape my ideas along the way. Needless to say, any errors or omissions are my own.

During my time at Cambridge University, where the scaffolding of this project took shape, Tim Harper was a generous and insightful supervisor who improved my work in numerous ways. My PhD examiners, Clare Anderson and Saul Dubow, provided rigorous feedback that was instrumental in helping me adapt a doctoral dissertation into a book. I would also like to thank my advisor, Alison Bashford, for helping me think through the international dimensions of the project, and the anonymous reviewers at Cambridge University Press for helping me to better understand my own arguments. Shruti Kapila was a great help in the early iterations of this work and provided incisive commentary that steered the research in productive directions. Special thanks are owed to Kim Wagner for reading the manuscript at multiple stages and providing patient and frank advice that has undoubtedly made this a far better book than it would otherwise have been.

For helpful feedback on earlier drafts of this work, I would like to thank Sandra den Otter, Christopher Andrew, Susan Pedersen, Surabhi Ranganathan, Devyani Gupta, and Upendra Baxi. Amitava Chowdhury has seen this research develop since its inception and has been an irreplaceable element in my intellectual development over the past eight years. If it wasn't for his encouragement, faith, and friendship at various stages throughout this process, this book might never have been completed. I am also thankful to the participants of numerous workshops, conferences, and conversations who provided advice and inspiration that helped strengthen the final product, including Nonica Datta, Deanna Heath, Lauren Benton, Durba Ghosh, Bhavani Raman, Mark Condos, Katherine Bruce-Lockhart, Ishan Mukherjee, and Partha Shil, as well as

Christopher Bayly and Keith Jeffery, both of whom are sadly no longer with us. I would also like to thank Michael Sugarman for the countless ideas shared over coffee and cardamom buns and Sophie-Jung Kim for always being a provocative interlocutor and confidante. As a sounding board, advisor, travel companion, and roommate, Alastair McClure is unmatched. Although there is no space to mention them all by name, a wide-ranging network of friends, teachers, and colleagues have enriched this experience in more ways than I can count.

I am grateful to scholars at the University of Toronto for first introducing me to the academic study of South Asia as an undergraduate, as well as providing me with an intellectual home while I shepherded this project into completion during two postdoctoral fellowships. The opportunity to work with bright and enthusiastic students while teaching in the Contemporary Asian Studies program has been as instructive for me as I hope it was for them. I am especially appreciative of my Research Assistant, Bonnie Lao, for her help fine-tuning the index. Colleagues including Christoph Emmrich, Beatrice Jauregui, Rachel Silvey, and Shannon Garden-Smith have helped make my years here a genuine delight. A special word is reserved for my mentor, Ritu Birla, who is always a source of equal parts wisdom and humour. Working with Robert Baines and several dozen talented interns as Editor-in-Chief at the NATO Association of Canada has helped me refine my own writing and, I hope, improved the readability of this text.

This research would simply not have been possible without the generous funding provided by the Gates Cambridge Trust. I would also like to thank the Trust staff for reliable and prompt responses to all matters, whether logistical, financial, or otherwise. Fellowships at the University of Toronto's Asian Institute, one funded by the Social Science and Humanities Research Council of Canada and one by the Richard Charles Lee Asian Pathways Research Lab, gave me the freedom and breathing room to complete this project. Other sources of funding over the course of this research include travel grants from Trinity Hall and from the Smuts Memorial Fund and a foreign language instruction grant from the Schools of Arts & Humanities and Humanities & Social Sciences at the University of Cambridge. The Master's research that provided the initial spark for this dissertation was funded by the Social Science and Humanities Research Council of Canada.

The global scope of this research required visits to archives around the world, where I encountered helpful and informative staff who made this project possible. First and foremost, Kevin Greenbank, Rachel Rowe, and Barbara Roe at the Centre for South Asian Studies, Cambridge always provided cheerful assistance with any inquiry, no matter how big or small. The staff at the National Library, Kolkata, helped me track down an out of print collection of the writings of Rash Behari Bose, which I have not seen cited anywhere else. Sugata Bose and Krishna Bose from the Netaji Research Bureau were prompt and gracious in responding to my inquiries. Jacques Oberson and his colleagues at the League of Nations Archives in Geneva provided such efficient guidance that what was intended as a preliminary one week reconnaissance trip ended up furnishing far more useful material than I anticipated. Naoya Inaba from Waseda University Library helped me track down the full collection of *New Asia* volumes, justifying my trip to Tokyo. Thanks are also due to the many archivists and librarians who responded to countless inquiries at the British Library, National Archives, Kew, and the National Archives of India, as well as the Jawaharlal Nehru Memorial Museum and Library, the University of Toronto Libraries, and the National Archives of Singapore. I am grateful to Shachi Chotia for her patient attempts to teach me Hindi, and to her family for their hospitality and kindness during my time in Jaipur. I am confident I speak for all of her students when I say that she is sorely missed. The superb editorial team at Cambridge University Press, especially Lucy Rhymer, Emily Sharp, and Neena Maheen, made sure that my publishing experience was as smooth and stress-free as possible. I also thank Beth Morel for an excellent job as copy-editor. A section of Chapter 5 providing context for India's joining of the League of Nations first appeared in the *Journal of Imperial and Commonwealth History*. I am grateful to the publishers of this journal for giving me permission to republish this section and to the *Journal of World History* for permission to republish some of the material on Rash Behari Bose.

On a personal note, I would like to thank my father for sharing with me his passion for history through a childhood filled with museum visits and books about the pharaohs. I appreciate that my sister Katherine visited me in England on multiple occasions during my time abroad. Family, both old and new, have provided cheer and encouragement throughout this process, and I am pleased to share the result with them all. Regrettably, two of the most important people in this process will never see the finished book. My grandfather, Richard Jennings, whose stories of the past started me down this path, recently passed away just months short of his hundredth birthday. It saddens me deeply that my mother, an avid reader who always encouraged me to write, will never have an opportunity to add this book to her impressive list.

My final and deepest thanks go to Emily, my partner in all things, who, along with our dog Finnegan, has been my staunchest supporter and closest companion during this process. For accompanying me to archives around the world when she could, tolerating my extended absences when she could not, and her heroic efforts to expunge the passive voice from my writing, I dedicate this book to her.

Abbreviations

BL	British Library
CID	Criminal Investigation Department
CRT	Comité Répression Internationale du Terrorisme
CUL	Cambridge University Library
HC	House of Commons
HL	House of Lords
IOR	Indian Office Records, British Library
LNA	League of Nations Archives, Geneva
NAI	National Archives of India, New Delhi
NLI	National Library of India, Kolkata
PRO	Public Records Office, Kew
SAAA	Sri Aurobindo Ashram Archives
SAADA	South Asian American Digital Archive

Introduction
The Colonial Prose of Counterterrorism

On 16 March 2011, an unmanned drone killed around forty people in Datta Khel, a town in Pakistan's rural region of North Waziristan. While initial reports claimed that the strike had been directed against a gathering of militants, it has since come to light that the meeting was in fact a tribal *jirga*, a traditional community gathering convened, in this case, to settle a dispute regarding ownership of a local chromite mine.[1] Even assuming that members of the Taliban were present, as some accounts do seem to confirm, the bulk of those killed in the attack were tribal elders, many of whom had previously provided a bulwark against radicalization among their communities.[2] Unlike most earlier drone attacks,[3] the Datta Khel strike immediately attracted the strong criticism of Pakistan's foreign ministry, who called it 'a flagrant violation of all humanitarian rules and norms'. An unnamed US official dismissed the criticism, telling the *Wall Street Journal*, 'These guys were terrorists, not the local men's glee club.'[4]

Although the Datta Khel drone strike is a particularly controversial example, there have been thousands of deaths caused by unmanned aircraft in the past two decades throughout the remote regions of a growing list of Muslim-majority countries that include Afghanistan, Pakistan, Yemen, and Somalia.[5] Human rights groups and investigative journalists have roundly condemned the uncounted civilian casualties produced by this aerial bombardment. Despite a clinical language of 'targeted', 'surgical', or 'precision' strikes, the civilian death toll is easily

[1] Salman Masood and Pir Zubair Shah, 'C.I.A. Drone Kills Civilians in Pakistan', *The New York Times* (17 March 2011).

[2] Chris Woods, 'Covert Drone Strikes and the Fiction of Zero Civilian Casualties', in Mike Aaronson et al., *Precision Strike Warfare and International Intervention: Strategic, Ethico-Legal and Decisional Implications* (London: Routledge, 2015), pp. 99–101.

[3] See, for example, Mark Mazzetti, *The Way of the Knife: The CIA, a Secret Army, and a War at the Ends of the Earth* (New York: Penguin Books, 2014), pp. 108–9.

[4] Tom Wright and Rehmat Mehsud, 'Pakistan Slams U.S. Drone Strike', *The Wall Street Journal* (18 March 2011).

[5] As of 2015, the estimate was 2,800 or more. See Woods, 'Covert Drone Strikes', p. 95.

in the hundreds and likely higher. In the first three years of Barack Obama's presidency alone, sixty-four children died as a direct result of these strikes.[6] This 'Secret War' is part of the 'Global War on Terror' that began as a response to the horrific attacks carried out by Al Qaeda against America on 11 September 2001. Originating under President George W. Bush, drone strikes increased in frequency during the Obama administration and have expanded further under the instructions of President Trump, who has rolled back the safeguards finally put in place by his predecessor to track civilian casualties.[7]

Of special concern to human rights groups are so-called signature strikes, a lethal form of aerial warfare that targets unknown individuals whose behaviour is considered similar enough to that of terrorists to warrant pre-emptive assassination. In regions where terrorists are known to operate, the simple fact of being a 'military-aged male' is sometimes considered sufficient grounds for establishing guilt. This heavily critiqued extrajudicial framework makes it virtually impossible, based on publicly available data, to assess how many of the alleged 'militants' executed in this manner were actually members of extremist networks. Counterterrorism expert Naureen Shah of Amnesty International has expressed the concern that the application of 'signature strikes' risks creating a new norm in which the US government, in assuming the a priori guilt of its targets, may be creating a positive feedback loop detached from the realities on the ground.[8] How does a liberal democracy, ostensibly grounded in the rule of law and a commitment to human rights, find no contradiction in waging a covert, extrajudicial assassination program in which a person can be targeted for execution based only on patterns of behaviour or physical markers? The simple answer is that political liberalism and an extrajudicial 'state of exception' are not contradictory, but rather adhere to a mutually constitutive logic embedded in the structures of nineteenth- and twentieth-century empire.[9]

While the technology that has enabled the recent proliferation of unmanned drones is quite new, historian Priya Satia has demonstrated how the underlying philosophy is a direct legacy of colonial aerial surveillance and bombardment conducted during the 'pacification

[6] George Monbiot, 'In the U.S., Mass Child Killings Are Tragedies: In Pakistan, Mere Bug Splats', *The Guardian* (17 December 2012).

[7] Dan de Luce and Sean D. Naylor, 'Report: The Drones Are Back', *Foreign Policy* (26 March 2018).

[8] Naureen Shah, 'Drone Attacks and the Brennan Doctrine', *The Guardian* (2 May 2012).

[9] The relationship between liberalism and empire is most famously explicated in Uday Mehta, *Liberalism and Empire: A Study in Nineteenth-Century British Thought* (Chicago: University of Chicago Press, 1999).

operations' of the interwar period.[10] Then, as now, military officials regarded the north-western frontier region that separates Pakistan from Afghanistan as an 'unruly' place full of 'barbaric' cultural practices and religious 'fanaticism'.[11] Aerial bombardment carried out by Britain's Royal Air Force (RAF) in interwar Afghanistan attracted the vociferous criticism of Indian activists like Mahendra Pratap, a revolutionary Pan-Asianist who petitioned the League of Nations in 1933, calling on the international community to raise their 'pious voices against every barbarous trespass on the rights of Man'.[12]

The idea that our current global order has been shaped by, or continues to be shaped by, the processes of nineteenth and twentieth century colonialism is certainly not new. Scholars from a range of disciplines have been making this point for years, seeking to 'provincialize Europe',[13] or indeed to show that current political conditions in Afghanistan, Iraq, or Palestine constitute a 'colonial present'.[14] Perhaps the most famous of these critiques is Edward Said's seminal text on 'Orientalism', wherein he describes the 'Orient' as Europe's 'cultural contestant, and one of its deepest and most recurring images of the Other'.[15] For Said, the forms of knowledge-production established under colonialism share a direct relationship with enduring Western representations of Asia and the Middle East, a fact with obvious relevance for the current 'War on Terror'.[16] Following the US-led invasion of Iraq in 2003, a growing number of scholars have located America's – now waning – global hegemony within a deeper history of imperialism, knowledge, and power.[17] With the dramatic reappearance of Western chauvinism articulated in the Brexit

[10] Priya Satia, 'Drones: A History from the British Middle East', *Humanity: An International Journal of Human Rights, Humanitarianism, and Development* 5, no. 1 (2014), pp. 1–31.

[11] Mark Condos, 'License to Kill: The Murderous Outrages Act and the Rule of Law in Colonial India, 1867–1925', *Modern Asian Studies* 50, no. 2 (2016), pp. 479–517.

[12] Mahendra Pratap to Secretary-General of the League of Nations, 1st August 1933, LNA, R3637/6266, p. 1.

[13] Dipesh Chakrabarty, *Provincializing Europe: Postcolonial Thought and Historical Difference* (Princeton, NJ: Princeton University Press, 2000).

[14] Derek Gregory, *The Colonial Present: Afghanistan, Palestine, Iraq* (Malden, MA: Blackwell, 2004).

[15] Edward Said, *Orientalism* (New York: Vintage Books, 1979), p. 1.

[16] See Said, *Covering Islam: How the Media and the Experts Determine How We See the Rest of the World* (New York: Vintage Books, 1997). The entangled relationship between colonial knowledge and European perceptions of Islam as a 'problem' are also addressed from the standpoint of the Dutch East Indies in Dietrich Jung, '"Islam as a Problem": Dutch Religious Politics in the East Indies', *Review of Religious Research* 51, no. 3 (2010), pp. 288–301.

[17] For example, Himadeep Muppidi, *The Colonial Signs of International Relations* (New York: Columbia University Press, 2012).

campaign in the United Kingdom, the presidency of Donald Trump in the United States, and the rise of ethno-nationalist populism in Europe, this scholarship will likely continue for some time.[18] Still, such approaches require a degree of care and sophistication. As Ann Laura Stoler points out, even when one recognizes the colonial trajectories or antecedents of current power relations, the very nature of the now-popular term 'postcolonial' can create an artificial sense of distance between researchers and a colonial history that is also alive and well even in less obvious, but no less durable, manifestations.[19]

Terrorism, Security, and the State of Exception

The three quotes with which this monograph opens capture three snapshots in an evolving 'prose of counterterrorism' that traces its roots to the early nineteenth century. When Bush made his famous address to the nation following the 9/11 attacks, in which Al Qaeda operatives hijacked and weaponized four commercial airliners to devastating effect, he was drawing on a repertoire of cultural idioms, categories, and narratives that were already familiar to Western audiences. While 9/11 brought 'terrorism' into the realm of public consciousness in an unprecedented manner, the term 'terrorism' already carried with it a malleable yet intelligible set of connotations. Terrorism was evil and indiscriminate, it was something carried out by 'them' against 'us', it implied a 'barbaric' worldview, culture, or religion, and it threatened not only America but everyone who desired 'peace and security in the world'. Throughout the early 2000s, international and domestic authorities, legal experts, activists, and law enforcement operatives would discuss and debate the possibility of a universally agreed-upon definition for 'terrorism', but the basic features emphasized in Bush's speech have become remarkably widespread.[20]

Bush's invocation of 'the terrorists' as a global foe that divides the world into a Manichean order of moral certitude – 'You're either with us or you're with the terrorists' – has generally been interpreted through the theoretical framework provided by mid-twentieth-century German jurist

[18] An excellent recent addition to this field that explicitly addresses phenomena such as Brexit is Robert Gildea, *Empires of the Mind: The Colonial Past and the Politics of the Present* (Cambridge: Cambridge University Press, 2019).

[19] Ann Laura Stoler, *Duress: Imperial Durabilities in Our Times* (Durham, NC: Duke University Press, 2016), pp. 4–10.

[20] Lisa Stampnitsky, *Disciplining Terror: How Experts Invented 'Terrorism'* (Cambridge: Cambridge University Press, 2013), pp. 3–4.

Carl Schmitt.[21] For Schmitt, the central legal innovation of the early twentieth century was the attempt to outlaw war, rather than simply bracket it as previous international legal regimes sought to accomplish. This criminalization of war, accomplished through the League of Nations' desire to enforce a perpetual peace, led to the transformation from a *justum bellum* – a war between just states – to a *justa causa belli* – a just war. Within such a war, 'the asserted juridical right and moral legitimacy of one's own cause and the alleged injustice of the opponent's cause only sharpen and deepen the belligerents' hostility', according to Schmitt.[22] This in turn would lead to what Schmitt called, 'the modern transformation of penal law into social pest control',[23] particularly with regard to insurgents or partisans, who would be regarded by their very nature as unjust 'foes' unworthy of recognition under the law. Schmitt's work has proved highly influential, providing the foundation for much of the current scholarship on critical terrorism studies.[24]

We can also observe the direct influence of Schmitt's thought in the work of Italian philosopher Giorgio Agamben, who identifies the sovereign as possessing the ability to designate not only who constitutes a foe, but also who may be excluded entirely from the body-politic. According to Agamben, sovereignty reflects the ability to divest certain persons of their claim to citizenship, marking them instead as *homo sacer*, a figure of 'bare life' with no protections under human or divine law.[25] The liminal designation of 'bare life' reflects the exclusion of an individual from the juridical rights which form the basis of the liberal rule of law – a framework that can be highly useful in seeking to understand the nature of emergency measures directed against criminal categories such as terrorists, pirates, or 'thugs'. Agamben points out that the categorization of suspected terrorists as 'detainees' in Guantanamo Bay, following the

[21] Stephen Legg (ed.), *Spatiality, Sovereignty and Carl Schmitt: Geographies of the Nomos* (London: Routledge, 2011). See also Reza Aslan, *Beyond Fundamentalism: Confronting Extremism in the Age of Globalization* (New York: Random House, 2010).

[22] Carl Schmitt, *The Nomos of the Earth in the International Law of the Jus Publicum Europeaum* (New York: Telos, 2003), p. 156.

[23] Ibid., p. 124.

[24] For some of the other work on contemporary terrorism as understood through a reading of Schmitt, see Louiza Odysseos and Fabio Petito (eds.), *The International Political Thought of Carl Schmitt: Terror, Liberal War and the Crisis of Global Order* (London: Routledge, 2007), Gabriella Slomp, *Carl Schmitt and the Politics of Hostility, Violence and Terror* (Basingstoke: Palgrave Macmillan, 2009), Tarik Kochi, 'The Partisan: Carl Schmitt and Terrorism', *Law and Critique* 17, no. 3 (2006), pp. 267–95, and Stuart Elden, *Terror and Territory: The Spatial Extent of Sovereignty* (Minneapolis: University of Minnesota Press, 2009).

[25] Giorgio Agamben, *Homo Sacer: Sovereign Power and Bare Life*, trans. Daniel Heller-Roazen (Stanford, CA: Stanford University Press, 1998), p. 12.

emergency Patriot Act of 2001, placed them in a liminal space as neither prisoners of war – with attendant rights afforded by the Geneva Convention – nor as criminals, subject to the ordinary juridical procedures of US criminal law.[26]

Although different national and historical legal regimes have used diverse terms to refer to the phenomenon, the current study follows Agamben's lead in referring to emergency legal decrees that demarcate the limits of 'ordinary' judicial processes as 'states of exception'.[27] While Western legal scholars typically situate the sovereign's ability to declare an extralegal 'state of exception' within a trajectory of European jurisprudence dating back to Roman law, there are important, though inexact, parallels in ancient India. For kings of the Mauryan and Gupta periods, the wilderness lying at the edges of sovereign territory represented an exception to ordinary norms of violence and non-violence. In these contexts, state violence against forest-dwellers throughout the subcontinent was historically legitimized through a paradigm that demarcated the wilderness as a zone of 'difference'.[28] Representations of the wilderness in ancient Indian scriptures are complex, sometimes connoting a military or economic resource to the state, sometimes indicating a realm of asceticism and renunciation. Nonetheless, the designation of tribal peoples as *mlecchas* (barbarians) and the incorporation of these peoples into the fold of the state through campaigns of 'pacification', assimilation, and elimination provides an important yet distinctive source of comparison with Eurocentric accounts – like that of Agamben – that locate the original 'state of exception' within the *homo sacer* of Roman jurisprudence.[29] Substantial continuities between pre-colonial and colonial legal regimes in India, especially as reflected in the fluid and malleable 'disturbed areas' in which military law often played a mediating role, further caution against assuming that European models of exception can be mapped directly onto colonial settings.[30]

The other problem with Eurocentric genealogies of the state of exception is that they do not adequately differentiate between states of exception deployed within colonial settings and colonialism itself as the state of

[26] Agamben, *State of Exception*, trans. Kevin Attell (Chicago: University of Chicago Press, 2005), pp. 3–4.

[27] Ibid., p. 4.

[28] Upinder Singh, *Political Violence in Ancient India* (Cambridge, MA: Harvard University Press, 2017), pp. 367–459.

[29] Ibid. See also James Scott, *The Art of Not Being Governed: An Anarchist History of Upland Southeast Asia* (New Haven, CT: Yale University Press, 2009).

[30] Bhavani Raman, 'The Making of "Disturbed Areas" in Early Colonial India: Genealogies of a Jurisdiction' (unpublished paper, 27 February 2020).

exception par excellence.[31] In focusing only on Western 'domestic' settings, we can be deceived into assuming a clear division between 'ordinary' law and extralegal executive power, whereas for historian Nasser Hussain, the colonial 'jurisprudence of emergency' illustrates how 'norm and exception … function in juxtaposition'.[32] Hussain draws on Schmitt's famous definition of the sovereign as 'he who decides on the exception',[33] and asserts that while the concept of emergency has been studied, the 'indicative function of emergency as a constitutive relation between modern law and sovereignty', as formative in our understanding of modern power, has not. Instead of understanding the state of emergency as existing outside the rule of law, Hussain argues that the relationship between the rule of law and emergency is 'as intimate as it is anxious', and that within the imperial context, emergency law is to be understood as an expression of colonial sovereignty.[34] At the level of colonial law in practice, Partha Chatterjee shows how anti-colonial violence ultimately served the same function as anti-colonial non-violence, in that both forced the state to expose its own 'legal' violence through the assertion of emergency measures that violated the ostensible principles on which colonial rule rested its authority.[35] As John Pincince argues, the very notion of 'political offences', while of central importance to British metropolitan and international law, was thus wholly excluded from the prosecution of anti-colonial revolutionary activities in India, which the imperial government instead criminalized as apolitical terrorism. For Pincince, the colonial state existed in a permanent state of exception, as challenges to colonial authority revealed the precarious order of the colonial state at precisely the same time that emergency measures and increased surveillance highlighted the further criminalization of the colonial subject.[36]

Many modern states, including those governing in colonial spaces, have sought to resolve the inherent contradiction of a permanent state of exception through the paradigm of security. Operating under the Roman principle of *salus populi suprema lex* – 'The safety of the people is the highest law' – the modern state can more easily reconcile tensions

[31] Achille Mbembe, 'Necropolitics', *Public Culture* 15, no. 1 (2003), p. 24.

[32] Nasser Hussain, *Jurisprudence of Emergency: Colonialism and the Rule of Law* (Ann Arbor: University of Michigan Press, 2003), p. 20.

[33] Carl Schmitt, *Political Theology: Four Chapters on the Concept of Sovereignty*, trans. George Schwab (Cambridge, MA: MIT Press, 1985), p. 5.

[34] Hussain, *Jurisprudence of Emergency*, p. 32.

[35] Partha Chatterjee, *The Black Hole of Empire: History of a Global Practice of Power* (Princeton, NJ: Princeton University Press, 2012), pp. 289–90.

[36] John Pincince, 'De-centering Carl Schmitt: The Colonial State of Exception and the Criminalization of the Political in British India, 1905–1920', *Politica Comun* 5 (2014).

between states of exception and a rule of law by casting 'exceptional' measures as necessary for public safety.[37] The modern discourse of security is regarded by French philosopher Michel Foucault as marking a transition towards new statistics-based modes of knowledge production that give us the modern governmental techniques of social, political, and economic management. For Foucault, a key characteristic of the modern state is the replacement of the early modern relationship between sovereigns and their subjects with a new dynamic between governments and populations, a fact reflected in the transformation of modern security regimes.[38] Although Foucault's arguments provide a useful framework for understanding the discursive strategies deployed by colonial authorities in legitimizing emergency measures in the name of security, his lack of engagement with colonial history nonetheless poses a problem for any attempt to transplant Foucault's theories directly into colonial genealogies of terrorism.

In *Discipline and Punish: The Birth of the Prison*, Foucault famously argues that 'discipline' – *surveiller* in the original French – replaced older forms of punishment premised on the violation and destruction of the criminal's body.[39] But while aspects of this shift can indeed be observed in the rigid prison schedules and disciplinary regimes deployed against 'thugs' and 'terrorists' in British India – or, for that matter, in the global surveillance activities of the National Security Agency (NSA) in the current 'War on Terror' – the violation or destruction of the body of the rebel nonetheless remains an important expression of colonial power. British authorities deployed a range of techniques explicitly designed to terrorize indigenous insurgents into submission by targeting their bodies, such as sewing Muslims into pig-skins,[40] forcibly transporting Hindus across the *kala pani* of the Indian Ocean,[41] and destroying the bodies of Sikhs by blowing them from the mouths of cannons.[42] Similarly, while many contemporary terrorists are indeed processed through the

[37] Lytton to Birkenhead, 11 December 1924, MSS Eur, F 160/12, p. 43.

[38] Michel Foucault, *Security, Territory, Population: Lectures at the Collège de France, 1977–1978* (New York: Palgrave Macmillan, 2009), p. 45.

[39] Michel Foucault, *Discipline and Punish: The Birth of the Prison*, trans. Alan Sheridan (New York: Vintage Books, 1995).

[40] Chandrika Kaul, '"You Cannot Govern by Force Alone": W. H. Russell, *The Times* and the Great Rebellion', in Crispin Bates et al. (eds.), *Mutiny at the Margins: New Perspectives on the Indian Uprising of 1857*, vol. 3: *Global Perspectives* (New Delhi: Sage, 2013), pp. 18–35.

[41] Kim Wagner, *Rumours and Rebels: A New History of the Indian Uprising of 1857* (Oxford: Peter Lang, 2017), p. 36.

[42] Mark Condos, *Insecurity State: Punjab and the Making of Colonial Power in British India* (Cambridge: Cambridge University Press, 2017), pp. 103–39.

disciplinary apparatus of a global surveillance state, others are subjected to measures that mark them as outliers to Foucault's framework. When we think of the humiliation and sexual abuse of detainees in Abu Ghraib,[43] the deliberate desecration of Taliban corpses by American soldiers in Afghanistan,[44] or the obliteration of suspected militants through remote drone strikes, we can observe a punitive response at odds with Foucault's assumptions regarding the bureaucratized and rational disciplinary techniques of the modern state.

Genealogies of Terrorism

Although most scholars acknowledge that terrorism has a long history, many see its existence prior to the Second World War as nothing more than a prelude that hints towards the prevalence of the phenomenon beginning in the latter half of the twentieth century and continuing to the present.[45] Scholarly works that do excavate the historical roots of terrorism generally fit into one of two approaches. One strand of work analyzes terrorism as a form of asymmetric warfare stretching back into antiquity, with examples such as the Jewish Sicarii, the Ismaili Assassins, or the Thugs of India serving as direct precursors to the terrorists of the modern age.[46] In an influential article published in 1984, political scientist David C. Rapoport explicitly sought to show how the current phenomenon of terrorism could be traced back to ancient practices connected to the Jewish, Muslim, and Hindu religious traditions.[47] The problem with this approach in the case of the 'thugs' is that Rapoport's reading of the colonial record is overly literal, taking at face value the accounts of officials who had a vested interest in establishing certain perceptions of 'thuggee' as a vast conspiracy stretching across the Indian subcontinent and inspired by the excesses of a superstitious and bloodthirsty Hindu cult of the goddess Kali. While there is not space in the current study to delve into the histories of the Sicarii or the Ismaili Assassins, the colonial construction of the 'thugs' is discussed below and is elaborated at greater depth in the following chapter. Rapoport's 'deep history' approach to the phenomenon of so-called holy terror has been popular in policy circles

[43] See Judith Butler, *Frames of War: When Is Life Grievable?* (London: Verso, 2009).
[44] Graham Bowley and Matthew Rosenberg, 'US Deplores Video of Marines Urinating on Taliban', *The New York Times* (12 January 2012).
[45] For example, Bruce Hoffman, *Inside Terrorism* (London: Victor Gollancz, 1998).
[46] See Gérard Chaliand and Arnaud Blin (eds.), *The History of Terrorism: From Antiquity to Al Qaeda* (Berkeley: University of California Press, 2007).
[47] David C. Rapoport, 'Fear and Trembling: Terrorism in Three Religious Traditions', *The American Political Science Review* 78, no. 3 (1984), pp. 658–77.

seeking to root current geopolitical crises in primordial traditions of religiously sanctioned violence, but has been soundly rebutted by historians such as Kim Wagner.[48]

The most dangerous manifestation of this school of thought can be found in the work of scholars like celebrated military historian John Keegan, who argued after 9/11 that *jihadist* terrorism constituted an 'oriental way of war' derived from an unchanging 'Islamic mind'.[49] In an article originally published in *The Times* in 2001, Keegan explicitly drew on the 'clash of civilizations' hypothesis put forward by Samuel Huntington to portray the 'War on Terror' as a conflict between two competing styles of warfare.[50] While Keegan described Western soldiers as fighting 'face to face' and observing 'what, to non-Westerners may well seem curious rules of honour', he wrote, 'Orientals, by contrast, shrink from pitched battle, which they often deride as a sort of game, preferring ambush, surprise, treachery and deceit as the best way to overcome an enemy.' Claiming that it was not his intention to stereotype adherents of Islam, Keegan went on to describe the terrorist attacks of 9/11 as conducted by 'Arabs, appearing suddenly out of empty space like their desert raider ancestors' who 'assaulted the heartlands of Western power, in a terrifying surprise raid and did appalling damage'.[51] In case there was any doubt of his political views, Keegan closed his article with a blatant display of what Partha Chatterjee coined 'the rule of colonial difference',[52] in a statement that could just as easily have been written in the 1830s: 'It is no good pretending that the peoples of the desert and the empty spaces exist on the same level of civilisation as those who farm and manufacture. They do not.'[53]

Consciously or not, Keegan's article emulated a central tenet of colonial counterinsurgency – that the 'savage' methods of colonial

[48] A leading historian of the 'thugs', Wagner has dissected Rapoport's argument at length, so I will not go into greater depth here. See Kim Wagner, '"Thugs and Assassins": "New Terrorism" and the Resurrection of Colonial Knowledge', in Carola Dietze and Claudia Verhoeven (eds.), *The Oxford Handbook of the History of Terrorism* (Oxford: Oxford University Press, 2016).

[49] John Keegan, 'In This War of Civilisations, the West Will Prevail', *The Telegraph* (8 October 2001).

[50] Huntington's argument that 'the West' and 'Islam' constitute distinct civilizations has come to be seen as common sense by many, despite its lack of historicity and failure to understand that boundaries between 'civilizations' have always been highly permeable, especially where the Islamic world is concerned. See Samuel Huntington, *The Clash of Civilizations and the Remaking of World Order* (New York: Touchstone, 1997).

[51] Keegan, 'In This War of Civilisations'.

[52] Partha Chatterjee, *The Nation and Its Fragments: Colonial and Postcolonial Histories* (Princeton, NJ: Princeton University Press, 1993), pp. 16–18.

[53] Keegan, 'In This War of Civilisations'.

populations required and justified an equally 'savage' response from imperial forces. Describing the brutality of British tactics deployed against the 'Mau Mau' rebels of Kenya in the 1950s, Frederick Cooper argued that '[t]he savagery of British counterterrorism in Kenya was built against the belief that the terrorist was a savage'.[54] In a recent article by Kim Wagner, we see that contemporary military historians and policy makers often draw on colonial-era texts such as C. E. Calwell's 1898 counterinsurgency manual, *Small Wars: Their Principles and Practice*, not as contextualized historical sources but as 'masterpieces' containing lessons for twenty-first-century operations in Iraq and Afghanistan. As Wagner argues, the problem with this approach is that the forms of 'savage warfare' adopted by nineteenth-century imperial forces were not 'tactical necessities' but instead reflect 'deeply encoded assumptions concerning the inherent difference of local opponents'.[55] Similarly, Achille Mbembe refers to colonies as 'the location par excellence where the controls and guarantees of judicial order can be suspended – the zone where the violence of the state of exception is deemed to operate in the service of "civilization."' Unlike recognized sovereign states, Mbembe argues, colonies are not constrained by typical legal principles, as the lack of humanity ascribed to the colonized means, 'In the eyes of the conqueror, *savage life* is just another form of *animal life*, a horrifying experience, something alien beyond imagination or comprehension.'[56] For Jewish philosopher Hannah Arendt, this unrestrained violence – manifested in innovations of modern warfare first pioneered under colonial rule, such as aerial bombardment and the concentration camp – served as a direct precursor to the horrors visited upon Europeans by Europeans during the first half of the twentieth century.[57]

In contrast to works seeking to locate the roots of terrorism within primordial histories of religious or cultural difference, a second scholarly approach identifies the origins of modern terrorism in the spread of 'propaganda by deed' following the rise of print capitalism and new

[54] Frederick Cooper, 'Mau Mau and the Discourses of Decolonization', *Journal of African History* 29, no. 2 (1988), p. 317.

[55] Kim Wagner, 'Savage Warfare: Violence and the Rule of Colonial Difference in Early British Counterinsurgency', *History Workshop Journal* 85, no. 1 (2018), pp. 217–37.

[56] Mbembe, 'Necropolitics', p. 24.

[57] Hannah Arendt, *The Origins of Totalitarianism* (New York: Harcourt Brace Jovanovich, 1973), p. 185. Arendt's thesis is further developed in Sven Lindqvist's excellent *'Exterminate All the Brutes': One Man's Odyssey into the Heart of Darkness and the Origins of European Genocide* (New York: The New Press, 1996).

communications technologies in eighteenth- and nineteenth-century Europe.[58] Broadly speaking, this second approach has provided a more productive framework for understanding the origins of modern 'terrorism' as a tactic of political communication directly linked to the shifting global landscape of the modern period. According to the conventional narrative, the first English-language usage of the term 'terrorism' or 'terrorist' dates back to conservative philosopher Edmund Burke's analysis of the French Revolution at the end of the eighteenth century. In 1795, Burke mentioned 'thousands of those hellhounds called terrorists', and the following year wrote in his *Letters on a Regicide Peace*, 'Scratch any ideology and beneath it you will find a terrorist.' The term 'terrorism' appears shortly thereafter, in the 1798 supplement to the *Dictionnaire de l'Académie Française*.[59] For intellectual historian Mikkel Thorup, the context of the French Revolution is key to understanding what makes modern terrorism distinct from tactics of assassination or asymmetrical warfare deployed in earlier times. What made the execution of Louis XVI such a significant turning point in the history of political violence, according to Thorup, was the fact that while previous acts of tyrannicide justified themselves on the principle of upholding justice through the murder of an unjust ruler, Louis was killed not for his specific actions but for his symbolic position as king. This means that what made terrorism a historically new form of violence was the fact that 'even though actual persons are being targeted, and perhaps their killing is being legitimated by specific actions they have committed, the real target of the attack is not the person but the abstraction of the system'.[60]

Despite Thorup's incisive analysis regarding the intellectual underpinnings of modern 'terrorism', most accounts that seek to explain its origins are more interested in defining or explaining terrorism as a phenomenon than interrogating the genealogies of terrorism as a concept. Many attempts have been made to create a framework within which all acts of terrorism carried out across a range of historical and geographical settings can be made legible as belonging to a singular – though multifaceted – category of analysis.[61] One of the most influential of these

[58] A particularly good study can be found in Richard Bach Jensen, *The Battle against Anarchist Terrorism: An International History, 1878–1934* (Cambridge: Cambridge University Press, 2014).

[59] Walter Laqueur and Christopher Wall, *The Future of Terrorism: ISIS, Al-Qaeda, and the Alt-Right* (New York: St. Martin's Press, 2018), pp. 28–30.

[60] Thorup, *Intellectual History of Terror: War, Violence, and the State* (New York: Routledge, 2010), pp. 9–10.

[61] For a penetrating critique of the overall field of terrorism studies, see Stampnitsky, *Disciplining Terror*.

approaches has been David Rapoport's argument that the terrorism of the modern era can be grouped into 'Four Waves' comprising anarchist, anti-colonial, New Left, and religious ideologies spanning the period from the 1880s to the present.[62] Although Rapoport presents this framework as possessing explanatory power across a global arena – even going so far as to confidently predict that the 'religious terrorism' wave will disappear by 2025 – the case of colonial India undermines Rapoport's neat periodization.[63] As the following chapters will show, the history of colonial states of exception in India cannot be divided into an 'anarchist' period from 1880 to 1920, followed by an anti-colonial period thereafter, as Rapoport's framework would suggest. While the pre-war revolutionary movement in Bengal certainly adopted 'Russian methods' connected with global anarchist networks, members of the radical Jugantar and Anushilan organizations did not see themselves as anarchists, but rather as patriots, millenarians, and anti-colonialists.[64] In addition, the central claim made by proponents of this 'new terrorism' framework, that 'fourth wave' *jihadism* represents a type of violence unprecedented in its irrationality and fanaticism,[65] directly mirrors arguments made regarding the 'murderous outrages' of India's north-west frontier as far back as the 1870s.[66]

The idea that 'terrorism' in the colonial world reflected a progression from the 'anarchism' of the late nineteenth century to the 'anti-colonialism' of the interwar period reflects an overly literal reading of the colonial archive, which does indeed often portray the revolutionaries in these terms. Ranajit Guha, a pioneer of the subaltern studies school of Indian historiography, was the first to challenge conventional narratives that classified insurgency in colonial India into a 'pre-political' phase in the eighteenth and nineteenth centuries, followed by a 'political' phase only with the rise of a nationalist movement in the twentieth century that adhered to a liberal understanding of politics.[67] Guha argued that

[62] See Jean E. Rosenfeld, *Terrorism, Identity and Legitimacy: The Four Waves Theory and Political Violence* (New York: Routledge, 2011).

[63] Approaches that seek to classify terrorism primarily on the basis of ideology typically fail to understand how 'radicalized' young men are drawn into these ideologies in the first place. See Jamil Jivani, *Why Young Men: Rage, Race and the Crisis of Identity* (Toronto: HarperCollins, 2018), pp. 117–67.

[64] Shukla Sanyal, *Revolutionary Pamphlets, Propaganda and Political Culture in Colonial Bengal* (Cambridge: Cambridge University Press, 2014).

[65] Walter Laqueur, *The New Terrorism: Fanaticism and the Arms of Mass Destruction* (New York: Oxford University Press, 1999).

[66] This will be discussed further in the following chapter.

[67] Ranajit Guha, *Elementary Aspects of Peasant Insurgency in Colonial India* (Delhi: Oxford University Press, 1983), pp. 2–5. See also Partha Chatterjee, *The Politics of the Governed: Popular Politics in Most of the World* (New York: Columbia University Press, 2004) and

understanding resistance and rebellion in colonial India requires critically reading 'against the grain' of the archive to identify the 'prose of counterinsurgency' through which colonial officials recorded and commented upon violent uprisings against their rule.[68] Taking its cue from Guha, the current study expands this field of inquiry into the twentieth century in an effort to better understand the 'prose of counterterrorism' deployed by the modern colonial state. By grounding itself within the setting of British India, *A Genealogy of Terrorism* highlights the limitations of attempts to understand the phenomenon of 'terrorism' that neglect a deep engagement with colonial contexts.

When the colonized world is factored into global histories of terrorism, it is mainly during the height of decolonization following the Second World War, whereas the significance of colonial states of exception before the 1940s – other than Ireland and sometimes Palestine – tend to elicit only cursory mention.[69] In other accounts, 'terrorism' in non-Western settings is presented only as a brief case study, in which European anarchist tactics were co-opted and imitated by anti-colonial activists. Writing from a perspective foregrounded in European history and political thought, the synchretist ideologies of India's revolutionaries are often depicted as a 'confusing mess of ideas' drawing on a 'mishmash of historical examples'.[70] As such, when the colonized world is considered, it is more as a domain acted upon by European agency than a productive space in which ideas about terrorism were generated, contested, or reshaped. Such an approach limits the impact of these analyses by occluding the extent to which 'terrorism' in its earliest incarnations was heavily inflected by the logics and languages of colonial 'states of exception' that stretched back well into the nineteenth century. This perspective also ignores the extent to which the anti-colonial thought of insurgents from throughout the colonized world was itself highly influential in shaping and transforming European radicalism itself.[71] As the

James C. Scott, *Weapons of the Weak: Everyday Forms of Peasant Resistance* (New Haven, CT: Yale University Press, 1985).

[68] Ranajit Guha, 'The Prose of Counter-Insurgency', in Guha (ed.), *Subaltern Studies II* (New Delhi: Oxford University Press, 1983). Scholars since Ruha have continued to advocate critical approaches to archival sources, especially in colonial settings. See, for example Ann Stoler, 'Colonial Archives and the Arts of Governance', *Archival Science* 2 (2002), pp. 87–109.

[69] For example, see Matthew Carr, *The Infernal Machine: A History of Terrorism* (New York: The New Press, 2006) or Michael Burleigh, *Blood and Rage: A Cultural History of Terrorism* (London: HarperPress, 2008).

[70] Laqueur and Wall, *The Future of Terrorism*, pp. 66–7.

[71] Priyamvada Gopal, *Insurgent Empire: Anticolonial Resistance and British Dissent* (London: Verso, 2019).

current study will show, many of the descriptions associated with modern terrorism such as its presumed apolitical nature, fanaticism, cowardice, and insanity, and the inherent danger it poses to international peace, were originally articulated and rehearsed most explicitly in colonial settings like British India.

Violence and Non-Violence in Colonial India

Despite its lack of centrality within existing scholarship on the history of global terrorism, Indian revolutionary violence was a topic of grave concern for British metropolitan politicians in the early twentieth century. On 1 July 1909, a young Indian student named Madan Lal Dhingra shot and killed Sir William Curzon-Wyllie, political aide-de-camp for British India's secretary of state. The attack occurred in the heart of London during a meeting of the National Indian Association at the Imperial Institute in South Kensington. Despite attempts to portray Dhingra as insane, motivated by personal grievance, or drugged with the use of *bhang* (cannabis), the young man's words and demeanour during his trial made it clear that the act was politically motivated.[72] Dhingra was a member of India House, a youth hostel that served as the centre of gravity for the secretive Indian Home Rule Society established by the radical anti-colonialist Shyamji Krishnavarma. While political agitators within the subcontinent were subject to harsh colonial censorship laws, the promotion of free expression within turn-of-the-century Britain ironically made the metropole a freer environment for Indian nationalists wishing to express dissatisfaction with circumstances back home.[73] Still, the relocation of anti-colonialists into metropolitan spaces in Britain and France also created a 'feedback cycle' wherein radical networks and security forces engaged in a mutually constitutive race to expand their operations, leading to increasingly illiberal policies in Europe as well.[74] Following the assassination, Dhingra was promptly executed, and due to his association with India House, the suspicion of the authorities also fell upon others associated with the hostel as potential

[72] *The Times of India* (7 August 1909), p. 10.

[73] Nicholas Owen, 'The Soft Heart of the British Empire: Indian Radicals in Edwardian London', *Past & Present* 220, no. 220 (2013), pp. 143–84.

[74] See also Daniel Brückenhaus, *Policing Transnational Protest: Liberal Imperialism and the Surveillance of Anticolonialists in Europe, 1905–1945* (New York: Oxford University Press, 2017), p. 2.

accomplices, under the assumption that the young Dhingra must have been only a puppet of sinister 'wire-pullers' such as Krishnavarma.[75]

With Krishnavarma having left Britain in 1907 to escape prosecution for an earlier sedition charge, the radical nationalist Vinayak Damodar Savarkar was India House's leading authority figure at the time of the assassination. Savarkar had gained fame – as well as notoriety – after the publication of a book titled *The History of the War of Indian Independence*, an account of the rebellion of 1857 that reframed the so-called mutiny as a nationalist-inspired revolt against colonialism. Widely interpreted as a call to arms for the revolutionary movement of the early 1900s, the book was banned throughout the British Empire and British metropolitan police placed Savarkar under surveillance. Following Curzon-Wyllie's assassination at the hand of Dhingra, Savarkar published an article applauding the deed as an act of patriotism, prompting British authorities to arrest him on charges of sedition, conspiracy, and treason. Detained in England, Savarkar was en route to India as a prisoner aboard a P&O liner the following year when he escaped through an open porthole while the ship was docked at Marseilles. Although Savarkar hoped that he would be detained by French authorities and protected from extradition due to the political nature of the charges against him, he was promptly arrested by British detectives who went ashore to capture him. French authorities protested this violation of French sovereignty and brought the case before The Hague Tribunal, which concluded that there was no obligation on the part of the British to restore Savarkar to the French government.[76] As planned, the British government sent Savarkar on to India, to be tried under the colony's sedition laws, which were considerably more robust than those of Britain itself. The Bombay High Court sentenced Savarkar to the maximum available sentence of two life terms, to be served in the notorious cellular jail in the Andaman Islands.[77]

Writing about the incident in his memoirs more than a decade later, Josiah Wedgwood, a Member of Parliament for the British Labour Party, described the incident as indicative of a 'natural evolution' through which the international law of Europe was inexorably 'closing down the hatches on every rebel against the existing order'. Wedgwood identified

[75] See Harald Fischer-Tiné, 'Mass-Mediated Panic in the British Empire? Shyamji Krishnavarma's "Scientific Terrorism" and the "London Outrage", 1909', in Fischer-Tiné, *Anxieties, Fear and Panic in Colonial Settings: Empires on the Verge of a Nervous Breakdown* (Houndmills: Palgrave, 2017), pp. 99–134.

[76] For the full story and its wider context, see Brückenhaus, *Policing Transnational Protest*, pp. 8–41.

[77] Janaki Bakhle, 'Savarkar (1883–1966), Sedition and Surveillance: The Rule of Law in a Colonial Situation', *Social History* 35, No. 1 (2010), pp. 51–66.

the central conflict of the twentieth century in Asia not as the tension between Britain and India or East and West, but rather between 'Liberty and Authority'. Wedgwood argued that while in previous centuries a political refugee could flee one sovereign by seeking refuge in the territory of another, there was now no such refuge possible from 'the straight-waistcoat of modern civilization'. The increasing bureaucratization of the international system was, according to Wedgwood, rapidly eliminating channels for political redress, and laying the groundwork for a potential 'bureaucratic tyranny', wherein individual liberty would give way entirely to the logic of national and international security.[78] A vocal critic of British colonialism in India and an advocate for the rights of refugees, Wedgwood exemplified many of the tensions that existed between metropolitan politics and high imperialism in early twentieth century Britain. While party leaderships – whether Liberal, Conservative, or Labour – were often complicit in maintaining the structures of Britain's global empire, dissenting voices like that of Wedgwood represented an important site of critique against imperialism that consistently forced the language of empire to adapt to changing international moral norms.[79]

The Savarkar incident reflects the deeply entangled relationship that existed in the early twentieth century between domestic political violence and international law. With the rise of anarchism in Europe and anti-colonial radicalism abroad towards the end of the long nineteenth century, an international system previously defined by the relationships between sovereign states became increasingly concerned with the threat posed to state sovereignty itself by the existence of radical insurgents capable of subverting domestic authority.[80] This occurred, however, at precisely the same time that state sovereignty was evolving to encompass the new political community defined by the territorially bounded nation-state. As a world of empires transformed into a world of nations following the global cataclysm of the First World War and the establishment of the new international society that achieved tangible expression through the League of Nations based out of Geneva, the spectre of 'the terrorist' began to stalk the margins of international law.[81]

[78] Josiah Wedgwood, *Essays and Adventures of a Labour M.P.* (London: George Allen & Unwin Ltd, 1924), pp. 144–53.

[79] See Nicholas Owen, *The British Left and India: Metropolitan Anti-imperialism, 1885–1947* (Oxford: Oxford University Press, 2008).

[80] The global dimensions of this revolutionary movement are explored in Maia Ramnath, *Haj to Utopia: How the Ghadar Movement Charted Global Radicalism and Attempted to Overthrow the British Empire* (Berkeley: University of California Press, 2011).

[81] See David Armitage, *Foundations of Modern International Thought* (Cambridge: Cambridge University Press, 2013), p. 191.

In 1917 James Campbell Ker, who previously served as personal assistant to the Director of Criminal Intelligence, published a summary of the first decade of revolutionary politics in India, with the title *Political Trouble in India, 1907–1917*. The government restricted the volume to official usage and circulated it among administrators and security services to provide a manual for understanding the history of revolutionary networks such as the Dacca Anushilan Samiti and the radical Jugantar group. H. W. Hale of the Indian Police composed the sequel to this volume, titled *Terrorism in India, 1917–1936*, following a temporary posting to the Intelligence Bureau. Aside from the useful primary material that these volumes provide for historians through their comprehensive documentation of various actions undertaken by revolutionaries throughout the early twentieth century, the titles of the books are themselves instructive of an evolving colonial prose of counterterrorism during this period. By the time that Hale composed his volume in 1937, the term 'terrorism' had definitively replaced older labels such as 'sedition', 'conspiracy', or 'political crime' as the primary lens through which acts of anti-colonial revolutionary violence were understood.

In the first page of his volume, Hale defined terrorism as follows:

> Terrorism, as distinct from other revolutionary methods such as Communism or the Ghadar Movement, may be said to denote the commission of outrages of a comparatively 'individual' nature. That is to say, the terrorist holds the belief that Indian independence can best be brought about by a series of revolutionary outrages calculated to instil fear into the British official classes and to drive them out of India. He commits outrages for the purpose of collecting funds for the purchase of arms, for the making of bombs and for the maintenance of his party, hoping that the masses will be drawn to his support either by fear or admiration.[82]

Hale's attempt to explicitly define terrorism in relation to other forms of revolutionary politics reflects a growing need in the late 1930s to clarify the meaning of a term that, by this point in time, became ubiquitous in its usage by government officials. The word 'terrorism', alongside its physical personification in the figure of 'the terrorist', appears so frequently in the colonial police records of 1930s India that a reader could easily be misled into assuming that this term was the natural definition through which revolutionary activities were always described. As a result, the growing field of scholarship surrounding the history of anti-colonial revolutionary violence in India has produced remarkably little critical engagement with the history of this term within the political

[82] H. W. Hale, *Terrorism in India, 1917–1936* (Simla: Government of India Press, 1937), IOR: L/P&J/12/403, p. 1.

and legal discourses of the colonial state. Most scholars of the Indian revolutionary movement have sought to clarify their own terminology to avoid replicating a colonial discourse of criminality or applying an unintended value judgement through an uncritical usage of the politically charged label of 'terrorism'. But none has yet provided a comprehensive genealogy of the term 'terrorism' within the context of colonial India throughout the height of British rule.[83]

A rich body of literature emerging from fields including postcolonial studies, South Asian studies, and colonial history have brought to light the significant contributions made by Indian revolutionaries to the independence movement, which earlier generations of historians portrayed as dominated by the non-violent activism of Mohandas Gandhi and the Indian National Congress. One of the first key texts in this field was Sumit Sarkar's magisterial work on the *swadeshi* movement, which has proved particularly influential, not only for the history of revolutionary 'terrorism' in India but for the political history of Bengal more broadly.[84] In it, Sarkar explains his own use of the term 'terrorism' by clarifying that for him the term connotes elite action in contrast to the more popular militancy that typically defines revolutionary insurgency. For Sarkar, the key terminological dividing line is not violence versus non-violence, but rather elite action as opposed to mass action. Explaining this distinction, Sarkar points out that out of 186 persons convicted of revolutionary crimes or killed committing them from 1907 to 1917, 165 came from the upper three castes of Brahmin, Kayastha, and Baidya.[85] Without disputing Sarkar's claim regarding the primarily upper-caste demographics of the revolutionary movement, I will nonetheless continue to use

[83] Partha Chatterjee has an excellent chapter on the uses of the term in twentieth-century India, but there has as yet been no full-length study of this colonial genealogy. See Partha Chatterjee, 'Terrorism: State Sovereignty and Militant Politics in India', in Gluck Carol and Anne Lowenhaupt Tsing (eds), *Words in Motion: Toward a Global Lexicon* (Durham, NC: Duke University Press, 2009), pp. 240–62. See also Philip Deery's article on the history of the term in colonial Malaya: 'The Terminology of Terrorism: Malaya, 1948–52', *Journal of Southeast Asian Studies* 34, 2 (2003), pp. 231–47.

[84] Sumit Sarkar, *The Swadeshi Movement in Bengal, 1903–1908* (New Delhi: People's Publishing House, 1973). See also A. C. Bose, *Indian Revolutionaries Abroad 1905–1922, in the Background of International Developments* (Patna: Bharati Bawan, 1971) and David M. Laushey, *Bengal Terrorism and the Marxist Left: Aspects of Regional Nationalism in India, 1905–1942* (Calcutta: Firma K.L. Mukhopadhyay, 1975). A re-examination of Sarkar's work can be found in the special issue *Swadeshi in the Time of Nations*, in *Economic & Political Weekly* 47, no. 42 (2012). See also Lisa Trivedi, 'Visually Mapping the "Nation": Swadeshi Politics in Nationalist India, 1920–1930', *The Journal of African Studies* 62, 1 (2003), pp. 11–41, Amit Bhattacharyya, *Swadeshi Enterprise in Bengal, 1900–1920* (Calcutta: Mita Bhattacharyya: Distributed by Seagull Bookshop, 1986).

[85] Sarkar, *Swadeshi Movement*, 63–76.

'anti-colonial revolutionaries' as the main label designating those that Sarkar and others define as 'terrorists'. The term 'revolutionary' is, of course, itself a fraught term, which, in the words of Kama Maclean and Daniel Elam, 'is as slippery as it is indispensable'.[86] For the purposes of the current study, 'revolutionary' is used as an imperfect, though useful, catch-all label meant to encompass a range of political actors, by no means confined to the word's more narrow Marxist implications. By contrast, the term 'terrorist' is used only insofar as it relates to how these figures were labelled either by their contemporaries, the colonial state, or future historians. There are three key reasons underlying this decision.

First, Sarkar's description of 'terrorism' as elite action risks oversimplifying the political thought of 'terrorists' like Rash Behari Bose, who, despite his own relatively elite background and reliance on individual acts of insurgency such as his bomb attack against Lord Hardinge, the viceroy and governor general of India, articulated a political philosophy that was no less revolutionary than that proposed by Communists such as M. N. Roy.[87] Here, I use Keith Baker's definition of 'revolution' not only as 'the rather mechanical change of political regime or as the necessary end result of a conflict between social classes', but rather as 'the ultimate moment of political choice, in which the givens of social existence seem suspended, the only power was the power of the imagination, and the world could be made anew'.[88] Such a description is absolutely applicable to the writings of Bose, who used the pages of his monthly journal *New Asia* to describe an emancipatory vision whereby the 'coloured people' of the world would reverse the global balance of power and remake the world along racial lines that would erase the disproportionate power of the Anglo-European imperial states.[89]

Second, as *A Genealogy of Terrorism* makes clear, the distinction between the 'individual' action ascribed to terrorism by Hale and the more collective form of insurgency that Sarkar defines as appropriately

[86] See Kama Maclean and Daniel Elam, 'Reading Revolutionaries: Texts, Acts, and Afterlives of Political Action in Late Colonial South Asia', *Postcolonial Studies* 16, no. 2 (2013), pp. 113–23.

[87] Roy himself also engaged in 'terrorist' plots prior to becoming committed to communist revolution, further complicating the artificial division between these figures. Kris Manjapra, *M.N. Roy: Marxism and Colonial Cosmopolitanism* (Delhi: Routledge, 2010).

[88] Keith Baker, *Inventing the French Revolution: Essays on French Political Culture in the Eighteenth Century* (Cambridge: Cambridge University Press, 1990), p. 3.

[89] *New Asia*, nos. 17 and 18, 1934, p. 2. See also Joseph McQuade, 'The *New Asia* of Rash Behari Bose: India, Japan, and the Limits of International, 1912–1945', *Journal of World History* 27, no. 4 (2016), pp. 641–67. By no means was Bose alone in combining 'terrorist' tactics with a Pan-Asian vision of global transformation. See Carolien Stolte and Fischer-Tiné, 'Imagining Asia in India: Nationalism and Internationalism (ca. 1905–1940)', *Comparative Studies in Society and History* 54, no. 1 (2012), pp. 65–92.

revolutionary is often very difficult, if not impossible, to clearly demarcate. Again taking Rash Behari Bose as an example, it is difficult to imagine a more 'individual' act of 'terrorism' than personally attempting to assassinate the viceroy of India through a spectacular bomb attack during the middle of a public procession. Taking Hale's or Sarkar's definition then, this would certainly constitute an act of terrorism. But less than three years after this incident, Bose was instrumental in planning an abortive uprising that intended to cripple Britain's war effort against Germany by stimulating mutinies among the British Indian garrisons across northern India. Reflecting upon the failure of this plot, Bose later concluded that a future rising would require arms to be distributed throughout the general population in order to be successful.[90] Despite this, he continued to be involved in gun-running operations connected to Sachindranath Sanyal's self-described 'terrorist' activities in the mid-1920s, and provided the animating force behind the formation of the Indian National Army, a military unit made up of captured Indian prisoners of war during the Second World War, which was ultimately taken over by the better known Subhas Chandra Bose.[91] The career of Rash Behari Bose thus demonstrates the inherently problematic nature of any attempt to draw a neat line of demarcation between 'elite terrorist' and 'popular revolutionary' activities.

Finally, given this book's emphasis on tracing a historical genealogy of the term 'terrorism', it is impossible to disentangle the complicated history through which this term came into common usage without a strong methodological scepticism towards using the word itself in such an analysis. While most historians of revolutionary India clearly spell out their intention to avoid moral judgements in referring to anti-colonial revolutionaries as terrorists, this misses the point. The question of whether revolutionaries such as Rash Behari Bose were morally justified in using violent means in pursuit of their goal of independence ignores the larger question of how the term 'terrorism' came to acquire a specific set of moral connotations in the first place. Asking whether a historical or contemporary figure, or set of figures, should or should not be considered a terrorist versus a freedom fighter is often a political question,

[90] Asitabha Das (ed.), *Rashbehari Bose Collected Works: Autobiography, Writing and Speeches* (Kolkata: Kishaloy Prakashan, 2006), p. 29.

[91] Sugata Bose, *His Majesty's Opponent: Subhas Chandra Bose and India's Struggle against Empire* (Cambridge, MA: Harvard University Press, 2011). See also Christopher Bayly and Tim Harper, *Forgotten Armies: Britain's Asian Empire and the War with Japan* (London: Penguin Books, 2005).

not a historical one. Furthermore, although the term 'terrorism' did indeed exist in the latter half of the nineteenth century, it did not come to be used as the primary category for describing revolutionary violence in India until the 1920s, making its uniform usage by historians referring to the 1900s or 1910s potentially anachronistic.

An admitted limitation of the current study is what some may see as an excessive engagement with colonial sources and colonial archives, at the expense of a detailed treatment of the political thought or methods of self-identification expressed by the revolutionaries themselves. The goal of the current study is to better understand how colonial authority was formed, articulated, and protected through an evolving prose of counter-terrorism that drew on categories of legal exception dating back at least as far as the late eighteenth and early nineteenth centuries. For this reason, while numerous documents produced by the revolutionaries do appear throughout the book, the bulk of the archival material on which this research draws is primarily derived from the British and Indian administrators, intelligence officers, bureaucrats, and legislators who ultimately articulated and legitimized the colonial prose of counterterrorism that forms our current object of study.[92]

Fortunately, there is already excellent research that does provide detailed and nuanced portrayals of how the men and women of the revolutionary movement expressed their goals, conveyed their ideas, and portrayed themselves to a wider Indian public. In broad terms, this literature can be grouped into three main areas of interest: the political thought of revolutionary 'leaders';[93] the organization, structure, and goals of various transnational revolutionary networks;[94] and the political messages that can be gleaned from various mediums including

[92] Although this approach may seem similar to that of Richard Popplewell on the surface, the key difference is that while Popplewell provides a thick description of the intelligence apparatus of the British Empire, *Assassins by Profession* interrogates the logics and discursive strategies through which colonial law and power was produced in the first place. See Popplewell, *Intelligence and Imperial Defence: British Intelligence and the Defence of the Indian Empire, 1904–1924* (London: Frank Cass, 1995).

[93] For example Harald Fischer-Tiné, *Shyamji Krishnavarma: Sanskrit, Sociology and Anti-Imperialism* (London: Routledge India, 2014), Peter Heehs, *The Lives of Sri Aurobindo* (New York: Columbia University Press, 2008), Carolien Stolte, '"Enough of the Great Napoleons!": Raja Mahendra Pratap's Pan-Asian Projects (1929–1939)', *Modern Asian Studies* 46, no. 2 (2012), pp. 403–23, and Manjapra, *M.N. Roy*.

[94] Maia Ramnath, *Haj to Utopia*, Durba Ghosh, 'Terrorism in Bengal: Political Violence in the Interwar Years', in Durba Ghosh and Dane Kennedy (eds.), *Decentring Empire: Britain, India and the Transcolonial World* (New Delhi: Orient Longman Private Ltd., 2006), pp. 270–92, and Peter Heehs, *The Bomb in Bengal: The Rise of Revolutionary Terrorism in India, 1900–1910* (Delhi: Oxford University Press, 1993).

pamphlets, images, and autobiographies produced and circulated by the revolutionaries.[95] In drawing from these accounts, we see a diverse, diffuse, and articulate range of anti-colonial perspectives undergirding the supposedly 'mindless' violence of Indian revolutionaries during the first half of the twentieth century. An underlying assumption of the current study, thoroughly buttressed by this meticulous research already conducted on revolutionary thought and praxis, is that colonial representations of anti-colonial 'terrorists' as 'lunatics', 'fanatics', and 'monsters' has little to no grounding in the reality of the Indian revolutionary movement. The central goal of this book is to excavate how these discursive representations of the revolutionaries informed and enabled the colonial states of exception through which they were policed.

Anxiety, Power, and the Making of Colonial Law

The initial quote with which this book opens is drawn from a comprehensive account compiled by William Henry Sleeman of the so-called thugs, a class of hereditary 'assassins by profession' who allegedly participated in an India-wide murder cult under the divine sanction of the goddess Kali.[96] In Sleeman's descriptions of the thugs and, indeed, in some recent scholarship as well, we can identify a kind of proto-terrorist – furtive, sinister killer, unmoored from local specificities or clearly demarcated territorial jurisdictions. This perspective is deeply flawed, constructing as it does a single, coherent category of criminality, while the reality most likely comprised a series of loose, amorphous, and often unrelated collections of brigands, highwaymen, bandits, and demobilized retainers. While the historiography of 'thuggee' will receive more attention in the following chapter, a common theme that emerges within this literature is the idea that representations of thugs often tell us more about the fears, obsessions, and preoccupations of their authors than they do about the 'thugs' themselves.[97]

[95] Durba Ghosh, *Gentlemanly Terrorists: Political Violence and the Colonial State in India, 1919–1947* (Cambridge: Cambridge University Press, 2017), Kama Maclean, *A Revolutionary History of Interwar India: Violence, Image, Voice and Text* (London: Hurst & Company, 2015), Michael Silvestri, 'The Bomb, *Bhadralok*, *Bhagavad* Gita, and Dan Breen: Terrorism in Bengal and Its Relation to the European Experience', *Terrorism and Political Violence* 21, no. 1 (2009), pp. 1–27, and Sanyal, *Revolutionary Pamphlets*.

[96] W. H. Sleeman, *Ramaseeana, or a vocabulary of the peculiar language used by the Thugs* (Calcutta: G.H. Huttmann, Military Orphan Press, 1836).

[97] Martine van Woerkens, *The Strangled Traveler: Colonial Imaginings and the Thugs of India* (Chicago: University of Chicago Press, 2002), pp. 6–9.

The broader role of fear, paranoia, anxiety, and other negative emotional states in the history of colonial governance has attracted increased scholarly attention in recent years.[98] The old image of the colonial administrator as a cool and detached bureaucrat has been replaced by the recognition that colonial knowledge was less a rational matrix of objective truth than a piecemeal web constructed out of imperfect, uneven, and often fictive interpretations of local customs and cultures.[99] From this perspective, attempts to capture or exterminate the thugs, dacoits, pirates, and fanatics of the nineteenth century highlight both the paranoia of colonial officials seeking to establish control over territories and peoples they poorly understood on the one hand, and the role of brute force in extending British control over the subcontinent through a coercive apparatus of legal and military control on the other.

This seemingly paradoxical relationship between anxiety and violence is less counterintuitive than it may seem. In many instances, moments of profound imperial insecurity could translate into spectacular outbursts of violence, such as the blowing of forty-nine Namdhari Sikhs from the mouths of cannons following the so-called Kooka outbreak of 1872, or the massacre of hundreds of unarmed protesters at Amritsar in 1919.[100] Furthermore, theorists of violence such as Hannah Arendt contend that violence and power should be understood as oppositional rather than equivalent. According to Arendt, power relies on consent or legitimacy,

[98] For some examples, see Fischer-Tiné, *Anxieties, Fear and Panic*; Condos, *Insecurity State*; Ann Laura Stoler, *Along the Archival Grain: Epistemic Anxieties and Colonial Commonsense* (Princeton, NJ: Princeton University Press, 2009); Robert Peckham (ed.), *Empires of Panic: Epidemics and Colonial Anxieties* (Hong Kong: Hong Kong University Press, 2015); Kim Wagner, '"Treading upon Fires": The "Mutiny" Motif and Colonial Anxieties in British India', *Past and Present* 218, no. 1 (2013), pp. 159–97; Maurus Reinkowski and Gregor Thum (eds.), *Helpless Imperialists: Imperial Failure, Fear and Radicalization* (Gottingen: Vandenhoeck and Ruprecht, 2013); Deep Kanta Lahiri Choudhury, *Telegraphic Imperialism: Crisis and Panic in the Indian Empire, c.1830* (Houndmills: Palgrave Macmillan, 2010); John Savage, '"Black Magic" and White Terror: Slave Poisoning and Colonial Society in Early 19th Century Martinique', *Journal of Social History*, 40, no. 3 (2007), pp. 635–62; D. K. Lahiri Choudhury, 'Sinews of Panic and the Nerves of Empire: The Imagined State's Entanglement with Information Panic, India c. 1800–1912', *Modern Asian Studies* 38, no. 4 (2004), pp. 965–1002; Ricardo Roque, 'The Razor's Edge: Portuguese Imperial Vulnerability in Colonial Moxico, Angola', *The International Journal of African Historical Studies* 36, no. 1 (2003), pp. 105–24; G. A. Oddie, 'Hook-Swinging and Popular Religion in South India during the Nineteenth Century', *Indian Economic & Social History Review* 23, no. 1 (1986), pp. 93–106.

[99] Harald Fischer-Tiné and Christine Whyte, 'Introduction' in Fischer-Tiné, *Anxieties, Fear and Panic*, p.1.

[100] See Condos, *Insecurity State*, 103–39 and Wagner, *Amritsar 1919*.

whereas violence acts as a tool of coercion in instances where true power is lacking.[101] As such, the operation of colonial rule in India as a form of what Ranajit Guha has called 'dominance without hegemony' can quite logically be regarded as simultaneously anxious and violent.[102] As we will see throughout the current study, it was often at times when officials felt most insecure about their own lack of knowledge regarding the activities of revolutionary organizations that they resorted to extraordinary measures to contain this threat.

At the same time, this point should not be exaggerated. While colonial rule was not as monolithic or stable as some would argue, it was nonetheless a system of government that, in the words of Partha Chatterjee, 'was at core absolutist and authoritarian'.[103] While officials may have felt anxiety at the prospect of secretive conspiracies lurking at the margins of imperial authority, the consolidation of British power throughout the subcontinent over the course of the nineteenth century ensured an increasingly expansive capacity for extreme brutality in both quotidian and spectacular forms.[104] An inability to identify individual perpetrators of real or imagined offences gave rise to a reliance on collective forms of punishment that indiscriminately targeted the innocent and the guilty alike.[105] Similarly, a 'rule of colonial difference', and the supposedly 'scientific' theories of racial difference that bolstered this ideology from the mid-nineteenth century onwards, provided the rhetorical justification for treating colonial subjects in ways that would have been unthinkable in metropolitan Britain.[106] Categories of 'extraordinary' legal standing such as thugs, pirates, criminal tribes, fanatics, and terrorists demarcate the outer limits of this 'colonial difference' by providing oppositional figures – beyond either law or politics – against whom colonialism could assert its legitimacy and expand its jurisdiction through the exercise of 'emergency' sovereign power.

[101] Hannah Arendt, *On Violence* (New York: Harcourt, Brace & World, 1970). See also Cornelia Beyer, *Violent Globalisms: Conflict in Response to Empire* (Aldershot: Ashgate, 2008), pp. 1–6.

[102] Ranajit Guha, *Dominance without Hegemony: History and Power in Colonial India* (Cambridge, MA: Harvard University Press, 1997).

[103] Partha Chatterjee, *Black Hole of Empire*, p. 119.

[104] Jordanna Bailkin, 'The Boot and the Spleen: When Was Murder Possible in British India?', *Comparative Studies in Society and History* 48, no. 2 (2006), pp. 462–93 and Elizabeth Kolsky, *Colonial Justice in British India: White Violence and the Rule of Law* (Cambridge: Cambridge University Press, 2010).

[105] See for example, Kim Wagner, *Amritsar 1919: An Empire of Fear and the Making of a Massacre* (New Haven, CT: Yale University Press, 2019).

[106] Partha Chatterjee, *The Nation and Its Fragments: Colonial and Postcolonial Histories* (Princeton, NJ: Princeton University Press, 1993).

Categories such as the 'pirate' and the 'fanatic' are precursors to the modern phenomenon of 'terrorism' only insofar as they provide us with the means to assess earlier iterations of a colonial 'state of exception' that met challenges to its authority with extrajudicial emergency measures designed to establish a clear monopoly on violence and to protect the commercial interests of empire.[107] In identifying the 'threat' of thuggee as an India-wide conspiracy, Sleeman provided one of the earliest articulations of an imperial right to exercise control beyond the narrow enclaves and corridors of colonial jurisdiction, encompassing 'every country in India' which 'could now be considered as under the protection of the Supreme Government'. Under the mandate given to it by 'the laws of humanity and of nations', the colonial administration could now, in the words of Sleeman, reclaim fugitive thugs from 'every State in which they might seek shelter'.[108]

It is this aspect of the early nineteenth-century Anti-Thug Campaigns that is most instructive for enhancing the emergence of 'terrorism' as a distinct category of global criminality in the twentieth century, and yet this aspect of the connection between 'thuggee' and 'terrorism' is, for the most part, only hinted at in the existing scholarship. A notable exception to this trend is Alex Tickell's monograph on representations of terror, terrorism, and insurgency in the Anglophone literature of colonial India. Focusing on the 'narrative mediation of violence', Tickell treats the colonial state of exception as the 'counterpart/context of terror', drawing upon a literary archive of novelists and journalists to show how terror was represented at different junctures in India's colonial history. Contesting the characterization of colonial and Indian writings as distinct 'hermetically sealed' sites of cultural production, Tickell explores the 'tense and often uneven exchange' between these literary traditions as they responded simultaneously to instances of state and non-state terror.[109]

More recently, Michael Silvestri has also shown how cultural stereotypes of thugs, dacoits, *sadhus*, and criminal tribes informed the perceptions of colonial intelligence operatives who sought to police the 'Bengali terrorism' of the twentieth century. In his study of colonial and international intelligence services, Silvestri refers to the matrix of colonial assumptions regarding the moral and physical degeneration of Indian society as comprising a 'kaleidoscopic vision of the Indian

[107] Radhika Singha, *A Despotism of Law: Crime and Justice in Early Colonial India* (Delhi: Oxford University Press, 1998), p. 170.

[108] Sleeman, *Ramaseeana*, p. 48–9.

[109] Alex Tickell, *Terrorism, Insurgency and Indian-English Literature, 1830–1947* (New York; London: Routledge, 2012), pp. 6–10.

underworld'.[110] Central to Silvestri's argument is the assertion that although intelligence operations 'were intended to be rational and objective forms of investigation, they were also deeply marked by colonial stereotypes of crime, criminality, and sedition, and this perspective needs to be incorporated into the story of British imperial intelligence in these decades'.[111] This is an apt description, which will serve as a point of departure for the current study's explication of the legal and discursive strategies through which imperial administrators constructed a distinctive prose of counterterrorism during the hundred-year period that marked the heyday of British rule in the Indian subcontinent.

Considering the reams of 'new imperial' histories that highlight the cross-fertilization of cultures, goods, and concepts from colonies to metropoles, it is no longer controversial to assert that events taking place in far-flung colonial settings could be just as productive in shaping modern Europe as European ideas were in supposedly 'making the modern world'.[112] Similarly, attention to the role of colonial law in the production of 'the market' as an object of governance reveals the complex interplay between 'vernacular capitalisms' and the universalizing project of liberal imperialism, which cannot be understood purely through a framework in which 'dynamic' European empires acted upon 'passive' local subjects.[113] Despite the efforts of modern reactionaries to try to rehabilitate empire as a positive good that is being unfairly slandered by 'politically correct' leftists, scholarly approaches to European imperialism are in fact far less concerned with weighing a moral 'balance sheet' to determine whether empire was 'good' or 'bad'.[114] That colonialism wrought havoc, racial injustice, and systemic violence upon the colonized world is well established. Weighing these effects against the 'benefits' generated by railways or telegraphs is a facile argument that says more about current political ideology than it does about the historical experience of colonialism for the vast majority of its subjects. For this

[110] Michael Silvestri, *Policing 'Bengali Terrorism' in India and the World: Imperial Intelligence and Revolutionary Nationalism, 1905–1939* (New York: Palgrave Macmillan, 2019), p. 26.

[111] Ibid., p. 30.

[112] Compare, for example, Niall Ferguson's celebratory *Empire: How Britain Made the Modern World* (London: Penguin Books, 2007) with C. A. Bayly's more nuanced *The Birth of the Modern World, 1780–1914: Global Connections and Comparisons* (Malden, MA: Blackwell, 2004). See also Jürgen Osterhammel, *Unfabling the East: The Enlightenment's Encounter with Asia* (Princeton, NJ: Princeton University Press, 2018).

[113] Ritu Birla, *Stages of Capital: Law, Culture, and Market Governance in Late Colonial India* (Durham, NC: Duke University Press, 2009).

[114] James McDougall and Kim Wagner, 'Don't Mistake Nostalgia about the British Empire for Scholarship', *Times Higher Education* (20 April 2018).

reason, the goal of most current scholarship is constructing a nuanced understanding of how colonialism shaped and was shaped by the new matrixes of power, knowledge, law, and technology that have emerged over the past few centuries.

India is certainly not the only possible case study for elucidating a colonial genealogy of terrorism. From within the British Empire, Kenya, Malaya, Ireland, and Palestine were all important hubs of anti-colonial insurgency in which emergency legislation, surveillance, and paramilitary force were deployed in innovative and influential ways.[115] Similarly, one need only look at the French experience in Algeria or Indochina, or the 'pacification' operations carried out by the Dutch in Indonesia or by the Americans in the Philippines, to observe important historical nodes in an evolving global prose of counterterrorism.[116] In her recent book on confinement, Laleh Khalili argues that what distinguishes liberal counterinsurgencies from those waged by illiberal regimes is 'the invocation of law and legality as structuring the conduct of war, an absolute dependence on a set of clearly defined procedures and administrative processes … and finally a discourse of humanitarian intent'. For Khalili, the racialization of one's opponent is central to liberal counterinsurgencies, as this racial differentiation is what 'resolves the tensions between illiberal methods and liberal discourse'.[117] In connecting the liberal counterinsurgencies of the twenty-first century with carceral strategies developed in multiple locations across the British, French, and American empires, Khalili shows how the forms taken by colonial violence can only properly be understood in relation to each other.

Still, there are good reasons for focusing on India for the current project. First, and perhaps most simply put, India was the largest colony in the world's largest empire during the heyday of global imperialism. Comprising the entire South Asian subcontinent that is now divided into the nation-states of India, Pakistan, and Bangladesh, British India was a behemoth in terms of population, resources, and strategic significance. Other colonial acquisitions such as the Suez Canal in Egypt were acquired by Britain with the express intention of protecting commercial and military linkages with the all-important subcontinent. The revenues extracted from India – and especially the production of consumer goods such as opium – provided the currency through which British officials and merchants

[115] Calder Walton explores many of these conflicts in *Empire of Secrets: British Intelligence, the Cold War and the Twilight of Empire* (London: HarperCollins, 2013).

[116] Martin Thomas, *Fight or Flight: Britain, France, and Their Roads from Empire* (Oxford: Oxford University Press, 2014).

[117] Laleh Khalili, *Time in the Shadows: Confinement in Counterinsurgencies* (Stanford, CA: Stanford University Press, 2013), pp. 4–5.

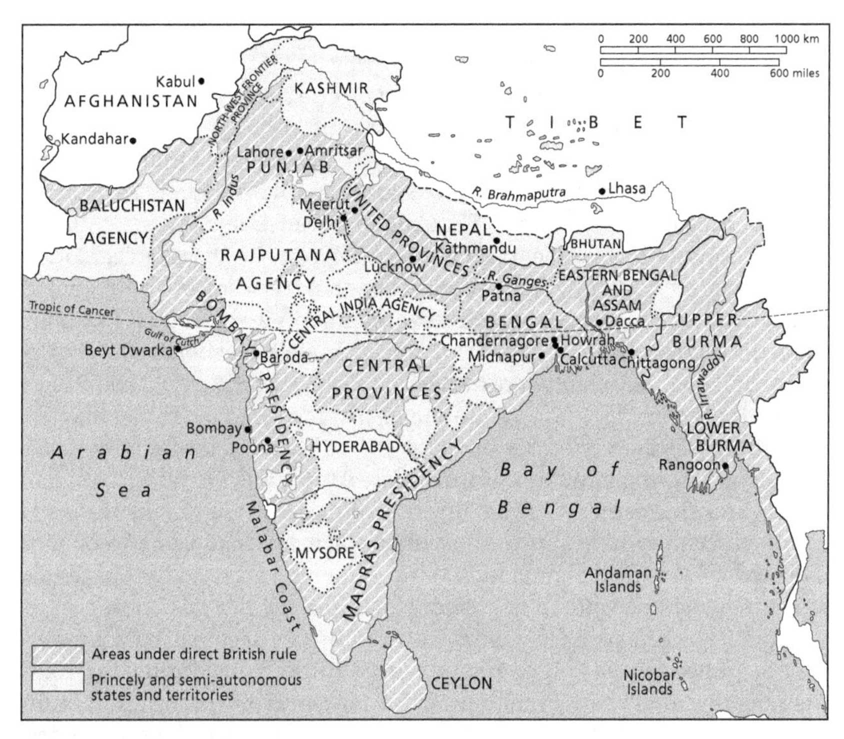

Figure 0.1 Colonial India and neighbouring states, 1909. Redrawn by Cox Cartographic Ltd from 'Map of the British Indian Empire from Imperial Gazetteer of India', Oxford University Press, 1909. Edinburgh Geographical Institute; J.G. Bartholomew and Sons (via Wikimedia Commons).

financed their 'triangle trade' with China, ensuring a steady supply of tea for a newly addicted British public. At moments of global crisis such as the First World War, retaining control over the so-called jewel in the imperial crown had a direct role in shaping policy elsewhere, such as during Britain's military campaign in Mesopotamia.[118]

Another factor that makes India a worthwhile starting point for excavating a colonial genealogy of terrorism is the role of the British raj as a 'subimperial centre'.[119] While historians are increasingly highlighting the wide range of cross-imperial connections that established horizontal links

[118] Popplewell, *Intelligence and Imperial Defence*, p. 6.
[119] Tony Ballantyne, 'Rereading the Archive and Opening Up the Nation-State', in Antoinette Burton (ed.), *After the Imperial Turn: Thinking with and through the Nation* (Durham, NC: Duke University Press, 2003), pp. 102–21.

across a variety of colonies, India formed a particularly crucial hub that, in the words of historian Thomas Metcalf, 'provided inspiration, precedents, and personnel for colonial administration' elsewhere.[120] Given that the current study is especially concerned with the making of terrorism as a legal category, it is significant that the Indian Penal Code formed the basis for legislation not only in India but also in colonies such as Burma, Ceylon, Singapore, the Straits Settlements, Brunei, and Aden. As such, legal innovations in India played a crucial role in shaping legislation throughout the Indian Ocean world, a fact that has attracted only limited scholarly attention. In addition, Indian migration was essential for many industries across the imperial world, especially after the abolition of slavery led merchants and plantation owners to seek out new cheap sources of labour.[121] Indian diasporic communities played a key role in shaping not only the political economies but also the cultures of far-flung colonies including Mauritius, Malaya, Burma, East Africa, Fiji, Guyana, Trinidad, Natal, and Suriname.[122] With the rise of anti-colonialism in the early twentieth century, these Indian expatriates living abroad came to occupy a central role in the dissemination of revolutionary arms and propaganda, a fact that will be explored at greater length throughout this book.

India also formed an essential hub for Britain's global security networks. Following its incorporation into British India during the mid-nineteenth century, the Punjab provided an especially important recruiting base for imperial policing. For example, the Malay States Guides, originally constituted as the Perak Armed Police and then the Perak Sikhs, were recruited from the Punjab in 1873 and remained the leading police force in Malaya until 1919. But the appeal of these 'manly' Sikhs was not limited to Southeast Asia – Punjabi police were prominent in colonies ranging from Hong Kong to Uganda to Somaliland.[123] Imperial recruitment relied heavily on conceptions of loyalty and disloyalty based on gendered discourses of masculinity and effeminacy that shared a mutually constitutive relationship with similar cultural assumptions within the British Isles. British accounts held up the 'martial races' of

[120] Thomas Metcalf, *Imperial Connections: India in the Indian Ocean Arena, 1860–1920* (Berkeley: University of California Press, 2007), p. 45.

[121] Amitava Chowdhury, 'Maritime Marronage and Trans-imperial Diplomatic Consequences of the British Emancipation, 1834–1848', in Hideaki Suzuki (ed.), *'Abolitions' as a Global Experience* (Singapore: National University of Singapore Press, 2016), pp. 149–60.

[122] Amitava Chowdhury, 'Narratives of Home: Diaspora Formations among the Indian Indentured Labourers', in Donald Akenson and Amitava Chowdhury (eds.), *Between Dispersion and Belonging: Global Approaches to Diaspora in Practice* (Montreal: McGill-Queen's University Press, 2016), pp. 240–53.

[123] Thomas Metcalf, *Imperial Connections*, pp. 68–102.

Sikhs and Gurkhas in India and Nepal as analogous to the fearsome Highland Scots that also comprised an essential component in British imperial forces. By contrast, stereotypes regarding the 'seditious *babus*' of Bengal shared a direct lineage with assumptions regarding the cowardice, treachery, and 'lack of manliness' displayed by Irish nationalists closer to home.[124] Key security personnel were often transferred from one site of unrest to another, often with the goal of deploying their knowledge of revolutionary tactics in India to combat 'terrorism' elsewhere. Michael Silvestri, for example, provides the example of Sir Charles Tegart, an Irish policeman trained in India to combat Bengali revolutionaries in the early 1900s, who would go on to contribute to imperial intelligence operations against Bolsheviks in France, Republicans in Ireland, and Zionists in Palestine.[125]

Chapters and Structure

This book comprises five chapters that progress chronologically from the Anti-Thug Campaigns that began in the 1830s to the international Convention for the Prevention and Punishment of Terrorism in 1937. While the current work is based on deep-sited archival research in and around colonial India, the relevance of its findings to a broader colonial genealogy of terrorism will be touched upon throughout. In some places, the book will engage with texts produced or statements made by the various 'subversive figures' who found themselves targets of colonial laws of exception, but the primary object of inquiry is the colonial state itself, as well as the legal and discursive strategies it pursued in dealing with extraordinary categories of criminality.

Chapter 1 analyzes some of the ethereal figures that populated the colonial imaginary in British India during the nineteenth century, including thugs, pirates, criminal tribes, and fanatics. The chapter argues that what was ethereal – that is to say, intangible or otherworldly – about these figures was not so much their existence, but rather their pervasive but ineffable presence within the colonial psyche and, by consequence, the colonial archive. Over the course of the nineteenth century, as British rule in India extended from a handful of loosely connected enclaves into

[124] Heather Streets, *Martial Races: The Military, Race and Masculinity in British Imperial Culture, 1857–1914* (Manchester: Manchester University Press, 2004).

[125] Michael Silvestri, '"An Irishman Is Specially Suited to Be a Policeman": Sir Charles Tegart & Revolutionary Terrorism in Bengal', *History Ireland* 8, no. 4 (2000), p. 41. This article also addresses some of the ambiguities and inconsistencies that resulted from a British reliance on supposedly disloyal Irishmen as police constables and soldiers in other colonial settings.

the paramount locus of sovereignty within the subcontinent, the identification and 'pacification' of various 'deviant' groups such as pirates, thugs, criminal tribes, and fanatics was central to the consolidation of imperial authority. Operating with a dearth of knowledge concerning regional practices, customs, and cultures, colonial officials tried to understand local populations by drawing upon a reservoir of overlapping yet distinct cultural tropes and stereotypes regarding the supposed barbarism, violence, and religious excess of indigenous society. The construction of categories of criminality lying 'beyond the line' of ordinary judicial processes in the nineteenth century would ultimately prove crucial to the later legal strategies adopted to police new, extraordinary forms of twentieth-century violence such as 'political dacoity' and 'terrorism'.

In Chapter 2, we see how many of the assumptions underlying colonial approaches towards thugs and criminal tribes were in turn projected onto early revolutionary organizations, especially the Dacca Anushilan Samiti in Bengal. Beginning by situating the political assassination of two British officials connected to the Poona Plague Commission in 1897 within the context of similar radical movements in Ireland and Russia, the chapter goes on to provide an in-depth examination of how an explicit strategy of 'terrorism' came to be adopted by anti-colonial secret societies in Bengal. By analyzing various publications put forward by Indian radicals expounding the 'philosophy of the bomb', the chapter argues that 'propaganda by bomb' was a form of political communication deployed against the structures of the colonial state in an attempt to undermine the legitimacy of British rule. The chapter concludes by detailing the various 'laws of exception' deployed by colonial officials with the intention of suppressing these revolutionary challenges to imperial authority in the prelude to the First World War.

The outbreak of global war placed new strains on British imperialism, requiring a massive mobilization of resources and stimulating the exponential growth of transnational networks of surveillance. At the same time, Chapter 3 shows how the 'state of emergency' provided by the war also provided an opportunity for officials to deploy unprecedented extraordinary powers of 'executive detention' against existing revolutionary organizations. In 1914, the Government of India passed the Ingress into India Ordinance in an attempt to limit the transgressive potential of Ghadar propaganda and transnational revolutionary networks based out of North America and parts of East and Southeast Asia. The following year, the passage of the wartime Defence of India Act sought to target revolutionaries who the government deemed to be either in league with Britain's German enemy, or whose acts of anti-colonial violence aided and assisted the German war effort. Following the conclusion of the war in 1918, colonial officials took steps to extend the repressive measures of the Defence of India Act into peacetime by issuing the controversial Rowlatt Act, despite the disapproval of an increasingly vocal Indian public. Moving beyond the security-centric analysis of previous scholarship, this chapter instead proves that the war was a space in which officials sought to create a new legal ordering of empire through the expansion of pre-existing corridors of imperial and, indeed, global jurisdiction. This chapter demonstrates that the wartime expansion of emergency laws was not only a response to security concerns or to the threat of foreign German interference, as scholars have typically regarded them, but also served as the colonial state's opportunistic answer to the more long-term political challenge presented by anti-colonial nationalism.

Following the Montagu-Chelmsford reforms after the end of the war, the continued discretionary power granted to the governor general in passing executive measures despite the opposition of the newly reorganized Indian legislature highlighted the emptiness of 'moderate' constitutional progression, giving greater impetus to revolutionary violence on the one hand and Gandhian direct action on the other. Chapter 4 assesses the complex relationship between the Indian National Congress and revolutionary politics, demonstrating that although the Gandhian faction ultimately won out, it did so only by a narrow margin in the face of the more radical political aspirations of important figures such as C. R. Das. The close connections between revolutionary organizations and 'mainstream' Indian nationalism forced colonial officials to develop new discursive strategies to justify the continued imposition of increasingly draconian 'emergency' legislation. In this context, the category of 'terrorism' became a useful rhetorical tool that was explicitly deployed with the goal of justifying controversial measures to the British Parliament on the one hand, and the Indian public on the other. In constructing 'terrorists' as a distinct category of evil assassins, officials could claim that controversial measures such as the Bengal Criminal Law Amendment Act or the Suppression of Terrorist Outrages Act were not directed against revolutionary nationalism, but rather against sinister 'enemies of their own country' with no political goal other than murder and mayhem.

The fifth and final chapter situates the book's earlier conclusions within a truly global context by exploring India's role at the League of Nations during the debates surrounding the Convention for the Prevention and Punishment of Terrorism in 1937, the first international law to target terrorism as a distinct category of global crime. A closer look at India's role in this convention provides new and important ways of understanding the larger context in which colonial officials framed their ideas about terrorism as a new and particularly dangerous form of global criminality, a 'world crime' that threatened not only the governing structures of an existing political regime, but rather the very notion of civilization itself. India's anomalous position as the only non-self-governing member of the League makes its enthusiasm for labelling acts of anti-colonial violence with the emerging internationally recognizable trope of 'terrorism' all the more intelligible. In signing on to the convention, the Government of India sought to secure international recognition for its existing domestic policies towards anti-colonial violence and, in doing so, it participated within a larger international discussion regarding the relationship between terrorism, territory, and sovereignty on a global stage.

In the conclusion, I point towards the ongoing legacies of a colonial 'prose of counterinsurgency', first in India and then in a wider global context. Legal measures first deployed against anti-colonial dissent, such as the Armed Forces Special Powers Act of 1942 or section 124-A of the Indian Penal Code from 1870, remain in force to this day, and their use shows no sign of abating. Similarly, the terms 'thug' and 'fanatic' now enjoy a global circulation in which, stripped from their original historical and regional context, they have come to stand in to connote an irredeemable criminal, often belonging to an 'unfamiliar' ethnic group or culture. The conclusion highlights the ongoing relevance of culturally based explanations regarding the nature of terrorism today and argues that a clearer definition – drawn from analytical observations rather than cultural assumptions – is needed if we are to finally move beyond a colonial prose of counterterrorism.

1 Ethereal Assassins

Colonial Law and 'Hereditary Crime' in the Nineteenth Century

The extension of British imperial power through the Indian subcontinent was, first and foremost, a process marked by violence and conquest. In the year 1600, a group of London merchants secured a charter from Queen Elizabeth I granting them a monopoly on trading rights in Asia and the authority to defend English interests by force if the need arose. This newly formed East India Company launched its first fleet in 1601, which immediately set sail for the profitable Spice Islands of Indonesia. Given the difficult competition provided by the firmly entrenched Dutch presence in South East Asia, the Company turned its attention to India, a vast subcontinent rich in textiles and spices, yet divided into hundreds of political, cultural, religious, and linguistic units. Although the mighty Mughal Empire ruled over much of northern India, the Company managed to carve out footholds along the coast, much as the Portuguese had done roughly a hundred years earlier. By the late 1660s, the East India Company had secured settlements at Madras and Bombay, and was in the process of expanding its reach into the wealthy Mughal province of Bengal. Although it is tempting to see the early phase of Company penetration into India as a primarily commercial endeavour governed by the twin logics of trade and profit, the political foundations of Company rule in India were present from its inception, and should not be understood as a later development that emerged only following the acquisition of Indian territory.[1]

It is essential to understand the Company as more than just a joint-stock trading enterprise, but rather as a state by the standards of its time. As an early modern corporation, the Company had the power to raise armies, conduct diplomacy, claim jurisdiction over territories and sea lanes within its ambit, and indeed to rule over subject peoples through taxation, law, and punishment. These functions did not emerge as incidental side effects of the Company's expanding territorial penetration

[1] See Philip J. Stern, *The Company-State: Corporate Sovereignty and the Early Modern Foundation of the British Empire in India* (New York: Oxford University Press, 2011).

into India but were part and parcel of its inception. In other words, the Company was not a commercial body that grew into a position of political sovereignty, but rather a political organization with commercial interests and functions.[2] In this capacity, the Company gradually worked to extend its reach into the subcontinent by constructing forts, forming alliances, and waging a series of 'forgotten wars' against various regional Indian powers.[3]

Viewed by the dominant Mughals as one small faction among many competing for influence across the subcontinent – and often a rogue, uncouth, piratical one at that – the Company did not play a major role in either the politics or commerce of India until well into the eighteenth century. By this time, Mughal power was in sharp decline due to a combination of factors that included costly wars in the Deccan, increasingly assertive regional forces such as the Marathas, and political infighting among the royal family following the death of the Emperor Alamgir (or Aurangzeb) in 1707.[4] In 1756, Siraj ud-Daula became Nawab of Bengal, inheriting the mantle from his recently deceased grandfather and occupying the important British port of Calcutta in June of that year following a dispute with the English. Siraj imprisoned the surviving members of the Company garrison in a tiny jail cell in Fort William, with some dying of suffocation overnight in what became infamous as the 'Black Hole of Calcutta'.[5] Although the exact details of this incident are disputed, the story of the 'Black Hole' served to bolster existing European prejudices regarding the supposedly barbaric and savage nature of Indian rulers. Company forces under the command of the young Robert Clive swiftly retaliated, and by 2 January 1757, Calcutta was back in English hands. Later that year, Clive won another victory against Siraj at the Battle of Plassey with the help of Mir Jafar, who then replaced Siraj as Nawab of Bengal with English support. Following another battle against combined Bengali and Mughal forces at Buxar, Clive was granted the *diwani*, or civil administration, of Bengal in 1765.[6]

[2] Ibid., pp. 3–15.

[3] For details, see Jon Wilson, *The Chaos of Empire: The British Raj and the Conquest of India* (New York: PublicAffairs, 2016), pp. 56–81. See also Christopher Bayly, *Rulers, Townsmen and Bazaars: North Indian Society in the Age of British Expansion, 1770–1870* (Cambridge: Cambridge University Press, 1983).

[4] For some of the leading theories on this decline, see Meena Bhargava (ed.), *The Decline of the Mughal Empire* (New Delhi: Oxford University Press, 2014).

[5] Partha Chatterjee unravels some of the myths and memories surrounding this incident in *The Black Hole of Empire*.

[6] A more detailed account of the Company's expansion in Bengal can be found in P. J. Marshall, *Bengal: The British Bridgehead: Eastern India, 1740–1828* (New York: Cambridge University Press, 1987). For the ways in which the conquest of Bengal fit

From 1765 to the middle of the nineteenth century, the British massively expanded their territorial possessions in India by waging a series of wars against the various regional powers that held sway across the subcontinent following the collapse of Mughal authority. Some of the most notable conflicts included wars with the Marathas of western India, the Sikhs of the Punjab, and the southern sultanate of Mysore.[7] As Company officials continued to extend their reach across the subcontinent, they also fought dozens of armed conflicts against countless smaller factions, which the British gradually subdued through a combination of pacification and patronage.[8] This period marked a profound reorganization in the structure of Indian society, as the flexible system under which the Mughals had held sway through a set of reciprocal rights and responsibilities between sovereigns and subjects gave way to the strict categorizations and fixed taxation structures favoured by the British.[9]

The extension of Company rule was also marked by persistent feelings of insecurity, anxiety, and paranoia on the part of colonial officials, who saw themselves as heavily outnumbered and surrounded by a culture that they did not understand.[10] This affected everything about the way that European colonists interacted with the local population, from the sharp demarcation of 'European' and 'native' zones mapped out in the planning of settlements and residences, to the disproportionate violence often meted out on Indian subordinates who in any way challenged the strict hierarchies through which colonial authority maintained itself.[11] While some of these categories were fixed, others remained usefully malleable and undetermined, complicating simplistic binaries between colonizers

into the longer histories of Britain's European wars, see G. J. Bryant, *The Emergence of British Power in India, 1600–1784: A Grand Strategic Interpretation* (Woodbridge: The Boydell Press, 2013).

[7] For an account of the Anglo-Maratha Wars, see Mesrob Vartavarias, 'Pacification and Patronage in the Maratha Deccan, 1803–1818', *Modern Asian Studies* 50, 6 (2016), pp. 1749–91, and Randolf G. S. Cooper, *The Anglo-Maratha Campaigns and the Contest for India: The Struggle for Control of the South Asian Military Economy* (Cambridge: Cambridge University Press, 2003). For the Anglo-Sikh Wars, see Hugh Cook, *The Sikh Wars: The British Army in the Punjab, 1845–1849* (London: Leo Cooper, 1975). The conflict between the British and Tipu Sultan of Mysore is well covered in Janaki Nair, *Mysore Modern: Rethinking the Region under Princely Rule* (Minneapolis: University of Minnesota Press, 2011), chapter 1.

[8] Vartavarias, 'Pacification and Patronage'.

[9] Mike Davis, *Late Victorian Holocausts: El Niño Famines and the Making of the Third World* (London: Verso, 2002), pp. 285–8.

[10] Ranajit Guha, 'Not at Home in Empire', *Critical Inquiry* 23, no. 3 (1997), pp. 482–93.

[11] Thomas R. Metcalf, *Ideologies of the Raj* (Cambridge: Cambridge University Press, 1995), pp. 171–85.

and colonized.[12] Despite the steady expansion of the Company's formal sphere of control throughout the early nineteenth century, British power remained heavily concentrated in a scattering of forts, settlements, and towns, with local taxation and law in the rural *mofussil* outsourced, for the most part, to local allies, clients, or subordinates. Given the paucity of reliable information on which officials often based their assumptions about Indian society, the cultural assumptions underlying discourses of the colonial 'other' are often at least as important as the actual 'facts' being reported upon by intelligence agents, soldiers, or explorers on the ground.[13]

This chapter analyzes some of the ethereal figures that populated the colonial imaginary in British India during the nineteenth century, including thugs, pirates, and fanatics. The terms 'ethereal' and 'imaginary' should not be taken to mean that these figures were purely fictional. Each of the above categories did indeed correspond to a tangible material reality, but in each case the reality was heavily distorted, embellished, or overlaid with existing or evolving cultural tropes and assumptions. What was ethereal – that is to say, intangible or otherworldly – about these figures was not so much their existence, but rather their pervasive but ineffable presence within the colonial psyche and, by consequence, the colonial archive. Pirates could be hunted down, captured, tried, and executed, but piracy continued to haunt the colonial administration right up until independence. Similarly, 'thugs' could be apprehended, interrogated, or transported, but the idea of 'thuggee' and the paranoia that it engendered regarding a perceived lack of colonial control within India's hinterland and waterways remained a recurrent theme in British administrative reports and popular culture.[14]

For this reason, I refer to the various targets of colonial anxiety in this period as ethereal assassins. This description is inspired by historian Julia Stephens' description of the 'Phantom Wahhabi' as 'merging a kernel of reality with overblown paranoia, haunt[ing] the imperial imagination as the embodiment of the intertwined threats of religious fanaticism and anti-colonial resistance'.[15] Although some of the figures featured in this

[12] Lauren Benton, 'Colonial Law and Cultural Difference: Jurisdictional Politics and the Formation of the Colonial State', *Comparative Studies in Society and History* 41, 3 (1999), pp. 563–88. See also Zoe Laidlaw, 'Breaking Britannia's Bounds? Law, Settlers, and Space in Britain's Imperial Historiography', *Historical Journal* 55, 3 (2012), pp. 807–30.

[13] Priya Satia, *Spies in Arabia: The Great War and the Cultural Foundations of Britain's Covert Empire in the Middle East* (Oxford: Oxford University Press, 2008).

[14] The word 'thug' has since evolved to imply a common criminal, robber, or unscrupulous killer, often with racialized connotations.

[15] Julia Stephens, 'The Phantom Wahhabi: Liberalism and the Muslim Fanatic in Mid-Victorian India', *Modern Asian Studies* 47, no. 1 (2013), p. 24.

chapter – such as the pirate or the rebel – did indeed represent resistance to the expanding authority of first the East India Company and then the British Crown, others – such as the thug or the 'criminal tribe' – were threatening not because they sought to challenge colonial rule, but rather because their patterns of life circumvented British ideas about what constituted a governable, and taxable, subject.[16]

While each of these figures had its own unique features, a significant degree of slippage and overlap can be found between them and – more importantly, for the purposes of this study – in the legal and security measures adopted by the colonial authorities to contain them. Time after time, the new threat posed by each successive target of colonial anxiety was said to justify greater executive powers, the imposition of new emergency laws, or the abrogation of the liberal rule of law – on which British imperialists in India claimed to ground their moral authority. Operations of 'pacification' undertaken with the goal of rooting out secretive groups of thugs, criminal tribes, pirates, or fanatics were typically directly linked to the project of establishing British sovereignty in and around the Indian subcontinent, by land and by sea. In this process, colonial administrators, judges, soldiers, police, and scholars produced, repurposed, and recycled a set of tropes portraying certain groups of Indian men as barbaric, violent, cowardly, secretive, superstitious, credulous, or fanatical. In drawing upon this reservoir of cultural stereotypes, various strands of colonial knowledge provided a strategic rationale for extraordinary legal measures that extended the reach of colonial rule.[17]

'So Intolerable an Evil'

The East India Company's conquest of India was an uneven and piecemeal affair marked by resistance, rebellion, and oftentimes chaos.[18] During the first four decades of the nineteenth century, British-led forces conducted a series of wars and 'pacification' operations against opponents that ranged from kings to chieftains to bandits. While the Company absorbed many of its former enemies' soldiers into the ranks of its own armed forces, many others were demobilized, leading to a surplus of

[16] Singha, *A Despotism of Law*, p. 170.

[17] On 'information panics' resulting from gaps in colonial knowledge, see Bayly, *Empire and Information*. For more on the field of colonial knowledge, see Bernard Cohn, *Colonialism and Its Forms of Knowledge: The British in India* (Princeton, NJ: Princeton University Press, 1996) and Ricardo Roque and Kim Wagner, *Engaging Colonial Knowledge: Reading European Archives in World History* (Basingstoke: Palgrave Macmillan, 2012).

[18] Wilson, *The Chaos of Empire*.

itinerant, battle-hardened men in need of alternative livelihoods. Many turned to brigandage as a source of income.[19] As a result, sections of India dissolved into anarchic cycles of violence that British officials held up as evidence of India's primordial propensity for disorder, but which were in fact direct consequences of the destabilizing impact of the Company's military expansion.[20]

A similar process can be observed at sea, where admirals and seafarers working in the service of local littoral states along India's coast were labelled as pirates or outlaws when they did not adhere to the impositions of the Company's new legal domain.[21] As Company rule extended beyond a handful of coastal enclaves to claim jurisdiction over the lucrative sea lanes of the Indian Ocean, the colonial logics of paternalism, protection, and commercial improvement drove officials to increasingly see themselves as guardians of oceanic trade, although the subcontinent's territorial revenues remained the priority.[22] From the Arabian Sea to the islands and inlets of South East Asia, existing systems of trade, plunder, or taxation that refused to recognize European supremacy or exceptionalism came to be regarded as deviant acts of piracy. Appealing to geographical determinism, colonial officials argued that the geography of the Indian Ocean was particularly conducive to piracy and that local littoral states and seafaring chiefs had thus been locked in a static condition of piratical behaviour and lawlessness from time immemorial.[23]

As historian Lauren Benton has demonstrated, the geographies of empire were not defined by contiguous coloured spaces on a map but rather by tendrils of sovereignty that extended along and around corridors, estuaries, hills, mountains, islands, and zones of varying degrees of direct authority.[24] In navigating, mapping, and codifying these various spaces of imperial rule, British colonial officials were often highly aware of the limits of their own knowledge and authority.[25] Uncertain of their

[19] Vartavarias, 'Pacification and Patronage', p. 1750. See also Seema Alavi, *The Sepoys and the Company: Tradition and Transition in Northern India 1770–1830* (Delhi: Oxford University Press, 1995), p. 40.

[20] Douglas M. Peers, *Between Mars and Mammon: Colonial Armies and the Garrison State in Early Nineteenth-Century India* (London: Tauris Academic Studies, 1995), pp. 59–61.

[21] Gwyn Campbell, 'Piracy in the Indian Ocean World: A Survey from Early Times to the Modern Day', *Interventions: International Journal of Postcolonial Studies* 16, no. 6 (2014), pp. 775–94.

[22] C. A. Bayly, *Imperial Meridian: The British Empire and the World, 1780–1830* (London: Routledge, 1989), p. 10.

[23] Simon Layton, 'Discourses of Piracy in an Age of Revolutions', *Itinerario* 35, no. 2 (August 2011), p. 84.

[24] Lauren Benton, *A Search for Sovereignty: Law and Geography in European Empires, 1400–1900* (Cambridge: Cambridge University Press, 2010).

[25] Bayly, *Empire and Information.*

surroundings, these officials conjured phantoms out of unfamiliar practices or rumours among local populations, often as a vehicle for expressing their own deepest fears or repressed desires.[26] While some of these categories, such as 'thugs', were considered distinctly 'Indian' forms of criminality, others, such as 'pirates', drew on pre-existing early modern and even classical discourses.[27] Officials neither invented these ethereal assassins out of thin air nor simply transplanted existing categories of criminality from different contexts. Instead, we can observe a process through which rumours and fears were rendered into comprehensible categories by re-appropriating and repositioning cultural tropes that already existed within British and international vocabularies.

Throughout the nineteenth century, colonial officials attempted to systematize a comprehensive understanding of *dacoit* bandit tribes, accused of ontological guilt through the simple fact of their membership in itinerant 'criminal' communities.[28] Distinct physical markers such as tattoos, clothing, and hairstyles, as well as the anthropometric measurements of one's skull, nose, or other physical features, were used by colonial ethnographers and police as indicators of potential criminality.[29] The idea that India was home to an underworld of criminals by birth predated the 'discovery' of thuggee, and in fact provided some of the legal framework with which thuggee was policed. The supposedly novel response to thuggee explored in this chapter was in fact preceded by major policing initiatives undertaken against dacoity in the late eighteenth century. Following a rise of banditry in the aftermath of the deadly famine of 1770, India's first governor general, Warren Hastings, implemented judicial reform in 1772. As Tom Lloyd argues, Article 35 of the regulations was particularly influential to the development of subsequent anti-thuggee legislation in the 1830s, as it provided for the summary execution of bandits and the enslavement of their families.[30] This new legislation was criticized by existing Islamic legal officers, who worried that insufficient attention would be paid to differentiating circumstantial

[26] Michael Taussig, *Mimesis and Alterity: A Particular History of the Senses* (New York: Routledge, 1993), pp. 65–6.

[27] Daniel Heller-Roazen, *The Enemy of All: Piracy and the Law of Nations* (New York: Zone Books, 2009).

[28] A thorough discussion of banditry and gang robbery in early colonial India is provided in Anand Yang (ed.), *Crime and Criminality in British India* (Tucson: University of Arizona Press, 1985).

[29] Clare Anderson, *Legible Bodies: Race, Criminality and Colonialism in South Asia* (Oxford: Bloomsbury, 2004), pp. 88–9.

[30] Tom Lloyd, 'Thuggee, Marginality and the State Effect in Colonial India, circa 1770–1840', *The Indian Economic and Social History Review* 45, no. 2 (2008), pp. 203–6.

criminals from habitual offenders. Just like the thugs of the early nineteenth century, dacoits were said to be 'robbers by profession … who have placed themselves in a state of declared war with our Government, and are therefore wholly excluded from every benefit of its laws', who could be readily identified through colonial knowledge and the implementation of extraordinary legal means.[31]

One figure that exemplifies the colonial anxiety of the early nineteenth century is the so-called thug. In popular accounts, ranging from the colonial era to the present day, thugs are depicted as fanatical worshippers of the goddess Kali, who murdered travellers in ritual strangulations as a kind of human sacrifice.[32] The phenomenon of thuggee was sensationalized by a soldier and administrator of the East India Company named William Henry Sleeman, whose imaginative and detailed account of the supposed practices of the thugs formed the basis for most popular understandings of the phenomenon.[33] The word 'thug' is derived from the Hindi word *thag*, which historically meant a cheat or swindler, and did not originally carry the connotations of ritual murder that it would accumulate in British accounts. The term *thag* along with the overlapping category of *phansigar*, or strangler, carried a range of contradictory meanings and certainly did not necessarily imply a uniform or universal criminal category as implied by the usage of the word 'thug' beginning in the 1830s.[34] The emphasis in later accounts on the alleged patronage of the thugs by Kali reflects deep colonial anxieties regarding this goddess. Depicted in many Tantric accounts as a goddess of time and death with dishevelled hair and a necklace of skulls, Kali exemplified British fears regarding the assumed depravity and violence of Indian religion.[35]

The idea that thugs occupied a space beyond the line of social law or of liberal rights was central to the manner in which thuggee was policed. An entirely new police department, the Thuggee Department (later the

[31] Committee of Circuit to Council at Fort William, 15 Aug. 1772, in J. E. Colebrooke, *Supplement to the Digest of the Regulations*, cited in Lloyd, 'Thuggee, Marginality and the State Effect', p. 205.

[32] For just a small selection of examples of how thugs were portrayed in nineteenth century literature, consider Philip Meadows Taylor's *Confessions of a Thug* in 1837, Eugene Sue's *Le Juif errant* in 1844–5, Wilkie Collins' *Moonstone* in 1868, and Mark Twain's *Following the Equator* in 1897.

[33] For a discussion of the extent to which the phenomenon of thuggee should be considered an orientalist fantasy versus a social reality, see Alexander Lyon Macfie, 'Thuggee: An Orientalist Construction?', *Rethinking History* 12, no. 3 (2008), pp. 383–97 and van Woerkens, *The Strangled Traveler*, pp. 6–9.

[34] For the etymology of the term, see Kim Wagner (ed.), *Stranglers & Bandits: A Historical Anthology* (New Delhi: Oxford University Press, 2009), pp. 3–5.

[35] Hugh Urban, *Tantra: Sex, Secrecy, Politics and Power in the Study of Religion* (Berkeley: University of California Press, 2003), p. 77–8.

Figure 1.1 A depiction of the goddess Kali. Images like these were sold to pilgrims and colonial British travellers and administrators, who would have brought them home as souvenirs, highlighting the 'exotic' nature of Indian religion. Creator Gabriel Huquier (French, 1695–1772).
(Photo by Heritage Arts/Heritage Images via Getty Images.)

Thuggee and Dacoity Department), was established in 1830 with the specific goal of eradicating thuggee and safeguarding the hinterlands of British India from highway robbery and other forms of dacoity.[36] The establishment of this new department coincided with Sleeman's first popular account of thuggee, published anonymously in the *Calcutta Literary Gazette* in the fall of 1830.[37] In it, Sleeman provided a sensational account of the hanging of eleven convicted thugs accused of

[36] In 1904, the Thuggee and Dacoity Department would transform into the Department of Criminal Intelligence, with the goal of policing the latest ethereal assassin – the 'political dacoit'. See Silvestri, *Policing 'Bengali Terrorism'*, pp. 36–43.

[37] The role of the press in feeding into the 'thug frenzy' will be considered in the next chapter. See also Maire ni Fhlathuin, 'The Campaign against Thugs in the Bengal Press of the 1830s', *Victorian Periodicals Review* 37, no. 2 (2004), pp. 124–40.

murdering thirty-five travellers. Central to Sleeman's narrative is the religious fervour of the condemned men who, despite four of them being Muslims and the others representing a diverse range of caste backgrounds, are reported to have all shouted the same invocation: 'Glory to Bindachul! Bhowanee's glory!'[38] Sleeman wrote that upon ascending the gallows, the condemned thugs took their own nooses in their hands, made another invocation to the goddess Bhawani, then placed the nooses around their own necks 'with the same ease and self-possession that they had first selected them; and some of the younger ones were actually laughing during this operation, at some observations that were made upon the crowd around them'.[39] The article went on to describe the thugs as members of an India-wide conspiracy centred on the temple of 'Bindachul' near Mirzapore, in which Hindu priests allegedly accept the bounty of the thugs as offerings to their goddess and dispatch gangs of assassins out in search of fresh sacrificial victims intended to 'propitiate' their 'blood-thirsty' goddess. The positioning of thuggee as a manifestation of indigenous religious excess set the thugs apart as a category unto themselves, in opposition to the 'civilizing mission' of colonialism, while simultaneously anchoring the practice within mainstream Indian religion and culture.[40]

Following the publication of this sensational article, Sleeman was promoted and placed in charge of the operations against thuggee. His subsequent book, *Ramaseeana; or, A vocabulary of the peculiar language used by the thugs*, became easily the most influential contribution to British understandings of thuggee, and served as the basis for most subsequent accounts of the phenomenon. In it, Sleeman claimed to provide a comprehensive digest of the Ramasee dialect, the argot or secret language supposedly used by thugs, including every word 'to which Thugs in any part of India have thought it necessary to assign a peculiar term'. For Sleeman, understanding this secretive language was central to understanding the thugs, even though subsequent research has determined that the terms found in the *Ramaseeana* are better described as a wide-ranging collection of working-class slang, used by various underground networks or communities, than as a coherent language.[41] The assumption that thugs spoke their own secret language connected to

[38] Bindachul was the alleged site of worship for the all-India thug criminal conspiracy. Bhawani (or Bhavani), like Kali, is an incarnation of the Hindu female divine.
[39] W. H. Sleeman, 'To the Editor of the Calcutta Literary Gazette (anonymous)', *Calcutta Literary Gazette* (3 October 1930), in Wagner (ed.), *Stranglers & Bandits*, pp. 174–82.
[40] Parama Roy, *Indian Traffic: Identities in Question in Colonial and Postcolonial India* (Berkeley: University of California Press, 1998), p. 49.
[41] Singha, *A Despotism of Law*, p. 208.

Figure 1.2 An artistic rendering of thugs strangling a traveller, drawn by Frances Eden in 1838.
(Photo by Apic via Getty Images.)

broader assumptions about the existence of similar patois or slang being used by other criminal communities, discernible by their mode of speech or even by distinctive body odours.[42] Aside from the emphasis on vocabulary, the *Ramaseeana* otherwise functions essentially as a colonial ethnological account of thuggee, reminiscent of other such ethnographies produced during this period.[43]

For Sleeman, the religious sanction apparently provided to the thugs by their divine patron goddess explained most of thuggee's distinctive features. In his preface, Sleeman wrote that the thugs were born into the cult of criminality, being taught by their elders that assassination was the will of their deity, and that 'the murders they perpetrate are pleasing to her, provided they are perpetrated under certain restrictions, attended by certain observances, and preceded and followed by certain rites, sacrifices and offerings'.[44] These restrictions included a prohibition on shedding blood – said to explain the thugs' choice of strangulation as their method of murder – and an injunction against the murder of women, which was said to violate the rules of the organization.[45] In practice, there

[42] Anderson, *Legible Bodies*, p. 128. [43] Metcalf, *Ideologies of the Raj*, pp. 119–22.
[44] Sleeman, *Ramaseeana*, p. i. [45] Ibid., pp. 44, 8.

were cases where so-called thugs did indeed use swords or other murder weapons that invariably drew blood, as well as cases where their victims were female, indicating that the actual practice of thuggee was considerably more varied and ad hoc than colonial accounts would suggest.[46]

In emphasizing the supposedly religious nature of thuggee, Sleeman assigned a distinctly Hindu dimension to what was, according to most earlier accounts, a flexible and non-denominational set of criminal practices rooted in local traditions of banditry and brigandage.[47] The notion that thuggee constituted a religious phenomenon fit well with British colonial perceptions of Indians as an inherently superstitious people held in the thrall of an exotic and barbaric religion. This explanation for thuggee also situated the phenomenon within a wider set of colonial assumptions about the supposedly predatory and savage nature of Hindu masculinity, reflected through concurrent debates on issues such as *sati*, child marriage, and infanticide.[48] The trope of an underground, Kali-worshipping cult of murderers defined by superstitious rituals and exotic practices would ultimately find new expression in the early twentieth century with the emergence of revolutionary nationalism in Bengal, the subject of the following chapter.[49] In constructing thuggee – and later terrorism – as illustrative of the broader failure of Hindu masculinity to uphold a 'civilized' code of conduct, the eradication of thuggee reported by Sleeman and subsequent colonial officials in the mid-nineteenth century highlighted the triumph of a British 'civilizing mission' premised upon the innate superiority of British masculinity and Protestant Christianity.[50] In other words, thuggee provided the rationale for a kind of 'authoritarian reform' that could marry the expansion of Evangelical and Utilitarian values with the articulation of an India-wide policing regime.[51]

Central to the 'eradication' of thuggee was the premise that criminal communities such as thugs had placed themselves 'beyond the pale' of civilized society, forfeiting their right to be surveilled, policed, or tried according to conventional legal procedures. As the British presence in

[46] Kim Wagner, *Thuggee: Banditry and the British in Early Nineteenth-Century India* (New York: Palgrave Macmillan, 2007), pp. 116–17, 146.
[47] Ibid., pp. 121–34.
[48] Daniel Grey, 'Creating the "Problem Hindu": Sati, Thuggee and Female Infanticide in India, 1800–60', *Gender & History* 25, no. 3 (2013), pp. 498–510.
[49] On colonial anxieties surrounding the worship of Kali by the thugs, see Urban, *Tantra*, pp. 75–85.
[50] Metcalf, *Ideologies of the Raj*, pp. 41–2.
[51] Singha, *A Despotism of Law*, p. 172–3. As Parama Roy has noted, the campaign against thuggee is not limited to this expansion of judicial authority, but also speaks to broader processes in the production of colonial identity. Roy, *Indian Traffic*, pp. 43–4.

India was shifting from a collection of loosely connected zones of control into a single paramount power that took as its target of governance the whole of the Indian subcontinent, regional approaches to banditry and thuggee came to take on an all-India significance, with thuggee itself reimagined as an all-India underground criminal conspiracy. It was no longer enough to expel thugs and dacoits from one region to another – instead officials viewed it as their responsibility to eradicate the system of thuggee entirely. From this standpoint, the campaign against thuggee also marks an early expansion of colonialism's 'rule of law' into more remote spaces of Indian culture and territory, laying the groundwork for the all-India legal jurisdiction that would ultimately be claimed by the British after 1857. It is also possible that the reason Sleeman decided to portray the annihilation of thuggee as a fait accompli was precisely because of the realization that it was impossible to actually establish the existence of any such all-India conspiracy.[52]

New legislation passed from 1836 to 1848 formalized the category of thuggee as a distinctly Indian form of crime while simultaneously failing to establish a clear or unambiguous definition of what exactly thuggee was or who exactly constituted a thug.[53] In a note from March of 1849, for example, a 'thug' is defined simply as 'a person who has employed poison as well as one who has employed strangling to effect his purpose'.[54] This rather open-ended definition raises obvious questions regarding the accuracy with which convictions of thuggee were obtained. From 1826 to 1841, 3,064 Indians were convicted of thuggee and sentenced to either imprisonment, transportation, or execution.[55] How many of those convicted actually belonged to a criminal organization – and indeed how many of these organizations truly fit the standardized mould of thuggee assumed by colonial authorities and popular audiences – has posed a serious question for later historians.[56]

The first piece of legislation to specifically target thugee as a distinct category of crime was Act XXX of 1836, which granted wide-ranging powers to Sleeman and the Thuggee and Dacoity Department in gathering evidence and prosecuting suspected thugs.[57] Arguably the

[52] Singha, *A Despotism of Law*, pp. 170–6.
[53] Act XXX of 1836, Extract Proceedings by the Governor General of India in the Legislative Department, 14 November 1836, BC, F/4/1685/68000, APAC, in Wagner (ed.), *Stranglers and Bandits*, pp. 189–90.
[54] 'Despatches to India and Bengal', 14 March 1849, IOR/E/4/799, pp. 890–91.
[55] Tom Lloyd, 'Acting in the "Theatre of Anarchy": The "Anti-Thug Campaign" and Elaborations of Colonial Rule in Early Nineteenth-Century India', *Edinburgh Papers in South Asian Studies* 19 (2006), p. 3.
[56] This question is taken up in Wagner, *Thuggee*.
[57] See Singha, *A Despotism of Law*, pp. 213-20.

most significant provision was the introduction of what Mark Brown calls the 'ontological crime' of 'being a thug' – in other words, the ability to prosecute a person based on their identity rather than the commission of a specific crime.[58] The following year, Act XIX further clarified the ability to use the evidence of approvers even in cases where capital charges were being pursued. Approvers were not to be used only in cases where a specific crime had occurred, but could also identify a suspect simply as being a thug or of belonging or having belonged to a thug gang.[59] Sleeman argued that ordinary criminal procedures could not apply to the thugs, due to their propensity for leaving no living witnesses to attest to their misdeeds. According to Sleeman,

> To suppress associations of this kind in such a country and such a society as those of India, a departure from rules like these, however suitable to ordinary times and circumstances, and to a more advanced and a more rational system of society, becomes indispensably necessary; and as they have matured their system to deprive all governments of every other kind of direct evidence to their guilt but the testimony of their associates, it behoves *(sic)* all Governments, in order to relieve society from so intolerable an evil, to mature another by which their testimonies shall be rendered effectual for their conviction without endangering the safety of the innocent.[60]

In other words, because a thug left no witnesses, and because the lack of physical markers other than an easily concealable knotted cord or scarf made the thugs so difficult to detect – let alone prosecute – the testimony of co-conspirators should be given greater weight than was normal under traditional British law. Approver testimonies were collected through a formulaic and dialectical process in which informants often told colonial officials what they wanted to hear as a means of reducing their sentence. Historian Shahid Amin describes the approver as one who could 'save his own skin and sacrifice those of his colleagues by his story-telling'. Amin notes that in contrast to the Inquisitorial model of interrogation found in medieval Europe, an approver's chances of saving his own life improved the more he implicated himself in the crimes of which he was accused, as it was this self-implication that established the approver's reliability as a source of information on his fellow criminals.[61] This complex process does not necessarily imply a conspiracy in which colonial officials invented thuggee out of thin air as a means of justifying their own presence in India. Nonetheless, it does speak to the production of

[58] Mark Brown, *Penal Power and Colonial Rule* (New York: Routledge, 2014), p. 49.
[59] Lloyd, 'The "Anti-Thug Campaign"', pp. 13–14.
[60] Sleeman, *Ramaseeana*, p. 54.
[61] Shahid Amin, *Event, Metaphor, Memory: Chauri Chaura 1922–1992* (New Delhi: Oxford University Press, 1995), pp. 75–85.

knowledge about thuggee as a process fraught with the potential for exaggeration, distortion, and the imposition of the cultural biases of the interrogators.[62] Colonial officials were not unaware of the potential risk of innocent men being implicated in thuggee 'through malice or stupidity by the approvers', but for the most part the system devised by Sleeman was thought to render 'the success of any such scheme of villainy almost impossible' as long as the proper procedure was followed.[63] Similar discussions would resurface in the early twentieth century with the policing of revolutionary nationalism, and would indeed play a central role in the construction of 'terrorism' as a distinct category of criminality, as the next chapter will show.

Never one to miss an opportunity for sensationalism, Sleeman warned that despite the great success of the colonial administration in extirpating the thuggee menace, it would be a mistake to settle into total complacency. For Sleeman, thuggee was deeply rooted in Indian society, with rural Indians allegedly covering up the crimes of their thug neighbours by disposing of strangled bodies left behind in wells and ditches in order to keep the activities of the thugs invisible to the prying eyes of the police.[64] This meant that colonial vigilance was required in continuing to monitor for any recurrence in thug activities, as to 'affirm absolutely that it has been suppressed while any seeds of the system remain to germinate and spread again over the land might soon render that has been done unavailing ...'[65] Thuggee had been defeated, according to Sleeman, thus validating the civilizing presence of British colonial rule. But in leaving open the possibility of a recurrence, Sleeman ensured that the imagined threat of thuggee would become an enduring trope in metropolitan culture.[66]

Just as it is today, the labelling of someone as a 'thug' became a useful way of critiquing a political opponent, with this idea circulating far beyond the confines of colonial India. Discussing the appointment of a Mr. O'Hagan to the High Court of Justice in Ireland, Irish parliamentarian T. M. Healy declared that people in Ireland 'did not care whether a man was a Thug or a Tartar, so long as he was an honest man'. In response, Mr. Blake remarked that no one would want to see the 'Thug Commissioner, in carrying out his religious convictions, now and then chopping off the heads of the landlords and tenants'.[67] A few years later, journalist and politician T. P. O'Connor accused the leader of the

[62] For a detailed examination of the process by which an approver's testimony was collected, see Lloyd, 'The "Anti-Thug Campaign"', pp. 18–22.
[63] 'Despatches to India and Bengal', 12 April 1844, IOR/E/4/780, pp. 780–7.
[64] Sleeman, *Ramaseeana*, p. 37. [65] Ibid., p. 21.
[66] Tickell, *Terrorism, Insurgency and Literature*, pp. 44–55.
[67] T. M. Healy, HC Deb, 20 July 1881, vol. 263, cc. 1397–1405.

Liberal Party of stirring up 'hatred and injustice to Ireland and the Irish people' and called him 'a Whig, and thug accustomed to rapid and violent changes of opinion, and to the treacherous treatment of Ireland'.[68] In 1853, Tory politician (and later Prime Minister) Benjamin Disraeli invoked the image of the seductive thugs as a metaphor for political duplicity:

> A Thug is a person of very gentlemanlike, even fascinating manners; he courts your acquaintance, he dines with you, he drinks with you, he smokes with you; he not only shares your pleasures, but even your pursuits; whatever you wish done, he is always ready to perform it ... but at the very moment when he has gained your entire confidence, at the very moment when you are, as it were, reposing on the bosom of his friendship, the mission of the Thug is fulfilled, and you cease to exist.[69]

In 1867, a doomed rebellion by anti-British Fenians in Ireland accompanied an upsurge in agrarian unrest, leading to concern among British parliamentarians regarding how to resolve the 'Irish Question'. In a House of Lords debate two years later, the Earl of Carnarvon likened the 'reign of terror' brought on by the Irish rebels to India's 'diabolical confraternity of Thugs', stating that just as the thugs had been suppressed by the 'unsparing exercise of executive authority', a similarly heavy-handed approach was required for Ireland.[70] In 1882, an Irish revolutionary organization orchestrated the assassination of two British officials in Phoenix Park, Dublin. The victims, Lord Frederick Cavendish and T. H. Burke, were stabbed to death with a weapon described by the *Irish Times* as an 'Irish Thug knife', an eight- to ten-inch dagger with a handle fixed at right angles to the blade, allowing for greater leverage.[71] Remarking on the assassinations, prime minister William Gladstone said that such a crime could not have been carried out without witnesses, arguing that while many might be keeping silent out of sympathy for the assassins, 'many more must be terrorized'.[72]

Theories proliferated regarding a vast conspiracy of underground radicals, reminiscent of the 'thug' secret societies of India. A series of articles published in *The Times* in 1887 sought to implicate Irish Home Rule League politicians in the murders, even publishing several letters purporting to show parliamentarian Charles Parnell's correspondence with a Fenian radical, in which Parnell allegedly condoned the assassination. Referring to the accusations against Parnell as libel, T. N. Healy

[68] T. P. O'Connor, HC Deb, 5 August 1885, vol. 300, cc. 1243.
[69] Benjamin Disraeli, HC Deb, 30 June 1853, vol. 128, cc. 1049.
[70] Earl of Carnarvon, HL Deb, 30 April 1869, vol. 195, cc. 1970.
[71] *Irish Times* (20 May 1880), p. 4. [72] *Boston Daily Globe* (7 May 1882), p. 1.

demanded an inquiry, and declared that if the English politicians refused, their honour 'will be placed on a level with that of an Indian Thug, and, for my part, I would rather be an Indian Thug, meeting my victims in the open, than a British gentleman'.[73] As a compromise, Parnell was offered a bill that would appoint a Special Commission to look into the allegations, called the Member of Parliament (Charges and Allegations) Bill. Scottish MP George Campbell, who had served as Lieutenant-Governor of Bengal from 1871 to 1874, referred to the bill – rather hyperbolically – as 'more sweeping and severe than the Act appointing the Thug Commission'.[74] *The Times* letters were ultimately proved to be forgeries, with the man behind them fleeing to Madrid and committing suicide, vindicating Parnell.

'The Terror of the Neighbouring Coast'

The transformation of 'thugs' into a religiously inspired sect devoted to human sacrifice roughly coincided with a shifting legal understanding of piracy within the wider world of European maritime power. Pirates in the early modern period tended to occupy a malleable position of fluid legality – sometimes working on the commission of a recognized state as a 'legitimate' privateer, sometimes engaged in 'illegitimate' piratical activities such as mutiny or unlicensed raiding.[75] With the expansion of European sea power and the formalization of international law throughout the eighteenth and early nineteenth centuries, these more loosely defined characterizations of piracy gave way to a more universalized understanding of pirates as *hostes humani generis* – enemies of mankind. Like thugs, pirates were viewed in early British accounts as a permanent feature of the Indian Ocean region that has existed since time immemorial. While many in the 'Golden Age' of Atlantic piracy deliberately positioned themselves as 'villains of all nations', rejecting the authority of the British government outright,[76] 'pirates' in the Indian Ocean typically maintained more ambiguous relationships to state patrons, often rejecting the criminal label imposed on them by the encroaching East India Company.[77]

[73] T. M. Healy, HC Deb, 6 May 1887, vol. 314, cc. 1154.
[74] George Campbell, HC Deb, 7 August 1888, vol. 329, cc. 1867.
[75] Benton, *A Search for Sovereignty*, p. 113.
[76] Marcus Rediker, *Villains of All Nations: Atlantic Piracy in the Golden Age* (Boston: Beacon Press, 2004).
[77] Simon Layton, 'Hydras and Leviathans in the Indian Ocean World', *International Journal of Maritime History* 25, no. 2 (2013), pp. 213–25.

While thuggee and piracy certainly refer to two distinct forms of criminality, each with its own unique histories and historiographies, it makes sense to examine the two within the same analytical framework.[78] Although the practices of accused thugs vary considerably from those of pirates, both represented a perceived threat to colonial trade routes and sovereignty because both ultimately undermined a central claim of the colonial government – its ability to police regions lying at the peripheries of its control, whether on land or at sea. In describing the activities of the thugs, India's governor general, Lord Bentinck, referred to them as 'inhuman monsters' who should be 'considered like Pirates, to be placed without the pale of social law and be subjected to condign punishment by whatever authority they may be seized and convicted'.[79]

As imperial claims began to take on an increasingly territorial dimension through the nineteenth century, a sovereign's ability to regulate the activities of subjects within an allotted sphere of control became an increasingly important marker of a ruler's legitimacy. One consequence of this shift was that groups who had previously occupied an irregular role within the dynamics of state power, such as bandits, raiders, or pirates, were increasingly reimagined as enemies of mankind located 'beyond the line' of normal legal processes.[80] By positioning these figures as 'exceptional' targets of extraordinary sovereign power, officials could reinforce the legitimacy of the state as the sole dispenser of violence and law by delegitimizing potential adversaries. At the same time, the expansion of territorial control relied upon the construction of these figures as oppositional reference points against which state authority could be re-inscribed. In other words, the state could often be positioned as 'legitimate' only in contrast to 'illegitimate' criminals, 'civilized' in contrast to 'barbaric' local practices, 'humane' in contrast to the 'inhumanity' of ethereal foes.[81]

[78] The comparison has been made, though not elaborated upon, in Lakshmi Subramanian, *The Sovereign and the Pirate: Ordering Maritime Subjects in India's Western Littoral* (New Delhi: Oxford University Press, 2016), p. 217 and Layton, 'Hydras and Leviathans', p. 221.

[79] Quoted in Sleeman, *Ramaseeana*, pp. 379–81. Similarly, as the trope of the 'thug' took on global dimensions, pirates increasingly came to be referred to as 'thugs', a trend that continues to this day. For a historical example, see 'Thugs in Court: The Alaska Pirates Arraigned by United States Commissioner Harsha', *Detroit Free Press* (17 August 1887), p. 8. For a bizarre example of the overlap between thugs and pirates in recent popular culture, see the 2018 film *Thugs of Hindostan*, directed by Vijay Krishna Acharya.

[80] Subramanian, *Sovereign and the Pirate*, p. 3.

[81] German jurist Carl Schmitt described this process, albeit in a different context, as the 'modern transformation of penal law into social pest control'. See Schmitt, *Nomos of the Earth*, p. 124.

Although the conquest of India was always a primarily terrestrial endeavour, the expansion of Company trade routes in the seventeenth and eighteenth centuries was also accompanied by a struggle to establish sovereignty over the sea routes that provided the lifeblood for the prosperous polities of India's western coast. Central to this project was the work of the Company's navy, the Bombay Marine. Originally established in 1613 to protect English factories from the Portuguese and the Dutch, the Bombay Marine was responsible for protecting Company interests along India's western coast.[82] At the turn of the eighteenth century, the Bombay Marine became embroiled in a protracted series of wars against Kanhoji Angria, an admiral and privateer working in service to the Company's opponent, the Marathas. Though regarded as a pirate by Company officials at the time, historians are now in agreement that the label is hugely misleading, and that the Angria in fact presented a sustained political challenge to Company hegemony in the western Indian Ocean.[83]

The explicit aim of Kanhoji's maritime raids was extending Maratha state power and resisting the European empires' claims to sole control over shipping lanes, making him precisely the kind of rational, pragmatic, political agent that colonial accounts sought to deny through the label of piracy. At this point the Company was still operating under the nominal sovereignty of the Mughals, but the expansion of Bombay's maritime jurisdiction though clashes against the Angria helped pave the way for English merchants and soldiers to extend their own reach along western India's coastline.[84] In this sense, the designation of the Angria as lawless pirates served as the 'maritime mirror' to the violence of colonial expansion, in the words of historian Simon Layton.[85] Even after the death of Kanhoji, his successors continued to periodically disrupt British shipping as far south as Calicut throughout the eighteenth century, only disappearing with the collapse of Maratha territorial rule in 1818.[86] With the

[82] Charles Low, *History of the Indian Navy (1613–1863)*, 2 volumes (London: 1877).

[83] See Derek Elliott, 'The Pirate and the Colonial Project: Kanhoji Angria', *Darkmatter* 5: Special Issue, *Pirates and Piracy* (2009), pp. 80–90, and 'The Politics of Capture in the Eastern Arabian Sea, c. 1700–1750', *International Journal of Maritime History* 25, no. 2 (2013), pp. 187–98.

[84] For a more comprehensive maritime history of the western Indian Ocean in this period, see Gwyn Campbell, *An Economic History of Imperial Madagascar, 1750–1895: The Rise and Fall of an Island Empire* (Cambridge: Cambridge University Press, 2005) and Ashin Das Gupta, *Indian Merchants and the Decline of Suraj, c. 1700–1750* (Wiesbaden: Franz Steiner Verlag, 1979).

[85] See Simon Layton, 'The "Moghul's Admiral": Angrian "Piracy" and the Rise of British Bombay', *Journal of Early Modern History* 17 (2013), pp. 75–93.

[86] Letter from Thomas Dorrill and Danvers Graves to Court of Directors, Honourable United Company of Merchants of England, 10 May 1743, IOR/E/1/32, p. 126.

consolidation of Company power between the Permanent Settlement of Bengal in 1793 and the final defeat of the Marathas in 1818, new efforts were undertaken to establish full control over the shipping routes of the Indian Ocean. By the 1830s, the earlier focus on providing convoy protection and passes of safe conduct along certain sea routes was replaced by the conviction that the Company now exercised a complete monopoly over trade and violence at sea. The Recorder's Court now demanded the right to intercept ships and claimed authority over 'all crimes perpetrated on the high seas by any person or persons'.[87]

Like thugs, pirates were also often classified according to supposedly hereditary classes, as 'piratical tribes'.[88] While cultural or geographical explanations had been invoked in seeking to understand earlier incarnations of Indian Ocean piracy, it is during the period from around 1780 to 1820 that religious and hereditary explanations came to dominate colonial discourse.[89] Sometimes the link between pirate groups and criminal tribes was explicit, as in the case of the Kolis (also referred to as 'Cooleys' in the colonial archive), a coastal seafaring community from Gujarat and the Konkan, some of whom were later enumerated as a 'criminal class'.[90] In the 1920s, W. J. Hatch explicitly identified the Kuravers as 'Land Pirates of India' – a class of supposedly hereditary criminals comparable to the pirates of India's coasts.[91] In other cases, what linked the two groups was the enumerative logic of nineteenth-century colonialism, which assumed the existence of static, hereditary occupational castes through which criminal predilections could be passed down from one generation to another.[92]

The distinction between acts of piracy and thuggee was not always self-evident. Many colonial officials were just as anxious in seeking to manage the security of inland waterways as they were in policing the better-documented cases of banditry on land or of piracy at sea.[93] Operating in a tangled space of legal overlap, river thugs, river pirates, and river

[87] Quoted in Subramanian, *Sovereign and the Pirate*, p. 237.

[88] Simon Layton, 'Discourses of Piracy in an Age of Revolutions', *Itinerario* 35, no. 2 (2011), pp. 85–6.

[89] Subramanian, *Sovereign and the Pirate*, p. 17. [90] Ibid., pp. 35–6.

[91] W. J. Hatch, *The Land Pirates of India: An account of the Kuravers a remarkable Tribe of Hereditary Criminals their extraordinary skill as Thieves Cattle-lifters and Highwaymen and their Manners and Customs* (London: Seeley, Service & Company, 1928).

[92] For a discussion of this process in wider context, see Nicholas Dirks, *Castes of Mind: Colonialism and the Making of Modern India* (Princeton, NJ: Princeton University Press, 2001).

[93] This point has been raised by Alastair McClure, 'Inland Piracy?: The River Dacoits of Colonial India', working paper presented at Pirates, Brigands and Smugglers in the Indian Ocean World, McGill University, 17 May 2018. See also Paul Winther, *Chambal River Dacoity: A Study of Banditry in North Central India* (unpublished PhD dissertation:

dacoits posed a significant nuisance for colonial administrators throughout the nineteenth century and into the twentieth.[94] In 1836, India's waterways were described by the Thuggee Department as 'infested by bands of fresh water pirates, having similar habits to those of the land thugs holding the same feeling, and different only from them in a few trifling particulars'.[95] That same year, it was reports of river thuggee specifically that provided the political will required for the passage of Act XXX, discussed earlier in this chapter.[96] By the 1850s, repeated reports of thugs, pirates, and dacoits operating along India's busy riverways led some colonial officials to call for the implementation of special measures such as the deployment of gunboats. Like the thugs who preceded them and the terrorists who would follow, river pirates were said to be especially difficult to prosecute given the secretive nature of the crime, the unfamiliarity (for colonial officials) of the riverine terrain, and the paucity of evidence as compared with 'ordinary' crime. As such, approvers continued to play a key role in the prosecution of river criminals.[97] While the references to river crime are scattered, they do appear frequently in the colonial archive, including one article published in the *Calcutta Review* in 1886 that referred to river dacoits as 'a disease in the body politic, requiring prompt and efficacious treatment'.[98] Concerns regarding river crime in the mid- to late nineteenth century represent the intersection of earlier anxieties regarding thuggee and dacoity on the one hand and coastal piracy on the other.

The consolidation of the colonial state's presence in the waterways of the subcontinent was accompanied by a hardening stance towards Indian pirates at sea. While European pirates were often romanticized in contemporary accounts, Indian and Arab pirates were not. European pirates often appear within the archive as freedom-loving buccaneers, whereas the pirates of the Indian Ocean were typically portrayed as barbarians following the dictates of culture, religion, or heredity.[99] Ethnographic

Cornell University, 1972), pp. 34–41. On rivers as 'treacherous places', albeit in an Atlantic context, see Benton, *Search for Sovereignty*, pp. 40–103.

[94] See for example W. Dampier, Views on prevalence of river Thuggee, 1844–1846, IOR/E/4, pp. 780–1.

[95] P. B. Bramley, *Report on River Crime and River Police Reorganization Scheme, Part 1* (Calcutta: The Bengal Secretariat Press, 1907), p. 1.

[96] Wagner, *Thuggee*, p. 214.

[97] Report on difficulty in coping with River Dacoits of the Doab, 2 September 1857, IOR/E/4/847, p. 373.

[98] *Calcutta Review* (January 1886), quoted in McClure, 'Inland Piracy'.

[99] Compare, for example, the descriptions of European and Indian pirates in John Biddulph, *The Pirates of Malabar and an Englishwoman in India two hundred years ago* (London: Smith, Elder & Co., 1907). See also Patricia Risso, 'Cross-Cultural Perceptions of Piracy: Maritime Violence in the Western Indian Ocean and Persian

accounts of various pirate groups became a popular means of providing a supposedly empirical rationale for understanding piracy as an innate indigenous propensity shaped by centuries of culture rather than local contingencies. These ethnographies increasingly described the pirates of the Indian Ocean as belonging to a diverse set of caste groups habitually addicted to piracy and whose acts of maritime plunder were said to be motivated by religion and superstition.[100]

With stories of the famous Barbary pirates of the Mediterranean gaining currency among European reading publics, Islam in particular came to be identified as a major force driving piracy in the western Indian Ocean and South East Asia during the first half of the nineteenth century.[101] The emergence of the Qawāsim 'pirates' of the Persian Gulf – referred to in colonial accounts under the corrupted form 'Joasmee' – was accompanied by a hardening of colonial attitudes and two major campaigns of 'pacification', conducted in 1809–1810 and 1819.[102] The Qawāsim themselves, on the other hand, may have seen their acts of maritime violence not as criminal piracy but as a form of morally sanctioned warfare against nearby Oman, a British ally.[103] According to British accounts, the Qawāsim captured around 216 ships from 1797 to 1819 in the region stretching from the Persian Gulf to southern Arabia and the Indian coast. Because these accounts often rely on a malleable interpretation of the term 'Joasmee', however, it is difficult for modern researchers to always identify when an attack was actually carried out by the Qawāsim. One consequence of the British construction of the 'Joasmee' as the quintessential pirate threat in the western Indian Ocean was the assumption that any piracy in the region must be carried out by 'Joasmees', thus created a self-perpetuating cycle of criminalization for the Qawāsim that was often unrelated to any actual criminal acts on their part.[104]

The absorption of the Qawāsim into the expansionist Wahhabi fold after 1808 provided the British with evidence that they were not just political opponents but universalist foes hostile not to both Christians

Gulf Region during a Long Eighteenth Century', *Journal of World History* 12, no. 2 (2001), p. 295.

[100] Subramanian, *Sovereign and the Pirate*, pp. 64, 124–38.

[101] Layton, 'Discourses of Piracy', p. 87.

[102] Charles E. Davies, *The Blood-Red Arab Flag: An Investigation into Qasimi Piracy, 1797–1820* (Exeter: University of Exeter Press, 1997).

[103] Risso, 'Cross-Cultural Perceptions', pp. 310–16.

[104] Hideaki Suzuki, 'The Making of the "Joasmee" Pirates: A Relativist Reconsideration of the Qawāsimi Piracy in the Persian Gulf', in Atsuti Osha (ed.), *In the Name of the Battle against Piracy: Ideas and Practices in State Monopoly of Maritime Violence in Europe and Asia in the Period of Transition* (Leiden: Brill, 2018), pp. 77–80.

and non-Wahhabi Muslims.[105] According to a letter from the Bombay Governor, one Qawāsim chief explained to the British that he and his people were 'compelled by the Wahabee chieftain to wage war against the Mahomedan powers in the Gulf, and to reduce them to the yoke and to the religion of the Wahabees'.[106] At the same time, the prevailing idea that emerges from colonial correspondence on the issue is that the 'Joasmees' had a hereditary addiction to piracy that could not be easily stamped out. The same Bombay letter goes on to lament:

> ... that every means of persuasion has for years past been exerted to induce the Piratical Tribes to abandon a course of proceeding so offensive to every regular Government but such have been their habits from their infancy, and upon which they have chiefly depended for their support, that neither our remonstrances nor the punishments inflicted on the Joasmees for their misconduct in 1809 have been productive ...[107]

The failure to properly 'civilize' the 'Joasmees' meant for some that the only solution left was to destroy them. Mahomed Yussuf, the 'Native Agent' at Sindh, encouraged the British 'to burn and destroy their Piratical Vessels, wherever they might find them, and in fact to extirpate them'.[108] In 1819, an expedition of 3,547 men departed Bombay and was joined by seven cruisers in the Persian Gulf. This combined force laid waste to the so-called Piratical Tribes along the Arabian coast and regional leaders were forced to sign treaties with the British promising 'to aid in the suppression of piracy should it again be practiced'.[109] In direct consequence of the suppression of the Qawāsim, the General Treaty for the Cessation of Plunder and Piracy by Land and Sea of 1820 sought to clearly define piracy in contrast to 'legitimate' warfare, stating that if any 'individual of the people of the Arabs' were to attack any travellers 'in the way of plunder and piracy and not of acknowledged war, he shall be accounted an enemy of all mankind'. The treaty defined war as 'that which is proclaimed, avowed, and ordered by government against government', while contrasting any comparable action that lacked government sanction as 'plunder and piracy'.[110]

[105] Ibid., pp. 90–4.
[106] Letter from Governor of Bombay, 22 August 1815, IOR: F/4/497/11931, p. 20.
[107] Ibid., p. 25.
[108] Translation by R. J. Goodwin of a letter from Mohammad Yussuf, Company Agent in Sindh to Governor of Bombay, 4 November 1815, IOR: F/4/497/11931, p. 98.
[109] F. C. Danvers, 'The Persian Gulf Route and Commerce', *The Asiatic Quarterly Review* 5 (1888), p. 406.
[110] General Treaty for the Cessation of Plunder and Piracy by Land and Sea, 5 February 1820, especially Article 2.

While the anti-piracy campaigns of the late eighteenth and early nineteenth centuries helped consolidate Company control over the shipping lanes of the Indian Ocean, the threat of piracy lingered. On 28 September 1859, an expeditionary force under British command left Bombay with the goal of capturing the stronghold of the Waghurs, a so-called piratical tribe who had rebelled against the Gaekwad of Baroda, a local ruler aligned with the British. Discussing the events in the London-based *Leader* newspaper, the Waghur uprising was attributed to 'the turbulence of the people' rather than the oppressions of the local ruler, 'if we are to judge from their history from remote time'. The region in question, a promontory encompassing Dwarka and the island of Bet, was known to colonial authorities as Okhamundul ('bad district') due to 'the thievish character of its people and the sterility of its soil'.[111] One contemporary account referred to the area has having been 'notorious for many years as a nest of pirates',[112] while another referred to the Waghurs as a 'mixed race of Muhammadans and Hindoos' who had long supplemented revenues derived from local pilgrimage with 'the profits of organized piracy'.[113] In a poem titled 'The Romance of Beyt', the Waghurs are depicted as '… a swarthy crowd / With nameless garb, and savage glee – / Their language rude, and fiercely loud – / Seizing the spoils that strewed the sea'. In this poem, the plunder of the Waghur is not connected to any specific socio-economic circumstances or broader historical context but is instead portrayed as an innate 'thirst for crime'. The poem locates Waghur piracy as timeless and eternal, referring to the Waghurs as a 'horde that, age on age, had been / The terror of the neighbouring coast'.[114]

As with the so-called thugs, representations of Indian pirates as a timeless menace lurking in the shadows of civilization served to reinforce the colonial project by providing a rationale for British intervention and occupation.[115] It is no coincidence that the publication of 'The Romance of Beyt' corresponded with the military campaigns of 'pacification' undertaken against Waghur seafarers. In an eyewitness account provided by a Captain Hodder, the assault on the Waghur stronghold by the

[111] *The Leader* (London) (12 November 1859), p. 1.

[112] *Launceston Examiner* (24 March 1860), p. 1.

[113] George Smith, *Life of John Wilson: For fifty years philanthropist and scholar in the east* (London: John Murray, 1878), p. 201

[114] J. R., 'A Romance of Beyt', in *Bombay Miscellany*, 1, no. 2 (Bombay: Chesson & Woodhall, 1861), pp. 158–63.

[115] The same holds true of piracy in the broader Indian Ocean world, including Malaya and the Arabian Peninsula. See Layton, 'Discourses of Piracy', p. 83–4.

Bombay Marine is described in detail, as is the sacking of a significant Krishna temple. A major pilgrimage site in the region, the temple at Dwarka, became the target of heavy looting by British troops, 'the gold plates stripped off the doors, and jewels of all kinds and money taken by the expeditionary force'.[116] Part of the intention behind the writing of 'The Romance of Beyt' appears to be a retroactive justification for the looting. The poem's protagonist, a fictional woman taken captive by the Waghurs, cries out in the poem's last verses for heaven to 'strike with vengeance this foul spot ... These shrines destroyed, which plunder fed, / Dark superstition's haunt of crime'.[117]

In the case of earlier predation along the northwest coast of India, colonial officials often sought to understand pirates with reference to ethnographic or historical accounts of their supposed antiquity.[118] Following developments in the policing of thuggee and dacoity through the first half of the nineteenth century, ethnographic approaches to understanding piracy achieved even greater importance by the 1850s and 1860s. In *The Administration of India from 1859 to 1868*, an official account of the first ten years of Crown rule in India following the transition from Company administration after the uprising of 1857, I. T. Prichard describes the Waghurs as having

> ... lived from time immemorial in idle dependence on its endowments and the votive offerings of the pilgrims. When these failed or time hung on their hands, they are said to have followed piracy for diversion or profit – a course for which their position, at the mouth of the Gulf of Cutch commanding the approach from the Arabian sea, afforded peculiar facilities.[119]

Describing the deployment of the Indian navy following the transfer of Okhamundel back into British hands following the 1857 uprising, Prichard stated that the need for immediate and sustained assaults on Beyt, and Dwarka provided evidence that the Gaekwad, having ruled over the area from 1820 to 1857, 'had wholly failed, even if he had attempted, to reduce to obedience that lawless tribe'. Prichard goes on to write:

> These people never wholly abandoned their restless and predatory habits; and whether under an idea that the vigilance of the British Government was relaxed,

[116] *Launceston* Examiner (24 March 1860), p. 1.
[117] J.R., 'A Romance of Beyt', pp. 160–3.
[118] Subramanian, *Sovereign and the Pirate*, pp. 103–50.
[119] Iltudus Thomas Prichard, *The Administration of India from 1859 to 1868: The first ten years of administration under the crown*, vol. 1 (London: Macmillan and Co, 1869), p. 299.

or that it had grown tired of coercion, or acting under some of those sudden impulses which occasionally drive half-savage races into wanton and fatal excesses, for the last year they have been incessantly giving trouble, plundering villages and slaughtering inoffensive villagers.[120]

Attempts made in the early nineteenth century to transform the 'piratical tribes' of India's north-western littoral into docile and governable subjects were clearly deemed to have been unsuccessful. But India's littorals were not the only spaces at the margins of empire in which officials struggled to maintain a sense of control over subjects who resisted incorporation – whether consciously or incidentally – into the colonial project. A widespread rebellion in 1857 prompted a vigorous military response from colonial authorities and the transition from Company to Crown rule. Obsessed with the intelligence failure of the 1857 uprising, officials sought out increasingly systematic and comprehensive ethnographic methods for understanding Indian society, as the following section will show.

'A Race Essentially Criminal'

Rebellions against the colonial state by India's various tribal communities during the nineteenth century were most often portrayed as apolitical acts of violence stemming from indigenous 'bloodlust' or innate 'savagery' rather than from legitimate grievances against British rule. An important example occurred in 1855 when an *adivasi* community called the Santhals rose up against railway engineers, planters, *zamindars*, and colonial officials in response to the loss of tribal lands and the clear-cutting of local forests for the purposes of cash-crop cultivation and the expansion of British-built railways.[121] Despite the clear view of the Santhals that their *hool*, or rebellion, represented a fight for social justice, colonial officials regarded it as nothing more than an act of criminality, a brand of dacoity with no political basis.[122] The hool was ultimately crushed by British Indian troops, and despite the romanticized depictions of the Santhals as the quintessential 'noble savage' in some British accounts, the prevailing perspective in colonial accounts was that Santhal

[120] Ibid., p. 300.

[121] See Guha, *Elementary Aspects*, Clare Anderson, '"The Wisdom of the Barbarian": Rebellion, Incarceration, and the Santal Body-Politic', *South Asia: Journal of South Asian Studies* 31, no. 2 (2008), pp. 223–40 and Prathama Banerjee, 'Historic Acts? Santal Rebellion and the Temporality of Practice', *Studies in History* 15, no. 2 (1999), pp. 209–46.

[122] Guha, *Elementary Aspects*, pp. 97–8.

resistance revealed a barbaric people in need of pacification.[123] Novelist Charles Dickens referred to the Santhals as the 'most savage and ferocious enemy' ever encountered by British soldiers.[124] Drawing on stereotypes of the infamous thugs, Dickens claimed that the Santhal revolt was precipitated by the need to assuage their 'sanguinary' goddess, subscribing as they did to what he called, 'a strange mixture of Hindu superstition, demon-worship ... and dread of, demons, ghosts and hobgoblins' in which the leap from 'intoxication to religion' was 'but one step'.[125] Rather than a political act of resistance directed against the extractive political economy of the colonial state, the Santhal revolt could be pathologized instead as a kind of superstitious fanaticism originating in the innate savagery of the so-called native mind.

The Santhal rebellion, and others like it, were precursors to the more widespread uprising of 1857 – referred to by the British as 'the Mutiny', or simply '1857'.[126] The uprising did indeed begin with a mutiny of Indian soldiers at Meerut, but it soon swept across much of northern India, incorporating a range of participants from local rulers to rural peasants. The most commonly cited proximate cause of the mutiny was the rumour that new rifle cartridges were greased with beef tallow and pig fat. Because soldiers needed to open the cartridges with their teeth and because cows are sacred to Hindus and pigs are viewed as unclean by Muslims, the cartridges simultaneously violated the precepts of both religions. Although there is no clear evidence that pig and cow fat were in fact used for the greasing of the cartridges, there is also no real evidence that they were not.[127] Regardless of the ultimate truth of this

[123] The 'noble savage' was a literary trope common to the romantic literature of the late eighteenth and early nineteenth centuries that celebrated indigenous peoples' supposedly uncorrupted and uncivilized characteristics.

[124] Charles Dickens, *Household Words XII*, 10 November 1855, p. 349.

[125] Ibid., p. 348.

[126] The so-called mutiny of 1857 (and what to call it) has been the subject of substantial scholarship for more than a century and a half. A sample of some of the more recent work includes: Bates et al., *Mutiny at the Margins*; Kim Wagner, *The Skull of Alum Bheg: The Life and Death of a Rebel of 1857* (London: Hurst & Company, 2017); Clare Anderson, *The Indian Uprising of 1857–8: Prisons, Prisoners and Rebellion* (London: Anthem Press, 2007); Wagner, *Rumours and Rebels*; Sharmistha Gooptu and Boria Majumdar (eds.), *Revisiting 1857: Myth, Memory, History* (New Delhi: Lotus Collection, Roli Books, 2007); Biswamoy Pati (ed.), *The Great Rebellion of 1857 in India: Exploring Transgressions, Contests and Diversities* (London: Routledge, 2010); Jill C. Bender, *The 1857 Indian Uprising and the British Empire* (Cambridge: Cambridge University Press, 2016); Ilyse R. Morgenstein Fuerst, *Indian Muslim Minorities and the 1857 Rebellion: Religion, Rebels, and Jihad* (London: I.B. Tauris, 2017); and Harleen Singh, *The Rani of Jhansi: Gender, History, and Fable in India* (Cambridge: Cambridge University Press, 2014).

[127] Wagner, *Rumours and Rebels*, p. 30.

rumour, it spread quickly, enhanced no doubt by the ease with which it fit into widespread Indian assumptions that the British were actively trying to undermine Indian religions in favour of mass conversion to Christianity. These fears did not come out of nowhere – they reflect widespread anxieties regarding the increasingly intrusive expansion of British interference in cultural matters following the rise of evangelical and liberal impulses through the 1830s and 1840s. Fears of a cultural or religious assault on Indian traditions also coincided with more prosaic grievances, as the Company's new doctrine of lapse forced Indian rulers without a direct heir to cede their territories to British rule. The most notable example of this was the kingdom of Oudh, annexed by the British in 1856 following accusations of misrule directed against the ruling Nawab. Oudh became a key site of rebellion, with the siege of Lucknow comprising one of the most important battles of the uprising. The issue of the greased cartridges, then, is better understood as the spark that ignited a broader conflagration fuelled by a variety of personal, local, and regional grievances.

After the initial mutiny at Meerut, the uprising spread to Delhi, Agra, Kanpur, and Lucknow, leading to a near-total collapse of British power across much of northern India, although Calcutta and the newly conquered Punjab remained in British hands. Upon seizing Delhi, rebels took on the aging Mughal emperor, Bahadur Shah Zafar II, as their figurehead, although his participation appears to have been highly reluctant.[128] The rebel troops at Delhi issued several proclamations calling on Indians of all faiths to rise up against the British in service of *dharma* (Hindu duty) and *din* (Islamic faith), most significantly in the Azamgarh Proclamation. Published in the *Delhi Gazette* on 29 September 1857, this manifesto called the uprising an 'Indian crusade' carried out in the name of the 'people of Hindustan', currently 'being ruined under the tyranny and oppression of the infidel and treacherous English'.[129] The proclamation went on to outline specific grievances relating to the East India Company's economic reforms including the loss of land rights by certain *zamindars*, the British monopoly on trade in commodities such as indigo and textiles, as well as the flooding of Indian markets with European goods and the consequent undercutting of local artisans.[130]

[128] William Dalrymple, *The Last Mughal: The Fall of a Dynasty, Delhi, 1857* (London: Bloomsbury, 2006).

[129] Appendix: The Azimgarh Proclamation, 25 August 1857, in *Essays in Honour of Prof. S.C. Sarkar* (New Delhi: People's Publishing House, 1976), pp. 495–8.

[130] For a deeper analysis of the proclamation, see Rudrangshu Mukherjee, 'The Azimgarh Proclamation and some questions on the revolt of 1857 in the northwestern provinces' in ibid., pp. 477–98.

The proclamation indicates that while the rebels framed their insurgency in religious terms, the range of factors that motivated Indians to take up arms against the British and their allies were considerably more complex, and were often rooted in specific socio-economic grievances shaped by colonial policy in the subcontinent.

Despite the initial successes of the rebellion, a lack of cohesion among the disparate pockets of insurgency, in contrast to the quick and efficient mobilization of troops loyal to the East India Company, led to the reconquest of Delhi by British-led troops in September 1857 and the formal cessation of hostilities by July 1859. Nonetheless, the scale and intensity of the uprising triggered an unprecedented panic on the part of the British. At a meeting held in Mansion House, London, a large gathering that included the mayor of London and a range of military and religious officials issued a resolution expressing their sympathy for the 'helpless sufferers of the recent mutinies', as well as its condemnation for the 'unheard of atrocities of the rebel army and its detestation of the rabble abettors of its cruelty to helpless women and children ...'[131] The idea that Indian rebels incapable of controlling their insatiable lust had violated or otherwise 'dishonoured' European women was a particularly popular trope in these accounts, with harrowing tales of mutilation, rape, and all manner of unspeakable acts forming staples of British press coverage of the uprising. There is no doubt that British officials and civilians, including women and children, were killed during the initial stages of the uprising, but sensationalist accounts in the press grossly exaggerated these atrocities and, in many cases, invented them entirely. In a memorandum drawn up with the explicit intention of uncovering the truth behind stories of Indian atrocities committed against European women, William Muir, the head of the Intelligence Department, concluded that 'the stories of dishonour done to European females are generally false'.[132] Similar conclusions were drawn from locations across India, although these conclusions largely ignored the plight of Eurasian or Indian women, some of whom were in fact abducted or assaulted during the course of the uprising.[133]

[131] *Illustrated London News* (29 August 1857), p. 227.

[132] William Muir, Memorandum containing the result of enquiries made by desire of the Governor-General into the rumours of European females having been dishonoured during the late mutinies, 30 December 1857, in William Coldstream (ed.), *Records of the government of the North-West Provinces of India during the Mutiny of 1857* (Edinburgh T. & T. Clark, 1902), pp. 368–72.

[133] Clare Anderson, *Subaltern Lives: Biographies of Colonialism in the Indian Ocean World, 1790–1920* (Cambridge: Cambridge University Press, 2012), pp. 146–9.

Despite the falsity of many rumours of Indian atrocities, the idea that rebels had tortured and violated European women provided justification for disproportionately violent reprisals by British soldiers as they reconquered rebel-held territory.[134] British counter-insurgency operations were more than merely punitive – in many places they were cruel and vindictive. Perhaps the most famous case of British retribution was the decision to execute some mutineers in spectacular fashion by strapping them to the mouths of cannons and then blowing them to pieces. Although this punishment had pre-colonial origins, it became a popular method of retribution during the chaos of 1857 as a means of desperately reasserting British dominance through a spectacular form of execution that both literally and symbolically sought to obliterate the threat of rebellious bodies.[135] Aside from executions by 'cannonade', British vengeance also took the form of mass hangings, summary shootings, and the razing of entire villages implicated in rebellion.[136] The indiscriminate violence meted out against rebels and their alleged sympathizers was so brutal that it needed to be explained and legitimized with reference to the atrocities – whether real or imagined – carried out by the rebels themselves.[137]

W. F. Mitchell, a sergeant of the 93rd Sutherland Highlanders, commented on the summary shooting of wounded rebels as follows:

> … the war of the Mutiny was a horrible … war for civilised men to be engaged in. The inhuman murders and foul treachery of the Nana Sahib and others put all feeling of humanity or mercy for the enemy out of the question, and our men thus early spoke of putting a wounded Jack Pandy [*sepoy*] *out of pain*, just as calmly as if he had been a wild beast; it was even considered an act of mercy … The only excuse is that *we* did not begin this war of extermination; and no apologist for the mutineers can say that they were actuated by patriotism to throw off the yoke of the oppressor. The cold-blooded cruelty of the mutineers and their leaders from first to last branded them in fact as traitors to humanity and cowardly assassins of helpless women and children.[138]

Those among the suspected rebels who escaped being shot out of hand by colonial troops were either hung or sentenced to transportation for life, a common form of punishment intended for both the practical

[134] For a detailed study of British retribution following the 1857 uprising, see Jacob Ramsay Smith, *Imperial Retribution: The Hunt for Nana Sahib and Rebel Leaders in the Aftermath of the Indian 'Mutiny' of 1857* (unpublished PhD dissertation: Queen Mary University of London, 2017).

[135] Wagner, *Skull of Alum Bheg*, pp. 175–89.

[136] Ibid., pp. 149–60.

[137] Taussig, *Mimesis and Alterity*, pp. 65–6.

[138] W. F. Mitchell, *Reminiscences of the Great Mutiny, 1857–59* (London: Macmillan and Co., Ltd., 1910), pp. 99–100.

purpose of furnishing the British with a cheap source of penal labour and the spiritual purpose of terrorizing an Indian population that viewed the crossing of the *kala pani* (dark water) of the ocean – and all that it entailed with regard to conditions on board transportation vessels – as a severe risk to one's caste and ritual purity.[139] One result of the uprising that would have particularly significant consequences for the history of political crime in India was the settlement of the Andaman Islands as a new penal colony. The islands form a long archipelago in the Bay of Bengal, located between southern India and the Tenasserim coast of Burma. Following an unsuccessful attempt to settle the islands in the late eighteenth century, British officials coincidentally revisited the idea of using the archipelago as a naval base and penal colony in 1857 before the outbreak of the uprising. The uprising resulted in massive jail breaks across India, as mutineers and rebels targeted prisons as symbols of colonial oppression and cultural violation, freeing some 23,000 prisoners across India during the rebellion.[140] As the British reconquered northern India from the rebels, they found themselves with a surplus of prisoners and a dearth of functioning jails in which to incarcerate them. Facing resistance from existing penal colonies in Burma and the Straits Settlements reluctant to accept new waves of political prisoners from India, colonial officials found the recent proposal to settle the Andaman Islands particularly appealing. Between April and November of 1857, the task of the newly appointed Andamans Committee shifted from assessing whether the islands could be settled to establishing which part of the archipelago would be the most conducive to a penal settlement. Between March 1858 and October 1859, the Government of India transported 3,697 convicts to the newly established penal colony of Port Blair, with a high number of these consisting of mutineers, rebels, or bandits otherwise associated with the chaos surrounding the uprising.[141] The Andaman Islands remained a key site of incarceration for political prisoners throughout the second half of the nineteenth century and, following the construction of a new cellular jail in 1906, became an infamous crucible in which the revolutionaries of the twentieth century forged their anti-colonial ambitions.

The uprising of 1857 and its suppression also had a transformative impact on the nature of colonial law, power, and sovereignty in the subcontinent.[142] Following the defeat of the rebels, control over British

[139] Wagner, *Rumours and Rebels*, p. 36. [140] Anderson, *Indian Uprising of 1857–8*, p. 2.
[141] Ibid., p. 144.
[142] The broader implications of this are discussed in Alastair McClure, *Violence, Sovereignty, and the Making of Colonial Criminal Law in India, 1857–1914* (unpublished PhD dissertation: University of Cambridge, 2017).

Figure 1.3 Execution of two rebels following the uprising, or 'mutiny', of 1857–1858.
(Photo by Photo 12 / Universal Images Group via Getty Images.)

territories in India passed from the East India Company to the Crown, with Queen Victoria assuming formal sovereignty in 1858. This accompanied a reorganization of Indian law through the imposition of a centralized Penal Code in 1860, as well as an increased ratio of British troops within the Indian Army and the establishment of the office of viceroy and governor general of India as head of the Indian government, directly answerable to Britain's secretary of state for India and the British parliament and monarchy.[143] The 'information panic' triggered by the rebellion led officials to seek out increasingly systematic methods of collecting apparently 'scientific' or 'objective' knowledge about Indian society. Driven by a desire to know, catalogue, and categorize the people over whom they sought to rule, British military and civil officers began to take a more comprehensive approach towards curing their ignorance of Indian society by producing accounts of various religions, castes, or tribes in which half-formed observations about authentic Indian practices and identities became overlaid with colonial cultural assumptions or fantasies.[144]

In 1871, assumptions regarding the hereditary nature of criminality were formally legislated through the Criminal Tribes Act, which designated certain ethnic, tribal, linguistic, and religious groupings as inherently criminal by virtue of their identity alone.[145] The act provided local

[143] There have been contrasting views on the extent of the impact of this transition. On the one hand, Tom Lloyd has argued that the extent of this transformation has been overstated, pointing towards the Anti-Thug Campaigns as examples of a 'state effect' that predate the events of 1857. By contrast, Alastair McClure has shown that the trial of the Mughal Emperor Bahadur Shah Zafar II ultimately forged a new social contract by recasting India's former sovereign as a punishable subject of the British Crown. While the imposition of Crown rule does indeed mark an important deepening of imperial sovereignty in the subcontinent, it must also be read within the context of a new global ordering that increasingly sought to rationalize and demarcate the bounded territorial limits of the modern state. See Tom Lloyd, 'Bandits, Bureaucrats and Bahadur Shah Zafar' in Bates et al. (ed.), *Mutiny at the Margins*, vol. 1: *Anticipation and Experiences in the Locality*, pp. 1–24, and McClure, *Violence, Sovereignty*, pp. 32–8.

[144] Bayly, *Empire and Information*, pp. 170–6.

[145] There is a wide literature on the construction of the 'criminal tribe' in colonial India. For further reading on the topic, see Anderson, *Legible Bodies*; Saurabh Arora, 'Gatherings of Mobility and Immobility: Itinerant "Criminal Tribes" and Their Containment by the Salvation Army in Colonial South India', *Transfers: Interdisciplinary Journal of Mobility Studies* 4, no. 1 (2014), pp. 8–26; Andrew Major, 'State and Criminal Tribes in Colonial Punjab: Surveillance, Control and Reclamation of the "Dangerous Classes"', *Modern Asian Studies* 33, no. 3 (1999), pp. 657–88; Jessica Hinchy, 'Obscenity, Moral Contagion and Masculinity: Hijras in Public Space in Colonial North India', *Asian Studies Review* 38, no. 2 (2014), pp. 274–94; Prabhakar B. Draxe, 'A Failed Revolt against the Raj: The Rebellion of the Berad, a Criminal Tribe, under the Leadership of Umaji Naik', *Social Change* 35, no. 2 (2005), pp. 127–30, and Brown, *Penal Power*, pp. 126–59.

governments with the authority to determine what tribes should be considered criminal by nature, and to intervene through the registration, resettlement, removal, or incarceration of any members of the specified communities found venturing beyond their prescribed territorial limits.[146] Members of itinerant social or ethnic communities across northern India were determined to be 'addicted to the systematic commission of non-bailable offences', and were placed under surveillance, their movements severely restricted.[147] This legislation had its roots in Act XI of 1848, which expanded the remit of the Thuggee and Dacoity Department to encompass itinerant communities across India, regardless of whether these communities could be specifically identified as thugs. In the 1910s, colonial intelligence officers attempted to further expand this legislation to also encompass 'criminal gangs', in a direct attempt to facilitate the policing of revolutionary organizations.[148]

In an examination of the skulls of seven men executed for supposedly being thugs, Robert Cox, a member of the Phrenological Society of Edinburgh, determined that the skulls showed 'a combination of large organs of the animal propensities with comparatively moderate organs of the moral sentiments'. According to Cox,

> The thugs belong to the class of characters in which I would place the captains and crews of slave-ships, and also the more desperate among soldiers; that is to say, men who individually are not quite so prone to cruelty ... but who, when temptation is presented to them, feel little or no compunction in yielding to it.[149]

This led Cox to conclude, in agreement with another phrenologist, Dr Spry, that 'many boys go on the roads as thugs because their fathers did, and not from any inherent ferocity of disposition'.[150] Still, phrenology played a contradictory role within the broader acquisition of colonial knowledge on criminality in the nineteenth century. On the one hand, Sleeman does not appear to have cited the findings of Cox and Spry to bolster his arguments regarding the thugs, illustrating the contested nature of phrenology, despite its broader impact on mainstream criminology. But the apparently 'objective' scientific evidence

[146] *The Times of India* (19 October 1871), p. 2.

[147] See Crispin Bates, 'Race, Caste and Tribe in Central India: The Early Origins of Indian Anthropometry', in Peter Robb (ed.), *The Concept of Race in South Asia* (Oxford: Oxford University Press, 1995), pp. 219–59.
See also Radhika Singha, 'Punished by Surveillance: Policing "Dangerousness" in Colonial India, 1872–1918', *Modern Asian Studies* 49, no. 2 (2015), pp. 241–69.

[148] Silvestri, *Policing 'Bengali Terrorism'*, pp. 50–3.

[149] Robert Cox, 'Remarks on the Skulls and Character of the Thugs', *The Phrenological Journal and Miscellany*, 8 (1834), p. 525.

[150] Ibid., p. 527.

provided by the study of these 'thug' skulls nonetheless served as an extension of the ethnographic project undertaken by Sleeman in collecting colonial knowledge on thuggee and helped disseminate blood-curdling stories about the phenomenon to a new metropolitan audience.[151]

The contested relationship between heredity and criminality can also be observed in similar debates regarding the supposedly biological impulses of other marginal groups such as dacoits, pirates, and members of other itinerant communities. Discussing the recent sentencing of sixty members of the Mina community as belonging to a hereditary criminal community, a note on the operations of the Thuggee and Dacoity Department in 1858 questioned Sleeman's characterization of the Mina as 'a race essentially criminal, and of a nature false and treacherous'. While agreeing that the Mina should not yet be 'trusted with any employment which would remove them from strict and constant supervision', the note's authors concur with the statement of Major Williams, the officer employed against the Mina, who stated that this group 'might readily be reclaimed by judicious management and extensive employment'.[152]

The note goes on to discuss a recent report by a Captain Lawrence, who wrote that the School of Industry established at Lahore for 'reformed' thug approvers and their families was meeting with great success. The sons of reformed thugs were said to have 'justified their employment by their conduct', and would soon be 'above the world, with a factory and machinery of their own and in a position to remunerate an overseer of their own appointing'.[153] Despite this apparent potential for reform, criminal tribes such as the Mina remained targets of colonial surveillance and suspicion right up until the end of imperial rule in India in 1947 and beyond. Classified as hereditary criminals under the Criminal Tribes Act of 1871, the Mina were referred to the following year as 'the most dangerous of all the predatory classes ... every Meena, whatever his ostensible occupation may be, should be regarded as without any doubt a dacoit or a burglar, and should be treated accordingly'.[154]

Central to the construction of 'hereditary' criminality were new advances in the biological and anthropological sciences, spurred by the

[151] Kim Wagner, 'Confessions of a Skull: Phrenology and Colonial Knowledge in Early Nineteenth-Century India', *History Workshop Journal* 69 (2010), pp. 27–51. For more on the history of phrenology, see Roger Cooter, *The Cultural Meaning of Popular Science: Phrenology and the Organization of Consent in Nineteenth-Century Britain* (Cambridge: Cambridge University Press, 1984).

[152] 'Despatches to India and Bengal', 11 August 1858, IOR/E/4/853, pp. 822–9.

[153] Ibid., pp. 830–2. [154] Quoted in Brown, *Penal Power*, p. 69.

publication of Charles Darwin's ground-breaking work on evolution, *On the Origin of Species*, published in 1859. The project of Victorian science was deeply intertwined with assumptions about racial difference, and the popularization of Darwin's theory of natural selection helped inspire a host of pseudo-scientific social theories such as eugenics and Social Darwinism. While the related fields of phrenology and anthropometry certainly existed before the publication of Darwin's findings, the theory of evolution seemed to offer a new scientific foundation for these theories. As such, 'scientific' theories of race did not so much replace older colonial classification tools such as language and culture, but rather emerged as a 'co-accomplice' that fit within the same intellectual framework.[155]

No one did more to integrate these dubious scientific methods with the study of criminal behaviour than Cesare Lombroso, an Italian physician credited with establishing criminal anthropology as a discipline. Believing that a person's level of evolutionary development directly corresponded to their innate capacity for criminality – as well as, of course, their race, class, and gender – Lombroso used anthropometric data to give widespread legitimacy to the long-suspected theory that some people were hereditary criminals by nature. Although Lombroso was ultimately forced to walk back on some of his arguments, his claim to have provided copious scientific data to buttress theories of criminality as a biologically inheritable trait sparked one of the nineteenth century's most heated scientific debates from the 1870s onwards.[156] While the relevance for the colonial situation is most pertinent to the current discussion, it should be noted that theories of hereditary criminality exercised powerful purchase within the metropole as well, where writers, reformers, and social critics such as Henry Mayhew sought to better understand the 'unknowable' poor of London through similar 'biological' typologies.[157]

'A Rebel Camp on the Frontier'

We have already seen how colonial ideas about the 'barbaric' nature of Islam informed legal approaches to 'Joasmee' piracy. Following the

[155] Shruti Kapila, 'Race Matters: Orientalism and Religion, India and Beyond c. 1770–1880', *Modern Asian Studies* 41, no. 3 (2007), pp. 485–8.

[156] For a more thorough discussion of Lombroso's theories and impact, see Stephen Jay Gould, *The Mismeasure of Man* (London: W.W. Norton, 1981), pp. 122–43, and David G. Horn, *The Criminal Body: Lombroso and the Anatomy of Deviance* (New York: Routledge, 2003).

[157] John Marriott, *The Other Empire: Metropolis, India and Progress in the Colonial Imagination* (Manchester: Manchester University Press, 2003), pp. 110–20.

events of 1857 and the more systematic and 'scientific' approach adopted towards colonial ethnography from the 1850s onwards, Muslims increasingly came to be seen as a distinct race predisposed towards acts of violence and 'fanaticism'. Like the thug and the pirate, the figure of the 'fanatic' became an analogy for the supposed religious extremism, irrationality, and violence of indigenous subjects. Whether in the mass uprising of 1857, the more individualized 'murderous outrages' conducted by Muslims across the north-west frontier and elsewhere, or the propensity for Malayan Muslims to 'run amok' on murderous rampages, colonial accounts sought to strip away the political agency of rebellious subjects, instead seeking to pathologize them as unreasoning 'fanatics'.[158] This section examines how colonial officials in the second half of the nineteenth century sought to pathologize the actions of Muslims who took up arms against the state by attributing this violence to inherent Islamic 'fanaticism' rather than political subjectivity.

Although the causes of the 1857 rebellion were, as we have seen, not limited to the grievances of any single religion, British officials quickly came to regard the uprising primarily as a war against Muslim insurgents. While violence was central to the colonial response to the rebellion of 1857, British pretentions to administer India through a 'rule of law' meant this violence had to be justified through a legal framework.[159] Colonial officials quickly designated the uprising as a 'war', thus justifying the suspension of legal norms. Extreme measures such as the State Offences Act XI of 1857 and Acts X and XI of 1858 provided draconian provisions for collective punishment for any non-European accused of 'crimes against the state'.[160] As the reluctant figurehead of the rebellion, Bahadur Shah Zafar was, ironically, simultaneously defined in legal terms as the *de jure* Mughal emperor and of committing treason by waging war against the state – a state of which he was, at least nominally, the head. To get around this idiosyncrasy, the Military Commission in charge of Zafar's trial sought to show that he was king in name only, and that his alleged role in masterminding the revolt was inspired by the primordial Muslim desire to establish a theocracy through violent upheaval.[161] After a twenty-one-day trial, the Commission sentenced

[158] Condos, 'License to Kill', pp. 479–517.

[159] Hussain, *Jurisprudence of Emergency*. For an older critique of the concept of a 'rule of law', see Carl Schmitt, *Legality and Legitimacy* (Durham, NC: Duke University Press, 2004), pp. 20–1.

[160] McClure, 'Sovereignty, Law and the Politics of Forgiveness in Colonial India, 1858–1903', *Comparative Studies of South Asia, Africa and the Middle East* 38, no. 3 (2018), pp. 385–401.

[161] Lloyd, 'Bandits, Bureaucrats and Bahadur', pp. 4–6.

Zafar to exile in Burma, where he would die a prisoner in 1862. By defining the rebellion as a war waged by 'fanatical' Muslims rather than a united uprising against British rule by India's Hindu and Muslim subjects, the Commission could strengthen the legitimacy of British colonialism while also formally replacing Mughal rule with that of Queen Victoria.[162]

Accompanying the positioning of the Mughal emperor as the leader of a 'Mahommedan conspiracy' was the transformation of Indian Muslims within the British imagination from cultural mediators between the Urdu- and Persian-speaking Mughal aristocracy and their British vassals to a suspect minority inextricably linked to insurgency and religious fanaticism. While Muslims had always comprised a demographic minority in the subcontinent, their privileged position under Mughal rule had afforded them a protected status within Indian society. Following the events of 1857–9, Muslims became a true minority in India in that they came to be seen as marginalized and dangerous outsiders to a majoritarian Hindu society.[163] During the retaking of Delhi by British forces, the Jama Masjid – the largest mosque in the city – was singled out for desacralization and desecration by British troops, who allegedly cooked pigs inside the structure and allowed dogs and soldiers to urinate in the sacred site.[164] This and other acts of violence that deliberately singled out Muslim bodies and institutions for retribution thoroughly terrified Indian Muslims, whether they had sided with the rebels or not. As the acclaimed poet Mirza Asadullah Khan Ghalib memorably wrote following the siege of Delhi, 'Each speck of Delhi dust, Is thirsty for the Muslim blood.'[165]

British retribution disproportionately targeted Muslims after the uprising due to racialized assumptions regarding the supposedly rugged, masculine, and fanatical characteristics of Indian Muslims in opposition to the stereotypically effeminate and unwarlike Hindus. As we have seen in previous sections, colonial anxieties regarding the supposed irrational superstitions of Indian religions have a deep genealogy throughout the entirety of the nineteenth century. While colonial officials entertained deep suspicions regarding the supposed superstition and religious excess of Indian religions in general, Islam came to be singled out as a

[162] McClure, *Violence, Sovereignty*, p. 36. [163] Fuerst, *Indian Muslim Minorities*, pp. 5–8.

[164] Bernard Cohn, *An Anthropologist among the Historians and Other Essays* (Delhi: Oxford University Press, 1987), p. 646.

[165] Ghalib quoted in Pavan Varma, *Ghalib: The Man, The Times* (New Delhi: Penguin Books India, 2008), pp.235–6. See also Masood Ashraf Raja, 'The Indian Rebellion of 1857 and Mirza Ghalib's Narrative of Survival', *Prose Studies* 31, no. 1 (2009), pp. 40–54.

particularly virulent strain of 'fanaticism', as we have seen in the case of the so-called Joasmee pirates of the Persian Gulf.[166] As such, the conflation of Muslims with fanaticism both built on pre-existing colonial typologies and simultaneously expanded these typologies in new directions. Prior to 1857, notions of Sikh masculinity and ferocity had shaped British attitudes, particularly during the Anglo-Sikh Wars in which colonial accounts portrayed the Sikhs as bloodthirsty and dangerous.[167] Following the uprising of 1857, similar stereotypes of Muslims were reinforced, while Sikh masculinity gradually came instead to represent their loyalty and steadfast nature – in a direct inversion of earlier tropes.[168]

Attitudes regarding the danger posed by 'unpacified' Muslims were particularly common on India's North-West Frontier, where restive Muslim tribes had long posed an obstacle to British expansion into Central Asia. Following the near-total annihilation of their forces in the First Anglo-Afghan War of 1839 to 1842, the lands to the west of the Punjab had become synonymous in the British imagination with rugged lawlessness.[169] As a result, British colonialism took on a particularly brutal form in India's North-West Frontier region, with officials relying on draconian emergency legislation and spectacular forms of punitive action in their attempt to keep the region under British control. A key example of this legislation was the Murderous Outrages Act of 1867, which granted the local government exceptional powers when dealing with sudden attacks carried out against colonial officials and their subordinates within the North-West Frontier by so-called fanatics. While the label of fanatic was not new, the term came to take on a more standardized meaning during the debates surrounding the passage of the Murderous Outrages Act. In his meticulous reconstruction of the debates and discussions surrounding the passage of this act, historian Mark Condos indicates how a standardized definition of 'fanatic' proved elusive to colonial officials, who experimented with several alternatives before settling on this term. Early correspondence relied primarily on the term *ghazis*, derived from the Arabic *ghazvah* which connoted religious

[166] For a good review of the literature on concepts of jihad in the specific context of South Asian Islam, see B. D. Hopkins, '*Jihad* on the Frontier: A History of Religious Revolt on the North-West Frontier, 1800–1947', *History Compass* 7, no. 6 (2009), pp. 1459–69.

[167] Anderson, *Subaltern Lives*, pp. 93–123.

[168] The topic of martial races, with special reference to Sikhs, is covered in greater detail in Chapter 3. For a discussion of colonial martial race theory, see Streets, *Martial Races*.

[169] For a recent account of the war, see William Dalrymple, *The Return of a King: The Battle for Afghanistan* (London: Bloomsbury, 2013).

warfare waged against non-Muslims. Wanting a more flexible term that could encompass the religious extremism of Hindus and Sikhs as well as Muslims, officials settled upon first 'political or religious fanatic' and then the more ambiguous 'fanatic'.[170]

The Murderous Outrages Act shared a close genealogy with earlier pieces of extraordinary legislation such as those targeting thugs and dacoits, but the most direct antecedent was the Act for the Suppression of Outrages in Malabar in 1854, also known as the 'Moplah Act'.[171] As we have seen, the Malabar coast had, since the time of Kanhoji Angria in the late seventeenth century, been associated by the British with piracy and unrest. During the period from 1836 to 1922, however, the region also became associated in the colonial imagination with periodic unrest generated by the Mappila community – 'Moplahs' within the colonial vocabulary. In a series of small-scale attacks spread out across the better part of a century, Mappila insurgents assassinated numerous Hindu landlords and their family members. The assassinations were motivated by a complex set of economic, political, and communal issues, but because the Mappilas often prepared for the attacks through ritual prayer, fasting, and the donning of white robes, colonial authorities at the time were quick to label the resistance as religiously inspired fanaticism.[172] The description of the Mappilas provided in an article from 1851 is typical. The article referred to the so-called Moplahs as belonging to a recently formed sect founded 'by the preaching of a mad Mussulman saint', notable for the 'extraordinary virtue they attach to the act of killing an idolator, which, together with dying in the cause of religion, they believe ensures them an immediate and peculiar reward in the next world'.[173] The following year, a local judge compiled a report depicting the Mappilas as an out-of-control menace that had reduced the Hindu landlords to a state of nervous terror, and which existing laws were 'wholly ineffectual' in combatting. In October 1854, the passage of the Moplah Act granted unprecedented power for colonial officials to inflict collective punishments and to detain and execute suspected 'fanatics'.[174]

Like the Moplah Act, the Murderous Outrages Act targeted Muslim 'fanatics', a loosely defined category of religiously inspired assassins. The act granted special tribunals the power to execute suspects and incinerate their remains based on a fairly loose standard of evidence. The extreme

[170] Condos, *Insecurity State*, p. 164–7. [171] Condos, 'License to Kill', p. 481.
[172] Condos, *Insecurity State*, pp. 145–9. For a review of some of the existing approaches to the topic, see David Arnold, 'Islam, the Mappilas, and Peasant Revolt in Malabar', *The Journal of Peasant Studies*, 9, no. 2 (1982), pp. 255–65.
[173] *New York Tribune* (10 November 1851), p. 6.
[174] Condos, *Insecurity State*, pp. 147–8.

measures enabled by this act reflect the deep-seated anxiety that these killings generated among colonial officials, representing as they did a threat to European lives and colonial authority. From 1849, when the British first took control of the frontier, to the passing of the act in 1867, sixteen Europeans and their Indian subordinates were either killed or wounded as a result of these 'murderous outrages'.[175] While these murders indicate that there was certainly some reality underlying colonial fears of subversion, British paranoia regarding a widespread and pervasive political plot to bring down the empire was greatly overblown.[176] Still, in the traumatic wake of the 1857 uprising, colonial lawmakers were increasingly convinced that only legislation allowing for quick and effective executive action would keep 'subversive' groups under control and ensure the stability of colonial rule.

On 20 September 1871, the spectre of the Muslim fanatic penetrated the heart of British judicial authority in India when the officiating chief justice of the High Court, Justice John Paxton Norman, was stabbed to death on the steps of Calcutta's Town Hall in broad daylight. His assailant, a Punjabi Muslim named Abdulla, stabbed Norman with a knife, first in the back and then in the abdomen before being subdued by the assembled crowd, with Norman dying of his wounds the following morning. The police were able to find no evidence of a conspiracy and Abdulla made no defence in his trial, simply stating that he previously presented a petition to Norman, whose refusal to take it made Abdulla angry.[177] It is possible that the petition in question was a response to Norman's refusal to grant a writ of habeus corpus to the Khan brothers in the well-publicized 'Wahhabi Trials' being conducted in Patna, Calcutta, and London, although this is conjecture.[178]

By most accounts, Abdulla was calm and collected throughout both the murder and the trial, with *The Saturday Review* reporting that he did not 'show any of the wild fury or unreasoning passion which might have given a clue to his motives in personal hatred or the fancies of a diseased brain'.[179] Private government correspondence, however, speculated that Abdulla was a religious fanatic. According to this unverified account, Abdulla lived from 1869 to February of 1870 in a mosque in Mirzapore

[175] Ibid., pp. 150–1. See also Elisabeth Kolsky, 'The Colonial Rule of Law and the Legal Regime of Exception: Frontier "Fanaticism" and State Violence in British India', *American Historical Review* 120, no. 4 (2015), pp. 1218–46.
[176] See Stephens, 'The Phantom Wahhabi', pp. 22–52.
[177] Commissioner of Police to Private Secretary to the Governor General, 8 October 1871. Home Department 1871 A, Judicial Proceedings, no. 22.
[178] Stephens, 'The Phantom Wahhabi', p. 39.
[179] *The Saturday Review* (28 October 1871).

and, while there, expressed the belief that 'a religious war with the English was lawful' and that he wanted to murder Norman so that Abdulla could become a *shaheed*, or martyr.[180] Ultimately, Abdulla was sentenced to death following his refusal to explain a clear motive, leading the judge to accuse him of a 'dark and ill-regulated mind'.[181] Later accounts took it as given that the murder had been carried out in the name of 'the fanatical rage of the Wahabi sect ... the duty of a holy war for the expulsion of their Christian rulers being constantly preached amongst them'.[182] Abdulla's murder of Norman, by his own account a result of an unanswered political grievance, thus came to take on a wider significance within the British imaginary, representing the broader threat of fanatical Muslim subversion.

Shortly after the assassination of Norman, his friend Sir William Wilson Hunter published *The Indian Musalmans: Are They Bound in Conscience to Rebel Against the Queen?*, a text that went on to become one of the most influential colonial treatises on Islamic 'fanaticism'. Hunter's short answer for his titular question was yes, the very nature of Islam marked Muslims out as fundamentally incapable of living under a non-Muslim ruler without rebellion arising as a religious duty.[183] The text begins in a sensational manner, referring to Indian Muslims as a 'rebel camp on our frontier' that occasionally sent forth 'fanatic swarms, who have attacked our camps, burned our villages, murdered our subjects, and involved our troops in three costly Wars'.[184] Like the thugs of the early nineteenth century, Muslim fanatics are portrayed as an India-wide underground network of conspiracy, connecting the mountains of the Punjab in the west with the tropical swamps of the Bengal delta in the east. Although Hunter divided the Muslim population into extremists and moderates, he claimed that the very nature of Islam provided the potential for even the moderates to rebel against their colonial rulers. Hunter wrote, 'While the more fanatical of the Musalmans have thus engaged in overt sedition, the whole Muhammadan community has been

[180] Mirzapore Magistrate to Simla Home Secretary, 10 October 1871. Judicial Home Department Proceedings, no. 38.

[181] *Empire* (Sydney) (5 December 1871), p. 3.

[182] *Annual Register: A review of public events at home and abroad for the year 1871* (London: Rivingtons, Waterloo Place, 1872), pp. 101–2.

[183] This is not unlike nineteenth century stereotypes of Jews as a disloyal minority at odds with mainstream European Christian society. See Aamir Mufti, *Enlightenment in the Colony: The Jewish Question and the Crisis of Postcolonial Culture* (Princeton, NJ: Princeton University Press, 2007).

[184] William Hunter, *The Indian Musulmans: Are they bound in conscience to rebel against the Queen?*, 2nd ed. (London: Trübner and Company, 1872) p. 9.

openly deliberating on their obligation to rebel.'[185] Based on a selective reading of Islamic documents that privileged *fatwas* that supported his argument and downplayed the significance of declarations of Muslim loyalty, Hunter believed that Islamic jurisprudence was intrinsically incompatible with infidel rule.[186] He also constructed Indian Muslims as a homogenous category primed for fanaticism and sedition, who would always put their religion ahead of any non-Islamic form of government.

Writing in response to Hunter, the eminent Muslim reformist and philosopher (later Sir) Sayyid Ahmed Khan published *Review on Dr. Hunter's Indian Musulmans: Are They Bound in Conscience to Rebel Against the Queen?* in 1872, just after the release of the second edition of the original *Indian Musulmans*. At the time of publishing, Khan was perhaps the most respected Indian Muslim intellectual within British circles, having written extensively about loyalty to the British Crown, as well as providing help to the British during the uprising of 1857, which ultimately earned him a knighthood in 1888.[187] Khan's *Review* dissected Hunter's arguments point by point, arguing that Hunter had fundamentally misread, mischaracterized, and misrepresented Islamic texts within his analysis.[188] One reason Khan's critique of Hunter was so effective was that, as a loyal modernist committed to aligning Islam with Western science, Khan represented exactly the type of Muslim that Hunter claimed didn't exist.[189] At the most basic level, Khan argued that Hunter failed to understand simple distinctions within Islam such as those between members of the Wahhabi sect and other Muslims, or between the concepts of *ijtihad* (textual exegesis) and *jihad* (struggle, as interpreted either in spiritual or martial terms).[190] Khan further maintained that Hunter's interpretation of the distinction between *dar al-Islam* (the realm of Islam) and *dar al-harb* (the realm of war) was wholly inconsistent with Islamic law and precedent. This is an important point, as Hunter's interpretation of anti-British jihad as a religious obligation to even moderate Muslims hinged upon his argument that any territory

[185] Ibid., p. 10. [186] Ibid., p. 70.

[187] For an analysis of Khan's sometimes contradictory roles as a religious reformer, cultural modernizer, and imperial apologist, see Faisal Devji, 'Apologetic Modernity', *Modern Intellectual History* 4, no. 1 (2007), pp. 61–76.

[188] A more comprehensive analysis of Khan's rebuttal can be found in Fuerst, *Indian Muslim Minorities*, pp. 86–122.

[189] Ibid., p. 86.

[190] Sayyid Ahmad Khan, *Review on Dr. Hunter's Indian Musalmans: Are they bound in conscience to rebel against the Queen?* (Benares: Printed at the Medical Hall Press, 1872), pp. 12, 37.

ruled by a non-Muslim authority constituted *dar al-harb*, a point which Khan thoroughly refuted.[191]

In 1872, the same year that Khan published his critique of Hunter, Lord Mayo, the viceroy and governor general of India, was assassinated by a convict while conducting a tour of the Andaman Islands on the 8th of February.[192] Having just completed his inspection of the penal settlement at Port Blair, Mayo was on his way back to his ship, the *Glasgow*, when an Afghan convict named Shere Ali leapt from cover and stabbed him twice in the back with a kitchen knife. In a telegram delivered four days later, a private secretary to the Government of India in Calcutta informed Queen Victoria of the murder, writing that there was 'no evidence of political motive – the act must have been suddenly conceived and executed'.[193] In an article published in *The Saturday Review* on 17 February, the author similarly stated that there was no political motive behind the attack, arguing instead that the assassination was largely explained by the disorderly environment of the Andamans penal colony:

> The assassin of Lord Mayo had therefore been living for a long period in a society where every thought and purpose of crime had been allowed to grow unchecked, and where deeds of violence had at least the sanction of the connivance or neglect of the authorities.[194]

The author contrasted this with the case of Norman's killer, Abdulla, 'who struck his blow in the midst of an orderly and calm society', representing a far more dangerous form of barbaric fanaticism. In the article, Shere Ali's crime is explained by the chaotic environment of both his current incarceration and his 'semi-barbarous' upbringing on the Afghan frontier, which had 'made violence and revolt seem to him the natural course of daily existence'.[195] The most common explanation for this shocking event drew on familiar stereotypes about Muslim fanaticism. In the British periodical *Good Words*, columnist T. Farquhar wrote that Mayo's murder had to have been premeditated, and referred to Shere Ali as a member of 'a class of assassins, who have blackened by their deeds the corner of India from which they have sprung'.[196] Upon announcing the murder in Parliament, Prime Minister William

[191] Ibid., p.32.

[192] The Andamans penal colony was a common destination for Muslims accused of participation in Wahabi conspiracies. See Satadru Sen, 'Contexts, Representation and the Colonized Convict: Maulana Thanesari in the Andaman Islands', *Crime, History & Societies* 8, no. 2 (2004), pp. 117–39, and Anderson, *Subaltern Lives*, pp. 124–56.

[193] Telegram from Private Secretary at Calcutta to Queen Victoria, 12 February 1872, in Queen Victoria's journals (electronic resource), pp. 37–8 (foldout).

[194] *The Saturday Review* (17 February 1872), p. 1.

[195] Ibid.

[196] *Good Words*, no. 13 (January 1872), p. 495.

Gladstone immediately referred to the assassination as 'a deplorable act of individual fanaticism'. The eighty-two-year-old Colonel William Henry Sykes, a naturalist, orientalist, and soldier with long experience in India, was quick to add that the murder was 'quite independent of any political feeling' and should be understood as an act of personal revenge carried out by a 'Mahomedan fanatic' in retaliation for his incarceration.[197] Although it was common for officials at the time to refer to the murder in terms of a jihad, Shere Ali does not appear to have gained any special status as a martyr following the assassination, despite his attempt to justify his actions by referring to Abdulla as his 'brother', thus ascribing some measure of religious legitimation to the murder.[198]

Writing in *Fraser's Magazine*, Robert H. Elliot, a coffee planter in Mysore, wrote that the assassination would precipitate 'a new phase of Oriental life', in which Indians would be emboldened to carry out more attacks against the British. According to Elliot, the murder of the viceroy, regardless of its intent, was 'a deed of the gravest political importance' that had irrevocably damaged British prestige and would inspire other Indians, disgruntled from more than a century of colonial oppression, to make similar attempts on the lives of British officials and colonists.[199] Contrary to explanations prevalent at the time, Elliot argued that whether or not the assassination bore religious connotations, its political and anti-colonial implications were undeniable. This political reading of the murder does not seem to have gained much traction in British metropolitan circles – an announcement regarding the unveiling of a bust in honour of the late Lord Mayo at St. Paul's Cathedral in London in 1886, *The Saturday Review* simply referred to Shere Ali as a 'barbarian assassin'.[200] The prevalence of this depoliticized reading of the assassination of Mayo explains why it, along with the murder of Judge Norman and other similar acts of 'fanaticism', are largely neglected in both past and current histories of the Indian revolutionary movement.[201] Despite the fact that Shere Ali was photographed as Mayo's killer, Ali's identity was kept secret by colonial officials nervous at the thought that Ali could be turned into a Muslim martyr, a fact that may also have contributed to his marginalization within later historiographies of Indian anticolonialism.[202]

[197] HC Deb, 12 February 1872, vol. 209, cc. 203–5.
[198] Helen James, 'The Assassination of Lord Mayo: The "First" Jihad?', *IJAPS* 5, no. 2 (2009), p. 18.
[199] *Fraser's Magazine*, April 1872, pp. 5, 28.
[200] *The Saturday Review*, 31 July 1886, p. 157.
[201] Guha, *Elementary Aspects*, pp. 2–5.
[202] Anderson, *Legible Bodies*, p. 161.

Later acts of violence carried out by Muslims against the colonial state continued to be regarded as attributable to the innate perversity of Islamic 'fanaticism' rather to any possible political grievances. In June 1915, two Muslim brothers belonging to the 8th Cavalry went on a killing spree in a military barracks in Jhansi that resulted in the deaths of their British officers and several others. A report at the time claimed that there was 'nothing whatever to indicate any political agitation or agency' behind the crime, and that the brothers were instead 'known to be surly, ill-disciplined fanatics'. The report goes on to describe the brothers as 'abnormally addicted to prayers and religious observances', providing as evidence the fact that both men obtained charms from their *Pir*, or spiritual guide, prior to committing the murders. Just as in the case of the Mappilas or the 'thugs', this supposed religious sanction behind the murders tells only a small part of the story. While the colonial intelligence branch described the first two charms as being intended towards the spiritual protection of the brothers, the third was apparently 'believed to protect the person in possession of it against a reigning tyrant'. The report similarly acknowledges that the brothers found the idea of going to war 'exceedingly distasteful to them and their relations', further hinting at the underlying political motivations that received sanction through the leveraging of the brothers' Islamic faith.[203]

As the above example illustrates, the 'prose of counter-insurgency' through which 'exceptional' acts of violence were understood continued to be inflected by a strong belief in the fanatical religiosity of colonial subjects on the one hand, and their pathological 'abnormality' on the other, well into the twentieth century. During this period, the idea of colonial subjects 'running amok' also became a common trope, connoting outbursts of sudden and unpredictable violence, usually resulting from some form of insanity or mental breakdown.[204] Originating in the Malay Peninsula, the term 'amok' became a catch-all medico-legal term to describe indigenous acts of violence, becoming intrinsically linked to colonial assumptions about culture, race, and violence.[205] Originally connoting an act of bravery carried out in war, amok was reimagined by colonial officials to fit alongside other 'pathologies' found in the colonized world, becoming seen as a hereditary 'culture-bound' form

[203] Weekly report of the Director, Criminal Intelligence, on the political situation for the month of July 1915, Home Political B, 516–519, pp. 6–7.

[204] Roland Littlewood, *Pathologies of the West: An Anthropology of Mental Illness in Europe and America* (Ithaca, NY: Cornell University Press, 2002), p. 26.

[205] Thomas Williamson, 'Communicating Amok in Malaysia', *Identities: Global Studies in Culture and Power* 14 (2007), pp. 341–5.

of mental illness that predisposed a person towards violent outbreaks.[206] Although the term was applied in a variety of contexts, it was especially prevalent in pathologizing acts of violence carried out by Muslims who, as we have seen, were considered particularly disposed towards such violent expressions of religiosity.[207] The theme of indigenous violence as a pathological mental disorder will reappear in subsequent chapters, as we will see how similar pathologies sought to strip revolutionary violence of its political meaning.

Conclusion

Speculation by Robert Elliot, the planter from Mysore, that the assassination of Lord Mayo was a 'deed of the gravest political importance', that would serve as a prelude to further assassinations of British officials carried out by disgruntled colonial subjects, turned out to be prescient. The turn of the twentieth century would see the rise of political assassination as an explicit tactic of anti-colonial resistance, marking a distinct new phase in the genealogy of 'terrorism' as a distinct category of modern crime. Still, despite the emerging novelty of 'terrorism' as a legal category, representations of 'terrorists' within the colonial archive would come to draw heavily on older tropes connected to the ethereal assassins of nineteenth century empire. This chapter has not sought to argue that these various categories of criminality were all similar in their motivations, beliefs, or objectives. What draws these various categories of criminality together is instead the interconnected tropes or idioms deployed by colonial officials in seeking to justify the imposition of draconian new laws and emergency measures designed to assuage the anxieties of a colonial state that saw itself as vulnerable to secretive and 'unknowable' conspiracies lurking at the margins of Indian society.

Whether in the clandestine Kali-worship of the 'thugs', the collective nature of dacoit gangs, the international nature of the pirate threat, or the unreasoning religiosity of Muslim 'fanatics', colonial assumptions regarding indigenous criminality would heavily inflect the genealogy of terrorism in ways that are still evident to this day. In the same way, colonial legislation in the twentieth century borrowed heavily from nineteenth century states of exception. As subsequent chapters will show, the

[206] Hissei Imai et al., 'Amok: A Mirror of Time and People. A Historical Review of Literature', *History of Psychiatry* 30, no. 1 (2019), pp. 38–57.

[207] See for example a letter from Commissioner, Peshawar District to Judicial Commissioner, 28 January 1865, IOR/L/PS/6/536, p. 2, in which an apprehended Muslim assassin named Lall Mahomed is described as 'rabid' and as answering questions regarding his motivations by repeating, 'Mad, mad.'

legal measures adopted to combat the rise of revolutionary secret societies would rely heavily on approver testimonies, summary sentencing, executive detention, and systems of mass surveillance, transportation, and resettlement, all of which had their inception in the extraordinary legislation of nineteenth century India. With the rise of mass media at the end of the nineteenth century and the proliferation of 'propaganda by deed' as a new strategy of political protest leveraged by anarchists, radicals, and anti-colonial revolutionaries, the genealogy of terrorism began to take coherent shape.

2 'The Magical Lore of Bengal'

Surveillance, Swadeshi, and Propaganda by Bomb, 1890s to 1913

Accounts of the revolutionary nationalist movement in India, whether written by colonial officials or contemporary historians, typically begin with the assassination carried out in 1897 against W. C. Rand, the chairman of the Poona Plague Committee.[1] As the previous chapter demonstrated, the origins of colonial legislation targeting so-called extraordinary forms of violence in India have a deeper genealogy, stretching at least as far back as campaigns against dacoity, thuggee, and piracy from the late eighteenth century to the 1830s. Still, the assassination of Rand marked the beginning of a new phase in the genealogy of 'terrorism'. For one thing, the assassin did not belong to any of the groups previously characterized as 'hereditary criminals' or 'assassins by profession'. Damodar Chapekar, the assassin, was a high-caste Brahmin lawyer – precisely the kind of Indian that colonialism ostensibly sought to cultivate. Newspaper reports of the assassination regularly referenced Chapekar's caste and profession as a means of further sensationalizing his 'strange career' as a radical.[2] With the rise of political assassination as an explicit tactic of anti-colonial resistance in early twentieth-century Bengal by secret societies primarily composed of upper-caste Hindus, colonial officials invented a new term – 'political dacoits' – to categorize this new class of criminal. While historian Durba Ghosh translates this term as 'gentlemanly terrorists' in her excellent recent book on the topic, the genealogy connecting the 'political dacoits' of the pre-war period to the 'terrorists' of the interwar is in fact more complicated.[3]

While earlier categories of extraordinary legal concern could be dismissed as 'savage' or 'barbaric' criminals operating at the fringes of society, a new vocabulary was required for colonial officials seeking to explain how educated members of India's upper castes could be induced to carry out the kind of 'outrages' previously reserved for the Muslim

[1] See, for example, Amit Kumar Gupta, 'Defying Death: Nationalist Revolutionism in India, 1897–1938', *Social Scientist* 25, no. 9/10 (1997), pp. 3–27.

[2] *Chicago Daily Tribune* (4 November 1897), p. 4.

[3] Ghosh, *Gentlemanly Terrorists*.

'fanatic' of the frontier. Religion retained potent explanatory power, as did the supposedly 'unknowable' nature of revolutionary secret societies operating beyond the reach of the intelligence apparatus of the colonial state. Like the thugs that came before, intelligence regarding 'political dacoits' was obtained chiefly through evidence given either by informants or by approvers – members of alleged criminal conspiracies willing to provide information about their accomplices in exchange for a more lenient sentence. Unlike the thugs, however, revolutionary organizations in early twentieth century India developed their own elaborate systems of counter-surveillance, information-collection, and reprisal, all of which worked to intimidate potential informants and reduce the capacity of the colonial state to prosecute members of these secret societies – or *samities*, as they were called.

This chapter explores the phenomenon of 'propaganda by bomb' in colonial Bengal, viewing the phenomenon as analogous yet distinct from the 'propaganda by deed' carried out by European anarchists and Fenian revolutionaries during the late nineteenth and early twentieth centuries. By tracing the inner workings of Bengal's revolutionary samities, this chapter unpacks how colonial perceptions of these organizations shaped official fears and anxieties and contributed to the genealogy of a new target of political concern called 'terrorism'. The use of the bomb in political assassinations by Bengali revolutionaries marked a new phase in colonial understandings of political violence and sparked a wave of emergency legislation that sought to police the interrelated propaganda tools of bombs and newspapers. Analyzing the relationship between bombs and ideas, this chapter argues that revolutionaries in this period used bombs as vehicles for disseminating an anti-colonial message to a wider audience than could be achieved through the circulation of radical newspapers or pamphlets. This strategy of propaganda by bomb culminated in the highly publicized attack on India's viceroy and governor general, Lord Hardinge, during his procession into Delhi in 1912, laying the groundwork for increasingly ambitious plots to overthrow British rule entirely following the outbreak of the First World War.

'Striking Terror to the British Heart'

On 22 June 1897, Damodar and Balkrishna Chapekar, brothers belonging to the Chitpavan Brahmin caste, assassinated W. C. Rand, the chairman of the Poona Plague Committee, and his guard, Lieutenant Charles Ayerst, on their way back from the 60th anniversary celebration of the coronation of Queen Victoria at Government House, Poona. The Chapekar brothers set an ambush for Rand's carriage and shot the chairman on his way back from the celebrations. Following the shooting of Rand, Damodar's brother Balkrishna shot Rand's military escort, Lieutenant Ayerst, in the head, killing him on the spot. Damodar was arrested and sentenced to death on the charge of murder, although the incident also sparked one of India's first major sedition trials when the radical nationalist Bal Gangadhar Tilak was accused of spreading disaffection against the colonial state based on articles published shortly before the assassination.[4] Following the execution of Damodar, other members of his association made two unsuccessful assassination attempts against the Poona Chief Constable before murdering two brothers who had provided information leading to Damodar's conviction. Four more of Damodar's accomplices were hanged for this, with another sentenced to ten years' rigorous imprisonment.[5]

According to the account of Damodar, written in prison, Rand was not targeted for assassination because of any personal characteristics or actions. Damodar specifically wrote that despite Rand's reputation as a wicked man of great perversity, surveillance of Rand revealed that he 'was a proud man like ourselves ... not addicted to any vice. There was no meanness in his character.'[6] The murder of Rand was instead articulated by Damodar as an inherently political action that came in response to quarantine measures adopted by the British colonial government following the outbreak of bubonic plague in Bombay and the surrounding area beginning in 1896. Following a period of devastating famine, the plague killed thousands across India, and prompted the imposition of harsh sanitation measures by colonial officials. These included forcible entry into the homes of locals, the destruction of personal possessions, quarantine measures, and forced relocation of those believed to be infected to hospitals and special segregation camps.[7]

Although British officials viewed these measures as prudent responses to a dangerous epidemic, many Indians were harshly critical of the heavy-handedness of the British response, accusing the colonial government of tyranny. Commenting on the murders of Rand and Ayerst in an interview with *The Manchester Guardian*, Gopal Krishna Gokhale, an

[4] As Sukeshi Kamra notes, this trial elucidates the manner in which writing, as well as the body, came to be framed as the site of sedition. Kamra, 'Law and Radical Rhetoric in British India: The 1897 Trial of Bal Gangadhar Tilak', *South Asia: Journal of South Asian Studies* 39, no. 3 (2016), pp. 546–59.

[5] Report of the Sedition Committee, pp. 3–4.

[6] Damodar Hari Chapekar, *Autobiography of Damodar Hari Chapekar* (Bombay Police Abstracts, 1910), p. 1014.

[7] Aidan Forth, *Barbed-Wire Imperialism: Britain's Empire of Camps, 1876–1903* (Berkeley: University of California Press, 2017), pp. 74–99.

important figure within the early Indian National Congress, said that there could be 'no doubt that the deplorable outrages of June 22 are to be connected with the measures taken in Poona against the plague'.[8] In the interview, Gokhale accused the British soldiers tasked with carrying out the anti-plague measures of entering kitchens and places of worship, 'contaminating food and spitting upon idols or breaking them and throwing them into the street. ... Women were dragged into the streets and stripped for inspection. ...'[9] Such accusations were widespread and appeared in the autobiography of Damodar Chapekar, who wrote that Rand was marked for death as an enemy of Indian religion, due to the work of the Plague Committee.

It is significant that the Chapekars targeted Rand not for his own personal actions during the plague but due to his position as a representative of the larger machinery of the colonial state. The devolution of state sovereignty over the nineteenth century from a single figurehead – the monarch – to a more diffuse abstraction – the state – created new avenues of political protest through the possibility of attacks directed against the officials or bureaucrats who served as personifications of state authority.[10] Rand's role as a stand-in for colonial sovereignty is evidenced by the Chapekar brothers' tarring of a statue of Queen Victoria prior to the assassination, which Damodar described in the following terms:

> There is a statue of the Queen of England situated at a certain crossing off our roads in the Fort in Bombay. ... This woman, after the Mutiny of 1857, acquired the universal sovereignty of India by making fair but deceitful promises. She alone is the real enemy of our people. Other white men are our enemies only in so far as they are her subjects. ... It is, however, to be deeply regretted that owing to our misfortune she is not here and it is not likely that she will ever come to this country. We, therefore, resolved to make an auspicious beginning by first dealing with her stone image. ...[11]

Originally intending to break the statue into pieces with a hammer, the brothers instead decided to disfigure the statue by blackening its face with tar and stringing a necklace of shoes around its neck.[12] Resolving not to go after any of the minor officers of the Plague Committee, the

[8] *The Manchester Guardian* (2 July 1897), p. 5. [9] Ibid.

[10] This can be situated within a broader intellectual transformation of political violence identified by Mikkel Thorup, in which 'even though actual persons are being targeted, and perhaps their killing is being legitimated by specific actions they have committed, the real target of the attack is not the person but the abstraction of the system'. See Thorup, *Intellectual History of Terror: War, Violence and the State* (New York: Routledge, 2012), pp. 9–10.

[11] Chapekar, *Autobiography*, p. 999. [12] Ibid., p. 1000.

brothers selected Rand as their target because, as chairman of the Committee, he provided the closest symbolic stand-in for the sovereignty of the Queen.

The assassination drew international media attention, especially given the global appetite for such stories driven by a recent rise in political violence across Europe.[13] Throughout the latter half of the nineteenth century and around the turn of the twentieth century, the rise of anarchist thought and particularly the doctrine of 'propaganda of the deed', which encouraged individual insurrectionary violence against the state, led to a spate of high-profile assassinations. These included the murders of Czar Alexander II of Russia in 1881, France's President Sadi Carnot in 1894, Antonio Cánovas del Castillo, the prime minister of Spain, in 1897, and King Umberto I of Italy in 1900. In 1901, the phenomenon of political murders, or so-called assassinationism, spread to the United States, with the sensationalized murder of President William McKinley.

The rise of political assassinations in the late nineteenth century was intimately connected to the proliferation of mass media. With the rise of print culture and the popular dissemination of newspapers to a mass audience, cheap and accessible print media created an expanded 'imagined community' of readers capable of participating in the public life of a country, region, or even global sphere of interest through their engagement with local and world news.[14] At the same time, the political economy of new print technologies ensured that individuals with greater access to capital or to political power could amplify their voices and determine what kinds of narratives average readers were able to access. For those lacking political power, the surest way to enter the pages of the press, thereby shaping public opinion and communicating a political message – however garbled, ventriloquized, or distorted it might become – was by somehow affecting the lives of the powerful.

[13] See especially Jensen, *Battle against Anarchist Terrorism*. See also Barbara Melchiori, *Terrorism in the Late Victorian Novel* (London: Croom Helm, 1985), Michael Hughes, 'British Opinion and Russian Terrorism in the 1880s', *European History Quarterly*, 41, no. 2 (2011), p. 257, Alex Houen, *Terrorism and Modern Literature: From Joseph Conrad to Ciaran Carson* (Oxford: Oxford University Pres, 2002), and Benedict Anderson, *Under Three Flags: Anarchism and the Anti-Colonial Imagination* (London: Verso, 2005).

[14] The idea of an 'imagined community' originates in Benedict Anderson's influential *Imagined Communities: Reflections on the Origin and Spread of Nationalism* (London: Verso, 1983). For specific reference to the rise of vernacular print culture in colonial India, see Anindita Ghosh, *Power in Print: Popular Publishing and the Politics of Language and Culture in a Colonial Society, 1778–1905* (New Delhi: Oxford University Press, 2006).

The assassination of prominent political figures became one method of achieving this goal.[15]

For those like Damodar Chapekar, who lacked access to a platform through which to disseminate their political message, the sensational killing of a high-ranking public official became an important alternative means by which to communicate with a broad popular audience. In his autobiography, composed after the assassination of Rand, Damodar wrote that such a memoir would be a 'needless waste of time' if written by one whose 'righteous conduct is barren in its effect in inculcating a wholesome moral or in gratifying the public taste'. For Damodar, a man could acquire fame only by either 'committing a reprehensible deed or by performing a very laudable act'. For a life to be worth writing about, it should succeed in accomplishing 'such righteous deeds as would engage the pens of several authors in describing them'.[16] This indicates that there was a clear and deliberate function behind the assassination of Rand beyond the act of killing itself, or the 'personal resentment and religious enthusiasm' attributed to it by historian Peter Heehs.[17] Killing Rand was on the one hand a symbolic rejection of the sovereignty of Queen Victoria, as evidenced by the tarring of her statue which preceded it. But, on the other hand, it was also a strategy of political communication through which Damodar ensured a readership for a memoir that would otherwise, by his own admission, not be worth reading.

The murder of Rand took place within a context where colonial officials were already on edge following a string of similar assassinations and public dynamite attacks carried out by the Irish Fenians. Fenians were an Irish organization centred in Dublin and New York who opposed the 1801 Act of Union that had consolidated Ireland within the larger body of Great Britain. Following the devastating famine of 1845 to 1849, Fenians blamed British rule for the social and economic problems that had become rampant throughout Ireland and began launching attacks against British officials and public buildings in an effort to generate terror and instability.[18] While the Fenians clearly articulated their campaign of political violence as a response to the poverty and starvation brought on by colonialism, British commentators dismissed these concerns by arguing that Irish poverty was brought on by the laziness of the Irish themselves. In this context, the secretive nature of Fenian assassination and

[15] Alex Schmid and Jany de Graaf, *Violence as Communication: Insurgent Terrorism and the Western New Media* (London: Sage, 1982), p. 12.

[16] Chapekar, *Autobiography*, pp. 955–7. [17] Heehs, *The Bomb in Bengal*, p. 11.

[18] For a fuller account, see Shane Kenna, *War in the Shadows: The Irish-American Fenians Who Bombed Victorian Britain* (Newbridge: Merrion Press, 2013).

dynamite plots was offered as evidence of Irish cowardice and racial inferiority, a theme that will resurface in our discussion of the revolutionaries of Bengal.[19]

British discussions of Fenian 'assassinationism', as it was called, similarly drew on cultural discourses drawn from other colonial settings. We have already seen how the label of 'thug' was sometimes used to imply the savage and brutal nature of Irish criminality, as in the case of the Phoenix Park murders and the use of the so-called Irish thug knife, discussed in Chapter 1. As a means of denying the political basis for Fenian violence, newspaper reports from the period also drew upon the term 'fanatic', which had originated as a means of explaining acts of violence carried out primarily by Muslims on India's north-west frontier. An informer deployed against an alleged plot for a Fenian rising based out of Cork in 1867, for example, declared under cross-examination that the information he provided on the conspiracy had 'put a stop to these miserable fanatics'.[20] Later, in a discussion of the trial of accused Fenian Joseph Mullet in Dublin in 1883, *The Manchester Guardian* declared that Mullet's diaries revealed 'an admixture of extreme nationalist politics and religious professions that was very striking' and stated further that papers found in Mullet's possession revealed him to be a 'fanatic' who 'looked upon political crime as being justifiable'.[21]

While some early accounts of Fenian violence did refer to it as 'terrorism', the looser association between Fenians and 'terror' was more common.[22] In a parliamentary debate in 1877, Lord Oranmore referred to agrarian and political crime in Ireland as casting 'a dark shade of grief and terror over all classes'.[23] Meanwhile in the American press, the *Cincinnati Enquirer* referred to the Fenians as 'striking terror to the soul of John Bull', while the *Chicago Daily Tribune* similarly reported that the Irish association was 'striking terror to the British heart'.[24] These descriptions of 'terror' refer more to a state of being than to a distinct category of criminality. In another parliamentary debate in 1883, for example, Randolph Churchill – a Tory radical and father of the famous future prime minister, Winston – described Ireland as being enveloped by 'terror, outrage, and crime of every description' that had culminated in the Phoenix Park assassinations. Churchill argued that earlier approaches towards Fenian violence had been too lenient and that it

[19] Patrick Brantlinger, *Taming Cannibals: Race and the Victorians* (Ithaca, NY: Cornell University Press, 2011), p. 138.

[20] *The Observer* (26 May 1867), p. 2.

[21] *The Manchester Guardian* (11 May 1883), p. 8.

[22] See for example, *The Irish Times* (6 April 1883), p. 5.

[23] Lord Oranmore, HL Deb, 16 July 1877, vol. 235, cc. 1298.

[24] *Cincinnati Enquirer* (25 October 1881), p. 1; *Chicago Daily Tribune* (21 June 1884), p. 5.

was only after Phoenix Park that order was finally restored 'to a land long distracted by anarchy and terrorized by unpunished crime'.[25]

The label of 'anarchy' or, indeed, 'anarchism' was the most common descriptor for late nineteenth century acts of political violence within a wider European context. The term 'anarchism' actually refers to an ideology originating out of radical strands of left-wing European political thought, which advocates the abolition of state-based forms of government in favour of voluntary self-governing institutions. During the late nineteenth century, however, anarchism came to be conflated in popular and governmental discourses with so-called assassinationism or propaganda of the deed, referring to bombings or assassinations carried out with the intention of undermining or challenging state authority. Although contemporary print media often depicted anarchism as a worldwide conspiracy, many of the acts of violence committed by disparate groups of nationalists, radicals, police spies, and the mentally ill during this period became conflated with the catch-all categorization of 'anarchism', lending the term an artificial degree of coherence.[26]

The policing of 'anarchism' took on a variety of forms in different countries, with some governments opting for preventive measures that aimed to stop anarchist plots before they could come to fruition, while other nations favoured the repression of anarchist networks following their commission of specific crimes. In general, more despotic regimes such as czarist Russia opted for preventive measures that included the prohibition of meetings, censorship, and mass arrests of suspected anarchists, while liberal or progressive governments sought to protect the rights of an individual until they committed an actual crime. In practice, the distinction was often not as clear-cut, and preventive policies aiming to monitor anarchist networks rather than destroy them were often the most successful in preventing political assassinations.[27] As this book argues, however, liberal governments such as Britain's were also prone to adopt markedly less liberal policies where their colonies were concerned.

Following the assassination of Elisabeth, the Empress of Austria and Queen of Hungary, by an Italian anarchist on 10 September 1898, the Italian government convened the 'International Conference for the Defense of Society against the Anarchists' from 24 November to

[25] Randolph Churchill, HC Deb, 20 February 1883, vol. 276, cc. 488–9.
[26] Jensen, *Battle against Anarchist Terrorism*, p. 3. See also Paul Knepper, 'The Other invisible Hand: Jews and Anarchists in London before the First World War', *Jewish History* 22 (2008), pp. 295–315.
[27] Ibid., p. 5.

21 December. This marked the first international conference to specifically target anarchism and would set the tone for future international cooperation on this issue. A key legacy of this conference was increased cooperation among European police forces as well as the expansion of the *portrait parlé* system that deployed a complex series of measurements and recordings of identifying markers in order to facilitate the recognition of suspected criminals.[28]

Following the Rome Conference, the assassination of President McKinley in 1901 resulted in the St Petersburg Protocol of 1904, in which a number of European powers came together in a second attempt to establish a concerted international response. This consisted of countries that would later stand on both sides of the First World War, including Russia, Roumania, Serbia, Bulgaria, Austria-Hungary, Germany, Denmark, Sweden-Norway, Spain, Portugal, Switzerland, and the Ottoman Empire. The protocol provided procedures for the expulsion of criminals designated as anarchists and called for the creation of central anti-anarchist offices in member countries, as well as cooperation between member police forces. Despite the urging of Berlin, London officials were unwilling to sign on to the protocol in 1906, with the excuse that British law already carried out most of the provisions in practice. The protocol ultimately fell through because national interests and political rivalries won out over coordination and multi-lateral cooperation, a theme that will be returned to in Chapter 5.[29]

'Political Dacoits'

Following the Chapekar brothers' assassination of Rand in 1897, the next major milestone in the evolution of political assassination within India was the decision of Lord Curzon, the viceroy and governor general of India, to partition the province of Bengal in 1905. Since 1765, Bengal, Bihar, and Orissa had been grouped into a single province, with an estimated combined population of around seventy-eight million people at the time of partition. The proposed partition would split the province into two new administrative units, which would be divided primarily along religious lines, with a Muslim majority in East Bengal and a primarily Hindu population in West Bengal. British officials justified

[28] Ibid., pp. 131–84. For more on the development of international policing itself, see Mathieu Deflem, *Policing World Society: Historical Foundations of International Police Cooperation* (Oxford: Oxford University Press, 2002).

[29] See Richard Bach Jensen, 'The First Global Wave of Terrorism and International Counter-Terrorism, 1905–1914', in Jussi Hanhimäki and Bernhard Blumenau (eds.), *An International History of Terrorism* (New York: Routledge, 2013), pp. 16–33.

the decision on the grounds of administrative efficiency, but privately Curzon admitted that he hoped that it would undermine the power of the incipient Indian nationalist movement. In a letter to John Brodrick, India's secretary of state, Curzon wrote that Calcutta was the centre of the Indian National Congress' political power and that

> ... its best wire-pullers and its most frothy orators all reside there. The perfection of their machinery, and the tyranny which it enables them to exercise are truly remarkable. They dominate public opinion in Calcutta ... the whole of their activity is directed to creating an agency so powerful that they may one day be able to force a weak Government to give them what they desire.[30]

For this reason, the partition attracted vehement opposition from the middle-class Bengali *bhadralok*, who campaigned vigorously against it by calling for mass boycotts of British goods. Invoking a language of Bengal as a dismembered motherland, politicians and intellectuals promoted *swadeshi*, the manufacture of locally produced goods that would replace British imports.[31] The swadeshi campaign drew on cultural symbols and religious idioms, often with a Hindu component, leading some to accuse the movement of sectarianism.[32] Although it is true that swadeshi tended to attract greater support from Hindus than from Muslims, Ruma Chatterjee argues that this fact should be understood in economic, rather than explicitly communal, terms. The western half of Bengal was predominantly Hindu and dominated by the urban centre of Calcutta, while the majority Muslim population of eastern Bengal was largely rural, with less access to capital. Chatterjee notes that although nationalists regarded the purchase of homespun goods rather than foreign products as a matter of loyalty, for the indebted peasantry of eastern Bengal, the choice was 'not between local and foreign fabrics as such, but between higher and lower prices'.[33] Despite this issue, the swadeshi movement was nonetheless able to mobilize an unprecedented level of support throughout Bengal, creating a mass base of anti-colonial agitation for the first time in India. It also produced unprecedented intellectual engagement with the wider world, as historian Kris Manjapra demonstrates. Disentangling the intellectual dimensions of the swadeshi movement from its cultural and social dimensions, Manjapra asserts that swadeshi ideology simultaneously

[30] B. L. Grover, *A Documentary Study of British Policy towards Indian Nationalism: 1885–1909* (Delhi: National Publications, 1967), pp. 224–5.

[31] For the classic in-depth examination of the swadeshi movement, see Sarkar, *The Swadeshi Movement*.

[32] Leonard A. Gordon. *Bengal: The Nationalist Movement 1876–1940* (New York: Columbia University Press, 1974), p. 114.

[33] Ruma Chatterjee, 'Cotton Handloom Manufactures of Bengal, 1870–1921' *Economic and Political Weekly* 22, no. 25 (1987), p. 992.

drew heavily on international reference points and sought to transmit itself to a wider global audience.[34]

Although the majority of this agitation was based around boycott and other methods of peaceful protest, it also laid the groundwork for the development of radical networks in Bengal that sought to undermine British authority through the use of targeted assassinations and revolutionary propaganda. Although numerous revolutionary organizations developed throughout this period, the two most significant in Bengal were the Jugantar group based out of Calcutta and the Anushilan Samiti, headquartered primarily in Dacca. Both of these organizations sought to seize on popular discontent with the partition of Bengal in order to recruit revolutionaries, particularly drawn from young, discontented men of the bhadralok class. Educated under the colonial regime but unable to access any benefits from it, many of these revolutionaries were disillusioned by the harsh reality of oppression that undergirded colonialism's universalizing promises.[35] Recruits to the revolutionary movement were further embittered by a colonial racial typology that dismissed Bengali men – derisively referred to as *babus* – as feeble and effeminate. The physical training offered by the secret societies and the opportunity to exert violence against their colonial oppressors provided young men with the opportunity to reassert their masculinity and find renewed pride in the religious traditions of Hinduism.[36]

In its earliest phase, revolutionary crime in Bengal often took the form of so-called political dacoities, or armed robberies carried out with the intention of acquiring funds to support the growth and operation of radical networks. F. C. Daly of the Bengal Special Branch saw the spread of the revolutionary samities as a natural outgrowth of the broader swadeshi movement. According to Daly, 'Violent political agitation of an open and practically unrestricted character had been rampant in Bengal from the time of the passing of the partition measure in July 1905. For years previous to that, the audacity of the Bengali agitator had been increasing year by year.'[37]

[34] Kris Manjapra, 'Knowledgeable Internationalism and the Swadeshi Movement, 1903–1921', *Economic & Political Weekly* 47, no. 42 (2012), pp. 53–62.

[35] Sanyal, *Revolutionary Pamphlets*, pp. 9–10.

[36] Mrinalini Sinha, *Colonial Masculinity: The 'Manly Englishman' and the 'Effeminate Bengali' in the Late Nineteenth Century* (Manchester: Manchester University Press, 1995), and John Rosselli, 'The Self-Image of Effeteness: Physical Education and Nationalism in Nineteenth-Century Bengal', *Past and Present* 88 (1980), pp. 121–48.

[37] F. C. Daly, Special Branch, Note on the growth of the revolutionary movement in Bengal, 7 August 1911, in Samanta, *Terrorism in Bengal: A Collection of Documents on Terrorist Activities from 1905 to 1939*, vol. 1 (Calcutta: Government of West Bengal, 1995), p. 3.

In a summary of the administration of the Government of India printed in 1916, the term 'political dacoity' is defined as 'implying dacoities committed by men not ordinarily of the professional criminal classes, as a part of the seditious campaign'.[38] Despite its widespread usage, some officials such as Lord Hardinge viewed the term with suspicion. At a meeting of the Imperial Legislative Council at Simla, Hardinge announced that he failed 'to see any difference between an ordinary dacoity and a political dacoity. They are both crimes of a heinous description, while the perpetrators, be they bhadralog *(sic)* or others, are all criminals of equal degree'.[39] Perhaps because of the predominantly bhadralok social basis of the revolutionary movement – distinct from earlier, more easily demarcated 'criminal' identities such as thugs or criminal tribes – incarcerated revolutionary nationalists were physically differentiated from other prisoners based on their clothing. So-called seditionists or political dacoits sentenced to transportation in this period were given uniforms marked with an 'S' for sedition and a 'C' for conspiracy. All were also marked with a 'D' for dangerous.[40]

Defying such colonial labels, revolutionaries did not call themselves dacoits, often referring to themselves simply as 'members of the samiti', or else deploying the term 'santan' in reference to the Bengali writer Bankim Chandra Chattopadhyay's 1882 novel *Anandamath*. Chattopadhyay was widely read in Bengali revolutionary circles, with *Anandamath* – a novel about a brotherhood of rebel monks called santans fighting the British during the famine of 1770 – providing literary inspiration to many in their pursuit of anti-colonial independence.[41] Revolutionaries justified robberies as necessary steps in the pursuit of freedom, with one article proclaiming, 'A nation yearning for freedom does not shrink even, if it's necessary, to collect money by committing theft and dacoity … the power of discriminating between right and wrong is gone. Every thing *(sic)* is sacrificed at the feet of the goddess of liberty.'[42] Other anti-colonial radicals sought to connect their work with that of the rebels of 1857. In 1909, following the fifty-year anniversary of the uprising, V. D. Savarkar wrote *The Indian War of Independence*, an influential text that used the

[38] *Summary of the Administration of the Government of India 1910–16* (Delhi: Superintendent Government Printing, 1916), p. 14.

[39] Meeting of Imperial Legislative Council at Simla, 17 September 1913, CUL, Hardinge Papers, p. 8.

[40] Anderson, *Legible Bodies*, p. 118.

[41] H. L. Salkeld, Magistrate on Special Duty, Anushilan Samiti, Dacca, Part 1, 1908, in Samanta (ed.), *Terrorism in Bengal*, vol. 2, p. 12.

[42] H. L. Salkeld, Anushilan Samiti, Dacca, Part I, 1908, in Samanta (ed.), *Terrorism in Bengal*, vol. 2, p. 106.

metaphor of a volcanic eruption to reframe the uprising as a natural phenomenon originating in colonial oppression and Indian patriotism that was to serve as a source of 'fiery inspiration' to the independence movement of the twentieth century.[43]

In practice, despite their lofty aspirations the early samities functioned much like criminal gangs, with harsh repercussions for members suspected of defection or disloyalty. Dacoity was not the primary goal of the associations, but was rather a necessary means to the end of securing funds that could support the broader anti-colonial work of training, assassination, and propaganda. As one revolutionary named Narendra Nath Banerji described it, 'The object of our society is not to commit dakaiti *(sic)* but assassination, with a view to remove from the field officers who have obtained an insight into our working, and to inspire fear amongst other officers.'[44] Although the samities are best known for their assassination of British officials, the most common victims of revolutionary plots were actually informants or defectors from within their own ranks, along with the police constables and Criminal Investigation Department (hereafter CID) spies who sought to extract evidence from these defectors. It is no coincidence that the CID was reconstituted directly out of the bones of the Thuggee and Dacoity Department, which was renamed and reoriented towards political crime in 1904. Much like the nineteenth century phenomenon of thuggee, colonial knowledge of the early revolutionary societies was derived almost entirely from the evidence of approvers, members of the samities willing to provide evidence against fellow revolutionaries in exchange for leniency or legal pardon.

As a result, the samities sought to protect themselves from infiltration or betrayal through a complex set of vows and rituals in which an initiate promised to forfeit their life should they disclose any secrets of the samiti to an outside source. The disclosure of martial training to the uninitiated was considered particularly dangerous to the societies. If a member was found to be providing instruction in 'play' – meaning lathi, sword, or dagger training – without compelling their pupil to take the required vows, samiti rules stated that efforts should first be made to induct the trainee through the initiation ritual but that if he refused to take the membership vows, 'then arrangements will have to be made for the

[43] V. D. Savarkar, *The Indian War of Independence* (London: 1909), p. vii.

[44] Statement of Narendra Nath Banerji of Chandernagore, 7 March 1911, in Samanta, *Terrorism in Bengal*, vol. 1, p. 330.

complete destruction of his knowledge'.[45] The 'destruction of knowledge' was a euphemism for murder, sometimes accompanied by the desecration of the victim's body. This was the case in the murder of Sukumar Chakrabarti, a 'santan' who, after being questioned by the police, was found decapitated and 'shockingly mutilated' to prevent his disclosing any further information.[46] For colonial authorities, it was this strategy of intimidation that marked out a 'further stage in terrorism' on the part of the samities.[47] In its earliest usages in the Indian context, terrorism most often refers not to attacks on public servants or the state, but to the intimidation of defectors, informants, and witnesses.

The initiation ceremony of the samities is described in great detail within the police records, although actual testimonies regarding the ceremony vary in key respects. It is impossible to know for sure whether this is indicative of a fluid and evolving set of practices among the revolutionaries themselves or the insertion of Orientalist fantasies on the part of British interviewers seeking to uncover ritual elements that would reinforce pre-existing tropes regarding the secretive and fanatical nature of older thug conspiracies. In some key features, the testimonies of revolutionary approvers from the early twentieth century bear striking similarity to those of arrested thugs from a hundred years earlier. The 1910 deposition of eighteen-year-old Sailendra Kumar Das, a recruit from a samiti run by the revolutionary Indra Nandi, placed a strong emphasis on the religious dimensions of the initiation ritual:

> The form of initiation was different from that in force now. The main portion of it was in Sanskrit. When I was initiated I had to sit on something like a mat. I held a 'Gita' in my left hand and a sword in my right. Ganges water was sprinkled over my body. I had to read out three times the clauses of the oath of initiation before a picture of Kali. A wooden fire was burning in front of me. There was also a picture of Sivaji in front of me.[48]

Describing his initiation into the same samiti during the same year, twenty-year-old Lalit Mohan Chakravarti's account similarly mentions an image of the Marathi hero Sivaji, although in Chakravarti's account it consists of a stone statue rather than a picture. Touching copper, a *tulsi*

[45] H. L. Salkeld, Magistrate on Special Duty, Anushilan Samiti, Dacca, Part 1, 1908, in Samanta, *Terrorism in Bengal*, vol. 2, p. 15.

[46] J. E. Armstrong, An Account of the Revolutionary Organization in Eastern Bengal with Special Reference to the Dacca Anushilan Samiti, Parts 1 and 2, Vol. 1, 1917, in Samanta *Terrorism in Bengal*, vol. 2, p. 308.

[47] H. L. Salkeld, Magistrate on Special Duty, Anushilan Samiti, Dacca, Part 1, 1908, in Samanta, *Terrorism in Bengal*, vol. 2, p. 15.

[48] Deposition of Sailendra Kumar Das, 9 March 1910, in Samanta, *Terrorism in Bengal*, vol. 1, p. 122.

plant, Ganges water, the Bhagavad Gita, fire, and a sword, Chakravarti called on god as his witness and allegedly burned a piece of paper on which he had written out his oath to the samiti.[49] Chakravarti's deposition, by his own admission, consists of multiple layers of omission and sudden remembering but clearly seeks to establish his role as both member and observer to the revolutionary movement, establishing his presence at key moments such as in the preparation of dacoities or in the incident – known to authorities – when the revolutionary leader Indra Nandi blew his own hand off while preparing a bomb.[50] For the colonial authorities, the significance of these initiation rituals was that they established the informant's membership within the group, as well as demarcating the boundaries of revolutionary membership through a conscious and undeniable ceremony that cemented one's commitment to the samiti.

Because of the danger posed to the samiti by defectors, revolutionary leaders sought to regulate and monitor the conduct of recruits through a complex system of surveillance. While the intelligence networks of the Raj are better known,[51] organizations like the Anushilan Samiti relied just as much on the collection and analysis of detailed information as did their colonial adversaries, even attempting at times to plant moles within the security services.[52] Led by the infamous revolutionary Pulin Behari Das during its earliest incarnation, the Anushilan Samiti was a wide-reaching organization comprising as many as twenty thousand total members distributed over more than five hundred branches across Dacca, Mymensingh, Faridpur, Tippera, and Pabna.[53] The reach of Anushilan is highlighted by its designation by colonial authorities as 'perhaps the most important of the outward and visible manifestations of the revolutionary movement in Bengal'.[54] Pulin was the key animating force behind the stunning early successes of Anushilan, with even his critics begrudgingly attesting to his 'strong personality and great organizing ability'. A low class of Kayastha by caste and a former lab assistant from Dacca college, Pulin quickly became the unchallenged leader of

[49] Deposition of Lalit Mohan Chakravarti, 23 March 1910, in Samanta, *Terrorism in Bengal*, vol. 1, pp. 66–8.

[50] Ibid., pp. 71–109. For more on the complex role of approvers within the colonial justice system, see Amin, *Event, Metaphor, Memory*, pp. 75–85.

[51] Popplewell's *Intelligence and Imperial Defence* remains one of the most influential accounts.

[52] Silvestri, *Policing 'Bengali Terrorism'*, p. 86.

[53] J. E. Armstrong, An Account of the Revolutionary Organization in Eastern Bengal with Special Reference to the Dacca Anushilan Samiti, Parts 1 and 2, Vol. 1, 1917, in Samanta, *Terrorism in Bengal*, vol. 2, pp. 297–8.

[54] Ibid., p. 271.

Anushilan, advocating the 'total surrender of one's personal independence in the hands of a leader'. Pulin believed that democratic principles could not hold up in military matters, because 'in these affairs speediness is the secret of success. The proper time for work passes by and the whole thing falls to the ground if the consent of everyone has to be taken.'[55]

Described as an 'ascetic disciplinarian', Pulin set strict standards of behaviour for members of the samiti, although it is unclear whether these ideal codes of conduct were followed in practice. A typical timetable written up by Pulin and his associate Ashutosh Das Gupta mandated that members rise at 4:30 in the morning to chant hymns and take care of their morning ablutions before heading outside for two hours of running, weapons training, and other physical activities. After a morning meal and bathing from 9 to 10:45 a.m., members of the samiti were expected to spend five hours in unspecified learning that likely focused on religious, cultural, and political education, before a further three hours of physical training and then further hymns and study of the *Ramayana* and *Mahabharata* following an evening meal around 7 p.m. The schedule would have left only five and a half hours for sleep following eighteen and a half hours of activity that included five to six hours a day of hard exercise in the heat, leading the police to conclude that following the prescribed regimen would have been impossible.[56] Nonetheless, the rigid structure that Pulin aspired to highlights the extreme levels of discipline that he believed were necessary for ensuring the compliance and obedience of Anushilan's members.[57]

To monitor members' behaviour, Pulin designated special 'vigilance committees' whose task it was to constantly spy on samiti members with the purpose of 'purifying the league from within by detecting the errors and deficiencies of the members of the league'. Pulin encouraged these informants to think of their work as being 'like that of a Govt. spy', capable of cross-questioning and cross-examining suspects in order to extract information without arousing the suspicions of their targets.[58] Agents of the vigilance committees grouped the transgressions of samiti members into four main categories: minor transgressions and mistakes, important transgressions that did limited or negligible harm to the samiti,

[55] Ibid., p. 281.

[56] H. L. Salkeld, Magistrate on Special Duty, Anushilan Samiti, Dacca, Part 4, 1908, in Samanta, *Terrorism in Bengal*, vol. 2, pp. 240–4.

[57] We can observe in this schedule the aspiration for the kind of disciplinary governmentality that Michel Foucault attributes primarily to the modern state and its institutions. See Foucault, *Discipline and Punish*.

[58] Armstrong, Account of the Revolutionary Organization, in Samanta, *Terrorism in Bengal*, vol. 2, 428–9.

serious transgressions such as spilling information or failing to complete a task, and finally very serious transgressions such as defecting to the enemy or refusing to follow the orders of a superior.[59] While the first three categories of infraction were punishable by varying degrees of demotion or social boycott, a transgression considered 'very serious' could result in a revolutionary being immediately put to death by their companions.

Sexual transgressions were also punishable by death. In cases where members broke their Brahmacharya vows of celibacy and engaged in extramarital or homosexual relations, the punishment could be swift and brutal.[60] British authorities were particularly obsessed with uncovering evidence of homosexual liaisons within the samities, even alleging that Pulin had one member killed to suppress information regarding Pulin's 'criminal intimacy' with a boy named Suresh Sen. It is difficult to say whether the allegations were based on actual evidence or merely reflect colonial anxieties regarding homosexual intercourse as an inherent 'great danger in bringing together in one building a large number of young men and boys'. The author of the report on alleged sexual impropriety within the samiti, H. L. Salkeld, later wrote that his account of homosexual liaisons among revolutionaries was intended to 'throw light on situations otherwise inexplicable' to British police officers.[61] Salkeld's statement reinforces the point that regardless of their veracity, such accounts provided a framework for colonial authorities to make sense of revolutionary secrecy and homosocial fraternal bonding through a predetermined cultural framework that linked so-called unnatural sexual intercourse with broader narratives of racial and sexual degeneracy.[62] In his popular book *Indian Unrest*, published in 1910, journalist Valentine Chirol explicitly linked political radicalism with sexual deviance, writing that revolutionary secret societies represented 'a form of erotomania which is certainly much more common among Hindu political fanatics than amongst Hindus in general'.[63] Across a variety of colonial contexts from Africa to South America, the British often viewed political dissent

[59] Ibid., p. 434. [60] Ibid., p. 393.

[61] H. L. Salkeld, Magistrate on Special Duty, Anushilan Samiti, Dacca, Part 4, 1908, in Samanta, *Terrorism in Bengal*, vol. 2, pp. 240–4.

[62] Anne McClintock, *Imperial Leather: Race, Gender and Sexuality in the Colonial Contest* (New York: Routledge, 1995), Anjali Arondekar, 'Without a Trace: Sexuality and the Colonial Archive', *Journal of the History of Sexuality*, 14, no. ½ (2005), pp. 10–25.

[63] Valentine Chirol, *Indian Unrest* (London: Macmillan, 1910), pp. 29–30.

as inextricably connected to moral degeneration and 'deviant' sexual behaviour, and India was no exception.[64]

In addition to imposing strict controls on members of the samiti, Pulin also sought to collect detailed information on potential external threats to the organization, designating a separate intelligence branch for that very purpose. In a series of 'village notes', members of this revolutionary intelligence branch were to collect social, political, and statistical data on villages throughout the newly created province of Eastern Bengal and Assam. Pulin considered the gathering of information to be one of the most important jobs, with the 'fittest man, intelligent, hardy, honest and the most responsible man' to be placed in charge of this department. Information that fell within his purview consisted of a town or villages' layout, including

> ... the principle roads, streets, lanes, bye-lanes, rivers and canals and bridges over them, tanks, wells, schools and colleges and the number of students therein, railway routes, stations, post office, police station, river jetty or port harbor, police clubs, churches ... number of the regiments and the number of the soldiers thereof. Number of Rifles, Pistols, Revolvers and quantity of ammunitions stored up.[65]

The collection of intelligence also extended to demographic information regarding the population such as numbers of Hindus and Muslims, males and females, Indian and European, as well as the numbers, locations, and movements of all known CID officers and their spies.[66] This facilitated counter-espionage and opened up colonial security forces to intimidation and assassination, leading the authorities to rely on increasingly drastic emergency laws to compensate for the increasing difficulty of winning the information war against their revolutionary opponents.

'The Secret of the Bomb'

Although the dacoities and assassinations carried out by revolutionary societies such as the Dacca Anushilan Samiti presented a challenge to colonial authority by undermining its claim to uphold law and order, it was the bomb attacks carried out by these same groups of political radicals that motivated the evolution of a new prose of counterterrorism.

[64] Urban, *Tantra*, p. 75. The place of homosexuality and 'sexual misconduct' within the imagination of colonial intelligence officials is also examined in Silvestri, *Policing 'Bengali Terrorism'*, pp. 53–5.

[65] J. E. Armstrong, An Account of the Revolutionary Organization in Eastern Bengal with Special Reference to the Dacca Anushilan Samiti, Parts 1 and 2, Vol. 1, 1917, in Samanta, *Terrorism in Bengal*, vol. 2, pp. 426–7.

[66] Ibid., p. 428.

The first bomb attack occurred on 6 December 1907, when revolutionaries connected to the Jugantar group derailed the train of Sir Andrew Fraser, the lieutenant-governor of Bengal near Midnapore by planting a bomb on the tracks. On 11 April 1908, revolutionaries threw a bomb at the mayor of Chandernagore, a sliver of French territory just outside Calcutta that was a popular route for smuggled arms and propaganda, but failed to kill him. Weeks later, on 30 April, a young revolutionary named Khudiram Bose, along with his accomplice Prafulla Chaki, threw a bomb into a carriage with the intention of assassinating Douglas Kingsford, a former chief presidency magistrate of Calcutta. The bomb instead killed two English women named Mrs. and Miss Kennedy by mistake.[67]

This deed transformed Khudiram Bose into the first revolutionary to enter the pantheon of 'freedom fighters' that would continue to expand over the course of the four decades that followed. In 'The Partition of Bengal', a poem confiscated by the colonial intelligence service, Khudiram is celebrated as a martyr who 'went to the celestial region with a fearless heart for his own country'. The poem implores its reader to remember Khudiram's 'smiling, lotus-like face',[68] a reference to reports that on the day of his execution, Khudiram climbed the scaffold with a cheerful smile on his face,[69] a narrative that hearkened back to Sleeman's very first account of thuggee, discussed in the previous chapter.[70] In the same raid, police discovered pictures of Khudiram and Prafulla hanging at the front entrance of a *samiti* headquarters, alongside images of Swami Vivekananda, the goddess Kali, and a stylized image of India as mother goddess.[71] Khudiram's venerated status even gave him the power to strike against the British from beyond the grave, according to some revolutionaries. In a letter composed in August 1908, Saraju Bala Sen Gupta wrote, 'Brother Khudiram in his lifetime has not finished doing

[67] *Sedition Committee*, pp. 31–2.

[68] 'The Partition of Bengal' excerpt in H. L. Salkeld, Anushilan Samiti, Dacca, Part I, 1908, in Samanta, *Terrorism in Bengal*, vol. 1, p. 139.

[69] Hitendra Patel, *Khudiram Bose: Revolutionary Extraordinaire* (Delhi: Publications Division Ministry of Information and Broadcasting Government of India, 2008), pp. 55–6.

[70] W. H. Sleeman, 'To the Editor of the Calcutta Literary Gazette (anonymous)', *Calcutta Literary Gazette* (3 October 1930), in Wagner (ed.), *Stranglers & Bandits*, pp. 174–82.

[71] H. L. Salkeld, Anushilan Samiti, Dacca, Part I, 1908, in Samanta, *Terrorism in Bengal*, vol. 1, p. 146. For a consideration of how early revolutionaries deployed the image of Kali as a means of inverting colonial stereotypes of Bengali masculinity, see Urban, *Tantra*, pp. 93–8.

his duty to his country. Even from the other world he will exterminate them to the root for his hanging on the gallows.'[72]

As the first 'successful' assassination by bomb in India, the murder of the Kennedy women attracted widespread media attention. The London-based *Times* described the deed as a case of 'deliberate murder, cruelly planned', while the *Illustrated London News* used the popular label of 'anarchy' to describe the incident.[73] An article from *Empire* reprinted in the Calcutta newspaper *Bande Mataram* remarked on the 'horror which the foul deed has awakened among the responsible members of the Indian community' and lamented the fact that the 'sanctity which formerly surrounded the life of the European in this country has been considerably invaded of recent years, and this terrible deed is not likely to enhance it'.[74] Many commentators were particularly troubled by the fact that it was a bomb that killed the Kennedy women. An article in *The Bengalee* emphasized the shocking and spectacular aspects of the killing by describing how 'a tremendous explosion startled the town'. The article pointed out with concern that the deadly results of the explosion indicated that the 'indigenous manufacturers of these infernal machines are becoming increasingly expert'.[75] Journalist Valentine Chirol referred to the killings at Muzaffarpur as the first time that 'any Indian had used this product of modern science with murderous effect'.[76]

In the report later drawn up by the Sedition Committee in 1918, which will be examined at greater length in the following chapter, assassination by bomb is singled out by colonial authorities as an inherently political crime. In a section detailing the definition of political assassination, the report states, 'there are of course certain classes of outrage which by their very nature proclaim themselves as revolutionary. Murder by bomb is practically certain to be of this character.'[77] Despite this, Lord Minto, the viceroy and governor general of India at the time of Khudiram's arrest, actively sought to deny any political motivation behind the attack, stating in a speech that 'the public at home will make a fatal mistake if they ascribe outrages such as that at Muzaffarpur to the efforts of a people struggling to liberate themselves from an oppressor'.[78] Although Minto referred to assassination by bomb as a foreign import, developed in Russia and subsequently 'sown amongst a strangely impressionable and

[72] Saraju Bala Sen Gupta to Dinesh Chandra Sen Gupta, 26 August 1908, H. L. Salkeld, Anushilan Samiti, Dacca, Part III, in Samanta, *Terrorism in Bengal*, vol. 1, p. 170.
[73] *The Times* (14 July 1908) and *Illustrated London News* (27 June 1908).
[74] *Bande Mataram* (5 May 1908), p. 1. [75] *The Bengalee* (2 May 1908), p. 5.
[76] Chirol, *Indian Unrest*, p. 55. [77] *Sedition Committee*, p. 26.
[78] Peter Heehs (1994), 'Foreign Influences on Bengali Revolutionary Terrorism, 1902–1908', *Modern Asian Studies* 28, no. 3 (1994), p. 555.

imitative people' in India, he refused to draw any parallels between the subjugation of the Russian and Indian people.[79] While Russian nihilists could be seen as fighting against government tyranny, official accounts precluded the possibility that the same could be said of assassination by bomb within the British Empire.[80]

By contrast, radicals saw the use of the bomb at Muzaffarpur as a symbolic victory of great importance. In a *Yugantar* leaflet written two months after the death of the Kennedy women, the author wrote: 'Bombs are not the only invincible weapons for the liberation of the country. … A few days ago you could not dream of Bengali youths using bombs.' The leaflet further proclaimed that the 'entire mechanism of British administration can be ground down simply with the help of bombs' and that preparations for a great war would be made irrelevant 'when we see the English struck with terror at the bursting of a bomb or two'.[81] An article published in *Yugantar* in July instructed its readers not to despair at the incident at Muzaffarpur, as, 'The time for wielding the pen is gone. Take now shelter in Manliness. There are in the country plenty of places still where bombs are manufactured.' Perhaps most significantly, the article further encouraged would-be revolutionaries to show their own initiative in taking up the politics of the bomb, proclaiming that 'the implements and materials for making bombs can be obtained plentifully in the market. Do not remain silent and inactive'.[82]

Having returned to his place at the forefront of Indian politics following the end of his earlier prison sentence, Bal Gangadhar Tilak was again put on trial for sedition because of articles that he published in *Kesari* following the Muzaffarpur incident. The first of these articles, titled 'Country's Misfortune', detailed the harm done to India by British colonial rule while the second, titled 'These Remedies Are Not Lasting', provided an extended analysis of the politics of the bomb. Tilak was charged under the Indian Penal Code under section 124-A, which prohibited exciting or attempting to excite feelings of disaffection towards the government, as well as under section 153-A, which made it unlawful to promote or attempt to promote feelings of hatred between different classes, and sentenced to six years in prison.[83]

[79] *The Times* (9 June 1909), p. 1.

[80] Hughes, 'British Opinion and Russian Terrorism', p. 257–8. See also Joseph McQuade, 'Political Discourse, Political Violence: Fenians, Nihilists, and the Revolutionaries of Bengal, 1907–1925', *Sikh Formations* 10, no. 1 (2014), pp. 43–55.

[81] *Yugantar* leaflet excerpt in H. L. Salkeld, Anushilan Samiti, Dacca, Part I, 1908, in Samanta, *Terrorism in Bengal*, vol. 1, p. 115.

[82] *Yugantar*, 6 July 1908, IOR: L/P&J/6/887, File 3037, p. 1.

[83] Annex 2 to the Secretary of State for India, IOR: L/P&J/6/877, File 2436, p. 2.

In 'These Remedies Are Not Lasting', published on 9 June 1908, Tilak sought to explain the motivation behind bomb assassinations in India and to differentiate them from the anarchist bombings that had become so prevalent in Europe. Tilak wrote that contrary to the official report, the bombs of Bengal were not subversive of society in the same way as the anarchist bombs of Europe. Referring to European anarchism as stemming from a hatred for 'selfish millionaires', Tilak argued it was instead an 'excess of patriotism that motivated the bombs of Bengal'. According to Tilak, the revolutionaries of Bengal were not anarchists, but simply adopted the weapon of the anarchist because of its effectiveness in forcing change. Pointing to examples from places like Portugal and Russia where governments were forced to modify their behaviour because of political assassinations – or, in his words, to 'bow down to the bomb' – Tilak wrote that assassination by bomb could be patriotic if it produced political reform.[84]

The article went on to criticize the Arms Act, as having slain the 'manhood of the nation' by ensuring that the administration could conduct any action they wanted without having to give any consideration to how it would be received by the disarmed population.[85] Tilak wrote that the advent of the bomb removed this imbalance and reduced the importance of military strength by providing the people with a means of registering their displeasure with governmental tyranny using the very tools of Western science that formerly oppressed them. According to Tilak, the bomb was an entirely new weapon and, completely unlike firearms, could not be taken away from the people through the Arms Act. Simple and easy to make, the bomb had 'more the form of knowledge, it is a [kind of] witchcraft, it is a charm, an amulet'. Although the knowledge of how to make bombs was still in India a 'secret knowledge', Tilak wrote that it would not be long before the 'magical lore of Bengal' spread throughout the rest of the country. Any attempt to prohibit the scientific knowledge that made bombs possible was in vain, as the knowledge was intimately connected to the edifice of European science on which colonialism supported itself, and the ingredients required for the production of bombs were relatively common materials used in a variety of industries, and thus could not be proscribed.[86]

Two more articles published in the *Kesari* further elaborated upon Tilak's theory of the bomb. In 'The real meaning of the bomb', published on 26 May, Tilak highlighted the significance of the advent of the bomb in India, writing that even the news of war in Afghanistan paled to

[84] *Kesari* (translation), 9 June 1908, IOR: L/P&J/6/877, p. 1. [85] Ibid., p. 2.
[86] Ibid., pp. 3–4.

insignificance before the news of the bomb, which became the 'sole subject of talk and writing in England'. According to Tilak, English public opinion maintained that 'if any extraordinary event has occurred in India since the year 1857, it is the birth of the bomb'.[87] Continuing along the same vein in 'The secret of the bomb', published on 2 June, Tilak wrote that there was a considerable difference between the 1897 assassination of Rand and the Muzaffarpur killings, entirely due to the use of the bomb in the latter. While pistols and muskets were old weapons, the bomb represented the latest discovery of Western science, which strengthened the power of rulers around the world but now provided the means of their undoing. While bombs alone could not destroy the military might of the government, they nonetheless carried the potential to undermine its authority:

> When the official class begins to overawe the people without any reason ... then the sound of the bomb is spontaneously produced to impart to the authorities the true knowledge that the people have reached a higher stage than the vapid one in which they pay regard to such an illiberal [policy of] repression.[88]

For Tilak, the bomb was above all else a tool of communication, through which the oppressed could speak out against tyranny through the propaganda of the deed.

These views were echoed in the writings of another prominent nationalist from the period, an Oxford-educated lawyer, journalist, scholar, and radical named Shyamji Krishnavarma.[89] A key figure in the early revolutionary movement, Krishnavarma opened India House, a youth hostel at Highgate, with the intention of providing scholarships for Indian students studying in London. Ironically, the British metropole provided greater freedom to Indian radicals than India itself, due to Britain's adherence to liberal principles of free expression and freedom of the press, which were often denied to colonial subjects abroad. For this reason, London became a hub for anti-colonial activism, with many Indian nationalists passing through the city over the first two decades of the twentieth century, including such well-known figures as Lala Lajpat Rai, Bipin Chandra Pal, Mohandas Gandhi, Har Dayal, V. D. Savarkar, and numerous others.[90] From his base in London,

[87] *Kesari* (translation), 26 May 1908, IOR: L/P&J/6/877, pp. 1–4.
[88] *Kesari* (translation), 2 June 1908, IOR: L/P&J/6/877, pp. 1–4.
[89] Fischer-Tiné, *Shyamji Krishnavarma*.
[90] Nicholas Owen, 'The Soft Heart of the British Empire: Indian Radicals in Edwardian London', *Past & Present* 220, no. 1 (2013), pp. 143–84. For the relationship between Indian revolutionaries and British anarchists, see Ole Birk Laursen, 'Anarchist Anti-Imperialism: Guy Aldred and the Indian Revolutionary Movement, 1909–14', *Journal of Imperial and Commonwealth History* 46, no. 2 (2018), pp. 286–303.

Krishnavarma edited a weekly newspaper called *The Indian Sociologist,* which published regular articles denouncing imperialism and criticizing the hypocrisy of Britain's failure to uphold its professed liberal values throughout the empire. Krishnavarma's writings were highly critical of British colonial rule, referring to it as a foreign despotism and advocating an alliance among victims of imperialism in India, Egypt, Ireland, and South Africa.[91] In 1907, Krishnavarma moved to Paris but continued to publish *The Indian Sociologist* out of London, with the radical V. D. Savarkar taking over operations at India House. The hostel subsequently gained new notoriety in 1909 when a Punjabi student named Madan Lal Dhingra shot and killed Sir William Curzon Wyllie, the political aide-de-camp for the secretary of state for India during a well-attended event at the Imperial Institute in London. This attack attracted global attention and brought fresh attention to the 'scientific terrorism' of Krishnavarma's ideology.[92]

Prior to the assassination, Krishnavarma published an article titled 'The Ethics of Dynamite' in the August 1908 issue of *The Indian Sociologist,* in which he referenced a famous essay by the British theorist and politician Auberon Herbert under the same name. The son of the 3rd Earl of Carnarvon, Herbert was a member of the British Parliament in the 1870s and became an influential theorist for classical liberals, libertarians, and anarchists due to his advocacy for the idea of *voluntaryism*, a political philosophy that asserted that all forms of association, including government, should be voluntary.[93] In the original 'Ethics of Dynamite' article, Herbert suggested that the use of dynamite could be a legitimate act of political resistance in cases where coercion made other means of redress impossible. Krishnavarma summarized the insights of Herbert's essay in *The Indian Sociologist*, writing,

> ... where the people have political power there is no need for the use of explosives. It only promotes reaction. But where the people are utterly defenceless, both politically and militarily, then one may look on the bomb or any other weapon as legitimate. Its employment then becomes merely a question of expediency.[94]

In the following issue of *The Indian Sociologist*, Krishnavarma applied Herbert's insights to the specific case of colonial India, launching a scathing critique of British rule. Having established that violence was

[91] *The Indian Sociologist*, 3, no. 9 (September 1907), pp. 35, and 3, no. 11 (November 1907), p. 42.

[92] Fischer-Tiné, 'Mass-Mediated Panic'.

[93] See Auberon Herbert, *The Right and Wrong of Compulsion by the State, and Other Essays*, ed. Eric Mack (Indianapolis: Liberty Classics, 1978).

[94] *The Indian Sociologist*, 4, no. 8 (August 1908), p. 30.

justified in cases where no other option was available to a subject population, Krishnavarma's next step was proving that circumstances in India justified the use of bomb attacks by Indian radicals. Krishnavarma first set out to demonstrate that the British held India for their own benefit and not for the benefit of the Indian people, arguing that the British were in India 'from base and selfish motives alone, for rapine and robbery', not altruism.[95] As his reading of Auberon Herbert makes clear, Krishnavarma was thoroughly conversant with British political theory, including liberal theories of property rights, which figured heavily in his critique of colonialism.[96] Krishnavarma viewed Britain's colonization of India as a usurpation, or 'wrongful gain', of Indian property. Because British law, specifically the Indian Penal Code, included the right to defend one's property even in cases where this defence caused the death of the robber, this implied that the assassination of British colonizers could be justified if carried out with the intention of defending Indian property rights from usurpation. In other words:

> Both in their own interest and in the interest of humanity, Indians must adopt such means as may be conducive to their success in resisting the alien aggressors who have enslaved them and who ... have no more respect for the lives of the people of India than for the beasts inhabiting that country.[97]

Krishnavarma concluded that British repression left Indians 'no other remedy except the exercise of their right to resist violence by violence'.[98]

In August 1909, another nationalist, Bipin Chandra Pal, was arrested for sedition and sentenced to one month's simple imprisonment for an article that he wrote in the London-based *Swaraj*, titled 'The Aetiology of the Bomb'. Although the term 'aetiology' can refer to broader processes of causation, it also carries medical connotations, often referring to the causes of a disease. Pal was not alone in trying to 'diagnose' the origins of the bomb in India, as the writings of both colonial sympathizers and revolutionaries alike are rife with medical metaphors.[99] In his article, Pal used the language of disease as a way of presenting his analysis of the history of the bomb in Bengal in seemingly objective terms, writing that

[95] *The Indian Sociologist*, 4, no. 9 (September 1908), p. 34.

[96] For more, see Fischer-Tiné, *Shyamji Krishnavarma.* [97] Ibid. [98] Ibid., p. 35.

[99] There is a prominent concern among colonial sources regarding the threat of 'infection' posed by those 'contaminated' with revolutionary ideas. See, for example, H. Wheeler, 29 August 1914, NAI, Home Department Political Branch A, September 1914, 211–224, p. 5. By contrast, colonial medical campaigns against disease and plague were similarly heavily inflected by the metaphors of counter-insurgency. See Forth, *Barbed Wire Imperialism*, p. 22.

there was no ethical justification for the use of the bomb, but that it nonetheless had a cause, just like any disease.[100]

Pal first compared the 'bomb-disease' to Russian nihilism, stating that even the 'greater inhumanities of the Russian despotism have offered no moral justification for these'. Despite this, Pal argued that there was no denying the fact that Russian nihilism was an inevitable and necessary product of Russian autocracy. The bomb, for Pal, 'is not an uncaused something, and there must, necessarily, be a similarity in its origin everywhere'. Assassination, by this logic, was ultimately due to 'a consciousness of the extreme helplessness of the assassin in relation to his opponent or oppressor, a strong sense of his utter lack of strength or moral and material resources to meet his enemy'. According to Pal, assassination by bomb was the most diabolical form of murder, as it endangered the lives of the innocent as well as the guilty. Despite this, like other forms of assassination, the politics of the bomb implied that the perpetrator did not believe that any legal recourse was available to him, implying a breakdown of public trust in the legitimacy or effectiveness of the government and its rule of law.[101]

Pal was careful to state that analyzing the psychology of the bomb was not the same as providing a moral justification for it. Pal compared the act of resorting to political assassination with acts of theft undertaken by those who are hungry – the action can be understood, even if it cannot be condoned. Acknowledging the fact that bomb assassinations frightened the government and staggered the people, making it difficult to take a calm and critical view of the phenomenon, Pal nonetheless referred to the psychology of the bomb in Bengal as 'a subject of supreme importance' for the Indian administration.[102] Pal further declared the following:

> However much we may condemn the fatal folly of the people who adopted these outlandish methods of political propaganda, we cannot shut our eyes to the ugly fact that the real responsibility of it lies far more with the quack statesmanship ... than with these impatient and inexperienced young men, who have been the victims of a mad impulse ... wrought upon by the repressive measures of the Government of Bengal.[103]

In the state of helplessness brought on by a heavy-handed governmental response to the swadeshi movement, Pal claims that people in India had come to view the bomb as a fundamental right that could be exercised in defence of one's person, property, honour, or religion, 'whenever these were attacked by lawless hooligans'. This appeal to violence in the

[100] *Swaraj*, I, no. 6–7, 31 August 1909, IOR: L/P&J/6/955, File 2887, p. 280. [101] Ibid.
[102] Ibid., p. 282. [103] Ibid., p. 283.

name of self-defence was for Pal a 'lawful appeal', a 'declaration of war, not against the Government, but against those who attacked private rights'.[104] For Pal, propaganda by bomb represented a reclamation of an elemental ability to kill, through which the powerless sought to protect themselves from the 'lawless hooligans' against whom the colonial state could not or would not intervene. The bomb was, in other words, a challenge to the authority of the colonial rule of law, simultaneously subverting the government's monopoly on violence while also calling into question the legitimacy of the colonial state in claiming this monopoly.

'No Terror for the Law-Abiding Citizen'

The challenge that such bomb attacks posed to the colonial order prompted a strong legal response from the state. The CID had been watching Khudiram's associates, based out of Manicktolla garden in Calcutta, for some time but neglected to share this information with local police. In fact, the CID became aware of the plot against Kingsford before it even occurred, when a member of the conspiracy bragged about it to Rajani Sarkar, a CID informant.[105] Despite dispatching an agent to Muzaffarpur to investigate, the security service was nonetheless unable to detect Khudiram and Prafulla until it was too late. Following the bomb attack, the CID finally raided Manicktolla garden, discovering a trove of weapons and 'seditious' literature.

This resulted in a highly publicized trial in Alipore, in which thirty-four were accused, with fifteen convicted by the High Court on 23 November 1909, including the famous revolutionary Barindra Ghose. In his judgment, the Chief Justice found 'a close and more than accidental correspondence between the propagandism of the Jugantar and the doctrines, objects and methods that were taught and practiced in the gardens'.[106] In fact, the Manicktolla group had indeed recently branched off from the Jugantar's eponymous newspaper, of which Barindra was originally a publisher. Over the span of a few months, circulation of the *Jugantar* soared from 200 to 7,000, and would soon exceed 20,000 copies. This circulation attracted the attention of the colonial government and

[104] Ibid., p. 290. [105] Heehs, *Bomb in Bengal*, p. 147.
[106] Note on the Growth of the Revolutionary Movement in Bengal, Eastern Bengal and Assam, and United Bengal up to May 1914 by Sydney Hutchinson, in *Terrorism in Bengal*, vol. 1, p. 229.

resulted in six separate prosecutions against the paper on charges of sedition.[107]

Prior to the Muzaffarpur attack, Barindra split with other radicals such as Nikhileswar Roy Maulick, who saw the paper as too valuable and too profitable to abandon. Barindra and the others agreed that the Chhatra Bhandar group, led by Nikhileswar, would continue publication of the *Jugantar*, while Barindra would embark on overt actions designed to subvert the power and authority of the colonial police. Barindra announced his intentions in an article titled 'Our Hope', in which he stated that 'if only a few determined men can, by their example, implant' in the mind of the people the notion that 'the English are not superior to us in strength … the diadem of the English shall roll in the dust'.[108] Peter Heehs argues that underlying Barindra's bluster for action was the concern that the paper was attracting too much attention from the authorities.[109] But understanding the politics of the bomb as a form of propaganda by deed indicates that Barindra's goal was also to adopt an alternate method of political communication, one that he viewed as more effective for inspiring anti-colonial resistance among his fellow Indians.

Another key figure in the trial, even more important than Barindra in terms of his impact on Indian nationalism, was his brother Aurobindo Ghose. A nationalist and spiritual thinker, Aurobindo provided important ideological inspiration to the early revolutionary movement through his writings and teachings, which argued that conventional political programs such as swadeshi, boycott, and education were only methods towards a goal and not the goal itself. For Aurobindo, the goal of anti-colonial resistance was an almost eschatological abolition of a system of government deemed foreign and unholy. In a speech given in 1908, Aurobindo stated that true nationalism was a 'religion by which we are trying to realize God in the nation, in our fellow countrymen. We are trying to realize him in the three hundred millions *(sic)* of our people'. To rebel against the colonial state was thus a project that was considered metaphysical as well as material, because

> … if you rely upon other forces supposing that you are a Nationalist in the European sense, meaning in a purely materialistic sense … if you want to replace the dominion of the foreigner by the dominion of somebody else, it is a purely material change; it is not a religion, it is not that you feel for the three

[107] See Sanyal, *Revolutionary Pamphlets*, pp. 30–5.
[108] Heehs, *Bomb in Bengal*, pp. 102–3. [109] Ibid., p. 103.

hundred millions of your countrymen, that you want to raise them up, that you want to make them all free and happy.[110]

Aurobindo's ideology carried strong appeal for disillusioned young men such as Khudiram Bose, who was known to have attended his speeches.[111] In the sweeping arrests that followed the Muzaffarpur bomb attack, the police sought to firmly establish a more direct connection between Aurobindo and revolutionary conspiracy. One police informant claimed of the Manicktolla conspirators, 'wherever any question arose, it was always Aurobindo to whom reference was made for a decision'.[112] The main piece of evidence to support such a claim was a letter from Barindra to his brother that said, 'now is the time. Please try and make them meet for our conference. We must have *sweets* all over India ready made for emergencies. I wait here for your answer.'[113] Despite the argument that sweets here served as an obvious code for bombs, the letter was ultimately dismissed as a forgery, leading the case against Aurobindo to unravel.[114] This was partly inspired by the suspicion towards police spies exhibited by the Sessions Court, whose judgment read as follows: 'Experience tells us that in cases when spies are employed documents do find their way into houses of suspected persons in a manner which cannot be explained by the accused.'[115]

Although Khudiram Bose – and Prafulla Chaki had he survived – could be tried for the specific crime of murder, the charge against his associates in the Manicktolla garden was conspiracy to wage war against the king. The central challenge for the prosecution was tying the overt acts committed by members of the association with an overarching conspiracy to deprive the king of the sovereignty of India. On the tenth day of the trial, the defence council put forward the argument that the attempt on the life of Kingsford, as well as the similar attempts made against the mayor of Chandernagore and Sir Andrew Fraser, did not amount to a waging of war against the Crown. C. R. Das, the advocate for the accused, contended that in the overt acts in question, personal

[110] Aurobindo Ghose, *Speeches* (Pondicherry: Sri Aurobindo Ashram Press, 1952), pp. 21–3.
[111] For the newest scholarship on the multifaceted life and thought of Aurobindo Ghose, see Peter Heehs, *The Lives of Sri Aurobindo* (New York: Columbia University Press, 2008), and Alex Wolfers, 'Born Like Krishna in the Prison House: Revolutionary Asceticism in the Political Ashram of Aurobindo Ghose', *South Asia: Journal of South Asian Studies* 39, no. 3 (2016), pp. 525–45.
[112] Quoted in Heehs, *Nationalism, Terrorism, Communalism*, p. 51.
[113] Bejai Krishna Bose, *The Alipore Bomb Case* (Calcutta, 1910), p. 4.
[114] See Heehs, *Nationalism, Terrorism, Communalism* and 'Foreign Influences on Bengali Revolutionary Terrorism'.
[115] Alipore Bomb Trial, Judgment of Sessions Court, 6 May 1909, SAAA, p. 171.

grudges against the victims as individuals motivated the accused, whose actions did not therefore represent a broader assault on imperial sovereignty. Das stated that attacks on individuals could not constitute the waging of war, as

> the essence of waging war was that there should be opposition and that it should not be restricted to particular individuals. ... In proving the waging of a war, the prosecution should prove not only the generality with regard to the scope of the particular acts but there must be such a thing from which it was possible for any human being to think that by that act they would be subverting the government of the country.[116]

According to Das, the attacks for which the accused were placed on trial did not fit these criteria.

Although the charges of waging war against the Crown were dropped, the High Court confirmed convictions under section 121-A of the Indian Penal Code against several suspects, including Barindra Ghose, Ullaskar Dutt, and Upendra Nath Banerjee. In contrast to section 121, which had to do with the waging of war against the sovereign, section 121-A applied to those who conspired to deprive the Crown of its sovereignty of British India, or to 'overawe' the Government of India or local government by use or threat of criminal force. It was thus conspiracy that provided the key legal framework through which the Alipore suspects were prosecuted, with the attack on Kingsford officially described as 'an act of terrorism ... in pursuance of the conspiracy'.[117]

Das sought to undermine the case of the prosecution by pointing out the inconsistencies that resulted from the archaic language of sections 121 and 121-A of the Indian Penal Code. Although not denying that the accused committed individual crimes, Das argued that these crimes did not amount to a waging of war against the king but should simply be prosecuted as individual acts of attempted murder or murder. Das contended that the attempt on the life of the mayor of Chandernagore was motivated by the mayor's decision to disallow a public meeting by nationalists. Similarly, he called the attempt against Kingsford an act of revenge. He further stated that to prove that war was being waged, the prosecution had to prove both the general intention to wage war lying behind any individual acts, as well as evidence that would indicate that by carrying out the individual act, the accused truly believed that they were subverting the Government of India. Along this same line of argument, Barindra Ghose admitted to the distant goal of revolution but claimed

[116] Alipore Bomb Trial, Appeals before High Court, SAAA, pp. 239–40.
[117] Judgment of Sessions Court, 6 May 1909, SAAA, p. 178.

that he never believed that any of his individual crimes would bring about national independence.[118]

The prosecution rejected this argument, as well as the one put forward by Das, who stated that it did not matter whether the accused were preparing for a far-off revolution or one in the immediate future. According to section 121-A, the moment that two of the accused 'conspired' to wage war, 'the offence was complete even if no overt acts were committed'.[119] In formulating his judgment, Sir Lawrence Hugh Jenkins of the High Court drew on the decision of an earlier conspiracy case, *Mucahy* v. *Reg.*, which referred to a conspiracy as the agreement, rather than intention, of two or more to commit an unlawful act by unlawful means. Quoting this case, Jenkins stated that when two or more agreed to put it into effect, 'the very plot is an act in itself, and the act of each of the parties, promise against promise, actus contra actum' was punishable if it was directed towards a criminal object or the use of criminal means.[120]

The significance of this legal strategy regarding conspiracy law is noted by political scientist and anthropologist Partha Chatterjee, who argues that the political nature of revolutionaries' crimes made them particularly challenging to prosecute through ordinary procedures. According to Chatterjee, using conspiracy as the key legal concept in constructing revolutionary politics as a crime meant that 'distinct and diverse activities by a large number of often-unconnected individuals' could be pooled together in order to constitute a 'single criminal offence with a single motive shared by all the accused'.[121] Since different members of a conspiracy might not be involved in specific overt actions, proving the existence of a conspiracy was essential for convicting revolutionaries who were not guilty of committing particular criminal acts. According to the legal standards of the time, it did not matter whether revolutionaries were preparing for an immediate uprising or for one in the distant future: 'The moment that two of these persons conspired to wage war the offence was complete even if no overt act were committed.'[122] In other words, by applying the legal doctrine of conspiracy to revolutionary societies, the state shifted the onus of the prosecution from proving that an individual committed a crime to proving that an individual belonged to a conspiracy. This transformation built on earlier legislation regarding dacoits, thugs, pirates, and criminal tribes, which had shifted the onus from

[118] Alipore Bomb Trial, Appeals before High Court, SAAA, p. 215.
[119] Alipore Bomb Trial, Appeals before High Court, SAAA, pp. 216–83.
[120] Alipore Bomb Trial, High Court Judgment, 1908, SAAA, p. 378.
[121] Chatterjee, *Black Hole of Empire*, p. 307.
[122] Alipore Bomb Trial, Appeals before High Court, SAAA, p. 283.

individual prosecutable acts to membership within a hereditary 'criminal' group.[123]

The first new law to address these issues of conspiracy and sedition was the Prevention of Seditious Meetings Act of 1907. This act empowered the government to prohibit political meetings convened by more than twenty individuals, 'for the furtherance or discussion of any subject likely to cause disturbance or public excitement or of any political subject or for the exhibition or distribution of any writing or printed matter relating to any such subject'.[124] Before its passage into law Rash Behari Ghose, a prominent politician, gave a speech opposing the proposed bill, stating:

> I am well aware that one of the first duties of the State is to preserve law and order, and if I thought that either law or order was menaced, or that public tranquillity could not be maintained unless the Government were armed with the power which they now propose to take, I would be the first to vote in favour of the Bill, and to vote for it with all my heart.[125]

Ghose declared that unrest in India was only skin deep, making such legislation wholly unnecessary. Referring to the proposed bill as an indictment of the whole Indian nation, Ghose argued that if the unrest was not widespread, a repressive law such as the one proposed was unnecessary, while if there was indeed widespread unrest, this should serve as an indictment of the colonial administration. Ghose warned that the bill would not fix the problem, but that the imposition of this bill would only make things worse by making the police into the 'absolute masters of the people' and thus deepening the divide between the government and its subjects.[126] The bill was similarly criticized by Gopal Krishna Gokhale, a prominent nationalist, who questioned the colonial government's use of the term 'sedition' by noting that different officials could define the term differently. Gokhale accused some officials of blaming sedition on any Indian who did not speak to them with 'bated breath and whispering humbleness', and said that others used the term to refer to any who offered legitimate criticism to the administration. Gokhale said that if any sedition did exist, it was a recent phenomenon caused by the impatience of the Indian people towards the slow progress being made in political reform.[127] The bill also attracted rigorous criticism from the Bengali vernacular press.[128]

[123] See Chapter 1.

[124] The Prevention of Seditious Meetings Act 1907, IOR: L/PJ/836, File 4060, p. 1.

[125] Rash Behari Ghose and Gopal Krishna Gokhale, *On Repression* (Adyar Madras: The Commonweal Office, 1916), p. 1.

[126] Ibid., pp. 2–9.

[127] Ibid., pp. 14–15.

[128] Sanyal, *Revolutionary Pamphlets*, p. 29.

In direct response to the Muzaffarpur attack, and contemporaneous with the ongoing Alipore trial, two new bills were introduced in the Governor General's Council in June of 1908 by Sir Harvey Adamson, a member of the Indian Civil Service. The first of these, which came into law as the Explosive Substances Act, sought to expand upon and supersede the Indian Explosives Act of 1884, which officials deemed ineffective in dealing with the deliberate manufacture of 'infernal machines' by revolutionary secret societies. This earlier law was framed to prevent accidents and did not provide for sentences of imprisonment, while the government deemed the Indian Arms Act of 1878 to be similarly inadequate both in terms of the penalties permitted under it and its lack of scope for dealing with preparations to manufacture bombs. By contrast, the Explosive Substances Act enabled the punishment of any person guilty of causing, or attempting to cause, an explosion likely to endanger life or property, as well as any person manufacturing or possessing an explosive substance with similar intent.[129]

Sir Harvey Adamson introduced the bill by listing the recent spate of bomb attacks and linking these with 'certain newspapers' guilty of inciting assassination. Adamson sought to make clear to the other members of the Governor General's Council that the culprits who this bill sought to address were not typical offenders 'of the lower criminal classes,' but were rather educated men bound together 'against all the interests that keep society alive, men who like pirates are the enemies of the human race'.[130] The bill received little discussion within the Council, with Sayyid Muhammad Bahadur expressing 'horror and indignation' regarding the Muzaffarpur killings, and giving the bill his assent.[131] Ripudaman Singh, a prominent Sikh who would himself later be accused of sedition in the 1920s, similarly gave his support to the measure, calling the recent bomb attacks deplorable and remarking that 'this sort of crime was unknown in this country till recently. It is every day happening in European countries, because, for good or evil, "democracy" is in the air, and India could not have escaped the infection.'[132] The bill was passed with no significant opposition.

[129] Sir Harvey Adamson, Explosive Substances Act, Statement of Objects and Reasons, 6 June 1908, IOR: L/PJ/6/875, File 2363, p. 1.

[130] Adamson, Meeting of the Council of the Governor General, Explosive Substances Act, 8 June 1908, IOR: L/PJ/6/875, File 2363, p. 1.

[131] Sayyid Muhammad Bahadur, Meeting of the Council of the Governor General, Explosive Substances Act, 8 June 1908, IOR: L/PJ/6/875, File 2363, p. 4.

[132] Ripudaman Singh, Meeting of the Council of the Governor General, Explosive Substances Act, 8 June 1908, IOR: L/PJ/6/875, File 2363, p. 5.

Following this, Adamson put forward 'a sequel to the Explosive Substances Bill' called the Newspapers (Incitement to Offences) Bill. Adamson said that this bill was designed to meet the same emergency as the previous one, and that the current situation had two key aspects, both of which needed to be dealt with if the 'evil' was to be stopped. The first, the actual making of bombs, was addressed through the Explosive Substances Bill. The second was the public incitement to murder carried out by the press. According to Adamson, these two factors were 'as inseparable as cause and effect. If you legislate for the effect without legislating for the cause, you do nothing'. For this reason, the Newspapers Bill was said to be every bit as important as the Explosive Substances Bill.[133] In the Statement of Objects and Reasons, Adamson declared that there was a close connection between bomb attacks and the incitements published by certain newspapers. The proposed bill thus restricted any publications that could be perceived as inciting murder, offences under the Explosive Substances Act, and broader acts of violence. It would empower the government to confiscate the printing press of an offending paper and to prohibit the lawful issue of that paper.[134]

In justifying the bill before the Governor General's Council, Adamson made specific reference to the *Jugantar* newspaper in his speech, pointing out that despite having been prosecuted for sedition on five separate occasions, the newspaper still existed and continued to publish articles that advocated the subversion of British rule. Adamson blamed the *Jugantar* for the Muzaffarpur murders, pointing out both that Barindra Ghose was an initial creator of the paper and that Khudiram Bose admitted to taking inspiration from articles within it. Still, Adamson was careful to clarify that the bill was not directed against sedition but was rather confined to the current emergency. According to Adamson, the bill would target only those newspapers that persistently defied the law, and that established themselves as 'schools of anarchy and outrage with the object of debauching young and immature minds and inciting men to murder, armed revolt, and secret and diabolical schemes of general assassination'.[135] Adamson claimed that the bill would not in any way be directed against the liberty of the press, and said that the measure would curtail 'no liberty that is legitimate', also stating that no

[133] Adamson, Meeting of the Council of the Governor General, Newspapers Act, 8 June 1908, IOR: L/PJ/6/875, File 2363, p. 1.

[134] Adamson, Newspapers Act, Statement of Objects and Reasons, 6 June 1908, IOR: L/PJ/875, File 2363, p. 1.

[135] Adamson, Meeting of the Council of the Governor General, Newspapers Act, 8 June 1908, IOR: L/PJ/6/875, File 2363, pp. 1–4.

newspaper 'in the civilized world has liberty to make such incitements'.[136]

Unlike the Explosive Substances Bill, the Newspapers Bill did receive criticism from other members of the Council.[137] Sayid Muhammad Bahadur expressed reluctance towards the bill, stating that it was wide in scope and too vaguely worded for the level of precision that would be required to ensure it did not restrict legitimate liberties, although he did ultimately give it his assent. Similarly, Ripudaman Singh said that the bill was not as urgent as the previous one and would affect a much larger number of potentially innocent people, concluding that further time would be needed to discuss its provisions. Despite these protests, the bill was passed nonetheless.

The next major piece of legislation to target revolutionary politics was called the Criminal Law Amendment Act of 1908 and came as a direct response to developments in the ongoing Alipore trial. The stated aim of this legislation was to provide for the quicker trial of certain offences and for the prohibition of associations deemed dangerous to the public peace. To this end, the first part of the act provided for the trial of certain offences by three judges of the High Court, circumventing the ordinary requirement of providing suspects with a trial by jury. The second part of the act empowered the Governor General in Council to declare certain associations to be unlawful, meaning that anyone belonging to or promoting any such criminalized association would be liable to severe punishments. Initially designed to extend to Bengal, Eastern Bengal, and Assam, the act could be extended to other provinces if it was deemed necessary by the Governor General in Council.[138]

The act also removed the right of bail for any accused against whom there was reasonable ground for further inquiry. It further stipulated that the evidence of witnesses already examined by the magistrate was still admissible in cases where there was reason to believe that the death or disappearance of the witness was caused in the interests of the accused. This was a direct response to the murder of Narendra Nath Gossain, the approver in the Alipore trial whose testimony provided a key piece of evidence against the accused. Originally a member of the Manicktolla garden group, Narendra agreed to act as an approver for the prosecution, giving evidence against his co-conspirators in exchange for leniency for

[136] Ibid.

[137] For a wider history of British press censorship in India, see N. Gerald Barrier, *Banned: Controversial Literature and Political Control in British India, 1907–1947* (New Delhi: Manohar, 1976).

[138] Adamson, Statement of Objects and Reasons, Indian Criminal Law Amendment Act, 9 December 1908, IOR: L/PJ/6/914, File 32.

himself. On 31 August 1908, two members of the conspiracy, Kanai Lal Dutt and Satyendra Nath Bose, lured Narendra to the infirmary of the Alipore jail on the pretence that they wanted to work with him to provide evidence against the others. Upon seeing Narendra, the two men opened fire with revolvers that they had smuggled into the prison. Although Narendra tried to flee, Kanai Lal Dutt pursued him and shot him again in the back, killing him.[139]

In December 1908 Adamson introduced the Criminal Law Amendment Bill in the Council of the Governor General, stating that in dealing with a conspiracy seeking to subvert British rule it was the duty of any responsible government to close any possible avenue that contributed to this objective. Adamson blamed revolutionary organizations for corrupting young men 'with no other criminal taint, the sons of respectable parents who do not belong to and have never associated with the ordinary criminal classes', but who were lured by seditious teachings into a 'misguided fanaticism' and led to the 'mistaken belief that in committing crimes of this nature they are working for the good of their country'. Although Adamson argued that the Prevention of Seditious Meetings Act of 1907 impeded the operation of seditious orators and that the Newspapers Act produced an almost total cessation of incitements to assassination within newspapers, he said that India's youth continued to be corrupted through secret associations that he referred to as 'nurseries for young anarchists'. Adamson quoted an unnamed (and potentially fictional) elderly Indian man, who apparently called these associations, 'the terror of the country' which pressed ordinary people into sedition out of fear of reprisal. According to Adamson, such people were only waiting for the government to demonstrate that it was strong enough to offer them reliable protection, in which case they would rejoice and cut off all connection with seditious agitators.[140]

Although there were some reservations, the bill acquired the support of the Council without much difficulty. Mr. Dadashoy concluded that although he was highly reluctant to see the introduction of any legal measures that would remove a person's right to be tried according to the established rules of his country, he nonetheless felt that the continued disturbances to the public peace were 'amply sufficient to prove the inefficiency of ordinary criminal procedure in times of stress and

[139] F. L. Halliday, Commissioner of Police in Calcutta, to Chief Secretary to the Governor of Bengal, 31 August 1908, No. 1876-C, SAAA, p. 1.

[140] Extract from the proceedings of the Council of the Governor General, 11 December 1908, IOR: L/PJ/6/914, File 32, pp. 2–4.

emergency, however well it may be suited to normal conditions'.[141] Ali Muhammad Khan, the Raja of Mahmudabad, said that although there was a notion abroad that harsh summary measures were not in keeping with constitutional measures of government, throughout history political offences were always treated separately from ordinary crime, even in 'civilized' England. Referring to revolutionaries as 'not only traitors to the Crown but … the worst enemies of their own country', Khan advocated for the necessity of precautionary measures that would allow the government to track 'that wild creature, called the anarchist, in his secret haunts'.[142] Even Rash Behari Ghose largely accepted the need for the legislation despite cautioning that anarchism could not be killed through coercive acts. Ghose said that unlike in Ireland, anarchy in India was a 'passing distemper', and he warned that the proposed bill could provoke alarm among Indians concerned by the discretionary power it gave to the governor general for suppressing associations. Still, Ghose reserved his strongest condemnation for 'anarchism' itself, stating that it promoted the 'dissolution of all that holds society together' and was opposed to the laws of both God and man.[143]

The imposition of these various bills provided a strong source of tension for British claims of legitimacy that rested upon an ostensible commitment to a liberal rule of law.[144] Lord Morley, the secretary of state for India, retained a cautious attitude towards repressive legislation throughout his tenure, although he ultimately supported the various measures adopted by the Government of India. Describing the difficulties of language within the drafting of the 1908 legislation, Morley argued that the offences covered by the Newspapers Act in fact differed substantively from acts of assassination and bombing covered by the other laws. He also expressed his agreement with British Prime Minister Herbert Henry Asquith, who referred to rebellion as 'too slippery a word' in seeking to devise a label by which revolutionary crime could be consistently defined. Morley also warned Lord Minto not to forget the vital importance of retaining support within the metropole for any extraordinary measures taken. Morley warned that if either the British press or House of Commons came to perceive a widespread public critique within India of the new measures, this would provide unprecedented legitimacy to the revolutionaries and render them far more difficult to police.[145]

[141] Ibid., pp. 8–9. [142] Ibid., p. 11. [143] Ibid., pp. 15–17.

[144] Of course, as we have already seen the supposed tensions between liberal values and repression in India should in fact be understood as deeply intertwined aspects of liberalism itself.

[145] Morley to Minto, 28 May 1908, Morley Collection, Mss Eur.D.573, NMML, pp. 174–5.

For this reason, Morley cautioned against an overreliance on 'Russian methods' of repression, which risked escalating the frequency and severity of retaliatory 'Russian methods' of reprisal in the form of political assassinations and subversion. Although Morley wrote that he did not want to compare British rule in India with Russian autocracy, he nonetheless stated that whenever he received news of a printer or writer being sentenced to years of penal transportation as a result of sedition charges, it made him feel as though he was 'an accomplice in Cossack Rule'.[146] When Minto reported that one of his colleagues referred to the consideration of pressure from the metropole as a humiliation for the Government of India, Morley called this pressure the government's only source of accountability, stating that without British oversight, rule in India would be 'the one irresponsible government in the world'. In a scathing reply, Morley told Minto to present Morley's compliments to the humiliated colleague and to beg him to 'reconsider impertinent nonsense of this description'.[147] Throughout his correspondence, Morley exemplified many of the tensions and inconsistencies of British claims to liberal government, writing that although he defended the use of harsh laws such as Regulation III of 1818 as needed, he was equally willing to fight against those who would seek to use such laws indiscriminately.[148]

Further laws that sought to extend the government's special powers against revolutionary politics included the Press Act of 1910, and an extension of the Seditious Meetings Act in 1911 and of the Criminal Law Amendment Act in 1913. These laws expanded the powers adopted under earlier legislation, with the Press Act further criminalizing 'seditious' articles as well as incitements to murder or other 'anarchical outrages'. The extension of the Seditious Meetings Act was met with criticism in the Imperial Legislative Council, where Gopal Krishna Gokhale, Bhupendra Nath Bose, and other Indian politicians put forward a memorandum stating that the only justification for such repressive measures was the presence of an exceptional state of affairs that no longer existed. Responding to this criticism, Hardinge said that the legislation 'need have no terrors for the law-abiding citizen' but that if the government relaxed its vigilance by allowing this law to lapse, 'there is very little doubt that sedition and political crime would once more spring into life and would thwart … the healthy evolution of political life and

[146] Morley to Minto, 7 May 1908, Morley Collection, Mss Eur.D.573, NMML, p. 145.
[147] Morley to Minto, 17 March 1910, Morley Collection, Mss Eur.D.573, NMML, p. 3.
[148] Morley to Minto, 27 January 1910, Morley Collection, Mss Eur.D.573, NMML, p. 2.

material progress'.[149] In this speech, Hardinge sought to demarcate legitimate politics from 'illegitimate political agitation', a distinction that would pursued more vigorously by subsequent officials in the 1920s.

On 23 December 1912, Hardinge was the target of a bomb attack that reverberated throughout British India. This attack came during Hardinge's triumphal procession into Delhi in an event meant to celebrate the transfer of British India's capital from Calcutta, a decision that drew strong criticism in Bengal despite the decision to reunite the province in 1911. Although Hardinge later claimed to have trusted himself 'more to the care of the people than to that of the police',[150] his procession was in fact been carried out under the watchful gaze of a security detail that included 497 Constables, 84 Head Constables, 34 mounted Constables, and more than a dozen Sub-Inspectors.[151] The bomb, thrown by the Bengali revolutionary Rash Behari Bose, nearly killed Hardinge, embedding shrapnel in his back and fatally injuring an attendant. Hardinge originally urged the procession to go on but then succumbed to his injuries and had to be carried away on a stretcher. News of the attempted assassination 'sent a thrill of horror and indignation through London' and attracted widespread media coverage. Many papers rejected the possibility that the attack was politically motivated, pointing out Hardinge's decision to cancel the partition of Bengal and the lull in revolutionary violence that occurred in that province surrounding the decision.[152] Nonetheless, the *Daily Telegraph*, *Morning Post*, and *Englishman* were all 'loud in their demand that repressive measures of a more severe kind than have hitherto been thought of should be resorted to' while less reactionary outlets instead treated the attack as 'the insane act of one man or a few, which has little or no political bearing and which, therefore, ought not to be allowed to affect the policy of Government'.[153]

Hardinge himself adopted an approach somewhere between these two extremes in his speech at the first meeting of the Imperial Legislative Council in January 1913, his first public appearance following the attack. Hardinge expressed his disappointment that the type of men who would carry out such a 'useless crime' could be found in India, particularly given that for the whole population of India, the crime ran contrary 'to

[149] Meeting of Imperial Legislative Council, 20 March 1911, Hardinge Papers, CUL, pp. 71–4.
[150] Lord Hardinge, First Meeting of Imperial Legislative Council at Delhi, 27 January 1913, Hardinge Papers, CUL, p. 456.
[151] Tarapada Lahiri, *Rashbehari Bose: The Indomitable Revolutionary* (Calcutta: Anushilan Samiti, 1984), p. 26.
[152] *The Bengalee* (25 December 1912), pp. 1–4.
[153] *The Bengalee* (26 December 1912), p. 4.

their own precepts and instincts of humanity and of loyalty, as well as to their religious principles'. Remarking that it was difficult to believe that the perpetrators of the attack were a class apart from society, Hardinge said that he hoped the storm of public outrage 'may give Indian terrorists cause for sensible and humane reflection and repentance'. Hardinge said that such crimes should not be dismissed as the isolated actions of 'irresponsible fanatics', but were usually the result of organized conspiracies in which the actual assailant was often not necessarily the instigator of the crime. For this reason, the only way to combat such groups was, according to Hardinge, 'to treat as enemies of society, not only those who commit crimes, but also those who offer any incentives to crime'. This included every 'intemperance of political language and methods which are likely to influence ill-balanced minds', a clear reference to the nationalist press and other radical publications.[154]

The meaning of the bomb attack was very clear to those who were involved in it. The anti-colonial credentials of Rash Behari Bose were beyond dispute – born in 1886 in Chandernagore, a small strip of French territory lying just north of Calcutta, Bose tried and failed on several occasions to join the Indian Army before ascending to a key role within the Anushilan Society, ultimately becoming liaison between a number of different revolutionary groups across northern India.[155] Bose would go on to mastermind an attempted all-India uprising during the First World War, details of which are examined in the next chapter. Following Bose's bold attempt to assassinate India's viceroy and governor general in a symbolic destruction of British sovereignty, Har Dayal, an Indian revolutionary best known for founding the infamous Ghadar party in 1913,[156] published the following circular from Yugantar Ashram in San Francisco:

> Who can describe the moral power of the bomb? It is concentrated moral dynamite. When the strong and the cunning, in the pride of their power parade their glory before their helpless victims, when the rich and the haughty set

[154] Lord Hardinge, First Meeting of Imperial Legislative Council at Delhi, 27 January 1913, Hardinge Papers, CUL, pp. 455–7.

[155] There is debate regarding whether his exact date of birth was the 15th of March or the 25th of May. See Takeshi Nakajima, *Bose of Nakamuraya: An Indian Revolutionary in Japan* (New Delhi: Promilla, 2009), p. 21.

[156] Aside from his founding of Ghadar, Har Dayal was a prominent intellectual with links to India Housein London and revolutionary networks throughout the British Empire. Moving to the United States in 1911, he briefly held a post at Stanford before being forced to resign due to his anarchist activities. For a biography of Har Dayal, see Emily Brown, *Har Dayal: Hindu Revolutionary and Rationalist* (Tucson: University of Arizona Press, 1975). The Ghadar party founded by Dayal is the subject of the following chapter.

themselves on a pedestal and ask their slaves to fall down before them and worship them, when the wicked ones of the earth seem exalted to the sky and nothing appears to withstand their might, then, in that dark hour, ... comes the bomb, which lays the tyrant in the dust.[157]

This pamphlet makes clear both the political motivation behind the assassination attempt as well as the discursive function of the bomb as a tool of political propaganda. For Har Dayal, a close associate of Bose, the significance of the bomb was that it pierced the illusion of impregnability with which the colonial regime cloaked itself, proving that even the sovereign figure of the governor general was not impervious to harm. While colonialism set the colonizers above the colonized in a hierarchy of domination, the bomb allowed the colonized to cast their oppressors down into the dust, levelling and inverting this hierarchy in a way that constitutional politics did not.

Conclusion

The rise of political assassination in India from 1897 to 1913 marked a new strategy of 'propaganda by deed', through which revolutionaries and radicals disillusioned with the colonial order sought to undermine the sovereignty of the state by exposing the mortality of its representatives. Although such assassinations were often carried out with firearms and can be situated within a longer trajectory of 'murderous outrages' that extends back into the nineteenth century, the advent of the bomb marked a distinct new phase in the politics of assassination. Cheap, relatively easy to make, and virtually impossible to wholly prohibit, the bomb provided an ideal answer for revolutionaries looking to subvert the government with violence. Such assassinations bore an intimate relationship to the Indian press, which was often accused of instigating or justifying instances of political violence through an appeal to the nineteenth-century category of sedition. In practice, however, the press did not simply comment on bomb attacks, but rather the bomb attacks themselves served a communicative function, capturing a wider audience than revolutionary literature could hope to reach through spectacular 'outrages' that sometimes made global headlines. From 1908 to 1913, various laws, both emergency and regular, were deployed and redrafted in an attempt to muffle anti-governmental criticism through both the press and the bomb. The introduction in 1908 of the Explosive Substances Act and the Newspaper (Incitement to Offences) Act as twin responses to the

[157] *Yugantar Circular*, 1913, SAADA, p. 3.

Muzaffarpur bomb attack illustrates the interconnected nature of bombs and newspapers in early twentieth-century India. The spectacular nature of Bose's attack on Hardinge marks the culmination of the politics of the bomb in this period in a highly public, and thus highly publicized, display of anti-colonial protest. The outbreak of war between Britain and Germany in 1914 only heightened both the scale of anti-colonial operations and the extremes to which imperial law would stretch itself in its attempt to keep up with a new, radical form of politics that challenged both the authority and legitimacy of the colonial rule of law.

3 'The Eye of Government Is on Them'

Anti-Colonialism and Emergency during the First World War

On 4 August 1914, England declared war on Germany following Austro-Hungary's attack on Serbia, and Germany's attack on Belgium. Although the immediate catalyst for the war was the assassination of the Austrian Archduke Franz Ferdinand by a Serbian revolutionary organization called the Black Hand on 28 June, the war was in fact the product of a more complicated set of factors including competing imperial rivalries and a changing balance of power within the European continent.[1] England's declaration of war was followed by an outpouring of support from many Indian subjects who saw the war as an opportunity to demonstrate their loyalty to the British Empire and thus prove their fitness for greater political participation. The Indian Army came to play an important role in the conflict, serving on battlefields in Flanders, British East Africa, the Suez Canal, and Mesopotamia, and incurring 121,598 casualties over the course of the war.[2] The First World War was also a time of great political ferment in many parts of the globe, as the economic implications of the war created greater opportunities for public engagement with nationalist ideologies. By 1919, wholesale food prices rose by 33 per cent above the pre-war level, and parts of India experienced price increases on staple commodities such as rice, wheat, and millets by as high as 73 per cent, 100 per cent, and 132 per cent, respectively.[3] The economic turmoil provided impetus for nascent strands of nationalism and political radicalism, which seized the opportunity of the war to internationalize their cause through global networks and, in some cases, German funds.

The First World War is widely regarded as a lynchpin in European history, the beginning of the 'short twentieth century' and the end of

[1] For more on the origins of the First World War, see Christopher Clark, *The Sleepwalkers: How Europe Went to War in 1914* (New York: HarperCollins, 2013).

[2] Budheswar Pati, *India and the First World War* (New Delhi: Atlantic Publishers and Distributors, 1996), p. 35.

[3] Ibid., p. 242.

nineteenth century positivism.[4] But the war needs to be recentred in Asian history as well, as its consequences for the development of national and transnational histories of Asia have not yet been adequately explored.[5] The war placed a heavy strain on British imperial resources, particularly in India from which 826,855 combatants and 445,582 non-combatants were mobilized over the course of the conflict.[6] Furthermore, the war undermined the prestige and the moral legitimacy of a Eurocentric world order that was already shaken by Japan's military victory over Russia in 1905.[7] Many viewed the wanton destruction of the First World War as an indictment of European civilization that seriously damaged the credibility of the British Empire. This led the ultranationalist Kokuryūkai of Japan, for example, to declare that 'the Great European War was [Europe's] suicide as a civilisation … [and] … the great opportunity for an Asian revival'.[8]

The war also stimulated the growth of global networks of imperial intelligence and unprecedented levels of cooperation between Britain and France, as security services sought to keep track of fluid and highly mobile anti-colonial organizations in North America, Europe, and Asia.[9] Historian Calder Walton refers to the First World War as 'the event that created the modern national security state', with total war requiring total surveillance.[10] There is strong merit to this argument, but at the same time a security-centric approach risks taking the official record too much at its word. While officials did indeed deploy an elaborate surveillance network against the forces of Indian nationalism during the war, this was less a response to the war itself than it was a seizure of opportunity on the

[4] See Eric Hobsbawm, *Age of Extremes: The Short Twentieth Century, 1914–1991* (London: Abacus, 1995).

[5] Tim Harper, 'Singapore, 1915, and the Birth of the Asian Underground', *Modern Asian Studies* 47, no. 6 (2013), p. 1786. For the impact of the war in Southeast Asia, see also Heather Streets-Salter, *World War One in Southeast Asia: Colonialism and Anticolonialism in an Era of Global Conflict* (Cambridge: Cambridge University Press, 2017).

[6] Pati, *India and the First World War*, p. 32. For more on the broader contribution of Britain's empire to its war effort, see also Ashley Jackson, *Distant Drums: The Role of Colonies in British Imperial Warfare* (Brighton: Sussex Academic Press, 2012).

[7] See Cemal Aydin, *The Politics of Anti-Westernism in Asia: Visions of World Order in Pan-Islamic and Pan-Asian Thought* (New York: Columbia University Press, 2007), p. 93, and Kris Manjapra, *Age of Entanglement: German and Indian intellectuals across Empire* (Cambridge, MA: Harvard University Press, 2014), p. 5.

[8] Uchida Ryōhei, 'Jo', *Ajia Taikan* (Tokyo: Kokuryūkai Shuppanbu, 1918) in Sven Saaler and Christopher Szpilman (eds.), *Pan-Asianism: A Documentary History*, vol. 1: *1850–1920* (Plymouth: Rowman & Littlefield, 2011), p. 128.

[9] Popplewell, *Intelligence and Imperial Defence*. See also Brückenhaus, *Policing Transnational Protest*, pp. 42–72.

[10] Calder Walton, *Empire of Secrets: British Intelligence, the Cold War and the Twilight of Empire* (London: HarperCollins, 2013).

part of a colonial regime seeking to justify the expansion of its imperial and oceanic corridors of legal jurisdiction. As this chapter will demonstrate, it was through law as much as espionage that the imperial government sought to clamp down on the forces of anti-colonial nationalism during the war. This mobilization of emergency law had less to do with protecting India and the empire from German military interests than it did with the cynical expansion of British executive authority and the stifling of anti-colonial dissent.[11]

This chapter analyzes the impact of the First World War on attempts by the colonial government of India to legislate against forms of political violence that sought to undermine or overthrow imperial sovereignty. Of special interest are those emergency laws that sought to extend the colonial government's right to detain suspects without trial, also known as 'executive detention'.[12] In 1914, the Government of India passed the Ingress into India Ordinance in an attempt to limit the transgressive potential of Ghadar propaganda and transnational revolutionary networks based out of North America and parts of East and South East Asia. The following year, the passage of the wartime Defence of India Act sought to target revolutionaries whom the government deemed to be either in league with Britain's German enemy, or whose acts of anti-colonial violence aided and assisted the German war effort. Following the conclusion of the war in 1918, colonial officials took steps to extend the repressive measures of the Defence of India Act into peacetime by issuing the controversial Rowlatt Act, despite the disapproval of an increasingly vocal Indian public.

By tracing the debates and discussions that surrounded the passage of these three pieces of 'emergency' legislation, this chapter demonstrates how executive discourses sought to construct and deploy distinct notions of 'the enemy' as a means of justifying and legitimizing the use of extraordinary laws to repress the political challenge of anti-colonial nationalism. Moving beyond the security-centric analysis of previous scholarship, this chapter instead proves that the war was a space in which colonial officials sought to create a new legal ordering of empire through the expansion of pre-existing corridors of imperial and, indeed, global jurisdiction. This chapter demonstrates that the wartime expansion of emergency laws was not only a response to security concerns or to the threat of foreign German interference, as scholars have typically regarded them, but also served as the colonial state's opportunistic

[11] See also Ramnath, *Haj to Utopia*, p. 89.
[12] A. W. Brian Simpson, *Human Rights and the End of Empire: Britain and the Genesis of the European Convention* (New York: Oxford University Press, 2004), p. 55.

Figure 3.1 Indian soldiers marching through France, 1914.
(Getty Images.)

answer to the more long-term political challenge presented by anti-colonial nationalism.

'A State of War'

Radicals within the Indian diaspora saw the First World War as an opportunity, and sought to exploit the temporary disarray of the British Empire.[13] The outbreak of war was swiftly followed by a call to arms issued by *Ghadar*, a revolutionary newspaper based out of San Francisco, with a wide readership extending through the Americas, Asia, Africa, and the Middle East. First published on 1 November 1913, *Ghadar* presented a call for an armed uprising against British rule from its very first issue; 'What is our name? Mutiny. What is our work? Mutiny. Where will the mutiny break out? In India. ... The time is soon to come when rifles and blood will take the place of pen and ink.'[14] Reaching a global readership of disaffected Indians suffering under immigration and labour restrictions that hampered their aspirations for work and dignity, *Ghadar* inspired the formation of hundreds of loosely affiliated cells and networks, with the central organization led by Har Dayal in San Francisco retaining its role as a hub for propaganda and revolutionary plots. As the British Empire became embroiled in its war with Germany, officials within the Government of India began to view the Ghadar organization and its transnational network of adherents as a serious threat to imperial security. This growing unease among the colonial authorities stimulated the development of an elaborate system of surveillance and an increasingly restrictive series of emergency laws aimed at stifling revolutionary activities.[15]

The rhetoric and imagery deployed by *Ghadar* made stronger use of military metaphors than earlier revolutionary organizations such as Jugantar or Anushilan, with an invocation of the mutiny of 1857 as a key symbolic rallying point. This was particularly true during the period

[13] The best account of these attempts, and of the interlocking political philosophies behind them, is provided in Ramnath, *Haj to Utopia*, pp. 34–94.

[14] Quoted in Government of India circular, 25 August 1915, Home Political Deposit, October 1915, NAI, File No. 43, p. 8.

[15] For the best recent account of Ghadar, see Ramnath, *Haj to Utopia*. For the history of the imperial security service, see Popplewell, *Intelligence and Imperial Defence*. The relationship between imperial surveillance and anticolonial radicalism is also explored by Seema Sohi, who argues that just as the political radicalism of South Asians in North America stimulated the development of imperial and domestic networks of intelligence and repression, these networks in turn served to further alienate and radicalize those on whom they sought to spy. See Sohi, *Echoes of Mutiny: Race, Surveillance and Indian Anticolonialism in North America* (New York: Oxford University Press, 2014).

Figure 3.2 Ghadar pamphlet depicting India as a mother goddess. This kind of imagery was common in revolutionary publications. (Courtesy of University of Toronto Libraries.)

of the First World War. Just before the outbreak of hostilities, the 28 July issue of *Ghadar* instructed its readers to set up a mutiny in India as soon as the war broke out in Europe. On 4 August 1914, the day that Britain declared war, *Ghadar* proclaimed; 'The bugle of war has sounded, and the war has begun. ... Now is the time for India ... if you set up a mutiny now, the English will come to an end; for on the one side Germany will smite them, and on the other side you.'[16] Despite its predominantly Punjabi composition, the Ghadar movement actively sought to foster a pan-Indian identity capable of channelling the particular grievances of a diverse diasporic community into a militant brand of anti-colonial patriotism.[17] As a result, the movement was particularly alarming to British officials, who found it difficult to police the loose collection of cells and networks developing both throughout and beyond their imperial

[16] Quoted in Malwinderjit Singh Waraich and Harinder Singh (eds.), *Ghadar Movement Original Documents*, vol. 1: *Lahore Conspiracy Cases I and II* (Chandigarh: Unistar Books Pvt. Ltd., 2008), p. 336.

[17] Ramnath, *Haj to Utopia*, p. 4.

jurisdiction. This was particularly true within the context of a global war in which Britain's enemies actively encouraged the spread of Ghadar ideas, arms, and propaganda.

The transgressive potential of transnational Indian communities for destabilizing imperial notions of security and stability is best highlighted by the famous voyage of the *Komagata Maru*.[18] Despite the supposed right of colonial subjects to circulate freely from one British colony to another, in practice the white settler colonies of Canada, Australia, South Africa, and New Zealand were deeply committed to a white supremacist agenda. In the early twentieth century, governments of these colonies sought to restrict the rights of indigenous peoples, Asians, and Africans within their borders and prevent non-white immigration from abroad.[19] As emerging nation-states sought to reify their borders in the name of national homogeneity, migration laws became one of the primary means by which governments could assert their sovereignty by regulating the movement of people across the borders of their territory.

Migration laws were complicated in the Indian context by local colonial protocols of recording identity, as well as issues of gender and class. As we have seen in the case of 'criminal tribes' and so-called hereditary dacoits, internal migration and mobility had been restricted in India since the nineteenth century. For this reason, contrary to John Torpey's argument that the emergence of the passport and other forms of restriction to the transnational circulation of people came about as a result of powerful states in the West seeking to control global migration, Radhika Singha argues that the introduction of compulsory passports in India during the First World War was shaped by considerations other than the simple binary of race and migration.[20] Nevertheless, for the white Dominions the exclusion of certain racialized bodies became an important tool in the construction of a national identity and the creation of particular labour regimes.

[18] For an excellent recent analysis, see Renisa Mawani, *Across Oceans of Law: The Komagata Maru and Jurisdiction in the Time of Empire* (Durham, NC: Duke University Press, 2018) and Anjali Gera Roy, *Imperialism and Sikh Migration: The Komagata Maru Incident* (Abingdon: Routledge, 2018). See also Ramnath, *Haj to Utopia*, pp. 47–50.

[19] For a more detailed analysis of the exclusionary immigration policies of Canada and the United States, see John Price, 'Canada, White Supremacy, and the Twinnings of Empire', *International Journal* 64, no. 4 (2013), pp. 628–38. For the global dimensions of these policies of racial exclusion, see Marilyn Lake and Henry Reynolds, *Drawing the Global Colour Line: White Men's Countries and the Challenge of Racial Equality* (Cambridge: Cambridge University Press, 2008).

[20] Radhika Singha, 'The Great War and a "Proper" Passport for the Colony: Border-Crossing in British India, c.1882–1922', *Indian Economic and Social History Review* 50, no. 3 (2013), pp. 289–315. See also John Torpey, *The Invention of the Passport: Surveillance, Citizenship, and the State* (Cambridge: Cambridge University Press, 2000).

In May of 1908, the Canadian government took steps to unofficially limit Indian immigration to Canada through a new law stipulating that only those travelling a continuous route from their point of departure would be allowed to enter the country, thereby excluding all voyages from India.[21] In a deliberate challenge to this exclusionary law, Gurdit Singh, a wealthy contractor based out of Singapore, arranged passage for 376 Indian passengers, mostly male Sikhs, to Vancouver. When the *Komagata Maru* arrived on 23 May 1914, immigration officials denied the passengers entry into Canada, leading to a tense standoff that lasted for weeks and finally culminated with the embittered passengers forced to return to India.[22]

The return of these passengers alarmed officials within the Government of India, who expressed concern that over the course of their voyage these passengers must have 'heard much bitterness of language against England and her colonies'. While officials admitted that perhaps only a minority of the passengers were 'undesirables', their actions at Vancouver were nonetheless 'scarcely conciliatory', meaning that their return should be closely controlled.[23] Although oceans are typically regarded as backdrops for movement with an association with lawlessness, this incident proves that during the colonial period oceans were, in fact, transected by jurisdictional corridors of law through which imperial sovereignty asserted itself.[24] Furthermore, as we have already seen in the case of Indian Ocean piracy, the legal boundaries between land and sea were often deeply intertwined under international law. In the case of the voyage of the *Komagata Maru* and of other ships that sought in various ways to challenge the Government of India by transgressing its borders, such as the *Annie Larsen* and the *Maverick* discussed later in this chapter, imperial officials devised new legal strategies that sought to extend imperial sovereignty along these oceanic corridors of jurisdiction.

It was in order to deal with the perceived threat posed by the return of the *Komagata Maru*, representative as it was of the larger fear of the return of potentially radicalized expatriate Indians, that the colonial

[21] Seema Sohi, 'Race, Surveillance, and Indian Anticolonialism in the Transnational Western U.S.-Canadian Borderlands', *The Journal of American History* 49, no. 2 (2011), pp. 420–36.

[22] A more detailed account is provided in Ramnath, *Haj to Utopia*, pp. 47–50, and in Ruth L. Almy, '"More Hateful because of Its Hypocrisy": Indians, Britain and Canadian Law in the Komagata Maru Incident of 1914', *Journal of Imperial and Commonwealth History* 46, no. 2 (2018), pp. 304–22.

[23] H. Wheeler, 29 August 1914, Home Department Political Branch A, NAI, 211–224, p. 5.

[24] Lauren Benton, *A Search for Sovereignty: Law and Geography in European Empires, 1400–1900* (New York: Cambridge University Press, 2010), pp. 104–11.

government passed the Ingress into India Ordinance in 1914. Because it was impossible to prevent Indian subjects from returning to India, this ordinance sought instead to police the subcontinent's porous borders by giving officials the authority to investigate Indians returning from abroad to determine any perceived threat they may pose to imperial security and decide accordingly whether to either detain them or place them under restrictions within their home village. Preventing the circulation of colonial subjects was all but impossible within an imperial context that relied upon a mobile, transimperial labour force and voluminous shipping routes across the Atlantic, Pacific, and Indian Ocean worlds. Instead, colonial officials sought to compensate by expanding earlier surveillance regimes designed to police 'criminal tribes' and dacoits within the subcontinent, in an attempt to ensure that returning expatriates could be 'made to realize that the eye of Government is on them'.[25] Although government officials initially claimed that in 'the practical application of this power, we shall proceed quite leniently',[26] in Punjab alone more than two thousand Indians returning home from abroad faced internment or temporary confinement within their home villages over the course of the war.[27]

Justification for these strong measures required careful consideration on the part of the colonial government. According to Sir Reginald Craddock, Home Member in the Governor General's Council, concern with Indian and British parliamentary opinion meant that the ordinary policy of the Government of India was to limit more drastic action only to cases where evidence of disaffection could be clearly demonstrated. Craddock wrote that although there were many in India who were hostile to the colonial regime, 'we watch them and see how they behave and the moment it seems necessary we take action against them'. According to Craddock, the onset of war with Germany triggered 'a warm wave of loyalty, carrying even the disaffected on its crest, which we do not wish to chill by any measure that involves asperity'. Despite this, Craddock felt that it was necessary to respond to the strong request of the government of Punjab for steps to be taken to deal with returning Sikhs, particularly from North America and the Far East, who were 'quite recently in a state of ferment, that the revolutionary paper the *Ghadar* has been circulating

[25] Michael O'Dwyer to William Vincent, 17 September 1917, Home Political A, NAI, No. 1–9 & K.-W., p. 2.
[26] Note by Reginald Craddock, 30 August 1914, Home Political A, NAI, 211–224, p. 6.
[27] Michael O'Dwyer to William Vincent, 17 September 1917, Home Political A, NAI, No. 1–9 & K.-W., p. 2.

among them, ... that [these Sikhs] were planning to come back and fight with their brothers to expel the British'.[28]

In order to articulate these repressive measures in a way that would not alienate moderate opinion, the Ingress into India Ordinance sought to label expatriate Indians returning from abroad as inherently different from subjects residing within India. Sir Charles Cleveland, the Director of Criminal Investigation, acknowledged that 'objections to dealing with returning Indians as "foreigners" are obvious', but argued that 'these people have brought punitive treatment on themselves by complicity of a great many of them in the villainous "Ghadar" campaign'.[29] This argument appears to have been fairly successful in dampening popular criticism of the ordinance, as Sir Michael O'Dwyer observed:

> One of the most striking facts connected with the administration of this Ordinance is the entire absence of any complaint levelled against the internments and restrictions imposed ... although these have in fact been more numerous, and of a more rigorous nature in the Punjab than those enforced under the Defence Act. This may, perhaps, be attributed partly to the character of the persons dealt with under the Ordinance. They are nearly all men who have spent several years abroad, after severing all close connection with their homes. In many instances they were ne'er-do-wells who had become estranged from their relatives, and on their return to their native villages their free and independent manners ... have won them no sympathy.[30]

While O'Dwyer attributed the unpopularity of returning expatriates to their foreign and alienated character, he argued that the main reason for the relative public indifference towards their fate in comparison to popular reactions to legislation such as Regulation III of 1818 and the Defence of India Act was 'the recognition that they have been engaged in intriguing against their own country with the enemy or with revolutionary organisations abroad'.[31]

The Ingress into India Ordinance thus provides a useful entry point into understanding the 'othering' of Indian revolutionaries during the First World War. It is significant that the first piece of exceptional legislation to target suspected revolutionaries after the outbreak of war targeted those colonial subjects that could most easily be disassociated from Indian society writ large, despite the fact that in a separate note, Sir Charles Cleveland called the radicals returning from North America

[28] Reginald Craddock, 30 August 1914, Home Political A, NAI, 211–224, p. 5.
[29] Note by Charles Cleveland, 28 August 1914, Home Political A, NAI, 211–224, p. 3.
[30] Michael O'Dwyer to William Vincent, 17 September 1917, Home Political A, NAI, No. 1–9 & K.-W.
[31] Ibid.

'boastful but not very effective'.[32] In describing the desirability of the ordinance, Alexander Muddiman stated clearly that the reason for its necessity was the volatility of the political situation in India, but observed that 'it is desirable not to draw undue attention to the actual reason that is behind the Ordinance. I venture to suggest that it should be as broad as possible so that it may be defended on other grounds than those actually of the moment.'

According to Muddiman, what was most important was ensuring that the ordinance be made watertight, but also kept 'short but extremely wide' so as to allow for it to be portrayed in a way that masked its true purpose by framing it as a war measure aimed at securing the safety of the state at a moment of crisis. This meant that it could 'as is unhappily not impossible' theoretically be applied to someone of British nationality if they were determined to be working as a German spy, 'as well as those persons who are specially aimed at'.[33] The ordinance was only tangentially connected to potential German plots, and was rather primarily concerned with the subversive potential of the returning revolutionaries themselves, a fact further reiterated in a subsequent note: 'Being widely drawn, the Ordinance can be justified on general grounds appertaining to a state of war rather than of internal sedition.'[34]

By publicly representing the ordinance as a necessity of the war, aimed solely against those who conspired with Germany, colonial officials constructed a very particular enemy, against whom public opinion could be more readily rallied. Here portraying the returning suspects as foreigners facilitated the process of conflating them with India's foreign German enemy. To this end, the Government of India issued a press communiqué explaining the supposed purpose behind the ordinance as being

> ... to ensure that the public peace is not endangered by the action of any persons who, in the interests of hostile Powers, might seek to return to India with the object of creating disturbances or of ascertaining facts likely to be of assistance to our enemies. ... The situation is one of emergency, and exceptional action is justified by the present state of war.[35]

In this sense, war provided an opportunity not only for Ghadar and other anti-colonial revolutionaries, but also for the imperial government, which used the language of war as justification for new laws that would

[32] Note by Charles Cleveland, 15 August 1914, Home Political A, NAI, 211–224, p. 1.
[33] Alexander Muddiman, 1 September 1914, Home Political A, NAI, 211–224, p. 7.
[34] H. Wheeler, 3 September 1914, Home Political A, NAI, 211–224, p. 9.
[35] Government of India press communiqué, 5 September 1914, Home Political A, NAI, 211–224, p. 10.

have required an entirely different strategy of legitimization if the authorities issued them in peacetime.

'The Appeal of Sikhs Was Specially Obnoxious'

Over the first fifteen years of the twentieth century, revolutionary groups in Bengal such as Jugantar and the Anushilan Samiti achieved varying degrees of success in expanding their operations and in staging attacks against colonial informants and imperial officials, most notably in the highly publicized bomb attack against Hardinge by Rash Behari Bose in 1912.[36] With the onset of war, these plans became more ambitious, and organizations in Punjab, Bengal, and central India sought to combine their resources to stage an all-India uprising, with Bose as a key organizer. Beginning on 12 February, Bose and his associates began making arrangements for a general rising on the 21st of that month, which was to be modelled after the mutiny of 1857. The Indian Army was the key element of the conspiracy, and revolutionaries attempted to disseminate revolutionary propaganda to troops stationed in Lahore, Rawalpindi, Ferozepore, and Meerut. Furthermore, the revolutionaries prepared bombs, arms, and ammunition, as well as flags, equipment for destroying railways and telegraph wires, and even a formal declaration of war.[37]

The police foiled the conspiracy by planting a spy named Kripal Singh into the inner circle of the revolutionaries. On 15 February, Singh overheard a conversation regarding the plans for the rising and informed the police. Although Bose realised that Singh was an informant and had the date of the rising moved up to 19 February, Singh was able to escape for long enough to signal his contacts in the CID, leading to a massive crackdown on revolutionary operations across India.[38] Following the failure of the conspiracy, Bose's lieutenant Sachindranath Sanyal attempted to carry on the fight, printing a new *Liberty* leaflet that implored its readers to honour the sacrifice of those captured by the police. 'You may die any day of plague, cholera or malaria,' Sanyal wrote in the *Liberty* leaflets confiscated at the time of his arrest. 'Why not die like a man in a noble cause? Look at the Germans who are dying in lakhs for their country. Dwellers in India, you must also die in lakhs.'[39] By juxtaposing Indian patriotism with that of the Germans, Sanyal articulated the revolutionary cause through the language of war. He also sought to reframe the defeat of

[36] See Chapter 2.
[37] Waraich and Singh (eds.), *Ghadar Movement Original Documents*, vol. 1, p. 161.
[38] Lahiri, *Rashbehari Bose*, p. 47.
[39] *Liberty*, July 1915, Home Political B, NAI, 516–519, p. 12.

his revolutionary companions as a kind of victory through sacrifice that he hoped would inspire others to join the anti-colonial cause.

Although Rash Behari Bose escaped the widespread crackdown, his co-conspirators, including V. G. Pingle, were prosecuted by Special Tribunal in the Lahore conspiracy trial, where the evidence provided by Kripal Singh played a key role in securing convictions. Singh's role as a paid police spy initially raised questions about the reliability of his testimony, but it was ultimately concluded that the government were 'no doubt justified in employing spies; and ... a person so employed [does not] deserve to be blamed if he instigates an offence no further than by pretending to concur with the perpetrators'.[40] Out of 291 conspirators arrested, 42 were executed, another 114 given life sentences, and the rest either acquitted or given sentences of varying degrees.

Following the failure of the plot, Bose decided to flee India. The experience of the failed uprising led him to conclude that soldiers alone would not be enough to stage a successful revolution against imperial authorities. Bose believed that if the civil population in Lahore were armed, overthrowing the government would have still been possible even with the arrest of mutinying troops, noting 'we had man-powers and a disciplined organisation, but no arms'. Bose's solution was to go abroad in search of arms and ammunition, which he could then distribute to people all over the country before a second attempt occurred. Bose also hoped that in going abroad it would be easier to acquire financial support from Germany, which was lacking in his earlier plot.[41]

Bose booked a ticket to Japan, as Rabindranath Tagore's highly publicized upcoming visit allowed him to deceive travel authorities by posing under the alias of P. N. Tagore and claiming that he was a relative travelling on ahead of the famed poet. At first glance, Japan may seem an odd choice for an exiled Indian revolutionary, given that Japan and Britain established an alliance in 1902 as a means of stalling Russian expansion in Asia and safeguarding their own interests in China and Korea. In 1915, this alliance was still in effect, and was one of the reasons for Japan's involvement in the First World War on the side of the British. But despite its relationship to Britain, Japan was also an emerging centre of Asianist thought, and the country's rapid industrialization and victory against Russia in 1905 cemented its reputation as a leader among Asian nations with the potential to challenge the hegemony of the West.[42]

[40] Waraich and Singh (eds.), *Ghadar Movement Original Documents*, vol. 1, p. 38.

[41] Das (ed.), *Rashbehari Bose Collected Works*, p. 29.

[42] See especially Aydin, *Politics of Anti-Westernism in Asia* and Pankaj Mishra, *From the Ruins of Empire: The Intellectuals Who Remade Asia* (New York: Farrar, Straus and Giroux, 2012).

Figure 3.3 A unit of Malay States Guides at Alexandra Barracks with Captain Moira Francis Allan Maclean, a European officer killed during the Singapore Mutiny of 1915.
(Courtesy of National Archives of Singapore.)

On his way to Japan, Bose's ship docked at Singapore, which was in the grip of martial law following the mutiny of the Indian 5th Light Infantry at Alexandra Barracks. The mutineers seized control of the island fortress for two full days before being crushed by a makeshift force composed of French, Russian, and Japanese troops. The 5th Light Infantry was previously the most important source of British security on the island, and the surprise and scope of the mutiny dealt a severe blow to imperial confidence in the region, particular given its close timing to the failed uprising in India.[43] The British responded by declaring martial law on 8 March, asserting that 'no male person of the Indian race over 18 years of age must leave Singapore ... without the sanction of the police'.[44] Colonial authorities also placed restrictions on Indians coming into Singapore, who were forced to obtain a police permit if they wished to enter the island. Despite providing a finger impression to the local authorities, Bose was able to keep up his disguise and continue on to Hong Kong and Japan unhindered, but immigration officials refused entry to twelve Sikhs travelling on the same ship.[45]

What made the Singapore mutiny and the attempted uprising in India particularly unsettling to imperial officials was the very concept of 'mutiny' itself and its relationship to the nature of Britain's imperial project during the First World War.[46] Ever since the events of 1857, where mutiny by British Indian troops sparked a series of connected uprisings that swept across northern and central India and shook the stability and confidence of the empire, the threat of mutiny retained a profound hold over the minds of British officials.[47] This led to a reorganization of the Indian Army, which sought to increase the proportion of European soldiers and discourage recruitment from groups deemed disloyal or seditious, particularly the literate middle-class of Bengal.[48]

[43] For more on the Singapore mutiny and its transnational and global significance, see Harper, 'Singapore, 1915' and Heather Streets-Salter, 'The Local Was Global: The Singapore Mutiny of 1915', *Journal of World History* 24, no. 3 (2013), pp. 539–76.

[44] *The Bengalee* (16 March 1915), p. 2.

[45] Das (ed.), *Rashbehari Bose Collected Works*, p. 47.

[46] This language of mutiny must also be situated within a longer history of treason and sedition as legal and political categories. A more in-depth examination of the nineteenth century lineage of these ideas was provided in Chapter 1, but it is worth noting that each of these three crimes was grounded in the loyalty or disloyalty of a subject to the sovereign, although in the case of mutiny this took on a particularly military dimension. See Benton, *A Search for Sovereignty*, pp. 59–68.

[47] See Wagner, 'Treading Upon Fires'.

[48] Rash Behari Bose had tried twice in his youth to join the Indian Army but, as a Bengali, was disallowed on both occasions. See Hemanta Sarkar, *Revolutionaries of Bengal: Their Methods and Ideals* (Calcutta: The Indian Book Club, 1923).

After the outbreak of war in 1914, these ratios became increasingly difficult to maintain, as the strain of war and reverses in the Mesopotamia campaign led to a heavy demand of Indian troops. The British particularly relied on troops drawn from the 'martial races' deemed historically loyal, with 446,976 of the 1,097,642 total troops of the Indian Army during the war drawn from the Punjab alone, of which less than one quarter were non-combatants. By contrast, only 59,052 Bengalis were recruited for the war effort and 51,935 of these were non-combatants.[49] These numbers meant that not only imperial security, but the European war effort itself rested precariously on the continued loyalty of Indian, and particularly Punjabi, soldiers. In its judgment on the attempted February uprising, the Special Tribunal at Lahore declared that the most important and 'undoubtedly the most dangerous' aspect of the plot was 'the seduction and attempted seduction of troops from their allegiance to His Majesty'.[50]

The colonial fear of mutiny expressed itself in a gendered and racialized language of loyalty and disloyalty. Growing distrust towards Indian and Irish nationalists in the late nineteenth and early twentieth centuries contributed to the popularity of a racial typology that attributed desirable masculine characteristics to colonial groups on whom the imperial military relied, such as Highland Scots, Gurkhas, and Sikhs. These attributes of loyalty, courage, and dependability contrasted with the supposedly effeminate characteristics of Irish Catholics and members of the Bengali middle class, whom the British depicted as weak, cowardly, and treacherous.[51] This meant the planned uprising of 1915 elicited a particularly strong reaction from colonial authorities not only because of its potential to destabilize imperial security, but also because it risked undermining the racial hierarchy on which colonial rule in India rested its legitimacy. As Sir Charles Cleveland, the Director of Criminal Intelligence, noted at the time, 'the appeal of Sikhs was specially obnoxious, because most of the Sikh immigrants served as sepoys, and on their return to India were likely to sow disaffection among the very classes from which Sikh regiments are recruited'.[52]

Beyond its impact on India, the possibility of subversion among Sikh troops threatened to destabilize Britain's entire Indian Ocean empire. Deployment overseas had been a regular feature of Indian Army life ever

[49] For a detailed breakdown of the composition of the Indian Army at this time, see David Omissi (ed.), *Indian Voices of the Great War: Soldiers' Letters, 1914–18* (London: Macmillan Press, 1999), p. 366.
[50] Waraich and Singh, *Ghadar Movement Original Documents*, vol. 1, p. 206.
[51] Streets, *Martial Races*.
[52] Government of India circular, 25 August 1915, Home Political Deposit, NAI, File No. 43, p. 7.

since the reorganization of the army following the transfer from Company rule in 1858. Indian, and particularly Sikh, troops played a crucial role in both extending and maintaining British imperial power in regions as diverse as East Africa, Malaya, and Mesopotamia from the late nineteenth century until the First World War.[53] Furthermore, the Punjab historically provided an important recruiting base for imperial policing. For example, the Malay States Guides, originally constituted as the Perak Armed Police and then the Perak Sikhs, were recruited from the Punjab in 1873 and remained the leading police force in Malaya until 1919. This was not limited to Malaya – Punjabi Sikh police were prominent in colonies ranging from Hong Kong to Uganda to Somaliland.[54] Aside from their presence within imperial military and police forces, Punjabi Sikhs were deeply embedded in a wide range of colonial societies, particularly in South East Asia, further enhancing the paranoia of imperial officials regarding the potentially destabilizing impact of this transnational community. While revolutionary unrest prior to the war was mainly centred out of Bengal, thus fitting colonial conceptions of the disloyal and effeminate Bengali, the predominantly Sikh composition of returning Ghadar revolutionaries and the February uprising's focus on instigating mutiny among supposedly 'loyal' troops in the Punjab thus posed a particularly strong threat to the racial underpinnings of Britain's Indian Ocean empire.[55]

The predominance of Punjabi Sikhs within the Ghadar movement also required a different notion of enmity than the one on which previous anti-revolutionary discourses relied. The outbreak of a world war and the new challenge posed by Ghadar to the stability of imperial martial race narratives of loyalty and disloyalty meant that subversive threats over the course of the war came to be reframed in the language of mutiny and conspiracy. This is not to say that the notion of sedition did not retain relevance throughout the period in question. The report drawn up by the committee assigned with assessing the nature and scope of the revolutionary movement in India and abroad, of which more will be discussed later in this chapter, was even named the *Sedition Committee Report of 1918*. But the idea of mutiny, and of conspiracy with a fixed German enemy, came to supplement, and at times even replace, the category of sedition in a number of important ways.

[53] Thomas Metcalf, *Imperial Connections: India in the Indian Ocean Arena, 1860–1920* (Berkeley: University of California Press, 2007), pp. 68–101.

[54] Ibid., p. 102.

[55] For more on the relationship between masculinity and race in Bengal, see Sinha, *Colonial Masculinity,* as well as Rosselli, 'The Self-Image of Effeteness'.

'It Must Be Regarded at Home as a War Measure'

This process is most clearly illustrated in the discussions that surrounded the passage of the Defence of India Act, an important piece of wartime legislation that the Government of India issued on 19 March 1915. The Defence of India Act was modelled closely after the Defence of the Realm Act, which the British Parliament passed on 8 August 1914, four days after the war with Germany began. The original act gave the British government powers similar to those of martial law, and aimed primarily at preventing persons from 'communicating with the enemy or obtaining information for that purpose or any purpose calculated to jeopardise the success of the operations of any of His Majesty's Forces or to assist the enemy'.[56] The importance placed on hostile association with a fixed foreign enemy had a strong precedent in Regulation III of 1818, which specifically stipulated in its preamble that the law sought to preserve British colonies from 'foreign hostility and from internal commotion'.[57] Originally drafted with Russia and post-Napoleonic France in mind, the Regulation's concern with a combination of internal dissent and foreign interference took on new significance during the global war with Germany and found a more fixed manifestation within the drafting of the Defence of India Act.

Within the British context, officials justified the Defence of the Realm Act based on the threat posed by German spies and informants, but it attracted a great deal of criticism from Irish nationalists, who viewed it as 'an instrument of terrorism, of petty persecution and bullying' through which 'free speech has been abolished, [and] freedom of the Press utterly destroyed', creating a 'state of tyranny that Russia would find difficult to equal'.[58] Despite this controversy, when Lord Hardinge introduced the Defence of India Act in a speech to the Imperial Legislative Council, he claimed that because 'law-abiding England accepted this measure without a murmur,' there should be no issue accepting similar measures in India, particularly because it would be up to the Indian people themselves 'to decide how far it may be necessary to put those clauses into force'.[59] Although the act gave wide rule-making powers to the governor general in Council, its provisions were only to be applied on a

[56] Christopher Andrew, *The Defence of the Realm: The Authorized History of MI5* (Toronto: Penguin, 2010), pp. 53–4.
[57] Text from *Bengal Regulation III* (7 April 1818).
[58] *Defence of the Realm Act in Ireland* (Dublin: Committee of Public Safety, 1915).
[59] Hardinge speech at Imperial Legislative Council, 18 March 1915, Lord Hardinge of Penshurst 'Speeches', vol. 3 (Calcutta: Superintendent Government Printing, 1916), Hardinge Papers, CUL, p. 72.

case-by-case basis in regions where it was deemed necessary. However, just three days after being issued, the Defence of India Act was implemented within certain districts in Punjab to deal with unrest, before being extended to Bengal in April and June, and then to Balasore, Benares, and parts of Burma thereafter.[60]

The decision to introduce the Defence of India Act was not immediate following the outbreak of war, as it was for the Defence of the Realm Act in Britain, but rather required careful consideration on the part of the Government of India. Just before the war began, Reginald Craddock expressed concern that the commencement of hostilities with Germany had the potential to seriously destabilize an already delicate political situation in India. Referring to anti-colonial revolutionaries as 'irresponsible enemies ... with a violent race hatred of the Englishmen', Craddock warned that a state of war would embolden anti-governmental violence and outlined the steps he viewed necessary for ensuring stability during the war.[61] The most important public discourse that Craddock insisted on maintaining was an affirmation of the government's belief in the people of India 'as loyal and patriotic subjects of His Imperial Majesty, to whom His Majesty looks ... for their help and support against the enemies of Great Britain'. This was to be achieved through a careful deployment of repressive measures only in cases where they could be justified based on specific occurrences. Nonetheless, Craddock made it clear that Regulation III of 1818 should be used 'unhesitatingly as need arises', but that the government 'must not show our teeth or display our various weapons until the temper of the people shows them to be necessary'.[62] This strategy sought to maintain a semblance of normalcy in which officials should emphasize the loyalty of the Indian people, thus reinforcing the legitimacy of the British imperial government, while at the same time the spectre of government repression would hang over this status quo, ready to be called up at a moment's notice whenever this legitimacy or security came under challenge.

For the first few months of the war, the Government of India was reluctant to adopt new measures to deal with the revolutionary movement, for fear of unnecessarily antagonizing public and parliamentary opinion. Nonetheless, this should not be read as evidence of leniency or of a genuine concern for the infringement of the rights of Indian subjects, but rather as a strategic decision based on a pragmatic desire to retain the

[60] *Summary of the Administration of the Government of India 1910–16* (Delhi: Superintendent Government Printing, 1916), p. 21.
[61] Reginald Craddock, 1 August 1914, Home Political Deposit, NAI, File No. 1, p. 3.
[62] Ibid., p. 6.

semblance of popular legitimacy. Hardinge specifically opposed a surveillance bill put forward by Lord Carmichael, the governor of Bengal, only out of a desire to 'avoid all legislation of a controversial nature and to keep everything as quiet as possible'. In a telegram to the secretary of state, Hardinge wrote that although he viewed the situation as dire, he nonetheless preferred to 'rely upon the powers that we already possess, even if I have to make use of Regulation III of 1818, ... in spite of what some of our Parliamentary friends at home might think. But I am determined to maintain order at all costs; and if I make use of the regulation ... it must be regarded at home as a war measure'.[63] The secretary of state wrote back, assuring Hardinge that he was 'prepared to place [his] blind eye to the telescope, and to regard any possible ... employment of it as a war incident; relying, of course, on your not using it unless in respect of some necessity for which that reason can be definitely explained'.[64]

After the discovery and disruption of the February uprising, Hardinge sent a telegram to the Earl of Crewe, the secretary of state for India, informing him that the situation in India was becoming desperate and stressing the need for stronger measures.[65] Following the passage of the Defence of India Act in March, Crewe wrote to Hardinge, expressing the hope that 'your Defence of the Realm provisions will do all you want' in curbing the revolutionary movement and restoring order.[66] As details regarding the scope of the February uprising came out in the Lahore conspiracy case, Hardinge wrote that the efficiency of the Special Tribunals vindicated the government's request for extraordinary legislation and proved the necessity for drastic measures.[67] By 20 June, 4,000 people had already been put on trial, with 538 convicted and 622 still under trial, demonstrating to Hardinge the 'astonishing efficiency' of the Tribunals.[68] Despite this supposed efficacy, Hardinge later admitted in a private letter to King George that the reason he decided to commute 16 out of the 23 death sentences ordered by the Special Tribunal in the Lahore trial was that his own legal advisor pointed out that the sentence given was 'absolutely illegal'. Fearing that a public awareness of this fact would cast doubts on the reliability and legitimacy of the Tribunals, Hardinge decided to grant clemency for political, rather than moral, reasons.[69]

[63] Hardinge to Crewe, 10 September 1914, Hardinge Papers, CUL, p. 46.
[64] Crewe to Viceroy, 9 October 1914, Hardinge Papers, CUL, p. 50.
[65] Hardinge to Crewe, 9 March 1915, Hardinge Papers, CUL, p. 13a.
[66] Crewe to Hardinge, 2 April 1915, Hardinge Papers, CUL, p. 19.
[67] Hardinge to Holderness, 6 May 1915, Hardinge Papers, CUL, p. 27.
[68] Hardinge to Holderness, 8 July 1915, Hardinge Papers, CUL, p. 38.
[69] Hardinge to King George V, 3 December 1915, Hardinge Papers, CUL, p. 121.

Although many revolutionaries throughout the early twentieth century were executed by the colonial government, most of those convicted were instead sentenced to various terms of penal transportation.[70] The numbers initially charged under emergency legislation during the war, as opposed to the number convicted and still further the number executed, indicates both the wide net cast by colonial security forces as well as the intrusive nature of surveillance on the lives of many Indians. As it became increasingly difficult to prove the existence of revolutionary conspiracies without disclosing information that would jeopardize intelligence sources or leave informants open to violent retribution, the expansion of emergency laws such as the Defence of India Act provided the means through which the government could throw a broad dragnet against potential conspirators. The Lahore trial is not at all unusual in significantly reducing the total number of death sentences originally decided upon, and seems to reflect the desire to prove sovereign power to both take and grant life to the colonized.[71]

'Criminal Acts of a Few Ill-Balanced Minds'

Despite the public enthusiasm with which Hardinge welcomed the Defence of India Act, it received a mixed reaction within the Indian press. The day before the passage of the act, an article in *The Bengalee*, a Calcutta-based newspaper with links to the nationalist movement, acknowledged that the 'growing complexity of the international situation … fully justifies our Government in being forearmed for whatever contingency might happen … And all offences that are likely to endanger the safety of the realm in a time like this, naturally demand summary and drastic treatment.' Nonetheless, the author expressed concern that the term 'public safety' could also be applied to ordinary crimes, 'which the

[70] For the most relevant literature on the history of penal transportation in a British imperial context, see Clare Anderson, 'Transnational Histories of Penal Transportation: Punishment, Labour and Governance in the British Imperial World, 1788–1939', *Australian Historical Studies* 47, no. 3 (2016), pp. 381–97 and *Legible Bodies: Race, Criminality and Colonialism in South Asia* (Oxford: Bloomsbury, 2004).

[71] Like the emergency measures that form the basis for this chapter, the politics of forgiveness have a deep genealogy in nineteenth century colonial law. See Alastair McClure, 'Sovereignty, Law, and the Politics of Forgiveness in Colonial India, 1858–1903', *Comparative Studies of South Asia, Africa and the Middle East* 38, no. 3 (2018), pp. 385–401. Such ostentatious acts of political clemency were not limited to the British Empire but reflected a wider global pattern in the exercise of imperial sovereignty. For example, on his visit to Taiwan in 1923, Crown Prince and future emperor of Japan Hirohito reduced the sentences of 535 political prisoners who had conspired against the Japanese state in 1915. See Herbert P. Bix, *Hirohito and the Making of Modern Japan* (New York: Perennial, HarperCollins, 2001), p. 138.

Indian police are so prone to characterise as political'. Quickly clarifying that this concern was not due to any desire to protect the perpetrators of these crimes from justice, the author went on to argue that special measures applied in such a way would not only fail to cure, but would actually 'immensely aggravate the very evil against which they may be directed'.[72] Here *The Bengalee* article drew an important distinction between acts genuinely directed against public safety through collaboration with British India's German enemies, as opposed to internal political agitation in India. In the latter case, the article presented emergency legislation as an unnecessary and unwanted infringement on the liberty of Indian subjects.

On 19 March 1915, government officials in India made a series of pronouncements explaining the need for exceptional legislation and seeking to win over public support for the Defence Act. As mentioned above, Hardinge sought to justify the act on the basis of its similarities to the Defence of the Realm Act in Britain, thus implying that nothing exceptional was being required of the Indian people other than the measures necessary for protecting their security in a time of war. Hardinge placed emphasis on India's 'striking reputation for loyalty', and argued that the 'criminal acts of a few ill-balanced minds' should not be allowed to tarnish India's reputation at a time when Indian soldiers were 'shedding their blood on the battlefield for the King Emperor and country'.[73] This speech very deliberately invokes the idea of patriotism as service to king and country, in an attempt to counter *Ghadar* publications that located patriotism in the rejection of colonial rule.[74] Hardinge's focus was on portraying the act as a burden of war that was to be shared between Indian and British people in common purpose for the defence of their respective homelands, rather than a repressive law meant to target political dissidents with nationalist aspirations.

The same tactic can be found in Craddock's speech, which carefully constructed the enemy against whom the Defence Act was directed as coming from abroad. In justifying the need for the act, Craddock referred to 'certain people' who were taking advantage of the outbreak of the war in order to break the peace. He went on to say that there 'has existed on the Pacific coast of America and in Far East a revolutionary organisation that endeavoured to create trouble in India', carefully refraining from

[72] *The Bengalee* (18 March 1915), p. 4. [73] *The Bengalee*, (19 March 1915), p. 1.

[74] One of many such examples can be found in the passage, 'Hasten and prepare for mutiny. ... Fight for the sake of your country, do not fear at all. It is a glorious thing to die fighting ...' in 'Gadr di Gunj' (Echo of Mutiny) published by the Yugantar Ashram, San Francisco, U.S.A. Proceedings, June 1914, Home Department Political A, NAI, Nos. 110–111, pp. 3–4.

explicitly referring to the members of this organisation as Indians themselves.[75] As with the Ingress into India Ordinance, a clear attempt was made to draw a division between the loyal subjects of India and the dangerous enemies coming from abroad to threaten public safety.

These assurances received a mixed reaction from Indian politicians and the press. Surendranath Banerjea, a prominent moderate politician, remarked that he remained unconvinced regarding several provisions of the act, which in his opinion could not be justified by the emergency of the war. Banerjea was willing to give 'whole hearted support' to the aspects of the act that pertained to military and naval considerations, but expressed concern regarding elements absent from the British version of the act. These included the prohibition of promoting feelings of enmity and hatred between different classes, as well as the creation of tribunals capable of trying offences under the Penal Code that were punishable with death or transportation. The Indian Association similarly protested the fact that the new law was issued by the government without any opportunity for public discussion beforehand. The *Leader* in Allahabad, which served as a platform for figures as influential as Motilal Nehru and Gandhi, worried about the act's 'needlessly and undesirably extended scope'. While the widely circulated Lahore *Tribune* admitted the necessity for drastic wartime measures, it nonetheless expressed concern that the government rejected 'even the most necessary' amendments that some politicians proposed to prevent abuses of power.[76]

By contrast, the reactionary *Englishman* wrote that the only problem with the Defence of India Act was that it had not been introduced sooner, as conciliation and repression could not 'soothe the savage beast of the "bhadralog" *(sic)* dacoit and Terrorist. ... To speak of "conciliatory statesmanship" – which is merely a euphemism for weakness – as a means of dealing with these disorders is contemptible rubbish.'[77] In softer language, the prominent Gujarati Muslim businessman Fazalbhoy Currimbhoy Ebrahim supported the act despite his distaste for 'drastic enactments and retrograde laws' because he felt convinced that 'in a moment of grave national crisis like the present one the political rights of the individual must give way. The one desire of every Indian was to help the Government to the fullest extent to prosecute this war to a victorious termination.'[78]

Although the act provoked a range of different reactions from disparate Indian and British newspapers and political figures, there was nonetheless a reasonably widespread consensus that special measures designed to

[75] *The Bengalee* (19 March 1915), p. 1. [76] Ibid., pp. 1–2. [77] Ibid., p. 4.
[78] *The Statesman* (19 March 1915), p. 8.

meet the emergency of the war with Germany were not necessarily distasteful in and of themselves. The Germans did in fact hope to exploit anti-British sentiment in India and other parts of the empire as a means of destabilizing the war effort of Britain and its allies. This tactic was first put forward in the widely read *Germany and the Next War* by Friedrich von Bernhardi, published in 1911.[79] Following the outbreak of war, German officials embarked on several plots for destabilizing British rule in Ireland, India, and parts of the Middle East.[80]

Although the Singapore mutiny and the Lahore conspiracy both ended in failure, both seriously destabilized British confidence while emboldening other revolutionaries by highlighting the precariousness of colonial rule. These also occurred within the context of a wider global outbreak of anti-colonial insurgency that would achieve its strongest culmination in the Easter Rising of 1916 in Dublin, when Irish republicans mounted a bloody revolt against British colonial authorities with German support.[81] While a small group of Indian students studying in Dublin at the time formed an ambulance corps to assist those injured in the rebellion, others, such as future president of India V. V. Giri, held close links with Irish revolutionaries and saw the war as an opportunity for anti-colonial nationalists from both Ireland and India.[82] For many Indian revolutionaries, especially members of the Ghadar party, Irish republicans – alongside their counterparts in the Egyptian anticolonial movement – were natural partners in the global war against British imperialism.[83]

A year before the Easter Rising, however, Indian revolutionaries in North America and South East Asia planned a less well known but equally ambitious insurgency when revolutionaries connected to the Ghadar movement sought to smuggle a large shipment of arms into

[79] Friedrich von Bernhardi, *Germany and the Next War*; trans. Allen Powles (London: E. Arnold, 1912).

[80] These plans are recounted in detail in Peter Hopkirk, *On Secret Service East of Constantinople: The Plot to Bring Down the British Empire* (London: John Murray, 1994). See also Popplewell, *Intelligence and Imperial Defence.*

[81] There is extensive literature on the Easter Rising. For a survey of the recent scholarship, see John Borgonovo, 'Review Article: Revolutionary Violence and Irish Historiography', *Irish Historical Studies* 38, no. 150 (2012), pp. 325–31. For some particularly good accounts, see Paul McMahon, *British Spies and Irish Rebels: British Intelligence and Ireland, 1916–1945* (Woodbridge: Boydell Press, 2008), Geoff Sloan, 'The British State and the Irish Rebellion of 1916: An Intelligence Failure or a Failure of Response?', *Intelligence and National Security* 28, no. 4 (2013), pp. 453–94, and Keith Jeffery, *1916: A Global History* (London: Bloomsbury, 2015).

[82] See Conor Mulvagh, *Irish Days, Indian Memories: V. V. Giri and Indian Law Students at University College Dublin* (Dublin: Irish Academic Press, 2016).

[83] Ramnath, *Haj to Utopia*, pp. 95–122.

Calcutta, with the aid of German intelligence services.[84] In March 1915, Ghadar revolutionaries in America in cooperation with German agents acquired two ships, the *Annie Larsen* and the *Maverick*, with the intention of transporting some 30,000 rifles and revolvers to the island of Java in the neutral Dutch East Indies. From there, they would be sent on to Calcutta on a number of small fishing boats in time for a large-scale uprising on Christmas Day. This would coincide with a second uprising in Burma, at the time still a part of British India, that would be instigated using weapons brought in from neighbouring Thailand. The final element to this bold plan would be a raid on the infamous Andaman Islands, where the numerous veteran revolutionaries under detention would be liberated to join the uprising against the Government of India.[85]

Despite its ambitions, this conspiracy fell apart due to a combination of the extensive scope of British intelligence operations in North America and South East Asia, as well as poor coordination on the part of both the Indian revolutionaries and their German accomplices.[86] Despite waiting for a month at the agreed meeting point, the schooner *Annie Larsen* was unable to meet up with the larger ocean-going *Maverick* in time to transfer the firearms that the revolutionaries loaded into the *Annie Larsen*'s cargo hold. Unable to find the *Annie Larsen* and the promised shipment of arms, the *Maverick* sailed across the Pacific only to arrive empty-handed in the Dutch East Indies. At the same time, some 5,000 rifles and 500 revolvers intended for the Burmese portion of the uprising were loaded on board the *Henry S.* in the Philippines, to be shipped across the South China Sea to a remote area of neutral Thailand. The discovery of a German spy named Vincent Craft in Singapore by British intelligence services resulted in the full details of the plot becoming known to imperial authorities, resulting in the confiscation of the cargo of the *Henry S.* by cooperative Dutch authorities. Hardinge expressed his relief in a telegram to Austen Chamberlain, the new secretary of state,

[84] Irish and Irish American sympathizers with India's freedom struggle also played a crucial role in this plot, as Matthew Erin Plowman has shown. Plowman, 'Irish Republicans and the Indo-German Conspiracy of World War I', *New Hibernia Review* 7, no. 3 (2003), pp. 80–105.

[85] *Sedition Committee Report*, p. 124.

[86] For fuller accounts of the *Annie Larsen* affair, see Hopkirk, *On Secret Service*, pp. 179–94, and Popplewell, *Intelligence and Imperial Defence*. See also Joan Jensen, 'The "Hindu Conspiracy": A Reassessment', *Pacific Historical Review* 48, no. 1 (1979), pp. 65–83, Don Dignan, 'The Hindu Conspiracy in Anglo-American Relations during World War I', *Pacific Historical Review* 40, no. 1 (1979), pp. 57–76, and Karl Hoover, 'The Hindu Conspiracy in California, 1913–1918', *German Studies Review* 8, no. 2 (1985), pp. 245–61. The earliest academic work on the subject was produced by Giles Brown immediately following Indian independence. See Brown, 'The Hindu Conspiracy, 1914–1917', *Pacific Historical Review* XVII (1948), pp. 299–310.

writing, 'the German plot for a merry Xmas in India has been scotched'.[87]

Despite these very real and tangible links between German intelligence services and the *Annie Larsen* affair, proving a German connection in the case of other revolutionary conspiracies was sometimes more difficult. As Rash Behari Bose and the other Lahore conspirators chose to place their trust in the Indian Army rather than in the German Foreign Office, colonial officials were unable to prove that the Germans provided any material assistance in the commission of the conspiracy. At issue was the so-called hostile association clause, or rule 12-A(1) of the Defence of India Act, which stipulated that the act applied to those who acted 'with intent to assist the King's enemies'.[88] Although the Special Tribunal admitted an inability to determine whether any communication occurred between the revolutionaries and a foreign enemy, the conclusion was nonetheless that the revolutionaries 'considered themselves as in league with the German enemies of the King Emperor'. Even though only 'suggestive indications' existed pointing towards the possibility of an understanding between Germany and the Lahore conspirators, the Tribunal determined that this provided sufficient legal grounds for the plot to fall under the purview of the Defence of India Act.[89]

The Tribunal justified this decision primarily on the basis of *Ghadar* publications that made reference to the war with Germany as an opportunity for revolution in India. These publications explicitly referred to the Germans as potential allies and emphasized the role of Britain as the shared enemy of India and Germany. On 4 August 1914, the day that Britain and Germany went to war, a *Ghadar* article entitled 'Bugle of War' exhorted Indian subjects to assist Germany, who could not win the war single-handed. In another issue published in November, *Ghadar* informed its readers that the Germans felt great sympathy for their movement due to their common enemy, and for this reason 'Germany can draw assistance from us, and they can render us great assistance also'.[90] A later issue declared, 'Our enemy is hemmed in by the German Lion ... our enemy ... is engaged with Germany ... this is not an opportunity to let slip ... let us start a rebellion.'[91] As indicated by these examples and corroborated by the details of the *Annie Larsen* affair, there is no doubt that many Indian revolutionaries looked to Germany during

[87] Hardinge to Chamberlain, 31 December 1915, Hardinge Papers, CUL, p. 78.
[88] Chief Secretary to the Governor of Bengal to Secretary to the Government of India, 10 March 1916, Home Political-A, NAI, 326–327, p. 1.
[89] Judgment of Special Tribunal in Waraich and Singh (eds.), *Ghadar Movement Original Documents*, vol. 1, pp. 336–8.
[90] Ibid., p. 75. [91] Ibid., p. 336.

the war as a potential ally in their struggle for independence. Nonetheless, prosecuting these conspirators under legislation publicly justified as a war measure directed specifically at German agents, or those in league with German agents, raised difficult questions regarding the nature of war and enmity.

In order to prosecute the Lahore conspirators under war measures, the Special Tribunal needed to determine that the failed uprising constituted an act of war. Referring to handwritten notes by Rash Behari Bose detailing plans drawn up for the uprising, the Tribunal concluded, 'That they were badly armed and generalled, that they were out on a hopeless and ridiculous task, makes no difference: they formed an actual array waging war.'[92] In the supplementary case that followed, the counsel for the defence put forward the argument that the facts under review, even if proven true, did not amount to a waging of war but rather would need to fall under the category of a lesser offence such as conspiracy. Accepting that in many cases it may be difficult to draw a line between an insurrection for a general purpose and an insurrection directed against the sovereignty of the king, the Tribunal claimed that the details of the Lahore conspiracy indicated that because it was directed against substituting imperial with swaraj rule, it could not be considered to be directed towards a general purpose. According to the Tribunal, this made it an act of war, which under Indian law meant that any conspirator who could be demonstrated to have been party to the agreement to wage war would be considered guilty of having waged war himself, regardless of his participation or lack thereof in any particular overt act of war. Based on this definition, there was thus no question that the revolutionaries had waged war against the king, 'and that every person who has committed any act in pursuance and furtherance of that war ... is guilty of abetting the waging of war'.[93]

Despite the verdict obtained in the Lahore conspiracy case, some officials viewed the specificity with which the Defence of India Act defined the enemy as overly restrictive. On 10 March 1916, the chief secretary to Lord Carmichael, the governor of Bengal, sent a letter to the Government of India, providing details of a raid in which police arrested around forty revolutionary suspects in Calcutta. Carmichael was concerned that rule 12-A(1) of the act, which specified that arrested persons had 'intent to assist the King's enemies', limited his ability to hold the suspected revolutionaries in custody, as there was no evidence that these men were involved in a conspiracy with foreign enemies. Carmichael

[92] Ibid., p. 321. [93] Ibid., p. 355.

wrote that the Intelligence Branch elicited valuable information from the prisoners and were confident of being able to learn more, but that under the current law doing so would be impossible. Carmichael thus requested 'whether those seven words could not be omitted from the rule'. In reply, the Government of India referred to Carmichael's reading of the rule as 'unnecessarily narrow', stating that not all individual cases would provide evidence of a precise connection with German intrigue. Because a close connection existed between the Indian revolutionary movement and German agents, and because the revolutionaries looked to the war as an opportunity for subversion, 'any attempt in this direction is direct assistance to the King's enemies'.[94]

Various officials proposed a number of other changes for the Defence of India Act at different points during the war, most of which sought to expand the powers provided under the act. In July 1916, the government of Bengal proposed that the act be extended to make punishable the possession of seditious literature. J. H. Kerr referred to the dissemination of seditious leaflets as an important aspect of the revolutionary movement, which facilitated and incited the spread of violence. Referring to the existing legal safeguards as insufficient, Kerr likened the proposed amendment to the Explosive Substances Act of 1908, which penalized the possession of explosives, and suggested that there was 'no apparent reason why the possession of the revolutionary literature ... should not be treated in the same manner'.[95] Some officials viewed this proposal with suspicion, such as G. R. Lowndes, who argued that rules under the Defence of India Act must be directly tied to the existing state of war. Because sedition and revolutionary violence in Bengal were not products of the war and existed long before the war began, Lowndes wrote that measures for their repression could only be regarded as war measures 'in so far as internal sedition is more dangerous in war time and handicaps us in the prosecution of the war'.[96] Reginald Craddock believed that the amendment could be acceptable if it was proposed in a more restricted form that differentiated revolutionary propaganda from 'ordinary' sedition. For Craddock, the 'relative degree of mischief likely to follow is the justification for discrimination between incitements to revolutionary crime, and mere seditious writings'.[97] Nonetheless, Hardinge ultimately

[94] Chief secretary to Governor of Bengal to Secretary to the Government of India, 10 March 1916, Home Political A, NAI, 326–327, p. 1.
[95] J. H. Kerr to the Government of India, 15 July 1916, Home Political A, NAI, 302–311, p. 12.
[96] G. R. Lowndes, 18 August 1916. Home Political A, NAI, 302–311, p. 3.
[97] R. Craddock, 21 August 1916. Home Political A, NAI, 302–311, pp. 3–4.

concluded that the proposal was open to too many potential legal and political objections, and rejected it at the last minute.

Another proposal put forward for modification of the Defence of India Act was the suggestion that British subjects born in Europe, and their descendants, should be made exempt from trial by Special Tribunal under the act. Although officials in the Legislative Department wrote that such a clause was 'intentionally omitted from the Act for political reasons', Henry Wheeler issued confidential instructions to ensure that in practice no European British subject should be tried for any offence by a Special Tribunal, 'as otherwise the defence might be tempted to raise the question of the validity of the Act'.[98] Annie Besant, a prominent British theosophist and advocate of Indian and Irish self-rule, who was detained under the act in June of 1917, did indeed challenge the validity of this law. Besant sent a petition to the king on 31 July, in which she stated that her arrest constituted an 'invasion of the liberty of your petitioner for which there is absolutely no justification in fact'. Denying that the Defence of India Act fit the stringent requirements of the Defence of the Realm Act in targeting only those involved in definitive operations calculated to prejudice the safety of the realm in a time of war, Besant called the Defence of India Act unconstitutional and illegal.[99]

Attempts were also made to enhance the Defence of India Act's provisions for transporting those detained under it. Because police information regarding revolutionary conspiracies relied so heavily on the testimony of detainees, one official pointed out that the examination of these people should be conducted as soon as possible following their arrest, and that the examination should be carried out by officers 'with an intimate and complete knowledge of all developments'.[100] This meant that in cases where revolutionaries travelled from one province to another, government officials sought a means of transferring suspects back to their home province as expediently as possible, so as to ensure that a thorough questioning could be conducted by intelligence officers familiar with the language and local context of the suspect. The Government of India approved this measure and added it as an amendment after sub-rule 3 of rule 12-A under section 2 of the Defence of India Act on 10 April 1917.[101]

[98] Henry Wheeler, 8 July 1915. Home Political A, NAI, 479–481, pp. 1–4.

[99] Mrs. Besant's petition to the King in Council, on the subject of the validity of the Defence of India Act, 31 July 1917, Home Political B, NAI, 334, p. 6.

[100] Hugh McPherson to Sir James DuBoulay, 11 March 1917, Home Political A, NAI, 175–177, p. 2.

[101] Government of India Home Department notification, 10 April 1917, Home Political A, NAI, 175–177, p. 5.

In June of the same year, officials sought a further amendment to empower local governments to deport a person out of British India, should it be deemed necessary for public security as defined under the Defence of India Act. This amendment was ultimately agreed to and the Government of India notified local authorities on 12 July 1918.[102] The central government viewed these attempts to amend the act as going too far, however, when the government of Burma requested that the Defence of India Act be extended to empower local governments to deport from military stations any women believed to be infected with venereal disease. The Government of India replied that such an amendment would 'involve a most unjustifiable and undesirable' straining of the act, and did 'not consider it desirable to pursue the matter any further'.[103] This incident indicates both the malleability of the concept of public security, as well as the way that this concept could be strained to its limit under the expansive interpretability of war measures.

'A Program of Violence and Terrorism'

Despite astonishing advances early in 1918, the German war effort collapsed following renewed offensives in the summer by Britain, France, and the United States of America, leading to the defeat of the Central Powers and the end of the First World War on 11 November. The end of the war in Europe raised questions regarding the fate of the Defence of India Act, which was justified all along as an explicit war measure. Government officials in India were always aware that the provisions of the act only extended up to six months following the end of the war, meaning that the question of how to proceed in peacetime provided an object of concern ever since the act had been first introduced. On taking over the governorship of Bengal from Lord Carmichael in 1917, Lord Ronaldshay announced in a speech that it could not be emphasized enough that 'sedition in Bengal began long before the war and that it will not end with the return of peace. It has to some extent been checked by the special measures adopted during the war, but if Government is no longer able to rely on such measures … there can be little doubt that outrages again become frequent.'[104] Despite initially insisting that the emergency measures adopted were required because of the exceptional

[102] Government of India to all local Governments, 12 July 1918, Home Political A, NAI, 64–65, p. 7.
[103] Secretary to the Government of India to the Secretary to the Government of Burma, 25 August 1916, Home Political B, NAI, 359–360, p. 7.
[104] Lord Ronaldshay speech in Legislative Council, 12 December 1917, Home Political, NAI, 1924 & K.-W.F. 379/I., p. 4.

circumstances of the war, the prospect of peace led officials to reframe the war measures as having done little more than to plaster over the cracks of a problem that would re-emerge the moment that the repressive laws expired.

To determine the value and effectiveness of this wartime legislation, the Government of India assigned two judges the job of assessing the arrests made under the Defence of India Act, Regulation III of 1818, and the Ingress into India Ordinance. The primary goal in appointing these judges was not to test the fairness of the war measures, but rather to diminish popular suspicion towards the provisions of the emergency laws, and to 'remove from the hands of certain politicians a weapon which they use against Government', according to Sir Michael O'Dwyer, the lieutenant-governor of the Punjab. According to O'Dwyer, the Defence of India Act was designed to help the executive government cope with exceptional conditions, meaning that the conclusions of the judges should not serve to undermine the act. For this reason, O'Dwyer proposed that the executive should have the freedom to decide which cases were to be reviewed, and when.[105] The idea for the secret tribunal, consisting of two judges eligible for promotion to the High Court, one of whom should be Indian, was first introduced by Sir William Vincent, who pointed out that the average person in India viewed the Defence of India Act as leaving power in the hands of the hated Criminal Investigation Department. Lord Willingdon agreed, arguing that it was not enough 'that a Government should be satisfied in its own mind that it is acting justly and fairly in each case', but was equally or even more important 'that the public at large should feel and appreciate that it is so acting'. Willingdon thus hoped that appointing a tribunal to review the work of the emergency laws would help remove public distrust for these measures, as well as removing the '"Star Chamber" character of the orders' and give the actions taken under them 'some sort of judicial guarantee'.[106]

The two judges selected for the review of the evidence were Sir Narayan Chandavarkar, a well-respected politician and Hindu reformer who served on the Bombay High Court, and C. P. Beachcroft, who presided over the famous Alipore bomb case from 1908 to 1909. In total, the judges examined 806 cases, including 702 prisoners interned under the Defence of India Act, as well as 100 being held under Regulation III

[105] Sir Michael O'Dwyer to Sir William Vincent, 17 September 1917, Home Political A, NAI, No. 1-9 & K.-W., p. 1.

[106] Lord Willingdon to Sir William Vincent, 17 September 1917, Home Political A, NAI, No. 1-9 & K.0-W., pp. 3–4.

and the remainder under the Ingress into India Ordinance. Of all these cases, the judges determined only six in which they found insufficient evidence to warrant charging the accused with acting 'in a manner prejudicial to the public safety or the defence of British India', but it is important to note that only 167 of the prisoners were willing or able to produce written testimony in their own defence. Aside from weighing the evidence collected against the suspected revolutionaries and assessing the efficacy of wartime legislation, the report prepared by Chandavarkar and Beachcroft also made an important argument regarding the difference between ordinary and revolutionary crime. According to the judges, ordinary crime was not concerned with 'upsetting the Government and striking at its very foundations and authority', whereas revolutionary crime was 'collective and continuous in its operation'.[107] This set revolutionary violence apart as a special kind of crime, containing within it an endless potential for violence that could only be met by indefinitely extended emergency measures.

Alongside the judgment drawn up by Chandavarkar and Beachcroft, officials also determined that it was necessary to produce a comprehensive report to assess the full scope of the revolutionary movement in India and its global connections. As with the work of the judges' tribunal, this committee would be tasked with justifying the extension of war measures in peacetime and pre-empting public criticism by lending judicial authority to the actions of the executive.[108] The committee was hand-picked through careful selection by the secretary of state and the Government of India, with Sir Sidney Rowlatt, who previously sat on the King's Bench Division of the High Court, chosen as committee president. Other members appointed to the committee included Sir Basil Scott, the chief justice of Bombay; C.V. Kumaraswami Sastri, a judge from the High Court of Madras; Sir Verney Lovett, a member of the Board of Revenue; and Provash Chandra Mitter, an additional member of the Bengal Legislative Council. The committee secretary was J. D. V. Hodge of the Indian Civil Service. Initially some officials recommended S. R. Das as a member of the committee, but others pointed out that despite his qualifications, his role as officiating standing council could 'detract from any weight which might otherwise be attached to his report'. Given that the goal of the report was to 'convince the sober-minded majority of the public of the gravity of the danger from the revolutionary conspiracy in

[107] *Report of Sir N. Chandavarkar and Mr. Justice Beachcroft on detenus and internees in Bengal*; P.P. 1918 (Cmd. 9198) viii, p. 110.

[108] S. R. Hignell to L. Davidson, 20 October 1917, Home Department Political A, NAI, 472–503, p. 6.

Bengal', it was desirable to 'avoid any possibility of an insinuation that the Committee [had] been packed'. For this reason, P. C. Mitter was viewed as a safer choice.[109] The Bombay government expressed some concern that this selection may not be suitable for the task at hand due to its overly judicial character and asked whether the committee might be strengthened by the addition of a government official with experience on the executive side. S.R. Hignell of the Government of India dismissed this argument, pointing out that maintaining the judicial appearance of the committee would provide greater weight to its conclusions.[110]

The official purpose of the committee, as described in the official resolution published in the *Gazette of India*, was to 'investigate and report on the nature and extent of the criminal conspiracies connected with the revolutionary movement in India' and to 'examine and consider the difficulties that have arisen in dealing with such conspiracies and to advise as to the legislation, if any, necessary to enable Government to deal effectively with them'.[111] To this end, the committee published a comprehensive examination and analysis of the revolutionary movement, beginning with the assassination of two British officials at Poona in 1897, and continuing through to describe the swadeshi agitation in Bengal and the global scope of revolutionary operations during the war. In the *Sedition Committee Report*, published in 1918, Rowlatt and his committee identified the 'terrorism of witnesses' as one of the main factors necessitating emergency legislation. The intimidation of witnesses, approvers, informants, and other members of the Indian criminal justice system was viewed as hampering the ability of the law to successfully prosecute revolutionaries. By emphasizing the longer history of political violence in India from 1897 to the time of writing, the Sedition Committee also sought to distance themselves from justifications made during the war for the Defence of India Act, which described it as a direct response to the state of war against the German enemy and their collaborators. Instead, the report described revolutionary violence as a fixed feature of current Indian politics that imperilled the rule of the law and the safety and security of the Indian people.[112]

In this report, the category of 'terrorism' appeared, albeit briefly, as a means of justifying the necessity of extending the war measures of the Defence of India Act into peacetime. Appearing in some sporadic

[109] H. L. Stephenson to S. R. Hignell, 31 October 1917, Home Department Political A, NAI, 472–503, p. 10.
[110] S. R. Hignell to L. Robertson, 22 November 1917, Home Department Political A, NAI, 472–503, pp. 13–14.
[111] *Sedition Committee Report*, p. i.
[112] See *Sedition Committee Report*, especially pages 181–212.

references before this point, the term 'terrorism' within the Committee's report connoted a very specific meaning – the use of violence to 'terrorize' witnesses, informants, juries, and other cogs in the apparatus of the imperial legal regime. The term 'terrorism' appears only eight times in the 226-page report, always with a very particular meaning. In the first usage, the report refers to a 'program of violence and terrorism', referencing a state of affairs generated by revolutionary activity, rather than a particular act of political violence. In the remaining references, however, the report refers to terrorism as underlying the difficulty of obtaining legal evidence duc to the murder or intimidation of witnesses and juries. The length of Indian trials is further provided as an explanation for the proliferation of this 'terrorism', as it is said to provide greater opportunity for revolutionaries to target members of the prosecution and thus ensure a favourable outcome for their co-conspirators.[113]

Through this rationalization, the legislation proposed by the Sedition Committee effectively sought to extend into peacetime the core principles of the Defence of India Act, such as the possibility for political offenders to be tried without a jury, as well as the detention of suspects without trial. This emergency law, called the Anarchical and Revolutionary Crimes Act of 1919 but popularly referred to as the Rowlatt Act, was warmly welcomed by British officials, as well as several Indian legal experts, who saw it as a necessary weapon in the continuing war against the Indian revolutionary organizations. Justice Mullick, an Indian judge, wrote of the revolutionary movement and the legislation proposed to counter it, 'the disease being now chronic, I have no hesitation in recommending that the remedies should be such as to be capable of permanent application'. Mullick worried that temporary legislation would be 'worse than useless', as it would provide a 'source of weakness' and provide 'the enemies of government a weapon for creating ill-will and suspicion at periodic intervals'.[114] Similarly, government official W. F. Rice argued that 'war legislation proper' did not need to remain permanently on the Statute Book because 'the emergency of the great European war will be recognised by all if it should ever recur. ... The existence of a state of war is a solid concrete fact that cannot be denied.' By contrast, the existence and potential danger of a renewal of revolutionary violence in India was, according to Rice, something that would be hotly debated by large sections of the Indian public, thus

[113] Ibid., pp. 151, 182, 188, 190, 201.
[114] Mr. Justice Mullick, 24 September 1918, Home Political A, NAI, Nos. 45–72 & Appx. & K.-W., p. 16.

slowing the ability of government to immediately implement new emergency laws.[115]

This question of public recognition was central to the goals of the Sedition Committee, which sought to publicize the activities of the Indian revolutionaries as a way of winning over support for emergency legislation. One suggestion made for communicating the findings of the *Sedition Committee Report* to a broader audience was that the report be published in vernacular newspapers. Given that vernacular papers were likely to quote parts of the report one way or the other, some officials asserted that at least an official translation would ensure authenticity. Sir Michael O'Dwyer was strongly in favour of this idea, stating that it would help allay the danger of the public being misled or misinformed by coverage of the report in Indian newspapers. O'Dwyer believed that the wider the readership of the actual text, the greater the likelihood of people accepting the recommendations of the Committee with regard to emergency legislation.[116] Sir Charles Cleveland suggested issuing a recommendation for local governments to publish vernacular translations of the report in order to disseminate the ideas contained within it to as wide a readership as possible, but also noted that translations also shouldn't be pushed onto an unwilling or indifferent public in parts of India where revolutionary violence was less prominent. Ultimately, the governments of Punjab and the United Provinces decided to issue official vernacular translations, but all other local governments refrained.[117]

The *Sedition Committee Report* and the accompanying Rowlatt Act attracted strong criticism from Indian politicians, lawyers, and nationalists. On 23 September 1918, Ganesh Srikrishna Khaparde, a well-known lawyer, political activist, and scholar, proposed a resolution in the Imperial Legislative Council recommending that the proposals of the Sedition Committee be held in abeyance until a 'thorough and searching' enquiry could be undertaken by a mixed committee of official and non-official Indians into the working of the Criminal Investigation Department. Khaparde raised concerns about the methods by which intelligence officers collected the information on which the report based its findings, and argued that a review of its work was a necessary first step towards accepting its recommendations. Concerns over the report were also raised by Muhammad Ali Jinnah, the future 'founding father' of Pakistan, who argued forcefully that 'no civilized Government will

[115] W. F. Rice to Secretary to the Government of India Home Department, 12 September 1918, Home Political A, NAI, Nos. 45–72 & Appx. & K.-W., p. 51.
[116] O'Dwyer to Vincent, 30 August 1918. Home Political Deposit, NAI, No. 31, pp. 3–4.
[117] Sir Charles Cleveland, 11 September 1918, Home Political Deposit, NAI, No. 31, p. 5.

accept, no civilized Government will ever dream of putting those recommendations in the form of laws'.[118] For many Indian lawyers and politicians, the proposed Rowlatt Act could too easily be deployed as a method of suppressing legitimate political dissent, despite the insistence of government officials that it was intended only towards the eradication of violent criminal conspiracies. As the Indian politician and freedom fighter Madan Mohan Malaviya pointed out in March 1919, the act referenced the word 'revolutionary' but did not provide a clear definition for this word, creating the potential for ambiguity and misuse. Sir William Vincent dismissed these concerns out of hand, arguing that 'to an ordinary man in the street the meaning of the word revolutionary was clear. ... It could not be applied to any but a criminal movement.' Vincent said that although the word 'might be used loosely by partisan newspapers ... it did not follow that responsible authorities would place any but the accurate definition upon the word'.[119]

Even Edwin Montagu, the secretary of state for India, held concerns regarding the provisions of the *Sedition Committee Report*, calling them 'most repugnant to my mind'. Despite a desire to stamp out revolution, Montagu confided to the new governor general and viceroy of India, Lord Chelmsford, that he despised the suggestion of preserving the Defence of India Act in peace time.[120] Chelmsford wrote back to say that he found Montagu's attitude troubling, as before the war, the inadequacy of the ordinary law created endless difficulties for the India Office, the Bengal government, and the Government of India. Chelmsford maintained that only the outbreak of war and the passing of the Defence of India Act allowed a temporary reprieve from revolutionary violence, and that only the maintenance of similar measures would keep Bengal secure following the end of the war.[121] Montagu clarified that he did not dispute the necessity for action to be taken, but simply that he was unhappy with the methods proposed in the report. Montagu wrote that he would like to introduce a process of law that would help ameliorate the situation, while what he would dislike would be the preservation of an act comparable to one issued in a time of war, pointing

[118] Extract from proceedings of Indian Legislative Council assembled under provisions of Government of India Act, 23 September 1918, Home Department Political A, NAI, No. 159, pp. 3–24.
[119] *The Bengalee* (14 March 1919), p. 6.
[120] Montagu to Chelmsford, 10 October 1918, Chelmsford Papers, Mss Eur E 264, p. 149.
[121] Chelmsford to Montagu, 19 November 1918, Chelmsford Papers, Mss Eur E 264, pp. 233–4.

out that such an act would never be accepted in Britain during a time of peace.[122]

The concern that the Rowlatt Act could be used to stifle non-violent forms of political protest gained greater impetus following the Jallianwala Bagh massacre in Amritsar. Protest against the act was not confined to the Imperial Legislative Council, but provided the catalyst for widespread disaffection throughout India, as nationalists felt that the repressive measures were a complete betrayal of the Indian people following the heavy losses incurred by Indian troops during the war. When thousands of Indians gathered in the garden of Jallianwala Bagh in the centre of Amritsar on 13 April 1919 – some to condemn the provisions of the Rowlatt Act, others simply to enjoy the use of the popular communal space during a religious festival – General Reginald Dyer ordered his soldiers to fire into the unarmed crowd, killing hundreds of civilians.[123] As Kim Wagner has shown in his recent study of the massacre, Dyer was 'not reacting to the actual crowd in front of him as much as to what he imagined that crowd to be – and the hostility and aggression that he ascribed to that crowd'.[124] In Wagner's meticulous account, it is possible to trace a direct line of imperial anxiety and paranoia from the 1857 rebellion to the fear of insurgency that sparked the disproportionate violence inflicted at Amritsar.[125] By extension, the massacre can also be understood as the tangible outcome of a colonial prose of counter-insurgency that had spent the better part of a century populating the imperial imaginary with ethereal and sinister conspiracies of thugs, fanatics, pirates, and terrorists.

The atrocity attracted widespread disgust and condemnation in both India and Britain, despite the efforts of the government to control coverage of the massacre within the press.[126] It was within this context that Mohandas Gandhi's mass politics of non-violent non-cooperation emerged as the locus of popular anti-colonial nationalism. Although Montagu and Chelmsford implemented a series of reforms six months later that transferred some executive responsibility to the provinces of

[122] Montagu to Chelmsford, 23 December 1918, Chelmsford Papers, Mss Eur E 264, p. 205.

[123] Patrick French, *Liberty or Death: India's Journey to Independence and Division* (London: Penguin, 2011), pp. 31–4. For more on the massacre and its consequences, see especially Wagner, *Amritsar 1919* and V. N. Datta and S. Settar (eds.), *Jallianwala Bagh Massacre* (Delhi: Pragati Publications, 2000).

[124] Wagner, *Amritsar 1919*, p. 164.

[125] See also Wagner, '"Calculated to Strike Terror": The Amritsar Massacre and the Spectacle of Colonial Violence', *Past and Present* 233, no. 1 (2016), pp. 185-225.

[126] Chandrika Kaul, *Reporting the Raj: The British Press and India, c. 1880–1922* (Manchester: Manchester University Press, 2003), pp. 199–225.

colonial India and expanded the franchise, these reforms came too late and provided too little to assuage public opinion. To make matters worse, under the Montagu–Chelmsford reforms, sovereign authority remained consolidated in the office of the viceroy, who remained accountable only to London. Despite the repeal of the Rowlatt Act and the promise of further constitutional reforms, the controversy surrounding the colonial government's attempt to extend war measures into a time of peace seriously undermined the legitimacy of British rule and fundamentally transformed the political landscape of colonial India.

Conclusion

While the occasion of the First World War provided an unprecedented opportunity for Indian revolutionaries to challenge imperial sovereignty through a series of ambitious plots, the conflict similarly provided the occasion for the Government of India to deploy emergency powers that were legitimized through the language of war. By erasing the longer anti-colonial pre-history of revolutionary organizations such as Ghadar, and instead portraying them as collaborators with the German enemy, imperial officials sought to legitimize the extension of extraordinary legislation that would otherwise have been much more difficult to justify. Despite their claim to be nothing more than war measures necessitated by a specific state of emergency, these laws retained a degree of malleability that allowed them to strain the limits of executive authority under the expansive category of public security. Towards the end of the war, officials returned to earlier arguments regarding the supposed dangers posed by 'political criminals', but in the increasingly politically charged context of the interwar period, these arguments were given far less credence. This is apparent in the comparatively mild reaction to actions taken under the Ingress into India Ordinance, as opposed to the mass agitation that followed the passage of the Rowlatt Act following the end of the war. In fuelling the expansion of both anti-colonial revolutionary networks and imperial laws of emergency, the First World War marked an important bridge between the pre-war language of 'political dacoity' and the construction of the new legal categories of 'terrorism' and 'the terrorist' that came to dominate interwar understandings of political violence.

4 Indefinite Emergency

Revolutionary Politics and 'Terrorism' in Interwar India

Although the First World War resulted in an unprecedented expansion of imperial networks of surveillance, it was during the period from 1919 to 1947 that British authorities in India massively expanded their security apparatus to counter the rapidly growing nationalist movement.[1] Contrary to the common assumption that British surveillance was primarily concerned with violent revolutionaries and paid little attention to more mainstream non-violent nationalists,[2] the release of the records of the Indian Political Intelligence department in the 1990s demonstrates the scale of surveillance to which Indian politicians were subjected during the interwar period.[3] During the war's immediate aftermath, India was rocked by inflation, an influenza epidemic, and the Third Anglo-Afghan War. Many Indians saw the introduction of the repressive Rowlatt Act as a betrayal, particularly in light of the role of Indian troops in helping to secure Britain's victory during the war. Although never intended for non-European colonial possessions, the promise of self-determination raised by the US President Woodrow Wilson also encouraged nationalist aspirations around the world.[4]

As a concession to public and political opinion following India's massive contributions to the war, liberal secretary of state Edwin Montagu introduced a small measure of constitutional reform meant to produce 'the increasing association of Indians in every branch of the administration and the gradual development of self-governing institutions with a view to the progressive realization of responsible government in India as an integral part of the British Empire'.[5] Montagu negotiated his proposals with the far more conservative governor general, Lord Chelmsford, and their joint action became known as the

[1] French, *Liberty or Death*, p. 97. [2] Popplewell, *Intelligence and Imperial Defence*, p. 66.
[3] French, *Liberty or Death*, pp. 97–101.
[4] See Erez Manela, *The Wilsonian Moment: Self-Determination and the International Origins of Anticolonial Nationalism* (Oxford: Oxford University Press, 2009).
[5] Quoted in French, *Liberty or Death*, p. 35.

Montagu-Chelmsford reforms, an important stepping stone in the constitutional history of India. These reforms promised Indians a degree of self-governance through shifting certain responsibilities such as agriculture, education, and health to provincial administrators responsible to an Indian electorate, while matters such as finance, law and order, and policing remained the jurisdiction of the colonial administration. Although these reforms, enshrined in the Government of India Act of 1919, expanded the number of Indians in administrative roles, many Indian politicians criticized the two-tiered provincial delegation of duties known as diarchy for retaining for the colonial government full executive powers, including the discretionary ability to circumvent the Indian legislature through the promulgation of ordinances.

In seeking to expand the role of Indians in government to a limited degree, the Montagu-Chelmsford reforms also reorganized the Indian legislature. The reforms expanded the number of Indians within provincial Legislative Councils, and the government created the Indian Legislative Assembly as the lower house of the Indian legislature. The Assembly consisted of 144 members – 103 elected and 41 nominated – with voting based on a heavily restricted franchise determined by income and land ownership. Although the Assembly had authorization to pass laws for the whole of British India, other than in matters falling under provincial jurisdiction, in practice the executive powers of the governor general could render the legislature impotent, particularly in any matters relating to the 'safety or tranquility of British India'. The governor general could veto any bill put forward by the Assembly and could similarly certify any bill for which the Assembly denied legislative approval.[6]

The Council of State replaced the Imperial Legislative Council as the upper house of the Indian legislature following the 1919 reforms. It consisted of 60 members, one of whom was chosen by the governor general to act as president, with the remainder divided between 34 elected members, 19 nominated officials, and 6 nominated non-officials. Franchise for the Council of State was even more restricted than that of the Legislative Assembly, with fewer than 15,000 voters throughout British India in 1925. Women could not vote, and the extremely high property qualifications required ensured that in practice the Council remained 'a citadel of vested interests'.[7] Although the creation of two levels of legislative power fell in line with most democratic

[6] Manik Lal Gupta, *Constitutional Development of India* (New Delhi: Atlantic Publishers & Distributors, 1989), p. 59.
[7] Ibid., p. 58.

countries of the time, the Council ultimately provided colonial authorities with an oligarchic Upper House that could be used as 'an organ of Government legislation' to counterbalance the establishment of a relatively democratic Assembly with an elected majority, albeit with a heavily restricted franchise in its own right.[8]

This fact was not lost on politicians of the time, who saw the reforms as an empty gesture that retained real executive power within the hands of the British imperial government. As a result, the interwar period in India was a time of great political upheaval, with the development of unprecedented mass support for the politics of anti-colonial nationalism. This period also marked the climax of the revolutionary movement in Bengal, as radicals disenchanted by the failure of the non-cooperation campaign soon returned to the tactics of assassination and political violence that they adopted before and during the war. In 1925, the return of revolutionary organizations prompted the Government of India to introduce the Bengal Criminal Law Amendment Act, despite vigorous opposition from within the newly expanded Indian legislatures. Deliberately labelling revolutionaries as 'terrorists' out of a desire to ensure that repressive measures would be acceptable to the British Parliament and to Indian moderates, colonial officials succeeded in temporarily suppressing the movement, only to see it return in 1930 in a daring raid on armouries in Chittagong. With political violence reaching unprecedented levels in the early 1930s, colonial officials became increasingly reliant on repressive emergency laws that for the first time began to target 'terrorism' as a distinct category of crime. Despite a decline in revolutionary violence after 1934, the concept of terrorism had by then become enshrined as a durable category of colonial law.

'A Standing Menace to Tyranny'

Following the end of the First World War, Mohandas Karamchand Gandhi emerged as the pre-eminent figure in the anti-colonial politics of India.[9] Gandhi is the subject of more scholarship than any other figure in South Asian history, with his own writings, correspondence, and speeches comprising some thirty million words.[10] Born in 1869 in the fishing town of Porbandar in Gujarat, then part of the Bombay

[8] Gupta, *Constitutional Development*, p. 57.

[9] 'Mahatma' is an honorific meaning 'Great Soul', which is often mistaken for Gandhi's first name. Although there are numerous biographies of Gandhi, one of the most recent and comprehensive covering the period in question is Ramachandra Guha, *Gandhi: The Years That Changed the World, 1914–1948* (Toronto: Random House Canada, 2018).

[10] French, *Liberty or Death*, p. 18.

Presidency, Gandhi obtained his education in London before going on to make a name for himself as a lawyer and political organizer in South Africa.[11] Gandhi became best known for his work on behalf of the Indian diasporic community, and particularly his campaign over the Transvaal Government's Asiatic Registration Bill. Returning to India in 1915, Gandhi supported the war effort and even welcomed a resolution by Chelmsford encouraging Indians to join the army.[12] Following the massacre of hundreds of Indian civilians at Jallianwala Bagh and the controversial Rowlatt Act, however, Gandhi became convinced of the repressive and destructive nature of colonial rule.

From the beginning, Gandhi was critical of revolutionary violence, viewing it as both an ineffective and an immoral strategy that could never produce true independence.[13] Condemning the assassination of Mr. Willouby, a Deputy Commissioner, Gandhi sought to distinguish his program of non-cooperation from movements in Ireland and Egypt that used violence as a political tactic.[14] Commenting on the Anglo-Irish Treaty of 1921 that followed a bloody civil war between British police and Irish Republicans, Gandhi refused to accept the idea that the Irish won freedom through violence. Gandhi argued that it was not the British blood shed by Irish revolutionaries that forced the British to negotiate a truce, but rather the 'gallons of blood' willingly shed by the Irish themselves. According to Gandhi, it was 'not the fear of losing more lives that has compelled a reluctant offer from England but it is the shame of any further imposition of agony upon a people that loves its liberty above everything else'.[15]

Gandhi's philosophy was thus not so much a wholesale rejection of violence, but rather a strategy that sought to expose the underlying violence of the colonial regime through a willingness for self-sacrifice. Non-violence for Gandhi was not about cowardice, and in fact Gandhi asserted that 'where there is only a choice between cowardice and violence I would advise violence'. Gandhi wrote that he would rather have India resort to violence than to see the country dishonoured through cowardice. This meant that non-violence was to consist of 'conscious suffering. It does not mean meek submission to the will of the evil-doer, but it means the putting of one's whole soul against the will of the tyrant.'

[11] For more on Gandhi's early life see Ramachandra Guha, *Gandhi before India* (London: Penguin Books, 2014).

[12] French, *Liberty or Death*, p. 26.

[13] For a more thorough review of the role of revolutionary violence in influencing his ardent adherence to non-violence, see Durba Ghosh, 'Gandhi and the Terrorists', *South Asia* 32, no. 3 (2016), pp. 560–76.

[14] *Young India* (1 September 1920), p. 2.

[15] *Young India* (15 December 1921), p. 12.

Such a stance did not come from a place of weakness, but rather of strength, what Gandhi referred to as the 'strength of the spirit' through which brute physical violence could be overcome and resisted through the application of *satyagraha*, or soul-force. Arguing that adopting violent methods for the overthrow of the colonial government amounted to blindly copying Europe's flaws, Gandhi wrote that although taking up the doctrine of the sword may grant India momentary victory, it would also mean forsaking India's true essence and would provide no true independence.[16]

Following Gandhi's arrest and the collapse of his political program of non-violent non-cooperation, revolutionary ideas began once again to gain traction in some political circles in India, particularly in Bengal. In an article titled 'What Became of the Bombs?' published in *Young India* following Gandhi's arrest, the author pointed out that revolutionary crimes vanished throughout the duration of Gandhi's political campaign, and attributed this to the non-violent philosophy of the Mahatma.[17]

Many saw the government's repression of Gandhi's campaign as evidence that only violent methods could successfully combat the autocratic authority of the colonial regime. Lord Lytton, the governor of Bengal, justified the repressive measures taken against nationalist protesters by stating that anywhere breaches of the law took place and disorder was fomented, it was an 'elementary duty' of government to suppress such agitation.[18] As revolutionary conspiracies once more began to be reported in 1923 following the dwindling of Gandhi's movement after an outburst of violence at Chauri Chaura, *Young India* lamented the fact that 'secret conspiracies for political violence have once again become a moral possibility. Such a situation was impossible in 1921'.[19]

In fact, some revolutionaries never gave up on the hope of instigating an armed rising against British rule, but simply required some breathing space to rebuild networks and stockpiles of arms decimated during the war. In 1920, immediately after the release of political prisoners initiated by the king's proclamation of amnesty in 1919, Pulin Behari Das of the Anushilan Samiti formed the Bharat Sevak Sangha, although this revolutionary society quickly disintegrated. Other revolutionaries from Jugantar still maintained the belief that only an armed revolution would bring about independence, but decided that it would be impossible to attract public sympathy due to the popularity of Gandhi's non-violent

[16] *Young India* (11 August 1920), pp. 3–4. [17] *Young India* (25 May 1922), p. 7.

[18] Lord Lytton, Reply to addresses presented at Khulna, 13 July 1922, NLI, G.P.3209415B436gov, p. 155.

[19] *Young India* (4 October 1923), pp. 3–4.

philosophy at that time.[20] In 1920, Anil Chandra Ray founded the Dacca Sri Sangha, a new revolutionary organization that successfully acquired a few revolvers by 1923 and reached a membership of around fifty by the end of 1924. Ray's goal was to slowly build up a strong, secret party that would not provide the government with easy opportunities to crush it by refraining from overt acts of political assassination or robbery. Instead, the Sri Sangha used open activity and social welfare to recruit members, focusing particularly on acquiring young members from well-to-do families capable of providing funds to the organization and thus avoid unpopular acts of brigandage, or so-called political dacoity.[21] Although Gandhi's famous program of non-violence vastly overshadowed such groups, a new genre of prison memoir began to emerge in this period as the accounts of Barindra Ghose, Sachindranath Sanyal, and later V. D. Savarkar began to romanticize revolutionary politics for public consumption, renewing interest in the politics of anti-colonial violence.[22]

During this period, the Dacca Anushilan Samiti was under the control of Narendra Mohan Sen, who strongly opposed dacoity and overt acts of violence due to the fear that it alienated public sympathy that would be necessary for a mass uprising. Sachindranath Sanyal, a young lieutenant of Rash Behari Bose, disagreed with Narendra's caution and from the early 1920s sought to establish a 'New Violence' party that would amalgamate the more radical elements from various revolutionary groups and orchestrate sensational acts of violence. This led to a schism within Anushilan between older members more sympathetic to the leftist goal of mass revolution and younger radicals who preferred methods that would come to be defined as specifically 'terrorist'.[23]

Another important factor in the development of anti-colonial violence during this period is the global impact of the Bolshevik revolution in Russia. In 1917, leftist revolutionaries led by Vladimir Lenin overthrew the provisional government that temporarily took power following an uprising against Czar Nicholas II earlier in the year. This revolution sparked international fears regarding the threat posed to national governments by leftist groups within their own borders, as the Bolshevik

[20] Special Superintendent of Police, CID, 6 March 1924, Home Political, NAI, File No. 61, pp. 2–3.

[21] R. E. A. Ray, Special Superintendent, IB, CID, Bengal, *Report on the Dacca Sri Sangha up to 1929* (Calcutta: Bengal Government Press, 1932), pp. 972–5.

[22] Barindra Ghose, *The Tale of My Exile* (Pondicherry: Arya Office, 1922), V. D. Savarkar, *The Story of My Transportation for Life* (Bombay: Sadbhakti Publications, 1950), Sachindranath Sanyal, *My Life in Prison* (Shakshi Prakashan, 2012). See Ghosh, *Gentlemanly Terrorists*, pp. 92–138.

[23] Activities of the Revolutionaries in Bengal from 1 September 1924 to 31 March 1925, in Samanta, *Terrorism in Bengal*, vol. 1, pp. 367–8.

revolution internationalized revolution in a way that previous uprisings had not done, despite some of the universalizing claims of nineteenth century revolutionary movements. Events in Russia cast a shadow over the proceedings of the Paris Peace Conference, and influenced the way the British government sought to police labour activists and other so-called subversives.[24] These events also affected the priorities of imperial intelligence services during the interwar period. Indian Political Intelligence files reveal that the primary targets of colonial security forces right up until independence in 1947 included left-wing revolutionaries, politicians, and activists.[25]

There is a huge degree of slippage and overlap between the revolutionary organizations covered in this chapter and the spread of communism in India, with the Dacca Anushilan Samiti, for example, transitioning to a leftist organization by the 1930s. Nonetheless, this chapter focuses exclusively on the language of 'terrorism' as it emerged in Bengal, and India more broadly. In H. W. Hale's *Terrorism in India, 1917–1936*, the key study of the revolutionary movement produced by the Intelligence Bureau, Hale makes a sharp distinction between terrorism and communism, omitting communism entirely from his narrative. Hale remarks that terrorism, 'as distinct from other revolutionary methods such as Communism or the Ghadr *(sic)* Movement, may be said to denote the commission of outrages of a comparatively "individual" nature'.[26]

A similar distinction was made by the renowned Indian communist M. N. Roy, who criticized 'sporadic terrorism' as being just as useless as constitutional nationalism. In his 1924 article 'Appeal to the Nationalists', Roy wrote, 'it is no more possible to win National Independence by killing a number of officials than by a series of Reform Acts passed by the British Parliament'.[27] In reality, the line between communists and 'terrorists' was often not so clear-cut, with Roy himself being involved in various plots to smuggle arms into India to be used by those designated as terrorists by the colonial government.[28] For the purposes of this

[24] Anthony Read, *The World on Fire: 1919 and the Battle with Bolshevism* (New York: W.W. Norton, 2008), pp. 79–83.

[25] For just a small sample of the many examples, see '"Bolshevism" – Govt of India memorandum prepared for the Imperial Conference', August 1923, L/P&J/12/188, File 9106; 'Indian Communists (Great Britain)', May–July 1923, L/P&J/12/143, File 6841A; 'Indian Labour: Strikes and Unrest', January 1935–September 1937, L/P&J/12/138, File 6835E.

[26] H. W. Hale, *Terrorism in India, 1917–1936* (Simla: Government of India Press, 1937), IOR: L/P&J/12/403, p. 1.

[27] Quoted in David Petrie, *Communism in India, 1924–1927* (Calcutta: Editions Indian, 1972), p. 91.

[28] See Manjapra, *M.N. Roy*.

chapter, however, Indian communism is largely excluded from the narrative in favour of an in-depth examination of the origins of the colonial language of terrorism.[29]

Following Gandhi's decision to call off his non cooperation campaign after the events of Chauri Chaura, Congress was split between the 'No-Changers', who supported his decision, and the Swaraj Party who criticized Gandhi for calling off the entire campaign due to a single violent incident. The Swaraj party, led by Chittaranjan Das – or C. R. Das – and Motilal Nehru, did not advocate violence – contrary to the claims of some British officials – but was unwilling to take such a dogmatic approach towards the ideal of non-violence at the expense of Indian independence. Although the Swaraj party adopted 'legitimate' political methods for its goals, with many elected to the central legislative assembly and provincial legislative councils in the 1923 elections, some members did have direct links to revolutionary secret societies. In this sense, the line between 'violent' revolutionaries and 'non-violent' politicians during the interwar period was far more blurred than most historiography has previously recognized.[30]

At a conference at Allahabad in February 1923, for example, representatives from the Swaraj party chosen to discuss the recent Congress split included renowned revolutionaries such as Pulin Behari Das and Sachindranath Sanyal.[31] This should not be taken as evidence that Swaraj politicians necessarily endorsed the adoption of violent means, or were in any way synonymous with the revolutionary movement. Following an alleged plot to assassinate colonial police officers, security forces arrested several suspected revolutionaries under the provisions of Regulation III of 1818. Although seven of the ten accused revolutionaries had links to the Bengal Swaraj party led by Das, radicals accused him of failing to protest strongly enough against these arrests, despite resolutions passed at a meeting in Cocanada in which Das and the Swaraj party demanded the immediate and unconditional release of political prisoners and the repeal of repressive laws.[32]

[29] For more on the communist or leftist aspect of Indian revolutionary politics, see David M. Lausey, *Bengal Terrorism and the Marxist Left: Aspects of Regional Nationalism in India, 1905–1942* (Calcutta: Firma K.L. Mukhopadhyay, 1975), and Peter Campbell, 'East Meets Left: South Asian Militants and the Social Party of Canada in British Columbia, 1904–1914', *International Journal of Canadian Studies* 20 (1999), pp. 35–65. For a detailed examination of workers' politics in Bengal throughout the period in question, see Subho Basu, *Does Class Matter? Colonial Capital and Workers' Resistance in Bengal, 1890–1937* (New Delhi: Oxford University Press, 2004).

[30] Maclean, *A Revolutionary History*, pp. 101–79.

[31] Special Superintendent of Police, CID, 6 March 1924, Home Political, NAI, File No. 61, p. 7.

[32] Ibid., pp. 8–9.

On 12 January 1924, a young Bengali man named Gopi Nath Saha shot and killed Ernest Day, an Englishman whom Saha mistook for Charles Tegart, the notorious Calcutta police commissioner known as a scourge to the revolutionary movement.[33] Put on trial for murder, Saha expressed regret at having killed an innocent man, stating to Justice Pearson in the High Court, 'I am extremely sorry for the innocent sahib that I have killed and for those who have been wounded. For the soul of the sahib I am praying to God. I do not consider a man my enemy because he is a sahib.' The next day, on 15 February, when Pearson sentenced Saha to execution, the revolutionary exclaimed, 'May every drop of blood of mine sow the seed of liberty in every Indian home.'[34]

These words were widely compared with those of Madan Lal Dhingra, the young revolutionary who assassinated Sir William Curzon Wyllie, the political aide-de-camp to the secretary of state for India in London in 1909. Following his death sentence, Dhingra famously stated that his only prayer was to be reborn and die again and again until India achieved its freedom. At the time, even the arch-imperialist Winston Churchill, while supporting the death sentence against Dhingra, called these words 'the finest ever made in the name of patriotism'. In a letter to the editor of *Forward* following Saha's execution in 1924, the anonymous author pointed out that it was entirely possible to separate motive from action and to applaud the patriotism of Saha while condemning his actions, just as Churchill did in the case of Dhingra.[35] Despite this, the political climate of 1920s India made Saha's action considerably more controversial.

The execution of Saha instigated a storm of coverage in the press. On 28 February, the Calcutta-based *Sarathi* published an article criticising Saha's use of violence, while simultaneously celebrating the brave resolve with which the revolutionary accepted his death sentence. The article went on to state that just as 'the heart of Gopi Nath's half-frantic mother is wailing out in lamentation, so the heart of all Bengal is wailing for this fearless youth … vowed to truth'.[36] The author wrote that as long as acts

[33] Tegart had taken a leading role in the suppression of earlier revolutionary networks, with some accounts claiming that he personally shot and killed Jotindra Nath Mukherjee, a prominent revolutionary leader, in a shootout in the jungle outside Calcutta. For more on Tegart, see Silvestri, '"An Irishman Is Specially Suited to Be a Policeman"' and J. C. Curry, *Tegart of the Indian Police* (Tunbridge Wells, 1960).

[34] A. N. Moberley, Chief Secretary to Governor of Bengal, to Secretary to the Government of India, 1 September 1924, Home Department Political Branch, NAI, F.379, p. 29.

[35] Letter to the editor of *Forward*, 19 June 1924, Home Department Political Branch, NAI, F.379, pp. 28–9.

[36] *Sarathi* (excerpt), 28 February 1924, Home Department Political Branch, NAI, F.379, p. 26.

of government 'terrorism' such as the Jallianwallah Bagh massacre continued, acts of violence like the murder of Day would escalate until India, like Ireland, was engulfed in a 'terrible Kurukshetra', a reference to the apocalyptic civil war described in the epic Mahabharata.[37] The *Pravartak* in Chandernagore wrote that Day's murder was proof that revolution in Bengal was back, but that it was 'quite natural for human beings to adopt such terrible methods if all other ways of achieving freedom are closed'.[38] While the assassination received the expected condemnation of the English press, many vernacular papers took the opportunity to heap criticism on the repressive nature of colonial rule, celebrating the courage of Saha while distancing themselves from his methods.

Some prominent politicians adopted a similar approach, particularly in Bengal. At its annual conference held at Sirajganj on 1 June, the Bengal Provincial Congress Committee passed a resolution acknowledging the sacrifice of Saha, while denouncing the violence of his actions. Gandhi opposed this resolution, and in turn moved a resolution at the Ahmedabad session of the All India Congress Committee, condemning Saha's murder of Day. In response, C. R. Das moved a counter-resolution at the same meeting where he reproduced the text of the Sirajganj resolution. Das was narrowly outvoted by 78 to 70, and the Committee backed Gandhi's resolution, reflecting the AICC's continued insistence on non-violence but also the thin margin of support by which it maintained this stance.[39]

Following the murder of Day, an attempt was made on Mr. Bruce, a member of Saha's jury, although this seems to have been another case of mistaken identity in which the intended target was again Charles Tegart. In March, police discovered a bomb factory in Calcutta, causing further panic. At the end of July, revolutionaries distributed propaganda pamphlets known as the 'Red Bengal' leaflets, announcing a campaign of police assassination and calling on Indians to rebel against their colonial oppressors. On 22 August, revolutionaries threw a bomb into a cloth shop on Mirzapur Street in Calcutta, killing one man and wounding another.[40]

Of these developments, the distribution of the Red Bengal leaflets marked the most coherent articulation of anti-colonial politics. Written

[37] Ibid.

[38] *Pravartak* (excerpt), 28 February 1924, Home Department Political Branch, NAI, F.379, pp. 27–8.

[39] Nitish K. Sengupta, *Land of Two Rivers: A History of Bengal from the Mahabharata to Mujib* (New Delhi: Penguin Books India, 2011), p. 342.

[40] Resolution published by the Governor of Bengal in an extraordinary *Gazette of India* Extraordinary, Calcutta, 25 October 1924, IOR: L/PJ/6/1886, p. 16.

by Sachindranath Sanyal, the leaflets proclaimed the failure of constitutional agitation and advocated instead the adoption of assassination and sabotage. These pamphlets are typically ignored within the historiography of Indian nationalism, as is the role of Sanyal, yet both are worthy of careful study. Revolutionaries circulated the first pamphlet to four High Court judges, the public prosecutor who represented the Crown in the Alipore conspiracy case, and the judge who convicted the accused in the Manicktolla Bomb Case, among others. The pamphlet informed the public that the Bengal Revolutionary Council passed a resolution for a 'campaign of ruthless assassination of police officers'. The text warned that anyone who obstructed the work of the revolutionaries in this endeavour or aided the government in the prosecution of the movement would be 'considered as doing acts highly prejudicial to the best interests of our country' and would thus be 'despatched forthwith'. The leaflet was signed 'President-in-Council, Red Bengal' and was surmounted by a picture of the goddess Kali.[41]

In a subsequent leaflet, Sanyal outlined the goals of the revolutionary movement, acknowledging that 'a few revolvers and bombs and police murders or a little white man's blood spilt here and there' would not be enough to bring independence. Instead, Sanyal and his compatriots pledged their commitment to acting as 'a standing menace to irresponsible tyranny, an abiding retaliation of flagrant misrule, and we mean to stay and work till these lawless laws are in fact wiped out, till government becomes responsible to the will of the people ...'[42] The goal was to wake up the 'sleeping leviathan of potentiality of India' and provide inspiration for an awakening of national consciousness that would render colonial rule impossible. To this end, the leaflet sought to rouse its readers with a stirring call to arms:

> The alien tyrant mad with power and pride, riding roughshod over law and justice proclaims there is need of us. ... Your Judiciary, who are hushing up dark crimes like these, proclaim from their seat of Justice, there is need of us. ... Your own women have come out before the world and in the story they repeat from the witness booth, in the story of their shame they proclaim there is need of us in this land, where the Executive ravish the women, the Judiciary condones them, and the representative of the King, the man at the head of the government insults them.[43]

[41] Weekly report of Director, Intelligence Bureau, 6 August 1924, IOR: L/PJ/12/220, pp. 1–2.
[42] Weekly report of Director, Intelligence Bureau, 27 August 1924, IOR: L/PJ/12/220, p. 6.
[43] Weekly report of Director, Intelligence Bureau, 27 August 1924, IOR: L/PJ/12/220, p. 6.

In November, a new pamphlet titled *Arise! Awake!* asked how long the people of Bengal would remain asleep and argued that all obstacles to independence must be removed. The pamphlet also pointed to examples in world history to demonstrate the need for violence and sacrifice in achieving national independence.[44] Following the mass arrests that resulted from the declaration of Lytton's ordinance, revolutionaries and radical sympathizers distributed this leaflet widely throughout Bengal, in an attempt to counteract the demoralizing effect of the governmental crackdown.[45] Unsurprisingly, the pamphlets attracted scathing criticism from much of the English-language press, with *The Statesman* contemptuously opining that the 'impression left is that the leaflet is the work of a dangerous lunatic who ... deserves not death but a skilled mental treatment till he recovers his balance and sees the world as it is'.[46]

'Easier to Defend in Parliament'

The polarized political context of the mid-1920s posed a serious challenge to British authorities seeking to suppress the re-emergence of revolutionary violence through a renewal of extraordinary legislation of the type deployed before and during the First World War. While emergency laws always provoked a certain level of protest and opposition from within Indian political circles and the vernacular press, the events of 1919 to 1923 created an unprecedented level of mass support for the notion that colonialism's promise of a just rule of law was nothing but a disguise for violent tyranny. As it became clear that revolutionary crime was once more on the rise due to a string of 'outrages' and foiled plots in Bengal Lord Lytton, the governor of Bengal, asked viceroy and governor general of India Lord Reading for new emergency powers to deal with suspected conspirators. Initially reluctant to sanction any new measures, Reading told Lytton to make use of the existing powers of arrest provided by Regulation III of 1818. Reading's concern was that the lack of 'dacoities' connected to the latest manifestation of the movement would make it more difficult to convince the public of the necessity of the emergency measures proposed. The removal of the war conditions that had stifled opposition to the Defence of India Act meant that draconian measures would find a much more critical reception within an increasingly vocal

44 Weekly report of Director, Intelligence Bureau, 26 November 1924, IOR: L/PJ/12/220, p. 9.

45 Weekly report of Director, Intelligence Bureau, 3 December 1924, IOR: L/PJ/12/220, p. 11.

46 *The Statesman* (28 August 1924), p. 3.

and politically engaged public. According to J. Crerar, the home secretary, the political atmosphere during the war was more favourable, and the additional justification of the 'special peril to a state at war' of revolutionary conspiracies helped minimize opposition to extraordinary measures that would have attracted heavy criticism during peacetime. Crerar worried that if war conditions enabled the success of the emergency powers, the logical conclusion was that during a time of peace such measures would require stronger and more careful reinforcement.[47]

Based on this assessment, Lytton replied that Regulation III did not provide an adequate solution, as although it allowed for the detention of suspects without trial, it lacked the preventive measures necessary for arresting revolutionaries before they could execute their plots.[48] Regulation III required an application to the local government and the Government of India, slowing down the ability of the authorities to act quickly and decisively in carrying out certain arrests. According to Alexander Muddiman, the home member of the Government of India and leader of the Legislative Assembly, the other problem with the regulation was that it was not conducive to the mass arrests required for crippling a widespread conspiracy. Regulation III provided drastic measures for dealing with the leaders of a conspiracy, but Muddiman asserted that the burden of evidence required by this law was too extensive. Muddiman stated that the case against a revolutionary might rest upon information that would be insufficient for taking action under the regulation, but that when widespread arrests were carried out against a large number of potential conspirators, the wider net provided 'a mass of information which threw a flood of light on the persons who took part in the movement and the part which each had played'.[49] In other words, the desire to conduct mass arrests based on less information was what made a new law desirable.

Officials were also concerned about the relationship between revolutionaries and more mainstream political leaders. Muddiman wrote that C. R. Das 'joining hands' with the revolutionaries gave a 'character and importance' to the movement that was beyond what it achieved throughout the long history of revolutionary agitation in India. Muddiman viewed the endorsement of the Sirajganj resolution by Das and such a large section of Congress as evidence that, contrary to the repeated

[47] Note by J. Crerar, 18 July 1924, Home Department Political Branch, NAI, F.379, p. 2.
[48] Earl of Lytton, *Pundits and Elephants. Being the experiences of five years as governor of an Indian province, etc* (London, 1942), p. 61.
[49] Alexander Muddiman, 23 July 1924, Home Department Political Branch, NAI, F.379, p. 15.

public insistence of the government, the revolutionaries enjoyed broad political support. In the eyes of Muddiman and other colonial officials, this indicated that for the first time, the revolutionary movement was 'able to find support in the political world and to command voices in the legislature and the public bodies'. Acting through the legislature in passing a new emergency law was out of the question, as it was necessary 'to strike swiftly and without opportunity for the escape of the enemy'. According to Muddiman, this could only be done through the promulgation of an ordinance, an act that must come directly through the sovereign authority of the governor general. In Muddiman's words, 'the authority which makes the ordinance must also be the authority which must judge of the existence of the emergency which would justify it'.[50] This is a succinct, though unintentional, articulation of the German jurist Carl Schmitt's dictum that the sovereign is he who decides upon the exception.[51]

In late July of 1924, Lytton visited Reading at Simla and argued that Regulation III was indeed proving ineffective at suppressing the growing revolutionary movement, and that such 'ineffective coercion ... was the worst of all policies'.[52] In September, the Bengal government laid out its three key justifications to the Government of India detailing why the ordinance was necessary. The first was the increase in assassination plots in 1923 and 1924, including the murder of Day. The second was the volatility of the political situation in Bengal that resulted from the growing influence of the Swaraj party and the increasingly hard-line nationalist stance taken by many politicians. The third, and perhaps the most significant of all, was the fear that revolutionaries outside of India would succeed at smuggling a large supply of weapons into Indian territory.

In September, it came to the attention of the colonial authorities that Rash Behari Bose, the notorious revolutionary involved in both the attempted assassination of Lord Hardinge and the aborted uprising of 1915, was planning to smuggle a large shipment of arms into India to be used by Sachindranath Sanyal and other radicals in Bengal.[53] Lytton worried that existing controls on smuggling were insufficient to prevent arms from arriving from other parts of Asia and could see

[50] Alexander Muddiman, 19 July 1924, Home Department Political Branch, NAI, F.379, p. 4.
[51] See Schmitt, *Political Theology*. See also Hussain, *Jurisprudence of Emergency*, pp. 15–6.
[52] Lytton, *Pundits and Elephants*, p. 63.
[53] Enclosure No. 1. Activities of Revolutionists in Bengal subsequent to August 1923, IOR: L/PJ/6/1886, p. 8.

no method whatever of defeating this part of the revolutionary programme other than that of dislocating the organisation entirely. … Unless steps are taken to deal with the revolutionaries in this country and to shut down the supplies of funds for the purpose of such importation, it will not be possible to keep out consignments of arms and ammunition, small or great.[54]

Lytton reminded the Government of India that the theft of fifty Mauser pistols from Messrs. Rodda & Co. in 1914 initiated a wave of violence that rendered Bengal almost impossible to govern during the war, and warned ominously, 'If only one consignment were to reach Bengal, it would produce a situation with which Government would be powerless to deal even by martial law.'[55] Lytton insisted that all of this provided evidence that an exceptional state of affairs existed in Bengal and that only exceptional measures would permit him to deal with it. Defining the exact limits of the exception, however, was not an easy task. In a letter responding to Lytton's request for emergency legislation, Reading indicated the difficulties of establishing exactly when an emergency began and, more important, when it could be said to be over. Reading's initial assumption was that an emergency would be a short and specified period of time, lasting less than six months, but on further reflection, he concluded that this would give

… an unnecessarily restricted meaning to the word and that the 'emergency' may continue for a longer period, but obviously not for an indefinitely prolonged period. … The meaning of the word is clear enough. The duration of the period must largely be a question of degree. It cannot be a given period in all conditions; indeed the use of the word 'emergency' in itself presupposes an indefinite period of time.[56]

In other words, Reading's main argument was that the parameters of an emergency would always be discretionary, and that by definition an emergency was finite in duration, despite the fact that this finite duration could have no previously decided limitations.

Lytton rejected these conclusions, arguing that 'if every time you have forged an effective weapon you throw it away again after you have used it, you will find the evil constantly returning, and you will always have to forge your weapon anew'. Reading objected that emergency powers could not be permanent, just as wartime legislation could not operate in times of peace. Lytton's proposed solution was emergency legislation that would remain permanently on the statute books, but could lie

[54] A. N. Moberley (Chief Secretary to Governor of Bengal) to the Government of India, 1 September 1924, Home Department Political Branch, NAI, F. 379.
[55] Ibid.
[56] Reading to Lytton, 5 September 1924, Lytton Papers, Mss Eur./F160/2, p. 276.

dormant during ordinary times, to be 'called into operation ... at a moment's notice if the need arose'. Reading initially conceded to a two-year limit for the proposed ordinance but after Lytton's rebuttal that such a limit would leave his successor defenceless against a recurrence of revolutionary crime, Reading agreed to an ordinance lasting for five years, to which Lytton concurred.[57] Reading's condition for this measure was that formal legislation would be submitted as a bill to the Legislative Council of Bengal, following the promulgation of the ordinance, which would remain a secret until its issuance on the night of 24 October. The issue of the ordinance was to occur in tandem with the sweeping arrests of several suspected revolutionaries including Subhas Chandra Bose, the chief executive officer of the Calcutta Corporation and one of C. R. Das' most significant lieutenants.[58]

Cognizant of the fact that such a display of executive authority would draw substantial criticism, the statement given by Reading in justifying the ordinance was drawn up with a great deal of care. While earlier repressive laws directed against the revolutionary movement explicitly targeted sedition, most notably following the Sedition Committee Report of 1918, Reading was careful to specify that the Bengal Criminal Law Amendment Ordinance would not give the government 'any extraordinary powers to deal with sedition, with industrial movements or with communal disturbances, even though they may menace the maintenance of order. ... It is aimed solely at the secret criminal conspiracy, which has terrorism as its object or method.'[59] The proclamation that the government ultimately circulated in the *Gazette of India* on 25 October 1924 made repeated reference to the 'terrorist movement' of Bengal, deploying a vocabulary that emphasized 'terrorism' more than any previous legal proclamation had done thus far.

This was not the case in earlier drafts of the proclamation, however, in which the terms 'terrorist' and 'terrorism' were not used once.[60] The original draft referred exclusively to 'revolutionaries', but in editing the draft, Secretary of State Sydney Olivier bracketed and underlined Reading's use of the word 'revolutionary', replacing it with the word 'terrorist' in red ink.[61] Writing back to Reading, Olivier recommended making these changes throughout the document, to which Reading replied,

[57] Lytton, *Pundits and Elephants*, p. 64–6.
[58] Subhas Chandra Bose would go on to become one of the most important nationalists in Indian politics, rivalled only by Gandhi and Nehru themselves. For his most comprehensive biography, see Bose, *His Majesty's Opponent*.
[59] *Gazette of India* Extraordinary, 25 October 1924, IOR: L/PJ/6/1886, p. 18.
[60] Reading to Olivier, 4 October 1924, Reading Papers, Mss Eur E 238/13, pp. 361–3.
[61] Olivier to Reading, 6 October 1924, IOR: L/PJ/6/1886, p. 156.

I quite appreciate that they made it slightly easier for you to defend in Parliament in England, although the words 'revolutionary' and 'revolutionaries' used by me are perhaps more appropriate in India. But I understand the difficulties you would have in any event to meet and did not attach sufficient importance to adhering to my own language and therefore changed these terms throughout as you desired.[62]

The emergence of 'terrorism' as the defining category to be used in subsequent legal and political pronouncements on the Indian revolutionary movement should thus be understood as a deliberate and calculated attempt on the part of colonial officials to make emergency measures more palatable both to the British Parliament back home and moderate opinion within India. Still, this linguistic manoeuvre did little to convince Indian nationalist politicians and newspapers, many of whom interpreted the ordinance as a direct assault on anti-colonial politics. Although apologists for government action maintained that the ordinance could not target nationalist politicians as it clearly stated that the law was directed against terrorism and terrorism alone,[63] C. R. Das referred to the ordinance as an obvious attack on the Swaraj party due to their growing strength, which he claimed was becoming unbearable for the government.[64]

From 26 to 31 October, nationalists held public meetings throughout Calcutta criticizing the government's action in promulgating the ordinance.[65] On 8 November, Gandhi, Das, and Motilal Nehru issued a statement arguing that the ordinance was directed not at criminals but at the Swaraj party in Bengal, and appealing for the cooperation of all political parties against the government's policy of repression.[66] On 15 November, various groups in India held more meetings accusing the government of stifling legitimate politics. These protesters did not stop there, but gave eulogies for dead revolutionaries like Khudiram Bose, Kanai Lal Datta, and Gopi Nath Saha.[67]

'Neither Terrorists nor Anarchists'

In January 1925, Sachindranath Sanyal, having evaded capture during the October arrests, anonymously produced a pamphlet called *The Revolutionary* in which he condemned the repressive measures taken against the revolutionary movement. The pamphlet circulated widely

[62] Reading to Olivier, 9 October 1924, Reading Papers, Mss Eur E 238/13, p. 194.
[63] *The Statesman* (30 October 1924), p. 8. [64] *The Statesman* (28 October 1924), p. 7.
[65] Report on Activities of Revolutionaries in Bengal, 1925, IOR: L/PJ/12/253, p. 5.
[66] Reading to Olivier, 6 December 1924, IOR: L/PJ/6/1886, p. 1.
[67] Report on Activities of Revolutionaries in Bengal, 1925, IOR: L/PJ/12/253, p. 6.

throughout northern India, with over three hundred copies received in eighteen districts of the United Provinces alone.[68] Responding to the proclamations of some politicians that the revolutionary movement was a figment of the colonial government's imagination, Sanyal wrote,

> Let no Indian deny the existence of this revolutionary party in order to denounce the repressive measures of the foreign rulers. The foreigners have no right to rule over India and therefore they must be denounced and driven out, not that they have committed any particular act of violence or crime. These are the natural consequences of a foreign rule.[69]

Responding to the language of terrorism deployed by Indian officials in promulgating the ordinance, Sanyal wrote that this word – as well as the term 'anarchism' – were 'invariably misapplied whenever any reference to the revolutionaries is to be made because it is so very convenient to denounce the revolutionaries under that name. The Indian revolutionaries are neither terrorists nor anarchists.' Sanyal pointed out that the goal of the revolutionaries was not spreading anarchy and that therefore the popular label of 'anarchism' was a clear misnomer. Furthermore, he argued that because terrorism was not the object of the revolutionaries, they should not be called terrorists either. According to Sanyal, the revolutionaries 'do not believe that terrorism alone can bring independence and they do not want terrorism for terrorism's sake, although they may at times resort to this method as a very effective means of retaliation'.[70]

Sanyal then turned the tables on the British with the accusation that the colonial government existed only because it succeeded at terrorizing the people of India. According to Sanyal, 'This official terrorism is surely to be met by counter-terrorism. A spirit of utter helplessness pervades every strata of our society and terrorism is an effective means of restoring the proper spirits in the society without which progress will be difficult.' He further asserted that terrorism also carried an international significance because such acts would draw the attention of England's enemies towards India and therefore promote the cause of Indian independence. Sanyal promised that the revolutionary party was not defeated, but had yet to embark upon its greatest and most deadly campaign of assassination thus far.[71]

[68] Chief Court of Oudh judgment in criminal appeals, delivered 22 August 1927, IOR: L/PJ/6/1910, p. 4.

[69] *The Revolutionary* (1 January 1925). *Terrorism in Bengal*, vol. 2, 'Activities of the Revolutionaries in Bengal from 1 September 1924 to 31 March 1925', p. 403.

[70] Ibid., p. 404. [71] Ibid., p. 405.

In February, Sanyal submitted a letter for publication in *Young India* that was printed under the title 'A Revolutionary's Defence'. Although this text received little attention in wider histories of the Indian independence movement, it provides a critically important rebuttal to Gandhi's political strategy of non-violence and a coherent defence of revolutionary tactics. In this letter, Sanyal began by reminding Gandhi that the year initially requested by the Mahatma for his experiment turned into more than four, with still no independence in sight. Sanyal argued that the response to Gandhi's programme was overwhelming and that its failure could not be blamed on the people of India, who mobilized by the thousands to engage in non-violent action against the colonial government. In response to those that claimed that non-violent non-cooperation failed because the people were not sufficiently non-violent, Sanyal wrote such a claim was to 'argue like a lawyer and not like a prophet'. He asserted that the people could not have been more non-violent, and that they were in fact 'non-violent to a degree which smelled of cowardice'.[72] Sanyal asserted that it was time for non-violent activists to retire from the political field and thus leave room for the return of the revolutionaries, who would no longer remain silent.

Sanyal addressed the accusation that revolutionaries were retarding India's progress, with the riposte that every small political concession made thus far came about on the heels of revolutionary agitation. He further asserted that the true progress made by the revolutionary movement was the 'moral advancement' of India. According to Sanyal, Indians were previously 'miserably afraid' of death, but the revolutionary movement had 'once more made the Indians realise the grandeur and the beauty that lie in dying for a noble cause'. Through their martyrdom, revolutionaries demonstrated that death was not always a bad thing, but could in fact serve as the highest ideal of patriotism. Sanyal asked, 'To die for one's own beliefs and convictions, to die in the consciousness that by so dying one is serving God in the nation ... is this no moral progress?'[73]

Gandhi responded in the same issue of *Young India*, stating that the world was sick of armed rebellions and that a bloody revolution could not succeed in India because the masses would not respond. He conceded that he did not deny the heroism and sacrifice of the revolutionary. However, according to Gandhi, 'heroism and sacrifice in a bad cause are so much waste of splendid energy and hurt the good cause by drawing away attention from it by the glamour of the misused heroism and

[72] *Young India* (12 February 1925), p. 6. [73] Ibid., p. 7.

sacrifice in a bad cause'. Gandhi wrote that the self-sacrifice of one innocent man was a million times more powerful than the sacrifice of a million men 'who die in the act of killing others'. The willing sacrifice of the innocent was, for Gandhi, 'the most powerful retort to insolent tyranny that has yet been conceived by God or man'. Still, Gandhi insisted that his criticism of the revolutionary did not imply intolerance towards him, but rather towards his methods.[74]

The authorities arrested Sanyal in Bhowanipur on 25 February and ultimately sentenced him to transportation for life following evidence that came out against him in the Kakori conspiracy trial following a train robbery near Lucknow. Despite his leading role in the revolutionary movement, Sanyal escaped capital punishment, a sentence that was often reserved for those who physically carried out assassinations themselves, such as Khudiram Bose, Madan Lal Dhingra, and Gopi Nath Saha.

'Legalised Brute Force'

Despite Reading's insistence that the Bengal Ordinance would only be granted on the condition that it would subsequently be passed in the Bengal Legislative Council, he expected all along that the Indian representatives would reject the bill and that it would in turn need to be certified by the government.[75] An article in *The Bengalee*, a Calcutta-based newspaper edited by Bipin Chandra Pal, attacked this process of certification, arguing that a certified bill was every bit as autocratic as an ordinance and lacked the moral sanction of ordinary law. The writer went on to declare that governing by ordinances and certified legislation was government by 'legalised brute force' and would never be acceptable to Indian opinion.[76]

The Bengal Legislative Council did indeed reject the proposed bill on 7 January by a vote of 66 to 57. Reading admitted that the strength of the vote against the bill was all the more impressive when the number of officials and nominated and European members in the House was taken into account.[77] Most Indian members of the Council criticized the bill, including Sir P. C. Mitter, a former architect of the infamous Rowlatt Act. Mitter argued that the proposed legislation departed from the recommendations of the Rowlatt Report and instead proceeded along the

74 Ibid., p. 8.
75 Reading to Birkenhead, 1 January 1925, Birkenhead Papers, NMML, Mss Eur. D703, p. 3.
76 *The Bengalee* (7 January 1925), p. 4.
77 Reading to Birkenhead, 8 January 1925, Birkenhead Papers, NMML, Mss Eur. D703, p. 2.

lines of the Defence of India Act which, although similar, contained some features unsuitable for peacetime legislation. Perhaps most significant was the removal of the right of habeas corpus under the ordinance, as opposed to the Rowlatt Act, which banned this right under part I but not under other conditions. The stipulations provided under the Criminal Law Amendment Bill for the investigation or scrutiny of steps taken under it were also more draconian than even those provided under the Rowlatt Act. On the other hand, the Criminal Law Amendment provided for allowances to the dependents of those held under it while Rowlatt had not, perhaps indicating a growing recognition of the political status of revolutionary detainees.[78] Mitter referred to the proposed bill as 'a quack's remedy and not a physician's treatment' and argued that if the bill were passed or certified, it would 'not only fail in its object but will perhaps be, quite unintentionally, helpful towards it'.[79]

Following its failure in the Legislative Council, the bill was certified by Lytton 'as being essential for the discharge of his duty in the administration of justice', after which it was signed by the King in Council on 17 March.[80] Two clauses from the original ordinance were introduced as a separate bill, one of which stipulated that those detained under the law possessed the right to appeal to High Court, while the other deprived the High Court of the power of issuing a writ of habeas corpus for those under detention. This bill was introduced in the Indian Legislative Assembly but attracted the criticism of opponents such as Motilal Nehru, who referred to it as a 'well-prepared trap', which, 'while pretending to concede a right ... really strikes at the very foundation upon which that right rests'.[81]

Indian politicians greeted the proposed Bengal Criminal Law Amendment Supplementary Bill with disdain. Nehru pointed out that the Assembly was given no opportunity to comment upon the original act, but that by agreeing to the Supplementary Bill, which granted the right of appeal for accused terrorists, the Assembly would be seen as giving their assent to the act in its entirety. Nehru referred to the right of appeal as bait that was being dangled before the Assembly to trick them into swallowing the whole thing.[82] Muhammad Ali Jinnah and

[78] For a more detailed examination of the technical differences, see Comparison of differences between the Rowlatt Act and Bengal Ordinance and Bill, 1925, Home Political, F.43/II, pp. 1–2.
[79] *The Bengalee* (8 January 1925), p. 4.
[80] House of Lords Parliamentary Debate, Vol. 60, 31 March 1925, p. 849.
[81] Legislative Assembly Debates, 23 March 1925, OP.3150.328.03(20), NLI, VOL. V, No. 40, p. 2805.
[82] Ibid., pp. 2806–7.

C. Duraiswami Aiyangar opposed the Supplementary Bill on the same grounds, stating that they would not support it out of concern that doing so would give legitimacy to the original 'illegal Act'.[83] Jinnah also disputed the claim that the bill was a matter of either national or public safety and pointed out that India was also not in a state of war.[84] The Legislative Assembly rejected the bill by a vote of 72 to 41.

Stating his opinion that the passage of the bill in its entirety was 'essential for the tranquility of the Presidency of Bengal', Reading certified the bill in the Council of State.[85] Even within this oligarchic institution, however, there was strong criticism to the proposed bill. G. A. Natesan, a nominated non-official from Madras, said that although he condemned the anarchist as an 'enemy of mankind', he implored the government to adopt alternate methods for policing anarchy, asking that India not be converted into 'another Ireland'.[86] Sevasila Vedamurti, an elected member of the Council, pointed out that there was an impression throughout India that the Council of State was nothing more than the 'handmaid' of the colonial government, and that the only reason for its existence was to 'register the decrees of the Government of India'. Vedamurti said that by being offered a bill already certified by the viceroy and governor general, the Council was being asked to pass the bill 'at the point of a bayonet'. He further declared that he regarded it an insult to the House to be called upon to pass the bill and called any discussion of it a waste of time, given that no amount of discussion or adverse voting would cause the Government of India to deviate 'even by a hair's breadth' from their predetermined course of action. Referring to the whole procedure as a farce, Vedamurti withdrew from the House.[87]

V. Ramadas Pantulu, an elected member from Madras, pointed out that the representatives of Bengal and of India already rejected the 'Black Bill' in no uncertain terms. Pantulu said that the government demanded that the bill be passed in its present form or rejected, but that, 'Reject it you dare not, nor are you allowed to amend it.' For this reason, he said any further discussion of the bill was pointless. Pantulu said it was obviously impossible to convince the governor general, who was

[83] Legislative Assembly Debates, 24 March 1925, OP.3150.328.03(20), NLI, VOL. V, No. 41, p. 2866.
[84] Legislative Assembly Debates, 23 March 1925, OP.3150.328.03(20), NLI, VOL. V, No. 40, p. 2812.
[85] Reading to Birkenhead, 2nd April 1925, NMML, Mss Eur. D703, pp. 1–2.
[86] Extracts from the proceedings of the Council of State, 26 March 1925, IOR: L/PJ/6/1886, pp. 3–6.
[87] Extracts from the proceedings of the Council of State, 26 March 1925, IOR: L/PJ/6/1886, p. 13.

influenced by the advice of 'the bureaucracy who are the steel frame of the Indian constitution'. For this reason, Pantulu similarly withdrew from the vote.[88] Although the Council of State nonetheless passed the measure by a comfortable margin of twenty nine votes to three, this represented a vote of only about half of the eligible electorate. Once the twenty six official and non-official nominated votes are accounted for, it becomes clear that even within the oligarchic limitations of the Council, the bill attracted negligible support from the elected members, many of whom, like Vedamurti and Pantulu, abstained from casting a vote.

By contrast, the bill attracted minimal opposition within the British Parliament, a fact no doubt impacted by the role of Ramsay MacDonald's Labour government in introducing the original ordinance in 1924. Shortly after the Labour government approved the Bengal Criminal Law Amendment Ordinance, the Conservatives defeated them in a general election on 29 October. By the time the Amendment Act came up for discussion under the Conservatives, Labour had no moral basis on which to oppose the measure, even if they wanted to, a fact that the Conservatives were happy to exploit. Writing to Lord Birkenhead, the new secretary of state, Lytton expressed his delight at the electoral success of the Conservatives, stating that he felt 'bottled up' under Labour. Lytton called it 'extraordinarily fortunate that the so-called "policy of repression" in Bengal was inaugurated while the Labour Government was still in power in England and cannot therefore be criticised as the first fruits of a Conservative reaction'. Because of this, Lytton wrote, 'the mouths of the Labour Party in opposition will be closed and they cannot accuse you of having inaugurated or sanctioned a reign of persecution in Bengal'.[89] This assumption proved broadly true, and aside from some opposition by individual members of Parliament, Labour mounted no sustained opposition to the passage of the Criminal Law Amendment Act the following year.[90]

By 1926, colonial police arrested forty-eight revolutionaries under Regulation III of 1818 and another 125 under the Bengal Criminal Law Amendment Act. The detainees were classified into four different categories of criminality. The first were simply called criminals, defined

[88] Extracts from the proceedings of the Council of State, 26 March 1925, IOR: L/PJ/6/1886, p. 22.
[89] Lytton to Birkenhead, 13 November 1924, Birkenhead Papers, NMML, Mss Eur F 160/12, pp. 2–4.
[90] For more on the relationship between the Conservative and Labour parties with regard to British imperial policy, see Owen, *British Left and India* and Stephen Howe, *Anticolonialism in British Politics: The Left and the End of Empire, 1918–1964* (Oxford: Oxford University Press, 1983).

as 'those who have committed crime and who would, it is believed, revert to crime if released'. After this came anarchists, 'those who are not addicted to crime but who are prepared to commit crime for revolutionary purposes', followed by revolutionary politicians who were designated as 'persons of violent revolutionary ideas who are, however, not themselves prepared to commit crime'. Finally, 'Bolsheviks' like Rash Behari Bose's gun-runner Hugo Espinoza were classified as 'irreconcilables'.[91] Despite its prevalence in the political discourse that surrounded the passage of the Criminal Law Amendment Act, the category of 'terrorist' had not yet been assigned a distinct legal classification.[92]

'The Blood-Stained Memory of the Easter Revolution'

In 1930, the five-year duration of the act was due to expire. The intervening years saw a lull in overt revolutionary activity in Bengal, although organizations like the Anushilan Samiti and Jugantar still actively recruited. This does not mean that the political situation throughout India was either quiet or stable. In 1928, colonial officials appointed the Simon Commission for a fact-finding mission that drew intense criticism across the Indian political spectrum due to its failure to include a single Indian within its ranks.

Police injured the celebrated nationalist politician Lala Lajpat Rai during a *lathi* charge when he led a protest against the commission during its visit to Lahore. Many Indians viewed Rai's death from a heart attack on 17 November as a direct result of the injuries he sustained during the protest. Following this, members of the Hindustan Socialist Republican Association in Punjab sought revenge against James Scott, the police superintendent who ordered the lathi charge. Intending to kill Scott, a group of revolutionaries, including Sanyal's disciple Bhagat Singh, instead assassinated a different policeman by mistake. In 1929, Singh and an accomplice named Batukeshwar Dutt threw two bombs into the Central Legislative Assembly and scattered radical leaflets while shouting, 'Inquilab Zindabad!', or 'Long Live Revolution!'[93]

[91] Despite his labelling as a 'Bolshevik', it is also possible that Espinoza was connected to a range of radical groups in India, China, and Japan, including the ultranationalist Kokuryūkai. I am grateful to Espinoza's granddaughter, Rana Caliskan, for bringing this point to my attention. For more on Espinoza's life, including his conversion to Islam and change of name to Abdur Raschid, see Silvestri, *Policing 'Bengali Terrorism'*, pp. 210–14.

[92] Arrests under Bengal Criminal Law Amendment Act and Ordinance and Regulation III from 1923–1926, BL, Mss Eur F160/37, p. 1.

[93] For a recent examination of Bhagat Singh and his significance, see Chris Moffat, 'Bhagat Singh's Corpse', *South Asia: Journal of South Asian Studies* 39, no. 3 (2016), pp. 644–61.

The executions of Singh and his accomplices in 1931 would later provoke widespread popular sympathy that forced Congress to walk a fine line between condemning violence while also acknowledging the revolutionaries' sacrifices.[94]

Writing in *Young India*, shortly after the attack, however, Gandhi argued forcefully that the bomb attack belonged to a philosophy of 'mad revenge and impotent rage'.[95] In January 1930, following an attempt by revolutionaries to bomb the train of viceroy and governor general Lord Irwin, Gandhi wrote an article titled 'The Cult of the Bomb' in which he rebutted the philosophy of revolutionary violence at greater length. Gandhi once more defended the necessity of non-violence, and stated that if the Indian people would only realize 'that it is not by terrorising the foreigner that we shall gain freedom, but by ourselves shedding fear and teaching the villager to shed his own fear that we shall gain true freedom, we would at once perceive that violence is suicidal'. Gandhi pointed out that in 1920 it was the principle of non-violence that aroused the participation of the Indian masses, 'as if by magic'. He wrote that India was entering a new era where the immediate objective was complete independence, and claimed that it was not enough to drive out the British through fear, but rather that mass civil disobedience was required to convert the colonial rulers and foster discipline among the masses.[96] Finally, Gandhi implored those 'who are not past reason' to stop endorsing bomb-throwing but rather to condemn such actions as inimical to the goal of Indian independence.[97]

On 26 January 1930, Congress declared a national Independence Day and unfurled the tricolour flag of independent India with shouts of 'Inquilab Zindabad!' On 12 March Gandhi launched the famous Salt March that became one of the most iconic moments of the Indian freedom struggle. Proposing a boycott of the tax levied against the Indian population on salt, a basic and necessary commodity, Gandhi undertook a symbolic march from his Sabarmati Ashram near Ahmedabad to a beach at Dandi, some 240 miles away. Accompanied by 78 hand-picked followers, Gandhi marched to the coast to boil his own salt in contravention of colonial law.[98] His actions marked the start of a new phase of *satyagraha* against colonial rule, in which thousands of non-violent protesters were ultimately incarcerated, including Gandhi himself. Significantly, before embarking on the march, Gandhi referred to the campaign

[94] Maclean, *A Revolutionary History*, p. 5. [95] *Young India* (18 April 1929), p. 4.
[96] *Young India* (2 January 1930), p. 4. [97] *Young India* (2 January 1930), p. 5.
[98] For a fuller account, see French, *Liberty or Death*, pp. 65–83.

Figure 4.1 Mohandas Gandhi leading the famous Salt March in 1930.
(Photo by Mansell / The LIFE Picture Collection via Getty Images.)

as an attempt to stave off 'the reign of terrorism that has just begun to overwhelm India'.[99]

This is the context in which the Bengal Criminal Law Amendment Act came up for review. It was due to expire on 23 April, which marked the end of the five-year period of operation initially agreed to by Reading. The government introduced and passed the Bengal Criminal Law Amendment (Part Continuance) Bill on 1 April, dropping the powers of preventive detention allowed under the previous act but retaining the other features of the law intact. Sir Francis Stanley Jackson, the governor of Bengal, promoted the bill through an appeal to the inherently non-political and nefarious nature of the figure of the terrorist. According to Jackson, 'The terrorist has no belief, or faith, in constitutional agitation or in the efficacy of political leaders. ... As a class the terrorist now, as always, pins his faith on violence as being the only method which will crown his efforts with success.'[100]

In response, Jitendra Lal Bannerjee referred to the Amendment Bill as 'an abuse of the powers of administration'.[101] Keshab Chandra Banerjee stated that although the bill was purged of objectionable features regarding detention without trial, the Indian people should nonetheless view it with suspicion. Banerjee said he appreciated the need for the maintenance of law and order at a time when 'violence and terrorist activities reign supreme'. According to Banerjee, however, the emergency measures enshrined in the bill could only be justified as a weapon to meet an abnormal situation, and would otherwise represent 'a direct negation of the principles of democracy'.[102]

Banerjee, however, noted that the preamble to the legislation indicated that it was meant to supplement the ordinary criminal laws of Bengal. This led Banerjee to argue that such emergency measures could only be justified if the government first proved that the ordinary law was not adequate to meet the situation. Banerjee said, 'If sufficient reasons could be brought forward to show an abnormal situation in the country, my clear duty would be to support the bill as one who is a lover of peace, order and constitution.' He argued that there was no clear indication of an immediate danger to public peace and therefore the criminal law should be sufficient to deal with any situations that may emerge, with

[99] Quoted in Maclean, *A Revolutionary History*, p. 7.
[100] Sir Francis Stanley Jackson, address to members of the legislative council on 25 March 1930, NLI, G.P.320.95415B436, p. 192.
[101] Council Proceedings, Bengal Legislative Council, Thirty-Fourth Session, 1 April 1930, NLI, Vol. 34, No. 3, p. 678.
[102] Ibid., pp. 680–1.

the understanding that should any 'extraordinary situation' develop, the bill could be considered in a special session of the Legislative Council.[103]

A. N. Moberly of the Bengal government responded that the authorities would never have dreamed of introducing the measure if they did not consider it 'absolutely essential' to the maintenance of law and order in Bengal. The bill, according to Moberly, was not aimed at the ordinary lawful citizen, but was instead aimed at 'the secret terrorist conspiracy, and our information is that secret terrorist conspiracy is still alive'. Moberly implored the Legislative Council to pass the proposed bill, stating that he was sure no member of the House would 'countenance the policy of these terrorists' by voting against the renewal of emergency powers.[104] An Indian member of the Council, Munindra Deb Rai Mohasai, referred to terrorism as being of 'exotic origin', incompatible with the adherence to *ahimsa* practiced by the people of India and accused the government of targeting the Civil Disobedience movement that was developing under Gandhi. Moberly denied this claim, stating that the law had no bearing on the Civil Disobedience campaign, as this was an open movement and the government had 'no objection whatever to any open movement'.[105] His claim, of course, stands in stark contrast to the tens of thousands of non-violent protesters ultimately arrested over the course of the Civil Disobedience campaign. Despite the objections raised by some Indian members of the Legislative Council, the Criminal Law Amendment Act was successfully renewed, though with the preventive detention portions removed.

Less than a month later, on 18 April, revolutionaries calling themselves the Indian Republican Army launched a daring raid against police and auxiliary armouries in Chittagong, Bengal. The name of the revolutionary organization and the timing of the raid, which occurred on Good Friday, indicate the strong inspiration provided by the revolutionary history of Ireland. Members of the Indian Republican Army drew inspiration from Irish nationalists who staged a dramatic insurrection in the heart of Dublin on Easter Sunday, 1916. This uprising ultimately sparked a civil war in which the Irish Republican Army and other Irish revolutionary forces succeeded in defeating British colonial rule and achieved independence under the Anglo-Irish Treaty of 1922. As one of the Chittagong raiders later wrote, 'The blood-stained memory of the Easter Revolution of the IRA touched our young minds with fiery enthusiasm!'[106] A number of the revolutionaries avidly read the Irish

[103] Ibid., p. 681. [104] Ibid., p. 682. [105] Ibid., p. 683.

[106] Quoted in Michael Silvestri, *Ireland and India: Nationalism, Empire and Memory* (New York: Palgrave Macmillan, 2009), p. 63. For more on the links between the Indian and Irish revolutionary movements, see also Silvestri, 'The Bomb, *Bhadralok, Bhagavad*

nationalist Dan Breen's *My Fight for Irish Freedom*, leading colonial officials to refer to it as a 'terrorist textbook'.[107] After capturing the armouries and cutting telephone and telegraph wires, the raiders retreated into the hill country surrounding Chittagong to wage an ongoing insurgency against British rule.

On the 19th, Secretary of State William Wedgwood Benn wrote to Lord Irwin promising that he would give his full support to any course of action taken by the viceroy.[108] That day, Irwin promulgated Ordinance No. I of 1930, an emergency law designed to 'suppress terrorist outrages'.[109] This ordinance allowed preventive detention, effectively bringing back into force the aspects of the Criminal Law Amendment Act that were just removed under the new Supplementary Bill. Irwin announced that the emergency created by the armoury raid demonstrated that revolutionaries had 'revived their methods of terrorism'. Irwin declared that the ordinance was meant to demonstrate the resolve of the government in preventing revolutionary outrages and taking all necessary measures to bring the terrorist movement under control.[110]

Gandhi immediately spoke out against both the Chittagong raid and the government's response to it, stating that although it was sad to see violence resorted to, the governor general's exercise of his extraordinary powers demonstrated that 'so long as the British people are determined to impose their rule upon the unwilling people, so long must they rule in reality without law'. Gandhi argued that the executive action of the colonial authorities proved the hollowness of constitutional reforms by shattering the illusion that elected Indians constituted the legislatures. He identified both the violence of government and the violence of revolutionary terrorists as twin opponents to be overcome through the non-violence of the Civil Disobedience movement.[111] Colonial forces surrounded and defeated the bulk of the Chittagong raiders on 22 April. Described by historian Sumit Sarkar as 'the most spectacular coup in the entire history of terrorism',[112] this incident marked the beginning of a new and particularly deadly phase of revolutionary violence in Bengal. Many of the leaders of the raid managed to evade capture and remained a

Gita, and Dan Breen'. The continuities between the earlier and later phases of Indo-Irish alliance are emphasized by Plowman, 'Irish Republicans and the Indo-German Conspiracy'.

[107] Report by R. E. A. Ray, Special Superintendent IB, CID, 1 Jan to 30 June 1927, *Terrorism in Bengal*, vol. 2, p. 603.

[108] SS to V, 19 April 1930, Halifax Collection, NMML, Mss Eur.e.152, p. 64.

[109] *The Bengalee* (20 April 1930), p. 4. [110] Ibid.

[111] *The Bengalee* (22 April 1930), p. 5.

[112] Sarkar, *Swadeshi Movement in Bengal*, p. 287.

thorn in the side of the Bengal Government for up to three years. In August, revolutionaries conducted another assassination attempt against Charles Tegart through a brazen daytime bombing in Dalhousie Square, Calcutta.

Accordingly, the Bengal government had no intention of allowing the ordinance to lapse at the date of its expiry on 19 October. In August, the government asked the Legislative Council to pass an act embodying the necessary elements of the ordinance. Just like the Criminal Law Amendment Act of 1925, the legislation would be limited to a period of five years, in the hope that by the time this period elapsed, 'conditions will have so altered that they can afford to take the risk of doing without this special preventive procedure'. Speaking on behalf of the official position, W. D. R. Prentice asked the Council to 'support Government in its fight against terrorism by giving us the minimum powers which we are convinced are essential'.[113] Prentice promised that the powers would not be used indiscriminately and would only be used against the loosely defined 'terrorist movement', meaning that 'civil disobedience or political agitation are entirely outside its sphere'.[114]

The politician and novelist Naresh Chandra Sen Gupta suggested that if this was indeed the case, the law should be subjected to public scrutiny. He argued that this legislation was in fact a 'negation of law' that would take away 'the elementary rights of the people' and that therefore the people had a right to scrutinize the proposed measures before they entered into force. Acknowledging that even in civilized societies, emergencies sometimes demanded that the government arm itself with special powers, Sen Gupta pointed out that the previous Bengal Criminal Law Amendment Act was still in force during the time of the planning of the Chittagong raid, and therefore clearly did not provide the authorities with any particularly useful tools in preventing this attack. Sen Gupta asserted that the problem with this emergency legislation was that evidence used against an accused terrorist was based on secret information provided by anonymous informants and therefore could not be tested through cross-examination.[115] Prentice opposed the proposal to solicit public opinion with regard to the bill, stating that because the bill followed the exact measures provided under the Act of 1925, public discussion was unnecessary. The motion to circulate the bill for public feedback was defeated by 69 votes to 29.[116]

[113] Bengal Legislative Council Proceedings, Vol. XXXV – Thirty-fifth Session, August 1930, NLI, p. 602.
[114] Ibid. [115] Ibid., pp. 603–5. [116] Ibid., p. 610.

Following this, Sen Gupta proposed that the bill be at least referred to a Select Committee, but this motion was similarly defeated by 65 votes to 25. Next, he proposed amending the duration of the proposed bill from five years to one, noting that in England the suspension of the Habeas Corpus Act was only ever carried out in intervals of one year at a time. He argued that even during the 'darkest days' of the Irish troubles, Habeas Corpus was suspended from year to year and that there was no reason why the same process should not be adopted in Bengal. Narendra Kumar Basu proposed a compromise of two years' duration, expressing the hope that the Simon Commission and Round Table Conference might increase the proportion of Indian elected representatives and that the proposed reforms may alleviate the motivations prompting revolutionary crimes. Prentice retorted that this argument was based on the proposition that political changes could stop the revolutionary movement, an idea that he soundly rejected, stating that 'the movement is entirely different from political agitation'. The proposal to reduce the duration of the bill from five years to two was rejected by 56 votes to 35.[117]

Sen Gupta continued to lead the opposition to the bill, declaring 'we are not advocates for the terrorist; if we are attempting to obstruct the passage of the Bill ... it is because the Bill is going to affect the subjects of the province in general and for the sake of giving adequate protection ... from the attention of the more zealous officers of the police'.[118] Jatindra Nath Basu remarked that the inability of the government to provide a safe trial without resorting to emergency measures served as evidence that the government was unable to fulfil its own basic responsibilities. He went on to say:

> The fact that after 175 years of Britain's connection with India ... a measure like the one which we have been considering should be sought to be placed on the statute book ... shows the failure of British policy in India and the bankruptcy of British statesmanship in dealing with Indian affairs.[119]

Another Indian member, Shanti Shekhareswar Roy, declared that as followers of non-violence, the Indian National Congress condemned the 'cult of the bomb' and said 'we all want to get rid of the terrorist'. Roy stated that real statesmanship would dictate that the feelings of despair underlying these acts of violence must be addressed, rather than a resort to panicked measures of repression that would only succeed in further alienating public opinion. Despite these protests, the bill was passed by a vote of 61 to 15.[120]

[117] Ibid., pp. 621–3. [118] Ibid., p. 625. [119] Ibid., p. 732. [120] Ibid., pp. 732–3.

'The Greatest Enemies of Their Own Country'

The re-introduction of the Bengal Criminal Law Amendment Act did not spell an end to the latest outbreak of revolutionary violence in Bengal. In August 1930, two revolutionaries named Anuja Sen Gupta and Dinesh Chandra Majumdar threw bombs at Charles Tegart's vehicle in Dalhousie Square but failed to kill him. The next day, a revolutionary bombed the Jorabagan police station, with another bomb thrown at the Eden Gardens police station the day after that. The same month, members of the Sri Sangha organization assassinated Lowman, the inspector general of police in Dacca. The following December, three revolutionaries dressed as Europeans shot and killed Lieutenant-Colonel Simpson, the inspector general of prisons. Following this escalation of violence, guards were provided to all district officers to protect them from assassination attempts, although D. R. Prentice, the home member to the Bengal government, remarked that they would provide only a partial protection 'against the rabid kind of terrorist who is prepared to be killed provided he kills first'.[121]

These events occurred within the global context of growing anti-imperial insurgency in places like Palestine, Ireland, Burma, and Cyprus. In 1934, Charles Gwynn published *Imperial Policing*, a manual that remains a classic among counter-insurgency specialists to this day. The book details British operations against a wide range of anti-colonial rebellions, with an emphasis on asymmetrical warfare and the pacification of restive populations. In this manual, Gwynn argued that despite public suspicion regarding the deployment of military forces in support of the civil administration, the army should in fact be used in a preventive capacity, rather than being called in only after the escalation of a disturbance. For Gwynn, policing and pacification were useful and necessary functions of the military. His approach would come to shape Anglo approaches to counter-insurgency operations from Malaya in the late 1940s to the American invasion of Afghanistan and Iraq in the early twenty-first century.[122]

The militarization of imperial policing was evident in the Amritsar massacre, where imperial troops opened fire on a crowd of non-violent protesters, killing hundreds. Beyond India, the rise of anti-colonial nationalisms around the world produced numerous sites of agitation that imperial officials sought to crush with the use of military force and

[121] D. R. Prentice to Sir James Crerar, 5 December 1931, Home Political, NAI, No. 291/1931, p. 22.

[122] Charles Gwynn, *Imperial Policing*, 2nd ed. (London: Macmillan, 1939).

emergency counter-insurgency legislation. A few key examples from the period include the British occupation of Iraq as a mandated territory under the terms of the Treaty of Versailles,[123] communal disturbances resulting from Jewish immigration to Palestine in 1929 and from 1936 to 1939,[124] and the Saya San rebellion in Burma from 1930 to 1932.[125] This context provided the framework within which colonial officials in India sought to understand and police the outbreak of violence triggered by the Chittagong raid.

In India, the situation in Chittagong remained particularly volatile, as several of the absconding raiders managed to avoid arrest and waged an ongoing insurgency from the hills. In April 1931, exactly one year after the initial raid, H. W. Emerson of the Bengal government reported the existence of 'a serious state of affairs both as regards the demoralisation of the official and non-official residents of Chittagong and the widespread sympathy in the district with the revolutionary party'.[126] In response to this situation, the government imposed a curfew that forbade anyone, whether Indian or European, from being out between the hours of 10 p.m. and 4.a.m. without a permit. Security forces established three patrols of two men each to look in on the wives of railway employees who would be home alone while their husbands went off to work and military authorities blocked all roads to the European area, with a 24-hour guard placed. All vehicles entering this area were stopped and searched, although this surveillance did not apply to Europeans.[127] These counter-insurgency measures echoed earlier systems of passes, curfews, and scorched earth employed against Afrikaner and African rebels during the Boer War from 1899 to 1902, and would resurface in later colonial campaigns in Malaya and Kenya.[128]

In October, Emerson reported that a large part of the district of Chittagong was still out of hand and that 'officials and a considerable

[123] Toby Dodge, *Inventing Iraq: The Failure of Nation Building and a History Denied* (New York: Columbia University Press, 2003), pp. 131–56.

[124] Robert Johnson, 'Command of the Army, Charles Gwynn and Imperial Policing: The British Doctrinal Approach to Internal Security in Palestine 1919–29', *Journal of Imperial and Commonwealth History* 43, no. 4 (2015), pp. 570–89, and Jacob Norris, 'Repression and Rebellion: Britain's Response to the Arab Revolt in Palestine of 1936–39', *The Journal of Imperial and Commonwealth History* 36, no. 1 (2008), pp. 25–45.

[125] Maitrii Aung Thwin, *The Return of the Galon King: History, Law, and Rebellion in Colonial Burma* (Athens: Ohio University Press, 2011).

[126] Minute by H. W. Emerson, 23 April 1931, Home Political, NAI, No. 291/1931, pp. 1–2.

[127] Ibid.

[128] Forth, *Barbed Wire Imperialism*, pp. 150–3. See also Caroline Elkins, *Imperial Reckoning: The Untold Story of Britain's Gulag in Kenya* (New York: Henry Holt, 2005).

portion of the civil population is under a reign of terrorism; the initiative is with the terrorists and the prestige of Government is very low indeed'. The Government of Bengal requested new emergency powers under the proposed Emergency Powers Ordinance, including unprecedented measures such as the power to take possession of buildings, to prohibit or limit traffic and regulate the use of transport and railways, as well as imposing collective fines on the inhabitants of particularly turbulent areas. Emerson wrote that even the introduction of these extreme measures did not go far enough and that he would prefer the imposition of martial law, as military support would improve moral and reduce the opposition of the civil population.[129]

The Bengal government's appeal for an extension of its special powers in this period was markedly more dire in tone than even the alarmist appeals of 1925.[130] This stemmed from a belief that 'terrorism' was no longer the result of a small group of irreconcilables, but now enjoyed the support of a growing proportion of the population. Many believed that 'the authority of Government has practically ceased to function' and that 'the majority of the Hindu population are definitely hostile'. The growing hysteria was the result of an information panic within the rural *mofussil*, where intelligence sources reported a complete breakdown of the information order. The CID found itself totally incapable of acquiring relevant intelligence on Surya Sen, the leader of the Armoury Raid, and his close followers who remained at large, and officials believed that even where information was available informants suffered from a loss of morale that rendered them unwilling to seek it out. By contrast, the CID reported, 'The gang of revolutionaries are fully informed of all movements against them and ... they find it a simple matter to defeat any half-hearted attempts that are made.'[131]

Widespread among officials was the perception that the government's inability to detect and arrest the phantom 'terrorists' was fatally undermining the authority and legitimacy of the state. Such a perception was heightened by the belief that 'if the morale of the local administration were satisfactory and the prestige of Government normal, necessary operations could be carried out without additional powers'. Taking

[129] Emerson to India Office, 19 October 1931, Home Political, NAI, No. 291/1931, pp. 4–6.

[130] Kama Maclean describes the anxieties of colonial officials and European expatriates throughout the interwar period in 'The Art of Panicking Quietly: British Expatriate Responses to "Terrorist Outrages" in India, 1912–33', in Fischer-Tiné (ed.), *Anxieties, Fear and Panic*, pp. 135–67.

[131] Political situation arising out of terrorist activity in Bengal, 1 November 1931, Home Political, NAI, No. 291/1931, p. 10.

strong action against the revolutionary movement required information, but the CID believed that such information would not be forthcoming 'until the population realise beyond any doubt that Government are masters of the situation'. To achieve this, officials proposed strong measures for controlling the movement of people, goods, and information within the affected areas, as a way of displaying to the people 'that Government are in earnest'.[132]

In this context, the language of terrorism took on an enhanced and particularly urgent meaning. In a letter to R. N. Reid, the chief secretary to the governor of Bengal, W. H. Nelson stated that terrorists 'should be treated as persons who have been exposed to infection from plague and should be isolated till the danger of their spreading it is over'. He further argued that police needed unlimited authority to keep an eye on anyone under suspicion, to demand proof of identity when desired, and to control the movement of individuals within designated areas. According to Nelson, police 'should not hesitate to shoot a man who attempted to run away when called on to halt'.[133] A government report on the topic likewise adopted the language of infectious disease, noting that 'if this plague spot is not dealt with summarily it will continue to contaminate the rest of the Province'.[134]

The question of how best to reassert governmental authority also prompted considerable discussion regarding whether counter-insurgency operations should be carried out by the police, the military, or by a joint operation between the two. In the past, the military was unwilling 'to undertake what they regard as police duties' and this was complicated by the fact that it was 'extremely difficult to define exactly what police duties are, [and] the civil authorities were afraid lest the military assistance might not give the relief to the police that was desirable'. The possibility of military deployment in Chittagong also raised the question of whether the province or the Government of India would be liable to cover the expenses.[135] The official stance of the Bengal government was a desire for the best of both worlds: 'You can be perfectly certain that we shall welcome the use of troops to show the flag, and that difficulties will only arise, if we are called upon to agree to pay for them.'[136]

[132] Ibid.
[133] W. H. Nelson to R. N. Reid, 17 September 1931, Home Political, NAI, No. 291/1931, pp. 19–20.
[134] Notes on the situation at Chittagong, November 1931, Home Political, NAI, No. 291/1931, p. 33.
[135] Ibid., p. 11.
[136] Bengal Criminal Law Amendment Ordinance, 29 October 1931, Home Political, NAI, No. 291/1931, p. 16.

Aside from the use of force and surveillance, the new secretary of state, Sir Samuel Hoare, suggested that the mass support of students should be enlisted by appealing to their self-interest. Hoare recommended adopting a policy by which the commission of terrorist crimes in precincts of educational institutions or by students belonging to any particular college or school would render all students from the relevant institution ineligible for government employment. Hoare saw it as inconsistent for the government to employ youths who allowed crime against government officials to be organized among them.[137] After consulting governors in Madras, Bombay, Burma, and elsewhere, Irwin wrote back to inform Hoare that the idea was universally rejected by all local governments. As numerous officials pointed out, the plan would not act as a deterrent to revolutionaries, who advocated the boycott of government services anyway, and would therefore accomplish nothing other than to enhance public resentment and increase sympathy for the revolutionary movement. Irwin suggested that a better approach would be to crack down on discipline within schools, but worried that the situation was likely to escalate significantly 'before there is anything like a general revolt against terrorists'.[138]

The repressive measures adopted by the colonial government did indeed attract widespread criticism, particularly given the broader context of the repression of the Congress-led Civil Disobedience campaign. In the Bengal Legislative Council, Munindra Deb Rai Mahasai criticized what he referred to as 'police terrorism', stating that the imposition of these 'lawless laws gave the police a splendid opportunity for the exhibition of their autocratic powers'. Mahasai asserted that the existing laws did not justify indiscriminate use of the lathi or the baton in breaking the heads of unarmed civil resisters, and said that it was 'a standing disgrace to any civilised Government to encourage the revival of this relic of the barbaric age in the twentieth century'. Mahasai went on to implore the government 'in the name of civilisation and humanity' to 'save the people from police terrorism'.[139]

As revolutionary attacks continued unabated into 1932, the Bengal government introduced the Suppression of Terrorist Outrages Act, the first piece of legislation in Bengal to explicitly name terrorism within its title. The government intended this act to replace the powers granted under the Emergency Powers Ordinance, which was due to lapse. These

137 Hoare to Irwin, 28 September 1931, Home Political, NAI, No. 4/35/31, p. 3.
138 Irwin to Hoare, 24 October 1931, Home Political, NAI, No. 4/35/31, p. 27.
139 Proceedings of the Bengal Legislative Council, Thirty-Eighth Session, 23 March 1932, NLI, Vol. 38, No. 3, p. 481.

included the power to detain and question anyone 'behaving suspiciously', to take possession of property, imposition of collective fines in 'turbulent' areas, as well as general powers of search. The provisions were specifically targeted against the ongoing troubled situation in Chittagong, although they could be extended to any part of Bengal by the governor general in Council. The other part of the bill, which provided for the use of special magistrates in trying 'terrorist' crimes, extended to the whole of Bengal immediately.[140]

Again, Narendra Kumar Basu spearheaded opposition to the bill, and argued that if repressive laws were effective at suppressing terrorism, they would have succeeded by now. He referred to the Government of India's reliance on ruling through ordinances as evidence of the bankruptcy of its statesmanship, and said that the reliance upon emergency laws demonstrated that the colonial administration had in fact ceased to function. Basu contended that the true underlying causes of revolutionary violence were political and economic in nature, and that reducing unemployment would be a far more effective strategy of counter-insurgency than the continued imposition of repressive laws.[141] Despite these and other objections, the bill was passed by a vote of 58 to 12.[142]

The government was not wholly blind to the economic argument put forward by Basu, however. At a speech given to the European Association in January 1934, Viceroy and Governor General Lord Willingdon declared that although the terrorist movement had existed for some time, it was fuelled in the past few years by the massive economic instability caused by the Great Depression that followed the Wall Street stock market crash of 1929. Although Willingdon referred to terrorists as 'the greatest enemies of their own country', he acknowledged that support for the movement was exacerbated by unemployment and a lack of career prospects for an increasingly educated youth.[143]

Although revolutionary attacks fell into marked decline from 1934 onwards and never ultimately resurfaced to such devastating effect for the duration of British rule, this does not mean that 'terrorism' ceased to be a concern for Europeans or for colonial officials in India. By 1935, revolutionary crime was substantially reduced, with only a few sporadic incidents in comparison to regular murders that occurred throughout the period from 1930 to 1934. H. W. Hale attributed this in part to the mass

140 R. N. Reid, Statement of Objects and Reasons, Bengal Criminal Law Amendment Act, 1 August 1932, IOR: L/PJ/7/399, p. 1.
141 Bengal Legislative Council debates, 6 September 1932, IOR/L/PJ/7/399, pp. 4–5.
142 Ibid., p. 132.
143 Speech by Lord Willingdon, 8 January 1934, Home Political, NAI, File No. 70/34-Poll, p. 14.

conversion of many revolutionaries to communist methods during this period, necessitating the building up of a mass base rather than individual acts of violence or political assassination.[144] During this period, new discourses surrounding the potential for terrorists to be 'reformed' also acquired fresh prominence, the idea being that if the malleability of the 'native mind' had made young Bengalis susceptible to revolutionary propaganda in the first place, they could similarly be reshaped into 'good citizens' through the pedagogical tools of colonial discipline.[145]

Still, officials continued to view terrorism as an active and ongoing threat to imperial security. At a speech given at a police parade in Dacca in 1935, Sir John Anderson, the governor of Bengal, said that although 'outrages' had declined, 'yet the terrorist virus is still active and malignant'. Anderson said that the persistence of conspiracies, even after the arrest of so many revolutionary leaders, revealed how deep-seated the 'poison' of terrorism had become. Arguing that the apparent decline in revolutionary crimes was only a result of the secret measures being undertaken for the good of the public by colonial intelligence services, Anderson argued that counter-insurgency measures could not be relaxed for even a moment.[146] Speaking at an Armistice Day dinner later in the year, Anderson expressed his appreciation for the soldiers of Bengal before going on to say that the conflict with terrorism could not be ended at any predetermined hour. He further declared, 'There can be no armistice with terrorism so long as there remain organisations that possess the will and may acquire the means to do mischief.' Claiming that the initiative had now passed into the hands of the government, Anderson cautioned that they should not 'win the war merely in order to lose the peace. We shall not relax our vigilance or neglect our front.'[147]

The obsession with terrorism as an ongoing 'menace' was also reflected in the press. In 1936, *The Statesman* published an article titled 'How War Is Waged on Terrorism', which referred to terrorism as an ongoing menace that was never fully eradicated, much like the 'thug' menace of the nineteenth century. The article declared that terrorism was not simply a matter of 'periodic outbursts of violence which attract public attention', but argued rather that in dealing with terrorism, the government was dealing with organizations that were in continuous operation for 30 years. According to the article:

[144] Hale, *Terrorism in India*, IOR: L/P&J/12/403, p. 7.
[145] Silvestri, *Policing 'Bengali Terrorism'*, pp. 158–67.
[146] Speech by Sir John Anderson, 11 July 1935, NLI, GP320.95415b436, p. 27.
[147] Speech by Anderson, 11 November 1935, NLI, GP320.95415b436, p. 140.

> Terrorism is never 'over now'. The army withdraws from the field of battle, perhaps to plan another attack or perhaps to develop some new strategical scheme or perhaps to form fresh alliances. ... On previous occasions Government has disbanded its 'army' immediately after a battle was over. This merely gave the enemy a chance to reorganize its scattered forces and prepare for a fresh attack.[148]

The article went on to say that while the majority of Bengalis were not necessarily disloyal, they were 'helpless against organized terrorism'. The author expressed with certainty the belief that, 'Another fresh attack is being planned ... So-called "public opinion" cannot be reached ... as long as the public see that the revolutionary forces are gathering strength day by day.'[149]

Reports submitted by colonial intelligence officials during this period also reflected this belief. By the late 1930s, the CID were operating in a state of almost perpetual emergency. In a report submitted in 1938, C. Fairweather warned that 'the next wave of revolution is being planned on a scale much greater than Bengal has ever known' and 'the ordinary civil or police powers will be unable to deal effectively with the numbers involved'.[150] Two months later, Fairweather warned that the widespread disaffection being promoted by nationalist agitators was 'a new form of sedition with which our penal code was never intended to deal'.[151]

Although studies of the revolutionary movement tend to ignore the period after 1935, one of the most significant assassinations in the movement's history occurred in 1940, during the Second World War. In February of that year Sir Samuel Hoare, a member of Churchill's War Cabinet, warned that failure to come to terms with the Congress leadership could result in a 'period of civil disobedience, if not of terrorism'.[152] This prediction was proven right in mid-March, when a Punjabi Sikh named Udham Singh shot and killed the former governor of Punjab, Sir Michael O'Dwyer, following a speech at Caxton Hall in London.[153] O'Dwyer had been governor at the time of the infamous Amritsar massacre in 1919. Not to be confused with General Reginald Dyer, who gave the order to fire on the demonstrators at Jallianwala Bagh, O'Dwyer was nonetheless widely reviled for having endorsed Dyer's actions. In a memoir written in 1925, O'Dwyer presented the Jallianwala Bagh

[148] *The Statesman* (27 July 1936), p. 18. [149] Ibid.

[150] Weekly CID Report, 27 October 1938, IOR: L/P&J/12/401, p. 7.

[151] Weekly CID Report, 1 December 1938, IOR: L/P&J/12/401, p. 23.

[152] Samuel Hoare in War Cabinet, 2 February 1940, CAB 65/5/30, TNA.

[153] The best recent account of this assassination and the circumstances leading up to it is Anita Anand, *The Patient Assassin: A True Tale of Massacre, Revenge, and India's Quest for Independence* (New York: Scribner, 2019).

massacre as a clash between 'the defiant Amritsar rebels and the forces of law and order'. O'Dwyer agreed with Dyer's assessment that the massacre had been a necessary show of force that prevented discontent in Amritsar from spreading elsewhere, describing Dyer's actions as appropriate and correct.[154]

During Singh's trial the prosecutor, G. B. McClure, quoted a statement allegedly made by Singh that read, 'I did it because I had a grudge against him. I do not belong to any society or anything else.'[155] Through the early phases of his trial, Singh is said to have exhibited a nonchalant attitude, reportedly saying at one point, 'I do not mind dying. ... You want to die when you are young. That is good and that is what I am doing.'[156] An anti-colonial radical who had previously been arrested in the late 1920s for possessing illegal firearms and copies of Ghadar propaganda, Singh's assassination of O'Dwyer was almost certainly a political act of revenge in response to the latter's heavy-handed suppression of revolutionaries during his tenure as governor of Punjab, and his endorsement of Dyer's actions at Jallianwala Bagh in particular.[157] While some newspapers reported on the incident with colourful headlines such as 'Hindoo runs amok at London meeting', most referred to the incident as a calculated assassination and referred to Singh as a 'Terrorist'.[158] In Parliament, Clement Attlee referred to the assassination as an 'abominable outrage', while W. Davidson asked Chamberlain if adequate protection was being given to other officials associated with India to protect them from similar 'fanatics'.[159]

Although the most well-reported, the killing of O'Dwyer was not the only political assassination that occurred in this period. The chaos of the war years saw a return of political dissent and popular unrest reminiscent of the early 1930s. New plots were hatched and new assassinations carried out, including the murder in 1941 of Kripal Singh, the spy who had been instrumental in foiling Rash Behari Bose's abortive northern India uprising back in 1915.[160] Although labour unrest, communism, communal tensions between Hindus and Muslims, and the widespread nationalism promoted by Congress absorbed much of the attention of colonial authorities through the 1940s, terrorism remained a constant concern right up until independence.

[154] Michael O'Dwyer, *India As I Knew It* (London: Constable & Company, 1925), pp. 283–5.
[155] *The Times of India* (5 June 1940), p. 7.
[156] *South China Morning Post* (3 April 1940), p. 9.
[157] Ramnath, *Haj to Utopia*, pp. 235–6. See also Anand, *The Patient Assassin*.
[158] *The Canberra Times* (15 March 1940), p. 1; *The New York Times* (6 June 1940), p. 5.
[159] HC Deb, 14 March 1940, vol. 358, cc. 1372–3. [160] Lahiri, *Rashbehari Bose*, p. 48.

Conclusion

Although the existing historiography regards the terms 'revolutionary' and 'terrorism' as largely interchangeable, the shift in governmental labelling of political radicals from revolutionaries to terrorists in fact marked a deliberate strategy within the 'prose of counter-insurgency'. Following the rise of Gandhi's non-cooperation campaign in the early 1920s, British officials began to consciously adopt the term 'terrorism' in 1925 as part of an attempt to render the Bengal Criminal Law Amendment Act more palatable to the British Parliament. By the 1930s, the term 'terrorism' became the standard label applied to revolutionary nationalists, despite the relatively infrequent usages of this term during the period before and during the First World War. Within the context of an increasingly assertive nationalist movement with a broadening base of popular support, the label of 'terrorism' became a useful way of delegitimizing the tactics of revolutionaries while simultaneously justifying the creeping expansion of executive rule, during precisely the same period in which colonial authorities were ostensibly devolving a share of power to elected Indian legislatures. Through this process, the figure of the 'terrorist' came to be constructed as an intangible threat that could be held up against the prospect of reform, even after terrorist crimes underwent a drastic decline after 1934.

The proliferation of this emergency legislation from the 1930s on highlights the empty nature of the Morley-Minto reforms by indicating the limits that executive discretion placed on the practical power of the elected legislatures. Although the Legislative Council in Bengal and the Indian Legislative Assembly provided important sites of debate and resistance within which Indian politicians could express their opposition to new emergency laws, the ultimate ability of the governor general to bypass the assemblies and certify these laws using his executive power indicates the truth behind Carl Schmitt's dictum that the sovereign is he who decides on the exception. By carefully deploying the vocabulary of terrorism in criminalizing the politics of Indian revolutionaries, the colonial state demonstrated the core of executive sovereignty that lay beneath the thin veneer of its legislative reforms. By deploying the category of 'terrorism' as the exception to the rule of law, colonial officials constructed an enemy wholly outside of the law, against whom only extra-legal solutions would suffice. This discourse also reaffirmed the 'elementary duty' of the colonial state in 'protecting' the people of India from terrorists, thus providing a plank of moral legitimacy at a time when colonialism as a system of government was coming under sustained domestic and international pressure.

5 Terrorism as a 'World Crime'

The British Empire, International Law, and the Invention of Global Terrorism

From 1 to 16 November 1937, the League of Nations hosted a special diplomatic conference with the goal of passing the world's first international law to target terrorism as a distinct category of crime. Among a diverse range of nation-states represented at the conference, twenty-four signed the Convention for the Prevention and Punishment of Terrorism. This convention was the result of a three-year process of drafting and debates undertaken by a Committee of Experts composed of representatives from Belgium, Britain, Chile, France, Hungary, Italy, Poland, Roumania, Spain, Switzerland, and the USSR. The Council of the League of Nations appointed this committee on 10 December 1934, following the highly publicized assassination of King Alexander I of Yugoslavia and Louis Barthou, the French foreign minister, by members of the Internal Macedonian Revolutionary Organization two months earlier in Marseilles. The assassination attracted international attention, particularly because it was the first regicide ever caught on film.[1] The assassin, a Bulgarian named Vlado Chernozemski, was immediately apprehended by French police with such violence that he died of his injuries. His co-conspirators escaped to Italy where they were safe from extradition due to an 1870 law that deliberately omitted political crimes from the list of extraditable offences.

The assassination of Alexander I was by no means the first incident of its kind, but was situated in a long history of internationally prominent assassinations that spanned the length of the nineteenth and early twentieth centuries. Early attempts to tackle 'assassinationism' and 'anarchism' through international legislation included the 'International Conference for the Defense of Society against the Anarchists' in 1898 and the St. Petersburg Protocol of 1904, as Chapter 2 has shown. Many of the same concerns that animated the formulation of the

[1] Although the video does not capture the murder itself on camera, both the build-up and aftermath were filmed and are now readily available online. See, for example, http://publicdomainreview.org/collections/live-footage-of-king-alexanders-assassination-1934/.

St. Petersburg Protocol were shared by the Committee of Experts in drafting the international Terrorism Convention of 1937. By this time, however, the category of anarchism was definitively replaced by a new target of international concern through the concept of 'terrorism'.

The novelty of this category meant that the first difficulty in drafting a counter-terrorism convention lay in establishing a precise legal definition for what terrorism actually was. To this end, the Committee of Experts held three meetings between 1935 and 1937.[2] At these meetings, they examined a series of proposals made by thirteen different governments, along with advice from relevant experts such as the International Criminal Police Commission based out of Vienna.[3] Throughout this drafting process, a number of important debates took place regarding the relationship between terrorism and politics, the problematic tautology of defining terrorism as an action that causes terror, as well as the tensions between international law and questions of territory and sovereignty. The convention ultimately compelled signatories to criminalize terrorist offences within their borders, while recommending that such offences should be exempt from the protection from extradition provided by the existing international law with regard to political offences.[4] The main function of the convention, however, was its goal to establish an internationally acceptable definition for terrorism as a distinct global category of crime. As such, it is the specificities of this definition that are of central importance to the current chapter.

In attempting to reach a consensus regarding an intelligible definition for 'terrorism', each representative came at the topic with their own ideas about political violence, usually motivated by their own national interests. Roumania proposed the idea of drafting a League of Nations treaty targeting terrorism back in 1926, and it was the Roumanian delegate, Professor M. Pella, who acted as chair of the Committee of Experts. The strong Roumanian presence in the 1937 debates can be explained by the recent assassination of Prime Minister Ion G. Duca in 1933 due to his attempt to suppress the Iron Guard, an ultra-nationalist fascist movement, which lent urgency to Roumania's position. Representative Koukai of Czechoslovakia also played a disproportionately vocal role in

[2] The first session took place some point during April and May of 1935, the second session was in January 1936, and the third and final session occurred in April 1937.

[3] League of Nations Archives, Geneva, 11 April 1935. Communications from International Organizations, International Criminal Police Commission, C.R.T. 2. This commission had been formed in 1923, with the aim of targeting the 'common enemy of humankind: the ordinary criminal.' See Deflem, *Policing World Society*, pp. 124–52.

[4] Ben Saul, 'The Legal Response of the League of Nations to Terrorism', *Journal of International Criminal Justice* 4, no. 1 (2006), p. 3.

Figure 5.1 Police chase after the assassin of King Alexander I of Yugoslavia during a state visit to Marseille. This high-profile killing provided the catalyst for a special League of Nations convention on international terrorism. (Photo by © Hulton-Deutsch Collection / CORBIS / Corbis via Getty Images.)

the debates, likely due to Czechoslovak fears triggered by the activities of the *Ordnersgruppe*, a paramilitary organization composed of ethnic Germans formed in 1933, who would go on to receive Nazi backing in 1938 prior to the German annexation of the Sudetenland. Sir John Fischer Williams, the British representative, also played a key role in the proceedings, although the British government never had any intention of signing on to the convention. An impressive scholar who produced books on international law, the League, and the League's goal of international peace, Williams consistently sought to steer the discussions in a way that reflected Britain's commitment to the right to political asylum guaranteed by the international law of the time.[5] When the representative for the Government of India, Sir Denys Bray, became indisposed, Williams also stood in for India and put forward India's main contribution to the convention, a clause regarding the sale and circulation of firearms.[6]

Despite the richness of these discussions, the Convention for the Prevention and Punishment of Terrorism has received very little scholarly attention, notwithstanding a recent outpouring of interest in the history of interwar internationalism and the League of Nations.[7] This is

[5] For some of Williams' earlier writings, see John Fischer Williams, *Some Aspects of the Covenant of the League of Nations* (London: 1934) and *International Change and International Peace* (London: Oxford University Press, 1932).

[6] International Conference on the Repression of Terrorism, Report by Sir Denys Bray, 1937, IOR: L/PJ/8/583, p. 223.

[7] For a review of the recent literature, see Susan Pedersen, 'Back to the League of Nations', *The American Historical Review* 11, no 4 (2007), pp. 1091–1117. For some of the recent scholarship on internationalism, see especially Glenda Sluga and Patricia Clavin (eds.), *Internationalisms: A Twentieth-Century History* (Cambridge: Cambridge University Press, 2016), Glenda Sluga, *Internationalism in the Age of Nationalism* (Philadelphia: University of Pennsylvania Press, 2013), Armitage, *Foundations of International Thought*, Daniel Gorman, *The Emergence of International Society in the 1920s* (Cambridge: Cambridge University Press, 2012), Mark Mazower, *Governing the World: The History of an Idea* (London: Allen Lane, 2012), and Margaret Macmillan, *Peacemakers: The Paris Conference of 1919 and Its Attempt to End War* (London: John Murray, 2001). For some of the recent work on the League of Nations specifically, see Susan Pedersen, *The Guardians: The League of Nations and the Crisis of Empire* (Oxford: Oxford University Press, 2015), Ruth Henig, *The League of Nations: The Peace Conferences of 1919–1923 and Their Aftermath* (London: Haus Histories, 2010), Patricia Clavin, 'Europe and the League of Nations', in Robert Gerwath (ed), *Twisted Paths: Europe 1914–1945* (Oxford: Oxford University Press, 2008), pp. 325–54 and Anne-Isabelle Richard, 'Competition and Complementarity: Civil Society Networks and the Question of Decentralizing the League of Nations', *Journal of Global History* 7, no. 2 (2012), pp. 233–56. Older scholarship on the League of Nations includes F. S. Northedge, *The League of Nations* (Leicester: Leicester University Press, 1986), F. P. Walters, *A History of the League* (New York: Oxford University Press, 1952), George Egerton, *Great Britain and the League of Nations* (London: Scholar Press, 1979), and *The League of Nations in Retrospect: Proceedings of the Symposium*, organized by the United Nations Library and the Graduate Institute of International Studies, 6–9 November 1980 (Berlin: Walter de Gruyter, 1983).

partly because with the breakdown of the League of Nations during the Second World War and its dissolution thereafter, the convention never entered into force. As a result, despite the interest it generated at the time and the fact that it attracted twenty-four initial signatories, the convention was only ever ratified by one country, India. In becoming signatories to the convention, the representatives of the twenty-four countries involved were expressing their willingness to move forward with the convention on the condition of ratification by their home governments. Because of the disruption of the Second World War, only the Government of India ever finished the ratification process signifying formal consent to abide by the terms of the convention.[8] Historian Ben Saul argues that despite these apparent failings, the convention provides important insight into more recent debates regarding terrorism and international law, which have largely replicated the ideas and problematics initially laid out in the discussions of the mid-1930s.[9]

While this is certainly true, the other important historical significance of this convention is the insight it provides into the origins of terrorism as a legal and political idea rooted in the international context of the interwar period. The convention is particularly important for understanding the processes through which terrorism emerged as a tool of government discourse in late colonial India, as explored in previous chapters. A closer look at India's role in this convention provides new and important ways of understanding the larger context in which colonial officials framed their ideas about terrorism as a new and particularly dangerous form of global criminality, a 'world crime' that threatened not only the governing structures of an existing political regime, but rather the very notion of civilization itself. In particular, India's anomalous position as the only non-self-governing member of the League makes its enthusiasm for labelling acts of political violence with the emerging internationally recognizable trope of 'terrorism' all the more intelligible. In signing on to the convention, the Government of India sought to secure international recognition for its existing domestic policies towards anti-colonial violence and, in doing so, it participated within a larger international discussion regarding the relationship between terrorism and domestic authority.

[8] The signatories were Albania, Belgium, Bulgaria, Czechoslovakia, Estonia, France, Greece, Monaco, the Netherlands, Norway, Roumania, Spain, and Yugoslavia from Europe, Argentina, Cuba, the Dominican Republic, Ecuador, Haiti, Peru, and Venezuela from the Americas, as well as Turkey, the USSR, Egypt, and India.

[9] Saul, 'The Legal Response of the League of Nations to Terrorism', pp. 78–102.

'A Political Curiosity'

Although India had long been the centre of multiple complex interregional trading networks, it was the First World War that catapulted it onto the international stage in a more formal manner.[10] Indian members played an active role at the Imperial Conference of London in 1907, with participation to such conferences restricted prior to this time because India was considered a mere dependency. As a result of India's massive contribution to the British war effort, India attended the first meeting of the Imperial War Cabinet in March 1917, with the secretary of state for India as its representative. India was afforded a status different to that of the Crown Colonies, as Lord Satyendra Prasanno Sinha and the Maharajah of Bikaner were also invited to attend. At the end of the session, British Prime Minister David Lloyd George announced that in all subsequent sessions of the Imperial Cabinet, whether in war or peace, India was to be separately represented by an Indian dignitary, with the secretary of state sitting as a member of the British Cabinet from then onwards. From June to September of 1918, Lord Sinha served as the Indian member, with the Maharajah of Patiala also attending. For the final session from December 1918 to January of 1919, Lord Sinha and the Maharajah of Bikaner took part as full members.[11]

Participation in the Imperial War Cabinet helped justify India's inclusion at the Paris peace negotiations in 1919, following the end of the war. As India's representative, alongside the Maharajah of Bikaner and the secretary of state, Sinha declared that the international position of India should not be differentiated from that of the Dominions with regard to its inclusion in the League of Nations. Sinha stated that although India was neither an independent state nor power, this was equally true of Canada, Australia, New Zealand, and South Africa. From the standpoint of international law, Sinha maintained that the position of India was exactly the same as that of the Dominions, none of which constituted a sovereign state with an independent foreign policy. Although Sinha acknowledged that the Dominions exercised greater internal autonomy, he pointed out that from a strictly legal point of view, the British Parliament was constitutionally able to legislate for the whole British Empire, and as such it should make no difference whether Britain's interference was more constant or continuous in India than in the Dominions.[12]

[10] See Metcalf, *Imperial Connections*.
[11] Note by Satyendra Prasanno Sinha, 22 January 1919, FO 608, PRO, Files 1614/5/1 to 1633/1/1, p. 257.
[12] Ibid.

Beyond these technical points, Sinha argued that the case for India's inclusion in the League of Nations could also be made on broader grounds. Referring to the British Empire as the 'best model' for a League of Nations, Sinha used the evidence of the Imperial Conferences to indicate that India's international standing could only be understood on equal terms with that of the Dominions. Noting that India's representation at these conferences marked a 'successive and continuous advance', Sinha remarked that it would be inconceivable that the British government could now backtrack on this position. As Sinha pointed out, any differentiation now between India and the Dominions 'will be looked upon not only as retrogression but a denial of privileges granted under the stress of war but withdrawn as soon as the pressure was removed'. Referring to the political consequences of denying India a place within the League as 'deplorable', Sinha also pointed out that the other Great Powers would be aware of India's massive contribution to the war effort and would not force a decision that would create difficulties within the empire. Noting that the League was to serve as a permanent institution, Sinha observed that it was not desirable to exclude a country with India's 'past traditions and glorious civilisation'.[13] As the terms of the debate moved into the public sphere, Sir J. C. Coyajee, a professor at Andhra University, later went so far as to claim that India's ancient tradition of non-violence was identical to the League's interest in disarmament, arguing that 'Indian mentality and culture have been ready for many centuries to welcome the advent of an institution like the League'.[14]

Because the Covenant of the League of Nations was made part of the Versailles Treaty, and because India obtained a place as a signatory to this treaty, India became an original member of the League on what could be termed a technicality. Although the Versailles Treaty was signed on 28 June 1919, the Covenant of the League became a separate treaty on 10 January 1920, after ratification by all signatories. As Article 1 of the League Covenant specified, subsequent membership would be open only to any 'fully self-governing State or Dominion or Colony not named in the Annex',[15] making India's role within the League a 'political curiosity' from the very beginning.[16] Writing an account of India's place within the League in 1932, V. S. Ram and B. M. Sharma referred to India's inclusion as an 'important departure in British Foreign Policy', that

[13] Ibid., pp. 258–60.
[14] J. C. Coyajee, *India and the League of Nations* (Madras: Waltair, 1932), p. iii.
[15] V. S. Ram and B. M. Sharma, *India and the League of Nations* (Lucknow: The Upper India Publishing House Ltd., 1932), p. 35.
[16] Ibid., p. 139.

Figure 5.2 The first session of the League of Nations in Geneva. India became the only non-self-governing member of the League as a result of the place afforded to it at the Paris peace negotiations following the First World War.
(Photo by Hulton Archive via Getty Images.)

'completely changed the international position of this country'.[17] As Ram and Sharma pointed out, India held no claim to membership under the rules laid out in Article 1, and if India had not become a member of the League through its role as a signatory of the Versailles Treaty, the country 'would have remained outside this important international body for a long time'.[18]

Such an anomalous position nonetheless raised important questions regarding what the label of 'India' actually meant, as well as how imperial sovereignty was to be understood. India during this period was not a cohesive political unit, and the political geography of the princely states raised important questions regarding how India as a category was to be understood at the level of the international.[19] India was composed of both the territories under direct British rule as well as a collection of hundreds of princely states ranging widely in territory and population across the span of the subcontinent. Local rulers administered these states under the watchful eye of British residents, and maintained a semblance of domestic independence constrained by ultimate British control over key features of sovereignty such as foreign affairs and succession. Although the princes comprised a diverse mosaic representing many different religions, priorities, and personalities, they shared much in common as a distinct social class within India, making it possible to speak – to some extent at least – of a broad princely order with some overarching features.[20] Despite the stereotypes of backwardness and barbarism that colonial authorities often deployed in the pursuance of British claims to civilizational superiority, the British attitude towards the princely states was broadly positive, given the inherently conservative tendencies of the princes. As a result, the states played a key role in the constitutional progression of India through the 1920s and 1930s, as the British increasingly came to see them as a counterweight to the growing influence of the Indian National Congress.[21]

Despite a domestically divided political landscape, India's status within the League allowed it to present a united front at the level of the

[17] Ibid., p. 137. [18] Ibid., p. 138.

[19] Stephen Legg, 'An International Anomaly?: Sovereignty, the League of Nations and India's Princely Geographies', *Journal of Historical Geography* 43 (2014), pp. 104–7.

[20] Ian Copland, *The Princes of India in the Endgame of Empire* (Cambridge: Cambridge University Press, 1997), p. 12.

[21] For more on the princely states of India, see Steven Ashton, *British Policy towards the Indian States* (London: Curzon, 1982), Barbara Ramusack, *The Princes of India in the Twilight of Empire: Dissolution of a Patron-Client System, 1914–1939* (Columbus: Ohio State University Press, 1978), and Robin Jeffrey (ed.), *People, Princes, and Paramount Power: Society and Politics in the Indian Princely States* (Delhi: Oxford University Press, 1978).

international. There it was to be regarded as a single political unit, at least from a purely legal standpoint, although the reality of this position was, of course, much more complicated. In an article printed in 1930, Dr Lanka Sundaram asserted that because international law did not recognize any cleavage between British India and the princely states, the juridical unity of India was definitely established and tacitly recognized by the League.[22] The most significant consequence of this juridical unity is that, according to historian Sunil Amrith, it 'allowed Asian colonial states and Asian nationalist intellectuals without state power to envisage their place in a world of nations'.[23]

The Indian delegation consisted of three members, one of whom was always a native prince. The Government of India appointed this delegation, which was not responsible to the Indian legislature, or to the Indian people more broadly. These delegates held the authority to participate in directing the affairs of the international community, while simultaneously lacking any right to govern the affairs of their own country. This contradictory relationship raised important questions regarding the role of the Indian delegation at Geneva, and its relationship to the delegation of Great Britain and its empire. The British Empire, after all, entered the League commanding six delegates - and thus six votes - due to the inclusion of the United Kingdom, Australia, New Zealand, Canada, South Africa, and India. Although each was recognized as a separate member, in practice the British delegation consulted extensively with the others before providing any formal position to the Assembly of the League.[24] India's position in the League represented an inherent contradiction, reflecting on the one hand a new international role filled with potential opportunities, and on the other a retrenchment or even expansion of the British Empire's international clout.

India's League delegation, however, should not be thought of simply as a second – or indeed, a sixth – British vote in the Assembly, even though this was often the case in practice. In some cases, the Indian delegation did take a position different to that of the British delegation. At the Genoa Maritime Conference of 1920, for example, the secretary of state instructed the Indian delegation to secure special treatment for Indian seamen involved in British shipping, even though there was a concerted effort on the part of the other empire delegations to limit

[22] Lanka Sundaram, 'The International Status of India', Reprinted from *Journal of Royal Institute of International Affairs* (July 1930), LNA: 1A/19516/19516, p. 452.
[23] Sunil Amrith, 'Internationalising Health in the Twentieth Century', in Sluga and Clavin (eds.), *Internationalisms*, p. 253.
[24] Ram and Sharma, *India and the League of Nations*, pp. 145–6.

Indian involvement in British shipping. The British and Indian delegations were similarly at odds over the question of compulsory disinfection of Indian wool, which was raised at the International Labour Conferences of 1921 and 1924. Despite British insistence that the failure of India to fall in line with the British proposal for compulsory disinfection would result in a charge on British industry, the Indian delegates took a firm stance and rejected the proposed measures.[25] Although the two were not necessarily at odds over the issue, the Indian and British delegations also took different positions regarding the Convention for the Prevention and Punishment of Terrorism of 1937. In this case, the Government of India ultimately ratified the convention, viewing it as useful in the policing of anti-colonial revolutionary politics, while the British delegation refused to sign, citing aspects of the convention that were deemed antithetical to British traditions of political freedom.[26]

Despite these small examples of the Indian delegation exercising some autonomy in its international positions, the nature of the Government of India and its relationship to the secretary of state ensured that ultimate sovereignty always rested with Britain. Although the choice of delegates rested in the Government of India, which at the time was still dominated by British colonial officials, this government was only itself accountable to the secretary of state and thus the British Parliament by extension. In this way, the secretary of state was simultaneously a part of the Government of India and the British government, creating a very complicated situation where Indian representation to the League was concerned.

As a result, the freedom and opportunity afforded to India by its involvement in the League was largely hollow at a political level, with ultimate sovereignty still resting firmly with the secretary of state and the British Cabinet. Furthermore, some officials deemed the less visible control through which London was able to maintain its Indian interests to be the perfect response to new challenges to imperial legitimacy. Despite the expansion of British and French colonial possessions under the mandate system established by the League, the legitimacy of formal imperialism came under attack following the First World War due to the dissemination of new ideas about self-determination and nationalism. As historian Erez Manela argues, these ideas 'weakened [the] underlying supports of the imperial edifice ... [and] ... presented a major challenge to the legitimacy and permanence of the imperial order in the

[25] Sundaram, 'The International Status of India', LNA: 1A/19516/19516, p. 460.

[26] For an overview of the convention, see Saul, 'The Legal Response of the League', pp. 78–102.

international arena'.[27] While the formation of the League of Nations did not do away with empire, as the anti-colonial critics of 1919 hoped, it did force empire to reinvent itself in order to maintain legitimacy within a changing international landscape where indefinite territorial annexation was rapidly becoming less feasible.

In a memorandum on League policy written in 1936, Lord Cecil of Chelwood referred to the League of Nations as 'an almost ideal machinery for the preservation of the British Empire'. Cecil wrote that the primary objective of British foreign policy at that time was the maintenance of peace, which of course also meant the maintenance of a status quo in which Britain retained a dominant role. Cecil argued that armament, alliances, and the force of world opinion never successfully prevented war once it was decided upon by a determined country. Noting that in previous times it was entirely reasonable to place matters of 'honour and vital interest' at the forefront of British foreign policy, such an approach was no longer the most viable option and it was instead preferable to give the new system a fair trial, as the maintenance of the League system was the best hope of retaining imperial control. Cecil pointed out that most of the Dominions would now strongly resist having their foreign policy dictated from London, but were entirely willing to co-operate with Britain in pursuing a 'world policy' at Geneva. Observing the strain to the structure of the British Empire that would result from being set at odds with the Dominions on an important international debate, Cecil concluded that it was 'only on the basis of the League of Nations that there is any prospect of an imperial foreign policy'.[28]

'A Dangerous Spot in the Heart of Bengal'

From its first inception, the Convention for the Prevention and Punishment of Terrorism was a topic of 'vital concern' for the Government of India, whose own experience with political violence over the past thirty years reified terrorism as a distinct category of governmental interest, as the preceding chapters have indicated. In drafting the letter to be submitted to the League of Nations regarding India's position on the subject, J. A. Throne wrote that his government was 'fully in accord with the principle of international co-operation for the prevention and

[27] Manela, *Wilsonian Moment*, p. 11.

[28] Lord Cecil of Chelwood, 26 May 1936, Cecil of Chelwood Papers, BL, Add Mss 51083, pp. 109–10. This view was echoed by some anti-colonial nationalists such as Rash Behari Bose, who argued that the League of Nations was nothing more than a tool for maintaining global white supremacy. See McQuade, 'The *New Asia* of Bose', pp. 641–67.

punishment of terrorism'.[29] In particular, the Government of India was interested in the question of territory, and hoped that signing on to the convention would provide legal recourse regarding the ongoing challenge posed by the French possession of Chandernagore, which was often used as a safe haven by absconding Bengali revolutionaries including Aurobindo Ghose of the Alipore conspiracy case in 1909. Subsequently establishing an ashram in the French territory of Pondicherry, Aurobindo remained a source of irritation to colonial authorities for the remainder of his career. Despite retiring from politics and pursuing a life of spirituality, Aurobindo continued to be visited by nationalists and revolutionaries, and his presence in the French territory made his activities notoriously difficult for the colonial police to properly monitor.[30]

A small strip of territory lying just north of Calcutta, Chandernagore was first settled by French colonists in 1673. Despite the British having twice captured this territory in the mid- to late eighteenth century, the land was ceded back to the French in 1815 and the French retained their colonial presence in India until 1962. In the early twentieth century, the main sources of employment in Chandernagore were the jute mills located at Kankinara, which contained 354 looms and more than 7,000 spindles. In 1911, the population was 25,293 with a mixed population that included Bengali Hindus, Muslims, European British subjects, Madrasi French subjects from Pondicherry, and a few French Europeans. Cross-border trade and travel were ubiquitous, and ever since the early nineteenth century the territory had retained a reputation as a haven for 'stolen goods, cheats, swindlers and fraudulent pawn brokers'.[31] In the first decades of the twentieth century, Chandernagore was particularly notorious as an entry point for arms-dealing and cocaine-smuggling, as the border with British India was 'crossed and recrossed daily by hundreds of people without any let or hindrance and any one having friends or supporters working in the jute mills ... would be able to procure arms and take them to any place without raising suspicions'.[32]

[29] Views of the Government of India on draft conventions for the creation of an international criminal court for the prevention and punishment of terrorism, 1936, Foreign and Political Department, NAI, File No. 547-X, p. 13.

[30] For some of the most recent work on Aurobindo, see Wolfers, 'Born Like Krishna in the Prison-House' and Heehs, *Lives of Sri Aurobindo*. Daniel Brückenhaus has recently explored the complicated but often heavily entangled relationship between British and French colonial security services during the first half of the twentieth century. See Brückenhaus, *Policing Transnational Protest*.

[31] Note on Chandernagore by Mr. Abdul Majid, Deputy Superintendent of Police, Criminal Intelligence Department, 7 September 1913, in Samanta (ed.), *Terrorism in Bengal*, vol. 3, pp. 312–13.

[32] Ibid., pp. 318–19.

With the rise of anti-colonial violence in the first half of the twentieth century, Chandernagore quickly became a sore spot for British imperial officials, who viewed it as a 'dangerous spot in the heart of Bengal' that afforded safe passage and refuge to violent criminals.[33] The border lines between British and French Indian possessions were all the more difficult to police due to their 'arbitrary and administrative nature', as historian Akhila Yechury phrases it. As Yechury points out, these lines 'did not break social, cultural or economic ties with contiguous regions' and as such created a messy jurisdictional morass that was difficult for police investigators to navigate. Such issues were not limited to political absconders, but encompassed a wide range of criminalized activities, such as the marriage of children under the age of fourteen following the passage of the Child Marriage Restraint Act throughout British India in 1929.[34]

Frustration over the perceived inefficiency of the administration of Chandernagore led the Government of India to push for the cession of the territory by France at the Paris peace talks of 1919. By 1918, Sir Henry Wheeler and other officials concluded that the cooperation of the French government was insufficient, due to 'the deplorable condition of the executive in Chandernagore, which was practically represented by Bengalis and was inadequate and inefficient'.[35] During the war, the Government of India demanded that French authorities pass emergency legislation similar to the Defence of India Act that would provide executive powers to deal summarily with seditionists and revolutionaries, including Rash Behari Bose. The French government agreed to a more mild form of punitive legislation, which was enough to placate the Government of India for the duration of the war, but the hope remained that after the war Chandernagore could be ceded to British India 'possibly as an element in general territorial adjustments all over the globe as a result of the war'.[36] In the lead-up to the peace negotiations, officials in Bengal insisted that if Chandernagore retained its position as a French colony, it would remain a constant threat to broader Indian interests, urgently warning the Government of India that 'as long as this town is not under British control so long it must continue to furnish a refuge for

[33] Letter from Governor of Bengal, 21 November 1918, Home Political A, NAI, Nos. 137–139, p. 1.

[34] Akhila Yechury, *Empire, Nation and the French Settlements in India, c.1930–1954* (unpublished PhD dissertation: University of Cambridge, 2012), p. 16.

[35] Note by Sir Henry Wheeler, 4 October 1913, Home Political A, NAI, Nos. 137–139, p. 1.

[36] Foreign and Political Department Note, 10 December 1918, Home Political A, NAI, Nos. 137–139, p. 3.

revolutionary murderers and robbers ... and a starting point for fresh plots against the British Government'.[37]

Despite this, other priorities won out in Paris, leaving Chandernagore as a constant source of frustration for British officials throughout the interwar period. The issue of Chandernagore became particularly important in the early 1930s, when political violence in Bengal reached its peak with regular murders in and around Calcutta and the raid on the Chittagong armoury in 1930, discussed in Chapter 4. Despite the initial help offered by French authorities in the apprehension of absconders from the Chittagong raid, the overall perception of British officials at this time was that the actions of the Chandernagore authorities in suppressing revolutionary crime 'cannot by any means be described as vigorous'.[38] The French were extremely reluctant to take action against criminals with political motives that were protected under international law. Even when the authorities were willing to cooperate with the British Indian police force, however, the specificities of French law provided a source of great frustration for the Government of India, who argued that 'the legal procedure obtaining in that territory is unsuitable to the success of any operation there'.[39] In one example cited by the superintendent of police for Hooghly, a series of French legal restrictions including the prohibition of night raids and the necessity of formal warrants listing the owner of any houses that were to be searched stymied an attempt to apprehend the murderers of the police commissioner, Mr Garlick.[40] In comparison to the executive authority granted by the laws of exception implemented in British India that have been outlined throughout this book, the Government of India viewed the legal safeguards of French procedure as unnecessary and unwieldy impediments to the swift and secret detention of dangerous terrorists.

The longer history of Britain's relationship with the French territories, including Chandernagore, provides important context for understanding the priorities of the Government of India regarding the Convention for the Prevention and Punishment of Terrorism in 1937. The main instructions that the Government of India provided for its representative, Sir Denys Bray, were to push for the inclusion of a provision within the

[37] C. Tindall (Additional Secretary to the Government of Bengal) to Secretary to Government of India, Home Department, 21 November 1918, Home Political A, NAI, Nos. 137–139, p. 6.

[38] C. E. S. Fairweather to R. N. Reid, 14 March 1933, Home Political, NAI, File 45/19/1933, p. 1.

[39] Note by Fairweather, 11 March 1933, Home Political, NAI, File 45/19/1933, p. 14.

[40] Report by the Superintendent of Police, Hooghly, 18 January 1933, Home Political, NAI, File 45/19/1933, pp. 6–12.

convention that would regulate and monitor the circulation of firearms in signatory nations. Bray proposed this measure at the convention, using the argument that the experience of terrorism in India, and especially in Bengal, demonstrated that 'the potential danger of a terrorist would be reduced very considerably if steps could be taken to prevent him from arming himself with revolvers and pistols' and that to this end 'the fullest co-operation should exist among contracting States to prevent the smuggling of such weapons from one State to another'.[41] Bray proposed an amendment that resulted in Article 12 of the convention – Article 13 in the final version – being reframed to require gun retailers and manufacturers to maintain a register of the names and addresses of all firearm purchasers. The other members of the convention accepted Bray's proposal without discussion, although his illness on the day of the formal proposal meant that the amendment was put forward by the British representative Sir John Fischer Williams on Bray's behalf, a fact indicative of the intimate relationship between British and British Indian interests and personnel at Geneva.[42]

The Government of India's emphasis on the firearm clause, and particularly its interest in preventing the smuggling of weapons between contracting states, was a direct response to concerns regarding the potential danger that French Chandernagore posed to the maintenance of British India's territorial integrity. Following the passage of the convention, members of the Government of India expressed disappointment that although France was a signatory, its colonies including Chandernagore were exempted from the terms of the convention under Article 25, which stated that signatories would assume no obligations on behalf of colonies, territories, or mandates.[43] This, combined with the unwillingness of the British government to sign on to the convention at all, significantly dampened the Government of India's enthusiasm for the new measures, as 'one of the chief advantages which [they] hoped to gain from the Convention was the prevention of the smuggling of arms into British India from the French possessions'.[44] The Government of India's preoccupation with Chandernagore, and with the transnational

[41] Replies from Governments, 16 April 1935, LNA, C.R.T.1(b), p. 1.

[42] International Conference on the Repression of Terrorism, Report by Sir Denys Bray, 1937, IOR: L/PJ/8/583, p. 223. Bray and Williams both stayed in the Carlton Parc Hôtel throughout the duration of the conference and there is every reason to believe that they were in close communication throughout. Liste des Délégués, LNA, C.R.T./P.V.1-10.

[43] See Convention for the Prevention and Punishment of Terrorism, 16 November 1937, LNA, C.R.T./P.V. 18.

[44] International Conference on the Repression of Terrorism, Report by Sir Denys Bray, 1937, IOR: L/PJ/8/583, p. 181.

circulation of firearms, indicates the central role of territorial control – or lack thereof – in shaping colonial anxieties towards terrorism. More specifically, it points towards reading the Convention for the Prevention and Punishment of Terrorism as more than simply a failed exercise in international legislation. Instead, the convention should be regarded as an attempt to compensate for the territorial limits of the modern state through the formulation of a standardized script by which challengers to state sovereignty could be made legible and punishable irrespective of their circulation or relocation within a global arena.

'An Internationally Dangerous Manner'

Of central importance to this project was the responsibility of states to effectively exert sovereign control within their own territory. Historian David Armitage argues that '[p]erhaps the most momentous but least widely understood development in modern history is the long transition from a world of empires to a world of states'.[45] While Armitage locates the intellectual origins of this process within the revolutionary moment of the American War of Independence, which contributed to world history the radical proposition that states could be conjured out of colonies, it was not until the formation of the League of Nations that this process came to be institutionalized in the formal structures of international relations.[46] Whereas nineteenth century imperialisms retained a dynamic and expansive quality that allowed for shifting territorial claims and balance of power politics, the international system inaugurated at Versailles sought to legitimize an inter-state system wherein sovereignty rested within the fixed territoriality of geographically contiguous nation-states situated within a bounded global space. This process contributed to an increasing international regulation of movement through the creation of passports and other forms of documentary identification. In addition to the monopoly on violence claimed by emerging nation-states, modern governments have also claimed a 'monopoly of the legitimate means of movement', making themselves the final arbiters for determining who or what may cross these fixed borders.[47]

In the international system of the interwar, national interests remained of primary importance to governments in the planning of international policing initiatives. In other words, while nation-states worked increasingly towards cooperation with one another, their primary focus remained the maintenance of their monopoly on legitimate coercion

[45] Armitage, *Foundations of International Thought*, p. 191. [46] Ibid., p. 215.
[47] Torpey, *Invention of the Passport*, pp. 1–2.

within their own national borders.[48] Central to this system was the concept of responsibility, whereby the sovereignty of a state was made contingent upon its ability to uphold a certain 'standard of civilization' by replicating the structures and technologies of Western government. As Susan Pedersen demonstrates in her comprehensive account of the League of Nations' mandate system, the transformation of former German colonies into mandates provided the means by which empire in the interwar period could be simultaneously reinvigorated and contested.[49] The mandates system was premised on the argument that certain people or cultures 'not yet able to stand by themselves under the strenuous conditions of the modern world' required the supervision and guidance of 'advanced nations' in order to progress to a stage at which self-government and international recognition could be made possible.[50]

The relationship between sovereignty and responsibility was not limited to the mandates, but was also important for international law more broadly. In 1935, the Roumanian delegation to the Terrorism Convention's Committee of Experts circulated a study by Thomas Givenovitch, a professor in the Faculty of Law at Belgrade. In it, Givenovitch argued that in order to properly prohibit the proliferation of terrorism, 'it would be necessary to make the States themselves ... penally responsible for the preparatory acts' carried out within their own territory. Givenovitch stated, 'While a State cannot, of course, be a legal-domestic delinquent, that is to say, itself declare itself delinquent in its sovereign territory, it can be declared a possible delinquent in the eyes of the law of the international legal community, personified in the League of Nations.'[51] According to Givenovitch, this would even include a state's failure to communicate to the international community information regarding a terrorist attack planned within its own territory and carried out elsewhere. For Givenovitch, 'political terrorist crimes', as he referred to them, were *delicta juris gentium*, or crimes against international law. Terrorists proclaimed this international nature, according to Givenovitch, both through their selection of public targets which increased the likelihood of foreign citizens being injured, as well as their tendency to transgress state borders in the process between their preparation and their implementation. More importantly, Givenovitch asserted that the 'property attacked by acts of political terrorism is thus *international property*, since it is attacked in an *internationally dangerous manner*, even

[48] Deflem, *Policing World Society*, p. 27. [49] Pedersen, *The Guardians*. [50] Ibid., p. 1.
[51] Study by Thomas Givenovitch circulated to the Committee at the request of the Roumanian delegation, 3 May 1935, LNA, C.R.T.9, p. 6.

if that property is not actually international property'. For Givenovitch, this meant that states should adopt the principle of universality in policing terrorist crime, entailing that acts contemplated or carried out in one state's territory should be regarded as directed against that state itself, even if the actual intended target was a foreign government.[52] This reflects a particular concern with the public nature of political assassinations. Unlike 'ordinary' murder, which typically occurred behind closed doors, either within the domestic sphere or otherwise obscured from public view, 'terrorism' represented not only an attack against an individual but an attack carried out within the public sphere where the state was especially responsible for maintaining security.

Although Givenovitch's suggestion that states be made penally responsible for acts of terrorism planned or executed within their territory was unsurprisingly omitted in the drafting of the convention, the convention retained the broader notion of territorial responsibility. In an amendment to the draft convention submitted in 1936, the Soviet representative pushed for the inclusion of an article that stipulated that each High Contracting Party must take appropriate measures 'to prohibit and suppress the existence in their territories of associations avowedly engaged in international terrorism ... including the organisation of armed bands for the purpose of infringing the inviolability of the frontiers of the contracting States'.[53] The USSR was particularly concerned about the possibility of states exploiting terrorist activities as a means for disguised intervention in the political affairs of other states, a fact that was both understandable in light of the early history of the Bolshevik Revolution, as well as deeply ironic given Soviet sponsorship for subversive political organizations around the world in the early interwar period.[54] This proposal was agreeable to Sir John Fischer Williams of the British delegation, who suggested that such a stipulation was entirely consistent with the existing law in Britain, which in his view already took sufficient measures towards this end.[55]

India's self-presentation within these discussions provides important insight into the balancing act that government officials sought to achieve

[52] Study by Thomas Givenovitch circulated to the Committee at the request of the Roumanian delegation, 3 May 1935, LNA, C.R.T.9, pp. 7–9.
[53] Draft Convention, Amendments proposed by the Government of the Union of Soviet Socialist Republics, 7 January 1936, LNA, C.R.T.18(a), p. 1.
[54] See Definition of terrorist offences, criticism of the general scope of Article 2, in Criticisms and Suggestions made by the Governments upon the draft conventions annexed to the Committee's Second Report, LNA, C.R.T.25, p. 3.
[55] Reports by the UK delegation, Sir John Fischer Williams to Foreign Office, 7 June 1935, PRO, HO 189/1.

in affirming the need for legislation to curb the problem of terrorism, while simultaneously conveying to the international community that the Government of India was living up to its responsibilities as a legitimate sovereign. India's anomalous position within the League made this balancing act all the more important. Although the 1935 Government of India Act dissolved some sovereignty to local Indian authorities, ultimate executive authority still rested in the hands of the British viceroy and the secretary of state, and therefore the British Parliament. India was not a state among states, despite the efforts of the Indian delegation to present it as such, which explains why the Government of India was particularly eager to categorize anti-governmental protest as terrorism and thus claim international support for its repression. Despite the fact that domestic legislation tackling the problem of terrorism was always justified through the argument that the ordinary law was insufficient and thus extraordinary powers were needed, the Government of India presented an entirely different argument at the level of the international. In addressing the proposed inauguration of an International Criminal Court, which was being discussed in tandem with the Terrorism Convention, J. A. Throne of the Government of India wrote in the statement to be delivered by Sir Denys Bray at Geneva, 'Terrorism in India has very little connection at present with that in European countries; the Governments in India have adequate legal powers to deal with it and it appears most unlikely that they would ever wish to resort to the proposed Court.'[56] In fact, the most obvious factor differentiating terrorism in India from its European manifestations was India's lack of political independence, and its status as the only non-self-governing member of the League.

Despite enthusiasm for the Terrorism Convention itself, the Government of India regarded participation in the International Criminal Court as an expensive venture that would provide little benefit to India, due to the great distances which would be involved in transferring prisoners and personnel back and forth from Europe. Privately, Government of India officials were quite blunt about their feelings towards the proposed court, with M. G. Hallet writing, 'This is one of the activities of the League of Nations which makes me feel tired; the suggestion that an expensive criminal court should be established is a half baked idea and the sooner it is killed the better.'[57] The Government of India sought to present itself in a way that made it clear that the need for new international legislation that targeted transnational terrorism was not a reflection of the colonial

[56] J. A. Throne, draft letter to be submitted to the League of Nations, 1936, NAI, File No. 547-X, p. 12.
[57] M. G. Hallet, 29 June 1936, NAI, File No. 547-X, p. 11.

government's inability to maintain law and order within its own territory. To this end, Throne noted that although alterations to local law would be required in some cases, 'the existing law is likely to be found to be adequate to implement the more essential provisions of the Convention'.[58]

Informing this insistence was the concern shared by many Government of India officials that existing measures for preventing foreign nationals from printing seditious materials were in fact woefully inadequate. In an official note, O. K. Caroe mentioned the many complaints received by the Government of India from foreign governments regarding activities carried out in India that sought to subvert or damage their states. Although Caroe noted that these complaints were primarily directed against newspaper propaganda and other forms of dissent that would fall within the purview of sedition, rather than terrorism, he expressed concern that 'the liberty of the Indian Press in this regard is too often extremely embarrassing'.[59] As Stuart Elden argues in the context of the twenty-first century's 'War on Terror', a state that is unable to maintain its own territorial integrity by controlling the actions of non-state actors within its borders finds itself in a position where its sovereignty may be called into question.[60] While Elden locates this process within the global circumstances of the late 1990s and early 2000s, referring to the idea that states exercise control within their own territories as 'the sovereign fiction on which the United Nations is constructed', this analysis neglects the particular historical contingencies of the early interwar period where this idea originated.[61] It was in this specific historical moment, following the cataclysm of the First World War and the initial collapse of Western narratives of civilization and progress, that European imperialism sought to reconstitute itself through a new interstate system that reframed nineteenth century ideas of empire as tutelage into a mandates system that instead positioned tutelage as development. This system rested on a new discourse of progress and historical time in which state sovereignty was positioned as a universally attainable goal that, in practice, maintained European hegemony through a new set of exclusionary restrictions. Because sovereignty under this system was thus made contingent upon ideas of territorial responsibility, a state's claim to legitimacy could be undermined by a number of factors, including an inability to control or prevent the proliferation of

[58] J. A. Throne, draft letter to be submitted to the League of Nations, 1936, NAI, File No. 547-X, p. 13.
[59] Note by O. K. Caroe, 23 June 1936, NAI, File No. 547-X, p. 9.
[60] Elden, *Terror and Territory*, p. 64. [61] Ibid.

terrorism within its territory. It is for this reason that the narrative projected by the Government of India at Geneva – that 'adequate legal powers' existed to deal with terrorism – stands in such stark contrast to domestic speeches and publications that emphasize the law's inadequacy and the need for increasingly drastic emergency powers.

'The Final Rights of Humanity'

Although the Convention for the Prevention and Punishment of Terrorism stimulated a great deal of debate, one item that was accepted with relatively little discussion was the definition of terrorism as violence directed against the state. In the final convention, terrorism was defined as 'criminal acts directed against a State and intended or calculated to create a state of terror in the minds of particular persons, or a group of persons or the general public'.[62] Within this definition, the possible targets of terrorism included heads of state, their descendants or spouses, and persons acting in a public capacity.[63] This definition is key to understanding the function of an emerging prose of counterterrorism in the 1930s.

As Chapter 2 has shown, the emergence of terrorism as a distinct category of crime had its roots in the French Revolution, and specifically in the execution of King Louis XVI. What made Louis' execution such a significant turning point was the fact that while previous acts of tyrannicide were based on the principle of upholding justice through the murder of an unjust ruler, Louis was killed not for his specific actions but for his symbolic position as king. This means that what made terrorism a historically new form of violence was the fact that, according to Mikkel Thorup, 'even though actual persons are being targeted, and perhaps their killing is being legitimated by specific actions they have committed, the real target of the attack is not the person but the abstraction of the system'.[64] In other words, terrorism is given primary significance, not by what it does, but by what it represents through its symbolic use of violence. This is why ideas of terrorism came to be so closely coupled with violence directed against the state, because terrorism, in the structural position of both its perpetrator and its victim, was an inherently political crime.

[62] Convention for the Prevention and Punishment of Terrorism, Article 1, 16 November 1937, IOR: L/PJ/8/583, p. 43.
[63] Convention for the Prevention and Punishment of Terrorism, Article 2, 16 November 1937, IOR: L/PJ/8/583, p. 43.
[64] Thorup, *Intellectual History of Terror*, pp. 9–10.

Defining terrorism in political terms posed immediate difficulties for early twentieth century legislators regarding the right of political asylum, an important aspect of international law. The right of asylum was a particular concern for British officials, who prided themselves on liberal traditions of free speech and political liberty. Although it is true that British law maintained stronger protections for political refugees than most Continental powers, and that Britain was a relative latecomer to the kinds of racially exclusionary laws that were common throughout its colonies and the Dominions, it was never the free political haven that it purported to be.[65] Still, as one official noted in a memorandum to the Home Office, public opinion in Britain would surely condemn many acts of a 'specifically "terrorist" character', but might likewise regard others as being legitimate forms of protest against a tyrannical government. According to this logic, if a country lacked constitutional means for redressing the wrongs of a bad government, 'it can only be changed by measures involving force or the display of force; and public opinion might not support legislation which would make it a crime ... to concert measures in this country ... for carrying out an armed insurrection in a foreign country'. As such, the British government instructed Williams to make it clear that the 'object of the proposed Convention is not to make it more difficult to change existing Governments by revolutionary methods, but to discountenance the use for political purposes of methods which all civilised opinion must condemn'.[66]

In an attempt to address these concerns, the convention provided an exception from the obligation of extradition in the case of crimes that fell within the definition of 'political offences' of a given country. Ultimately, a great deal of discretion was left to member states to determine according to their own laws 'whether the terrorist aspect of the extraditable act outweighed its political aspect or vice versa'.[67] This was partly a result of the insistence of the British delegation, who viewed defining the political character of an offence as outside of the scope of an international convention.[68] British officials further maintained that British and

[65] See Alison Bashford and Jane McAdam, 'The Right to Asylum: Britain's 1905 Aliens Act and the Evolution of Refugee Law', *Law and History Review* 32, no. 2 (2014), pp. 309–50, and Alison Bashford and Catie Gilchrist, 'The Colonial History of the 1905 Aliens Act', *The Journal of Imperial and Commonwealth History* 40, no. 3 (2012), pp. 409–37.

[66] Memorandum by the Home Office, 1937, PRO, HO 189/9, p. 3.

[67] Proceedings of the International Conference on the Repression of Terrorism, 1–16 November 1937, LNA, C.R.T./P.V.18, p. 86.

[68] Draft Convention on Terrorism, Notes as to Legislation, April 1937, PRO, HO 189/2, p. 2. John Fischer Williams believed that this disagreement over what constituted a

Continental definitions of political crime were legally incompatible.[69] Most European states judged that 'the political character of an offence may be established solely by the motive of the offender',[70] whereas under British law the political nature of a crime was determined by whether or not the perpetrators committed their act in the course or furtherance of a political rising.[71] This meant that, from the British point of view, in order to maintain sufficient precision to defend political freedoms, the convention would need to make a clear distinction between 'cold-blooded assassinations or isolated incendiarism' as opposed to acts that constituted or led up to a legitimate civil war. As noted in a memorandum on the subject, 'Acts intended to cause death or grievous bodily harm ... are the normal incidents of any revolt or rising even before it has reached the stage of civil war' and cooperating with or assisting such acts was not necessarily unlawful, depending on the nature of the foreign insurgents. For the British, it was thus not political violence itself, but rather 'the drawing of the line between acts which everyone would condemn and political movements attended by violence ... which is ... the real difficulty in framing legislation on the lines of the Convention'.[72]

For some commentators, the political distinction between legitimate and illegitimate forms of violence was inherently misguided. T. W. H. Inskip, the British attorney general, argued in 1935 that adhering to such a distinction went too far towards granting potential legitimacy for rebellions conducted against foreign governments. Although Inskip, like his contemporaries, acknowledged that a political uprising could be justified in cases where no mechanism existed for constitutional change, he nonetheless maintained that the potential pitfalls of including such a stipulation outweighed the benefits. Remarking on the difficulty of drawing a distinction between legitimate and illegitimate forms of rebellion, Inskip wrote that it was 'not only illogical but unreasonable to prohibit ... the preparation of an insurrectionary expedition to proceed against a friendly State and at the same time to make it

political crime had severely damaged the practical utility of the Convention. John Fischer Williams to Leslie Brass, 29 March 1937, PRO, HO 189/11, p. 1.

[69] A third dimension to this conversation, missing due to the absence of the United States from the League of Nations, is extradition law in America, which by 1900 had established more extradition laws than any other country. See Katherine Untarman, *Uncle Sam's Policemen: The Pursuit of Fugitives across Borders* (Cambridge, MA: Harvard University Press, 2015).

[70] Account of the Third Session by John Fischer Williams, 21 May 1937, PRO, HO 189/12, p. 12.

[71] Memorandum by the Home Office, 1937, PRO, HO 189/9, p. 4.

[72] Notes by the Home Office DPP, Mr McClure, and Sir Norman Kendal, July 1935 and April – June 1937, PRO, HO 189/2, p. 1.

possible for a body of foreign revolutionaries or of British sympathisers to conspire to subvert a foreign Government by acts of violence'.[73]

The question of legitimate versus illegitimate forms of rebellion was also intimately connected to Britain's historical relationship with Europe. Many British officials viewed political violence as essentially a Continental problem, with G. B. McClure remarking at one point that it 'seems a little unreal that the word terrorism should be used or defined in an Act of Parliament in this country'.[74] However, there were also those who recognized the utility of the Terrorism Convention for helping to solve colonial difficulties. In November 1937, while the final version of the convention was being debated, J. G. Hibbert of the Colonial Office sent a message to the Home Office pointing out that although there was little desire for the colonies to be brought within the scope of the convention, it may nonetheless be of value in dealing with territories such as Palestine.[75] The British delegation at Geneva was also approached in confidence by the delegate for Egypt, who asked whether Britain intended to sign the convention on behalf of Palestine or Sudan in order to simplify the task of managing insurgency in these locations.[76] This concern with policing dissent within the British Empire cannot be understood purely through the lens of managing existential threats to a colonial regime, but must also be considered from the standpoint of political economy. While coding itself in a language of protecting imperial security, imperial policing often sought to manage industrial disputes within British colonies, something that the Terrorism Convention explicitly excluded from its mandate.[77] As such British interest in potentially applying the terms of the convention to these territories should also be

[73] Memorandum by the Attorney General, T. W. H. Inskip, 12 April 1935, PRO, HO 189/2, p. 1.

[74] G. B. McClure, Memorandum, 17 June 1937, PRO, HO 189/2, p. 4. It is surprising that in all of these discussions, no reference was made to Ireland, which must surely have factored into British officials' understanding of political crime and 'terrorism', given the predominance of Irish revolutionaries within the domestic history of political violence in Britain. Houen, *Terrorism and Modern Literature*, pp. 21–30.

[75] J. G. Hibbert (Colonial Office) to Dowson (Home Office), 3 November 1937, PRO. HO 189/7, p. 1. For more on the contested nature of Britain's relationship with the mandate of Palestine, see Zeina Ghandour, *A Discourse on Domination in Mandate Palestine: Imperialism, Property, Insurgency* (London: Routledge, 2009), Weldon Matthews, *Confronting an Empire, Constructing a Nation: Arab Nationalists and Popular Politics in Mandate Palestine* (London: I.B. Tauris, 2006), and Jacob Norris, *Land of Progress: Palestine in the Age of Colonial Development, 1905–1948* (Oxford: Oxford University Press, 2013).

[76] Leslie Brass, Draft Report, 10 December 1937, PRO, HO 189/8, p. 12.

[77] Martin Thomas, *Violence and Colonial Order: Police, Workers and Protest in the European Colonial Empires, 1918–1940* (Cambridge: Cambridge University Press, 2012), p. 2.

read within the context of imperial attempts to manage the economic and political aspirations of colonized subjects.

Recognition of the right of revolt as a legitimate political weapon against tyranny raised problematic concerns for British imperialism, as these narratives of legitimization were central to the project of many anti-colonial activists, who claimed that their actions were an expression of legitimate politics. When British intelligence services discovered Rash Behari Bose's presence in Japan during the summer of 1915, his extradition posed major legal challenges because of the political nature of his crime.[78] A message to Lord Hardinge from the British Embassy in Tokyo explained, 'The position is that the Japanese Government will not arrest persons, Indians or others, accused of merely political crimes such as "sedition."'[79] Hardinge was forced to admit that 'although the offences were punishable in India under ordinary Criminal Law we could not say that the motives for the crimes were entirely free of political character'. Despite this, Hardinge stressed that this was a case of great importance and urged the embassy to 'press most strongly for his deportation to India or to a British Territory under effective arrest'.[80] After a flurry of diplomatic correspondence in which Hardinge presented Bose's actions as neither political nor criminal but as part of a larger German plot to undermine the Allied war effort, the Japanese government finally agreed to issue a deportation order against Bose. Aided by friends linked to the Japanese ultranationalist Kokuryūkai and Gen'yôsha, Bose went into hiding in a small studio at Nakamuraya in Shinjuku, where he remained until the deportation order was withdrawn in March 1916, following the firing upon the Japanese ship *Tenyō-maru* by a British naval vessel and the forcible seizure of seven Indians traveling on board.[81]

[78] Political crimes were exempted from extradition in many countries during this period, including both Britain and Japan. The case of Bose was made even more challenging by the fact that despite attempts made in 1905 and 1915, British and Japanese officials had not been able to come to terms on an extradition treaty. Proposed extradition treaty between the United Kingdom and Japan, 1926, Foreign and Political Department, NAI, File No. 476-I. Efforts were renewed by the British government in 1927 and 1937, but still with no progress. See also Proposed Anglo-Japanese Extradition Treaty, External Affairs Department, NAI, File No. 321-X.

[79] British Embassy to Hardinge, 9 October 1915, Home Political-B. November 1915, NAI, File No. 72-83, p. 17. The right to asylum for political refugees was a well-established principle of international law by this time, which was also reflected in British legislation such as the Extradition Act of 1870, which exempted political criminals from extradition.

[80] Hardinge to British Embassy, 15 October 1915, Home Political-B, NAI, File No. 72-83, p. 20.

[81] For a detailed account, see Nakajima, *Bose of Nakamuraya*, pp. 78–111. For the full diplomatic correspondence, see Proposed deportation from Japan of one Thakur (Rash Behari Bose), November 1915, Home Political-B, NAI, File No. 72-83.

From his position of safety in Japan, Bose continued to challenge Britain's presence in India by appealing to principles of international law and what he called 'the cause of humanity'. In his writings, Bose often articulated the cause of anti-colonialism through universalist language reminiscent of that deployed by the League of Nations itself.[82] In 1930, several of the insurgents responsible for the Chittagong armoury attack fled to Chandernagore where British authorities, with the permission of the French police, stormed the house where these revolutionaries were taking refuge and apprehended them. This incident drew the condemnation of the directors of the Pan-Asiatic League, including Rash Behari Bose, who petitioned the League of Nations to condemn this 'gross breach of the international laws'. In their petition, the directors pointed out that as a French possession, Chandernagore was considered to be a foreign country under international law. They further argued that India was at war with Britain due to the resolution of national independence passed at Lahore by the Indian National Congress on 1 January 1930, and that the arrested persons took refuge in Chandernagore 'in the capacity of belligerents'. Citing other historical examples where belligerents received the right of asylum in foreign countries, the directors declared that in ceding to the demands of the British authorities, the French government 'abdicated its sovereign rights when it permitted the British police to enter its territory and exercise police rights there'. For the directors, this incident was nothing short of naked British imperialism, making their actions a violation of international law, referred to as 'not the cause of India ... [but] the cause of humanity'.[83]

In this declaration, Rash Behari Bose and the other directors deployed the category of humanity in a manner that was familiar to their international interlocutors. In charging the British colonial police with violating the cause of humanity through their violation of international law, this declaration made use of the same logic through which British officials expressed concerns regarding European and Oriental despotism. Although the French delegation wanted assassination excluded entirely from the list of offences that could be considered political,[84] a note drawn up for the British representative indicated that although homicide was a 'most heinous crime', it could nonetheless be justified in rare circumstances in which 'no other method exists of protecting the final rights of

[82] McQuade, 'The *New Asia*', pp. 641–67.

[83] Declaration of the Pan-Asiatic League in regard to the unlawful arrest of Indian revolutionists by the British police in French territory, received in registry 6 October 1930, LNA, 1A/19516/19516, p. 1.

[84] Preliminary Draft Convention drawn up by the Executive Bureau of the International Criminal Police Commission, 11 April 1935. C.R.T.3, p. 25.

humanity'.[85] Thus, the category of humanity provided a potential source of critique for laws that sought to punish terrorism through the repression of political rights. In addition to discussions surrounding the legitimacy versus illegitimacy of certain forms of insurgency, this also carried implications for broader political freedoms such as the freedom of workers to conduct a legitimate strike.[86] These concerns regarding the potential misuses of the convention in being deployed to curb the 'rights of humanity' also included left-leaning political organizations.[87] International groups such as the International Women's League for Peace and Freedom also cautioned against 'the present tendency of governments to assume that the maintenance of order and stability is possible only under a regime of suppression of liberty and normal rights'.[88]

'The Universal Conscience of Mankind'

The concept of humanity played another important function within international discourses of terrorism as a means of universalizing the particularities of local insurgencies into a more global narrative that maintained the interests of the state governments of whom the international community was composed. In crafting this universally oriented discourse, the convention made three key interpretive moves. First, it distinguished terrorism from forms of political violence that targeted a specific government or state. Second, this version of terrorism – not regional or local, but global in its supposed ambitions – was reframed as an attack upon international order and peace, as embodied by the international society of Geneva. Third, the convention narrated this attack upon international order through existing discourses of civilization and humanity in a way that set terrorism apart as a particularly reprehensible moral crime. This rhetorical strategy sought to shore up the conflation of the international with the category of humanity in a way that reinforced the role of nation-states in representing the collective interests of a global humanity, which could be more effectively envisioned through

[85] Meaning of 'political crime': Note by the British expert, 1 May 1935, C.R.T.8, p. 3.
[86] The British government worried that the convention could potentially be applied in non-terrorist contexts, such as tramway workers staging a strike, if aspects of the strike became violent and entailed damage against public tramway lines. Correspondence with the Foreign Office on the UK observations during the Assembly, July – October 1936, PRO, HO 189/5, p. 2.
[87] The Threat to the Right to Asylum, the International Convention against Terrorism, Article in Communications on the Conditions of Political Prisoners, 30 December 1937, Labour History Archive and Study Centre. LP/WG/REF/24.
[88] International Repression of Terrorism Correspondence with the International Women's League for Peace and Freedom, Geneva, LNA, 3A/17788/15085, p. 1.

its juxtaposition against the global threat of terrorism. While accepting historian Faisal Devji's intervention regarding late twentieth- and early twenty-first-century terrorism as a project in search of a global politics, this chapter asks how such a politics should be understood in the period before the atom bomb and the space age rendered humanity as a singular global category through its understanding of its own destructibility. In the interwar period, humanity as a category bore a different set of stakes and assumptions, which must be understood in their historical context if we are to situate the ideological provenance of the notion of humanity that emerged after the Second World War.[89]

First, it is important to note the repeated emphasis of delegates to the convention that terrorism was not to be understood as political violence directed towards a particular political system or government. At the final conference in November, the Roumanian delegate Mr Pella admitted that there was a great deal of difficulty in drawing a distinction between acts of terrorism and political crimes, because it was almost universally agreed that political offences were not 'of an anti-social character and did not shake the foundations of social life'. Because political offences were of a specifically anti-governmental character, 'they conflicted only with the principles of a quite special morality – namely, principles which were often connected with the form of government of each State and varied from one country to another. ... It was therefore advisable that other States should not intervene in questions which concerned the political life of a given State.' According to Pella, if a state aided in the repression of political offences directed against the interests of another state, that participation would be regarded as an interference within the latter state's internal affairs and hence an infringement on its sovereignty. For Pella, however, state sovereignty was not a sufficient justification for non-interference when it came to repressing acts of terrorism, precisely because these acts 'did not merely endanger the order of a given State but social order in general'. When a political offender or movement expressed their will 'in acts of barbarity and terrorism', the non-collaboration of states in suppressing these acts constituted for Pella 'the most flagrant repudiation of the duties of international solidarity'.[90]

Pella's argument reflected the belief in a shared set of state concerns and responsibilities at the level of the international that cut across national or regional divisions. Mr Chatelain of Haiti argued at the third meeting of the conference that 'no Government worthy of the name'

[89] See Faisal Devji, *The Terrorist in Search of Humanity: Militant Islam and Global Politics* (London: Hurst & Company, 2008).

[90] Provisional Minutes, Eighteenth Meeting, 16 November 1937, C.R.T./P.V.18, p. 66.

could afford to remain indifferent to such a cause, because the interdependence of states rested not only in economic, social, and intellectual matters but also in the principle of collective security.[91] The legal advisors to the British government shared this concern and worried that the particular danger of acts of terrorism was their ability to transgress national boundaries, thus containing within them an inherent potential for damaging relations between friendly states and undermining a key goal of the League: the maintenance of international peace.[92] More important, however, was the fear that terrorism was an action that sought to 'undermine the credit of the State' by 'destroying discipline, increasing poverty and suffering, and ... paralysing the State's powers of reaction'. This imperiled not only the sovereignty of a given state, but also the mutual recognition of sovereignty upon which the international order of Geneva rested its authority and legitimacy. Because the existing international law was, according to some, structured in such a way as to safeguard the rights of national subjects, while doing nothing to guarantee the 'highly valuable legal rights of the State itself', international criminal law was deemed insufficient for preventing or punishing crimes that violated the 'universal conscience of mankind' by simultaneously injuring the interests of all states.[93]

The idea of a 'universal conscience of mankind' was enshrined in the international order of the interwar through the concept of civilization. Prior to the First World War, and particularly in the late nineteenth century, the universal language of civilization held a powerful appeal for non-Western peoples seeking to enter the international society centered on Europe. During the late nineteenth century, European military and technological dominance on the world stage greatly impressed intellectuals in Asia, who sought to replicate European power through the development of their own societies along European lines. While Europe's global hegemony faced a few early setbacks, such as Japan's victory against Russia in 1905, it was the First World War that truly 'confirmed the moral crisis of the European world order'.[94] The apocalyptic scale of the war, as well as its destruction of ideas of European civilizational superiority, caused nationalist groups in Asia such as the Kokuryūkai of Japan to declare 'the Great European War was their suicide as a civilisation ... [and] ... the great opportunity for an Asian

[91] Third Meeting, 2 November 1937, C.R.T./P.V.18, p. 56. This concern was shared by the Polish representative, Mr Beckerman, who referred to terrorism as 'a scourge and a danger to peace and international relations.' Fifth Meeting, 3 November 1937, LNA, C.R.T.1(a), p. 100.

[92] Legal aspect and definition of terrorism, 16 April 1935, C.R.T.1(a), p. 2.

[93] Ibid., pp. 3–4.

[94] Aydin, *Politics of Anti-Westernism in Asia*, p. 93.

revival'.[95] While the nineteenth century saw the deployment of civilization as a barrier to the legitimacy and sovereignty of non-European states seeking to enter international society,[96] the crisis of the First World War refracted this challenge back onto European states, which were themselves forced to uphold the theory, if not the practice, of a particular standard of civilization.

To this end, political violence that challenged state sovereignty through its subversion of the governmental monopoly on violence within a given territory needed to be described in a way that would not jeopardize international society's larger claim to represent a global standard of civilization. While earlier narratives juxtaposed civilization with barbarism through a notion of historical time that trapped certain cultures or practices in what Dipesh Chakrabarty calls the 'waiting room of history',[97] terrorism was instead viewed as not simply an antithesis of modernity, but also as modernity's product. In the opening speech of the international conference on terrorism, the conference president, Court Carton de Wiart, argued that although the progressive march of European civilization succeeded in many instances 'in toning down the savagery and brutality of primitive times', the sinister companion to this progress was the way that, 'advancing knowledge and improved communications have served in their turn ... to promote acts designated by that new term "terrorism"'.[98]

The conflation of terrorism with modern technology and progress served an important function in setting it apart as a new form of criminality that sat in inherent contradistinction to the civilization of advanced society. In other words, terrorism was a new form of 'barbarism' that, despite its trappings of modernity, remained fundamentally incompatible with the functioning of a civilized international order. While barbarism carried historical connotations of a 'primitive' culture that failed to live up to the standard of civilization, terrorism threatened civilization through a deployment of entirely modern scientific tools of destruction such as the bomb, discussed in Chapter 2. For Mr Koukai of the delegation from Czechoslovakia, terrorism threatened the 'common heritage of the whole civilised world'[99] and constituted a particular moral crime, or 'world crime', on par with other targets of global concern from

[95] Uchida Ryōhei (1918), 'Jo', in Saaler and Szpilman (eds.), *Pan-Asianism*, p. 128.
[96] Gerrit Gong, *The Standard of 'Civilization' in International Society* (Oxford: Clarendon Press, 1984).
[97] Chakrabarty, *Provincializing Europe.*
[98] Proceedings of the International Conference on the Repression of Terrorism, 1 November 1937, IOR: L/P&J/8/583, p. 77.
[99] Third Meeting, 2 November 1937, C.R.T./P.V.18, p. 60.

this period such as human trafficking, piracy, counterfeiting currency, and the illegal drug trade.[100] What connected these 'world crimes' was not only their transnational scope, but also their immoral or 'uncivilized' nature, which carried within it an innate threat to an international order that sought to buttress its legitimacy on the claim to uphold and enforce a universal standard of civilization.

'Enemies of the Human Race'

Terrorism as a 'world crime' must be understood within the context of an emerging alignment of international interests that was, at the level of violence and sovereignty, more united than historians have previously recognized. In 1917, the same year as the Bolshevik Revolution in Russia, Vladimir Lenin wrote *Imperialism, the Highest Stage of Capitalism*, a book that rejected and condemned European economic and imperial practices. In response, American President Woodrow Wilson issued his famous Fourteen Points in 1918, spelling out an alternative vision for a post-war settlement that would seek to address some of the roots causes of the First World War.[101] Because Lenin's political vision gave rise to the Third International, or Comintern, and Wilson's formed the basis of the Versailles Treaty and the League of Nations, most historians regard the two as envisioning conflicting ideas of international order that competed throughout the interwar period to win over European and global public opinion.[102]

Still, the Convention for the Prevention and Punishment of Terrorism illustrates one way that the stark divide between Wilsonian and communist internationalisms is traditionally overemphasized in understanding the category of the international during the interwar period. The entry of the USSR into the League of Nations in 1934 signalled a shift in priorities for the Soviets, who became increasingly conciliatory towards the League as hopes of a world revolution declined and the two previously competing internationalisms aligned themselves against the emerging anti-internationalism of fascism.[103] More than this,

[100] Provisional Minutes, Eighteenth Meeting, 16 November 1937, C.R.T./P.V.18, p. 14.
[101] See Mazower, *Governing the World*, p. 127.
[102] See Arno Mayer, *Wilson vs. Lenin: Political Origins of the New Diplomacy, 1917–1918* (Cleveland, OH: World Publishers Co., 1964). See also Sebastian Conrad and Dominic Sachsenmaier, 'Introduction', in Conrad and Sachsenmaier (eds.), *Competing Visions of World Order: Global Moments and Movements, 1880s–1930s* (New York: Palgrave Macmillan, 2007), p. 7, and Manela, *The Wilsonian Moment*.
[103] Mazower, *Governing the World*, pp. 177–9. For a different version of this argument, see Brigitte Studer, *The Transnational World of the Cominternians* (Houndmills: Palgrave Macmillan, 2015), p. 7.

however, the broad alignment of priorities between disparate nation-states including the USSR regarding the danger posed by terrorism illustrates the ways that the international system of the interwar stimulated new concerns that transcended particular ideological or political orientations. This was the product of an increasing normalization of 'vertebrate' structures of statehood, which sought to bulwark themselves against the threat posed by new 'cellular' forms of political organization.[104] As historian Ben Saul notes, 'criminalizing terrorism was not designed to protect only democracies from political violence, but to protect all forms of political organization from violence'.[105] The international criminalization of terrorism rested on the notion that there was a 'feeling of solidarity and cooperation which exists between the States in the campaign against the activities of terrorists, who are enemies of the human race, and must be relentlessly tracked down and prevented from injuring their fellow creatures'.[106] The diplomats at Geneva spoke of an international solidarity, or 'le système de la solidarité des États', that existed between the disparate states of the world, and that ensured that the threat of terrorism should be dealt with through a unified and concerted response at the level of the international.[107]

International solidarity was, of course, not without limits. The political gulf between Britain and the USSR, as well as the emerging threat posed by fascist regimes in Germany and Italy, remained a source of tension, particularly for British security services.[108] When the British government consulted the superintendent of the Special Branch regarding the advisability of signing on to the convention, he pointed out that the new legislation would cause a great deal more work for Special Branch, as it would obligate them to take action against alien refugees plotting against authoritarian regimes, such as that of Mussolini.[109] In June 1937, Norman Kendall wrote to Leslie Brass of the League of Nations delegation, reiterating that the convention would likely result in many requests for the deportation of subversive elements from Germany, Italy, and Yugoslavia, with little benefit in return for the British government.[110] Other officials said that it was 'fundamentally absurd' to believe that a

[104] This language is drawn from Arjun Appadurai's analysis of terrorism in *Fear of Small Numbers: An Essay on the Geography of Anger* (Durham, NC: Duke University Press, 2006), pp. 87–114.

[105] Saul, 'The Legal Response of the League of Nations', p. 5.

[106] C.R.T./P.V.18, p. 23. [107] Liste des Délégués, C.R.T./P.V.1-10, p. 8.

[108] Walton, *Empire of Secrets*. See also Andrew, *Defence of the Realm*, pp. 139–87.

[109] Proposed convention for the suppression of Terrorism, 6 July 1935, PRO, Mepo 3/2048, p. 22.

[110] Norman Kendal to Leslie Brass, 18 June 1937, PRO, HO 189/2, p. 1.

Russian or German Court would hold to the convention with good faith in prosecuting Russians or Germans who plotted terrorist outrages against England.[111] These concerns, among others, ultimately outweighed British interest in the convention, meaning that when the convention was passed later that year in November, the United Kingdom was not a signatory.

Despite the practical limitations of the convention, the concerns animating it are instructive in understanding the emergence of terrorism as a category of international interest. As argued above, the threat of terrorism provided a common enemy against which all forms of government could unite, regardless of their different political systems. Thus, the category of terrorism provided a new language whereby international authority could assert itself as representing the interests and security of a common civilization. Such a categorization occurred not only at the level of law and rhetoric but also through the pooling of information regarding suspected terrorists, as well as fingerprinting, photographing, the collection and circulation of history sheets, and the 'constant supervision of all bodies ... which cannot establish their bona fide character and ... the detention and careful identification of the members of such organisations without prejudice to the appropriate legal penalties'.[112] Although Britain was not a signatory in November 1937, the British representative Sir John Fischer Williams played a key role in drafting the convention, and the definition of terrorism upon which it relied. Despite being reluctant to formally commit itself to the laws of the convention, the British government nonetheless bore the 'greatest sympathy with the object of the Conference' and claimed that they would uphold in practice all necessary measures for preventing and punishing any acts of terrorism carried out or planned within the United Kingdom.[113]

The states that did ultimately sign on to the convention reflect a wide political and geographical diversity, including France, Yugoslavia, Spain, Argentina, the USSR, Turkey, Egypt, and India, among others. This diversity reflects the broad concerns shared by members of the international system of the interwar, regarding the threat that non-state

[111] Observations of His Majesty's Government furnished to the League of Nations, 27 March 1937, PRO, HO 189/9, p. 1.

[112] Replies from governments (Argentine Republic), 8 August 1935, PRO, HO 189/4, p. 13.

[113] Instructions for United Kingdom delegation at diplomatic conference, 5 October 1937, PRO, HO 189/4, p. 2. Even the United States expressed sympathy with the motives of the convention, despite not being a League member. Replies from Governments, 28 February 1935, LNA, C.R.T.1, p. 2.

violence posed to their own sovereignty and, by extension, the legitimacy of an international order premised upon the mutual recognition of this sovereignty. By framing terrorism as a 'world crime' or a 'crime against civilization', the governmental representatives at Geneva sought, in their own words, to 'ensure the safety of all States, regardless of their social or political organisation, and to protect international order as such'.[114] The purpose of this convention was not simply to prevent and punish a set of politically motivated crimes, but rather to shore up international authority with the articulation of a new threat that could be described in universally intelligible terms through the category of 'terrorism'. In this way, terrorism can be understood not as a universal category, but as a universalizable trope capable of transcending national boundaries precisely because of the ease with which it could be applied to describe a wide range of acts of anti-state political violence.

Conclusion

The Convention for the Prevention and Punishment of Terrorism provides an important window into understanding the emergence of terrorism as a category of international concern during the interwar period. As the first international law to target terrorism as a distinct category of criminality, the convention sheds light on the definitions and debates that informed interwar ideas about political violence, territory, and sovereignty. The convention is particularly useful for understanding the context within which colonial officials framed their understanding of revolutionary violence in India, as well as the ways that their own experiences of anti-colonial politics shaped the Indian delegate's concerns and priorities at Geneva. The emphasis placed on terrorism as a problem of territory, the relationship between terrorism and political crime, and the framing of terrorism as a threat to civilization itself all serve to highlight the importance of situating India's colonial laws of terror within a larger contextual framework. The convention also indicates the highly contingent nature of modern understandings of terrorism, and the ways that they were produced through a particular set of local and international circumstances. By reading colonial India's counter-terrorism laws alongside its participation in a larger international discussion regarding the challenge that non-state violence posed to state

[114] Legal aspect and definition of terrorism, 16 April 1935, LNA, C.R.T.1(a), p. 3.

actors, it becomes possible to locate terrorism as a form of violence intimately linked to questions of authority and state formation. If terrorism and international authority are to be understood as competing yet complementary aspects of modern governance, the question of terrorism then becomes an important entry point not only into issues of political violence, but also into the very nature of the modern international system itself.

Conclusion

Empire, Law, and Terrorism in the 21st Century

While the exceptional legal measures adopted by the colonial state to suppress 'terrorist' attacks in the 1920s and 1930s attracted the sustained criticism of India's mainstream nationalist politicians, these measures did not disappear when the country gained independence at the stroke of midnight on 15 August 1947. To the contrary, the spectre of 'terrorism' would haunt the independent nation-states of India and Pakistan – and later Bangladesh – for the next seventy years and beyond. While the postcolonial states of South Asia finally returned sovereignty to the people of the subcontinent, many of the legal and bureaucratic structures that had provided a framework for colonial rule remained in place. These included various extraordinary laws that targeted terrorism, sedition, and armed insurgency. Born out of the brutal violence of partition, in which hundreds of thousands died and millions were displaced in communal clashes between Hindus, Muslims, and Sikhs, both India and Pakistan emerged at a time of bloody crisis.[1]

On 30 January 1948, independent India suffered its first major assassination when Mohandas Gandhi was shot three times at close range by a young radical named Nathuram Godse, at a multi-faith prayer meeting at Birla House in New Delhi. Godse was a former member of the Hindu nationalist RSS, but had left the organization in the 1940s to start his own militant association called Hindu Rashtra Dal.[2] Gandhi was carried back to his room but was declared dead within half an hour, while Godse was apprehended on the spot and beaten with sticks by the angry crowd before being taken into custody by the police. Just as had been the case approximately four decades earlier following the assassination of Curzon-Wylie by Madan Lal Dhingra, V. D. Savarkar fell under suspicion as the alleged mastermind behind the plot, although he ultimately escaped

[1] Yasmin Khan, *The Great Partition: The Making of India and Pakistan* (New Haven, CT: Yale University Press, 2007).

[2] Thomas Blom Hansen, *The Saffron Wave: Democracy and Hindu Nationalism in Modern India*, (Princeton, NJ: Princeton University Press, 1999), p. 249.

conviction. Godse blamed Gandhi for the partition of India and saw his killing as revenge for the chaos inflicted by this partition upon the Hindu community. Ironically, the assassination and the mourning rituals that followed it served only to consolidate the sovereignty of the Nehruvian state dominated by the secular Indian National Congress.[3]

Following the murder of Gandhi, Godse was variously called a 'Hindu fanatic'[4] or simply an 'assassin' in the press,[5] while Jawaharlal Nehru referred to him as a 'madman'.[6] The question of whether Godse should be regarded as an assassin, terrorist, or even patriot remains a hotly contested political issue in contemporary India. A 2013 article in *Mainstream Weekly* referred to Godse as the 'First Terrorist of Independent India',[7] while in 2014 an MP for the Bharatiya Janata Party (BJP) named Sakshi Maharaj controversially referred to Godse as a nationalist who 'did a lot for the nation.'[8] In 2015, the BJP's IT specialist Amit Malviya attracted criticism for tweeting a link to an unverified copy of Godse's final statement to the court, titled 'Why I Killed Gandhi', and writing 'Nathuram Godse had his reasons to assassinate M K Gandhi. A fair society must hear him out too.'[9] The motivations of Godse, his place in India's history, and the extent of his involvement with the RSS remain the subject of polarized debate between the BJP and the Indian National Congress.[10]

Such controversy is not limited to the killer of the Mahatma. Ongoing separatist movements in India's north-east, a Kashmiri resistance movement increasingly inflected by jihadist idioms, and a 'Red Corridor' across eastern India held by Maoist insurgents all contribute to an ongoing politically charged public conversation in independent India regarding the relationship between 'terrorism' and the state. Continued debates regarding emergency laws, freedom of expression, and the scope of permissible political dissent all carry echoes of the colonial prose of counterterrorism that formed the topic of this book. Recent insurgent

[3] Yasmin Khan, 'Performing Peace: Gandhi's Assassination as a Critical Moment in the Consolidation of the Nehruvian State', *Modern Asian Studies* 45, no. 1 (2011), pp. 57-80.

[4] *The Manchester Guardian* (31 January 1948), p. 1.

[5] *The Hindu* (31 January 1948), p. 1.

[6] *The New York Times* (31 January 1948), p. 1.

[7] *Mainstream Weekly*, LI, no. 49 (25 November 2013), https://mainstreamweekly.net/article4603.html

[8] *India Today* (11 December 2014), http://indiatoday.intoday.in/story/gandhi-killer-nathuram-godse-nationalist-bjp-mp-sakshi-maharaj-assassin-parliament-rajya-sabha/1/406344.html

[9] Quoted in *Daily O* (3 October 2017), https://www.dailyo.in/politics/amit-malviya-gandhi-godse-bjp-modi-government/story/1/19858.html

[10] *NDTV* (5 July 2018), https://www.ndtv.com/india-news/rss-talks-about-mahatma-gandhi-but-follows-nathuram-godse-rahul-gandhi-1878094

Figure 6.1 Funeral procession of Mohandas Gandhi in Allahabad, following his assassination at the hand of Hindu nationalist Nathuram Godse in 1948.
(Photo by Keystone via Getty Images.)

attacks in India include the bombing of a passenger train heading from Bhopal to Ujjain by radicals allegedly inspired by ISIS, the murder of eight Hindu pilgrims on their way to the Amarnath Temple in the Kashmir Valley, and a Maoist IED attack in Chhattisgarh that left nine police dead and six others injured. The Indian government consistently responds to these incidents with enhanced security measures, many of which trace their genealogy directly to the emergency laws of the colonial state. As just one example, the controversial Armed Forces Special Powers Act, introduced to combat unrest in Nagaland in 1958, was based on the act of the same name used to suppress the Quit India movement in 1942.[11]

In even a cursory glance at the history of insurgency in independent India, it becomes clear that a colonial discourse of sinister thugs, dacoits, or terrorists residing in criminal neighbourhoods and posing a threat to ordered society and civilization has, in many cases, been directly borrowed and appropriated by the upper-caste-dominated ruling parties.[12] The bureaucratic and administrative rationale of the independent Indian nation-state did not emerge *ex nihilo*, but relied heavily on the infrastructure of rule created by the colonial state, particularly in terms of policing, taxation, and law. The bureaucratic apparatus of high-caste, middle-class administrators and functionaries remained largely intact, and in fact even expanded over decades of largely uncontested Congress rule. As anthropologist Thomas Blom Hansen puts it, the Indian state carried on a 'double discourse' that 'governed middle-class society through law and rational procedure, and ruled popular communities through rather repressive means and through the long-standing connivance and shared political imaginaries of local social elites and the local representatives of the state'.[13]

With the rise of the Hindu nationalist BJP in the 1990s and the early twenty-first century, the prose of counterterrorism shows no sign of abating. Nor does the ontological guilt with which certain communities remain branded, particularly in the case of Muslims in India, who are seen – as in so many other parts of the post-9/11 world – as innately predisposed towards terrorism and other acts of sabotage or violence against the state.[14] Where a colonial architecture of knowledge once slotted thugs and 'habitual' dacoits into biologically determined

[11] See full text of the Armed Forces Special Powers Act of 1958 at: https://indiacode.nic.in/handle/123456789/1527?view_type=search&sam_handle=123456789/1362
[12] Hansen, *Saffron Wave*, p. 51. [13] Ibid, p. 46.
[14] *The Independent* (18 September 2018), https://www.independent.co.uk/news/world/asia/india-rohingya-muslims-deport-burma-40000-supreme-court-terrorists-bangladesh-myanmar-a7953851.html

Figure 6.2 BJP President Amit Shah paying tribute to anti-colonial revolutionary Khudiram Bose during a political rally in Kolkata in 2018. More than a century after his death, Khudiram and others like him continue to be commemorated by Indian politicians, while many colonial-era counter-terrorism laws remain in place.
(Photo by Shubradip Ray / *Hindustan Times* via Getty Images.)

categories of criminality, a new globally oriented prose of counterterrorism seeks to categorize Muslim communities around the world as terrorists-in-waiting due to a supposedly set and unchanging religio-cultural predisposition. These assumptions echo with uncanny similarity the writings of Sir William Hunter, who asked in the 1870s if Indian Muslims were 'bound in conscience to rebel against the Queen'. When Hindu nationalists refer to Indian Muslims as a third column for Pakistani interests, or when US President Donald Trump advances discredited conspiracy theories that thousands of New Jersey Muslims cheered when the World Trade Center fell on 9/11, they are advancing a one-dimensional perspective on Islam that has scarcely changed in a century and a half.

Colonial Genealogies of the 'War on Terror'

Although this book has drawn heavily from archival documentation connected to the history of colonial India, India was only one node – albeit an important one – in the production of 'terrorism' as a global category of criminality. More work is needed that will trace the cross-imperial and, indeed, trans-imperial trajectories of the prose of counterterrorism. While this book has illustrated the relationship between colonial law in India and the international law of the League of Nations, it has had space to provide only some tentative gestures towards the wider applicability of its insights within a larger global context. This book's title, A *Genealogy of Terrorism* rather than The *Genealogy of Terrorism*, is certainly not accidental, and the current study does not claim to provide a complete picture of this multifaceted phenomenon. After all, the twentieth century saw budding insurgencies break out in far-flung corners of the British Empire that included Ireland, Malaya, Burma, East Africa, Iraq, and Palestine. As we have seen, British imperial officials often borrowed personnel and tactics from different colonial possessions in responding to these insurgencies. But what has been less understood, or even remarked upon, is the extent to which an emerging imperial prose of counterterrorism became consolidated throughout this period. Such an investigation need not limit itself to the British case alone, but would provide a fertile lens of comparison for understanding how events within the French Empire – notably Algeria and Indochina – and the Dutch Empire – notably Indonesia – contributed to an imperial prose of counterinsurgency that was truly global in character. Unfortunately, such an inquiry has been beyond the scope of the current project.

Given the polarized nature of contemporary global debates on emergency measures designed to tackle terrorism, a deeper historical context for these discussions is sorely needed. *A Genealogy of Terrorism* provides important grounds for rethinking 'terrorism' as the product of a specific set of historical circumstances and concerns, rather than a natural category of international criminality. In fact, by examining the 1937 League of Nations convention on terrorism, this book has illustrated the ways in which a normative acceptance of terrorism as the default category of analysis for understanding global manifestations of political violence was shaped by a distinct range of concerns tied to issues of territory, politics, sovereignty, and authority. This approach both provides insight into the nature of colonial rule in India during the height of British power and provides the beginnings of a framework for sketching out what French philosopher Michel Foucault referred to as 'a history of the present'.[15] As future research continues to build upon this terrain by expanding beyond the temporal and geographical limits of the current project, insight into the origins and legacies of terrorism as a political and

[15] Foucault, *Discipline and Punish*, p. 31.

legal category of analysis will render possible a deeper understanding of both past and present.

Explicating the colonial genealogies of the current 'War on Terror' is of more than just academic interest. Current counterterrorism proposals and policies advanced by politicians and scholars alike often rely on the same implicit logics of 'hereditary' or 'culturally determined' criminality that structured colonial law in the nineteenth and twentieth centuries. While the 'excesses' of the Bush administration – including the abuses at Abu Ghraib or the extralegal status of Guantanamo Bay – are often critiqued by liberals, the role of liberalism itself in structuring a global prose of counterterrorism is often ignored. Just as early colonial discourses regarding indigenous 'barbarism', 'backwardness', or 'fanaticism' were predicated upon a liberal conception of cultural difference and civilizational advancement, so too do contemporary commentators advance the 'common-sense' conclusion that some parts or peoples of the world are inherently predisposed towards religious militancy.[16]

Extensive research has highlighted the fact that religious extremism is only one of many factors that pushes people – most often men – to commit acts of ideologically motivated violence against civilians or state officials.[17] Nonetheless, commentators frequently continue to draw an artificial distinction between the culturally inspired 'terrorism' of 'outsiders' versus acts of domestic mass violence carried out by cultural 'insiders'. As researchers have pointed out, a Muslim carrying out an act of mass murder in a Western country will almost always be labelled a terrorist, whereas a similar attack carried out by a white European or North American, no matter how explicitly ideological in nature, will often be prosecuted under the lesser category of 'hate crime'.[18] While Muslim attackers since the nineteenth century have been labelled 'fanatics' and the Malayan insurgents of the twentieth century were said to 'run amok' due to distinctive and primitive cultural pathologies, 'lone gunmen' such as Dylan Roof or Alexandre Bissonnette are most often understood through the lens of mental illness or individual grievances,

[16] Neuroscientist Sam Harris has been a leading proponent of this perspective, referring to Islam as 'the motherlode of bad ideas' while simultaneously justifying the torture of suspected terrorists with troubling strawman arguments such as, 'it seems obvious that the misapplication of torture is far *less* troubling to us than collateral damage: there are, after all, no *infants* at Guantanamo Bay.' Sam Harris, 'In Defense of Torture', 1 June 2006, https://samharris.org/in-defense-of-torture/

[17] Robert A. Pape, *Dying to Win: The Strategic Logic of Suicide Terrorism* (New York: Random House Trade Paperbacks, 2006).

[18] Jonas R. Kunst, Lisa S. Myhren, and Ivuoma N. Onyeador, 'Simply Insane? Attributing Terrorism to Mental Illness (Versus Ideology) Affects Mental Representations of Race', *Criminal Justice and Behavior* 45, no. 12 (2018), pp. 1888–902.

and are not similarly positioned as representatives of the 'savagery' or 'backwardness' of their culture.

In recent years, heads of state and their intelligence agencies have increasingly come to emphasize far-right and white supremacist organizations as significant 'terrorist' threats, as evidenced by New Zealand PM Jacinda Ardern acknowledging that the horrific massacre of Muslims carried out in Christchurch in 2019 could 'only be described as a terrorist attack'.[19] The same year, Public Safety Canada added, for the first time, two neo-Nazi groups to its list of outlawed terrorist organizations, marking an important riposte to the global proliferation of freshly emboldened white supremacists.[20] According to data produced by the Anti-Defamation League's Center on Extremism, 71 per cent of fatalities generated by extremist violence in the United States from 2008 to 2017 was caused by far-right and white nationalist groups, while Islamist extremists were responsible for 26 per cent.[21] As such, it is more important than ever to establish a coherent and consistent genealogy of terrorism that eschews polemical or cultural explanations in favour of a more nuanced approach that takes into account the global imperial context in which this term originated.

Public perceptions of terrorism in many parts of the world remain deeply connected to fears of foreign or unfamiliar cultures, most notably Islam. Based on public attitude questionnaires conducted by the Pew Research Centre, the majority of Europeans in eight of the eleven countries surveyed expressed the belief in 2016 that accepting refugees from North Africa and the Middle East increased the likelihood of terrorist attacks within host countries. In countries such as Germany, the United Kingdom, and Sweden, the fear of terrorism outweighed other concerns about refugees such as the potential economic or social consequences on employment or healthcare.[22] In another survey conducted in the United States in 2018, 73 per cent of respondents identified terrorism as the top priority for President Trump and Congress, with other issues such as education, healthcare, and the economy receiving slightly lower

[19] BBC News (15 March 2019), https://www.bbc.com/news/av/world-asia-47579433/new-zealand-pm-jacinda-ardern-this-can-only-be-described-as-a-terrorist-attack

[20] *Global News* (26 June 2019), https://globalnews.ca/news/5432851/canada-adds-neo-nazi-groups-blood-honour-and-combat-18-to-list-of-terror-organizations/

[21] 'ADL Report: White Supremacist Murders More Than Doubled in 2017', (17 January 2018), https://www.adl.org/news/press-releases/adl-report-white-supremacist-murders-more-than-doubled-in-2017

[22] Richard Wike, Bruce Stokes and Katie Simmons, 'Europeans Fear Wave of Refugees Will Mean More Terrorism, Fewer Jobs', *Pew Research Center* (11 July 2016), https://www.pewresearch.org/global/2016/07/11/europeans-fear-wave-of-refugees-will-mean-more-terrorism-fewer-jobs/

percentages.[23] While the survey did not differentiate between domestic and international terrorism, Trump's victory in the 2016 election following his proposals to ban Muslims from entering America, restore the use of 'enhanced interrogation' techniques such as waterboarding, and force Muslim Americans to carry special identity papers illustrates that Muslim minorities remain a 'security concern' for a decisive segment of American voters.[24]

While scholars have pointed out the imperial implications of the US-led 'War on Terror' that began under President Bush and continued with his successors, less has been said about the genealogies of 'terrorism' itself as a legal and political category of 'colonial difference'. In tracing the legal and discursive shifts that began in the early nineteenth century and continued well into the twentieth, this book has shown how terrorism emerged as a category of exceptional criminality within the context of broader global forces such as colonialism, nationalism, and international law. Only by rigorously interrogating the premises and cultural perceptions that underlay early discourses of 'terrorism' in the colonial world does it become possible to understand how the term came to acquire its current connotations. Ultimately, such an approach is key to any attempt to understand the modern phenomenon of 'terrorism' in analytical, rather than political, terms.

[23] John Gramlich, 'Defending against Terrorism Has Remained a Top Policy Priority for Americans since 9/11', *Pew Research Center* (11 September 2018), https://www.pewresearch.org/fact-tank/2018/09/11/defending-against-terrorism-has-remained-a-top-policy-priority-for-americans-since-9-11/

[24] The Washington Post (15 March 2019), https://www.washingtonpost.com/opinions/2019/03/15/short-history-president-trumps-anti-muslim-bigotry/?utm_term=.02946c981bc5

Glossary

Adivasi	Indigenous and tribal peoples of the Indian subcontinent.
Ahimsa	Principle of non-violence found in Hinduism, Buddhism, and Jainism.
Amok	Medico-legal term for supposedly uncontrollable acts of violence.
Babu	Derogatory term for Bengali man.
Bhadralok	Bengali middle class.
Bhang	An edible mixture made of cannabis.
Dacoit	Bandit.
Dharma	A term in Hinduism and Buddhism that roughly corresponds to universal order.
Din	Islamic faith.
Diwani	Rights for control over land revenue.
Fatwa	A resolution on a point of Islamic law, issued by an authority.
Ghazi	Term for a Muslim soldier.
Ghazvah	An Arabic term for religious warfare.
Hool	Rebellion.
Ijtihad	Textual exegesis.
Jihad	A spiritual or physical struggle in the Islamic tradition.
Jihadist	A Muslim who participates in *jihad*.
Jirga	A traditional tribal gathering in Pashtun culture.
Kala pani	Black waters, a term for the Indian Ocean.
Khilafat	A transnational movement that protested the removal of the Ottoman caliph.
Lathi	Bamboo stave.
Mlecchas	Sanskrit for barbarian or foreigner.
Mofussil	Rural area.
Phansigar	Strangler.
Sadhu	Hindu ascetic.
Samiti	Society or association.

Sati	Practice in which widows immolated themselves on their husband's funeral pyre.
Satyagraha	Literally truth-force, also refers to Gandhi's non-violence campaign.
Sepoy	Indian soldier.
Shaheed	A martyr.
Swadeshi	Self-sufficiency, also refers to economic boycott of British goods.
Swaraj	Self-rule, can carry either personal or political connotations.
Thag	Hindi term for cheat or swindler, root for the term thug.
Tulsi	Plant cultivated for religious purposes in Hinduism.
Zamindar	Landowner.

Select Bibliography

Archival Sources

National Archives of India, New Delhi

Proceedings of the following departments:
External Affairs
Foreign and Political
Home and Political
Political and Secret

Nehru Memorial Museum and Library, New Delhi

Private Papers and Manuscripts

National Library of India, Kolkata

Foreign Official Documents
Newspapers and Periodicals
Manuscripts

Public Record Office, The National Archives, Kew

Colonial Office records
Foreign Office records
Home Office records
War Office records

India Office Records, British Library, London

Legislative, Political and Secret department records
European Manuscripts

League of Nations Archives, Geneva

Comité Répression Internationale du Terrorisme records
League of Nations Secretariat records

Waseda University Library, Tokyo

Microfilm and Manuscripts

South Asian American Digital Archive

Mahesh and Ishwar Chandra family materials

Sri Aurobindo Ashram Archive

Documents in the life of Sri Aurobindo

National Archives of Singapore

Photographs

Private Papers

Birkenhead Papers, Nehru Memorial Museum and Library, New Delhi.
Cecil of Chelwood Papers, European Manuscripts, British Library, London.
Chelmsford Papers, Nehru Memorial Museum and Library, New Delhi.
Halifax Papers, Nehru Memorial Museum and Library, New Delhi.
Hardinge Papers, Cambridge University Library.
Linlithgow Papers, Nehru Memorial Museum and Library, New Delhi.
Lytton Papers, European Manuscripts, British Library, London.
Morley Collection, Nehru Memorial Museum and Library, New Delhi.
Reading Papers, European Manuscripts, British Library, London.
Tegart Papers, Centre of South Asian Studies, University of Cambridge.

Newspapers

Amrita Bazar Patrika (Calcutta)
Asiatic Quarterly Review (London)
Bande Mataram (Calcutta)
BBC News (London)
The Bengalee (Calcutta)

The Canberra Times (Canberra)
Cincinnati Inquirer (Cincinnati)
Detroit Free Press (Detroit)
Empire (Sydney)
Foreign Policy (Washington, DC)
The Hindu (Madras)
Illustrated London News (London)
The Indian Sociologist (London)
India Today (Noida)
The Irish Times (Dublin)
Launceston Examiner (Launceston, Tasmania)
The Manchester Guardian (Manchester)
Mainstream Weekly (New Delhi)
The New Asia (Tokyo)
The New York Times (New York)
The People (London)
San Francisco Chronicle (San Francisco)
The Saturday Review (London)
South China Morning Post (Hong Kong)
The Statesman (Calcutta)
The Times (London)
The Times of India (Bombay)
The Wall Street Journal (New York)
Young India (Bombay)

Published Primary Sources

Annual Register: A review of public events at home and abroad for the year 1871. London: Rivingtons, Waterloo Place, 1872.

Bernhardi, Friedrich von, *Germany and the Next War*; trans. Allen Powles. London: E. Arnold, 1912.

Biddulph, John, *The Pirates of Malabar and an Englishwoman in India two hundred years ago*. London: Smith, Elder & Co., 1907.

Bose, Bejai Krishna, *The Alipore Bomb Case*, Calcutta, 1910.

Bose, Sisir K. and Sugata Bose (eds.), *The Essential Writings of Netaji Subhas Chandra Bose*. New Delhi: Oxford University Press, 2014.

Bramley, P. B., *Report on River Crime and River Police Reorganization Scheme, Part 1*. Calcutta: The Bengal Secretariat Press, 1907.

Chapekar, *Damodar Hari, Autobiography of Damodar Hari Chapekar*, Bombay Police Abstracts, 1910.

Charge to the Jury in the Case of Queen-Empress v. Bal Gangadhar Tilak and Keshav Mahadev Bal in the High Court of Bombay, Bombay: Thacker & Co., 1898.

Chirol, Valentine, *Indian Unrest*, London: Macmillan, 1910.

Coldstream, William (ed.), *Records of the government of the North-West Provinces of India during the Mutiny of 1857*. Edinburgh T. & T. Clark, 1902.

Cox, Robert, 'Remarks on the Skulls and Character of the Thugs', *The Phrenological Journal and Miscellany*, 8 (1834): 524–30.

Coyajee, J. C., *India and the League of Nations*, Madras: Waltair, 1932.

Danvers, F. C., 'The Persian Gulf Route and Commerce', *The Asiatic Quarterly Review* 5 (1888): 406.

Das, Asitabha (ed.), *Rashbehari Bose Collected Works: Autobiography, Writing and Speeches*, Kolkata: Kishaloy Prakashan, 2006.

Defence of the Realm Act in Ireland, Dublin: Committee of Public Safety, 1915.

Donogh, Walter Russell, *The History and Law of sedition and cognate offences in British India, penal and preventative*, Calcutta: Thacker, Spink & Co., 1914.

Ghose, Aurobindo, *Speeches*, Pondicherry: Sri Aurobindo Ashram Press, 1952.

Ghose, Barindra, *The Tale of My Exile*, Pondicherry: Arya Office, 1922.

Ghose, Rash Behari, and Gopal Krishna Gokhale, *On Repression*, Adyar Madras: The Commonweal Office, 1916.

Gopal, S. (ed.), *Selected Works of Jawaharlal Nehru*, vol. 14. New Delhi: Orient Longman Limited, 1972.

Grover, B. L., *A Documentary Study of British Policy towards Indian Nationalism: 1885–1909*, Delhi: National Publications, 1967.

Gwynn, Charles, *Imperial Policing*, 2nd ed., London: Macmillan, 1939.

Hatch, W. J., *The Land Pirates of India: An account of the Kuravers a remarkable Tribe of Hereditary Criminals their extraordinary skill as Thieves Cattle-lifters and Highwaymen and their Manners and Customs*. London: Seeley, Service & Company, 1928.

Hunter, William, *The Indian Musulmans: Are they bound in conscience to rebel against the Queen?* 2nd ed. London: Trübner and Company, 1872.

J. R., 'A Romance of Beyt', in *Bombay Miscellany*, 1, no. 2, Bombay: Chesson & Woodhall, 1861.

Kaye, John and G. B. Malleson (ed.), *Kaye and Malleson's History of the Indian Mutiny, II*. London: Allen, 1889.

Khan, Sayyid Ahmad, *Review on Dr. Hunter's Indian Musalmans: Are they bound in conscience to rebel against the Queen?* Benares: Printed at the Medical Hall Press, 1872.

Low, Charles, *History of the Indian Navy (1613–1863)*, 2 volumes. London: 1877.

Lytton, Earl of, *Pundits and Elephants. Being the experiences of five years as governor of an Indian province, etc*, London, 1942.

Mansergh, Nicholas (ed.), *The Transfer of Power, 1942–7*, vol. III. London: Her Majesty's Stationery Office, 1971.

Mitchell, W. F., *Reminiscences of the Great Mutiny, 1857–59*. London: Macmillan and Co., Ltd., 1910.

O'Dwyer, Michael, *India As I Knew It*. London: Constable & Company, 1925.

Petrie, David, *Communism in India, 1924–1927*, Calcutta: Editions Indian, 1972.

Prichard, Iltudus Thomas, *The Administration of India from 1859 to 1868: The first ten years of administration under the crown*, vol. 1. London: Macmillan and Co, 1869.

Rai, Lala Lajpat, *The story of my deportation*, New Delhi: Metropolitan, 1908.

Ram, V. S. and B. M. Sharma, *India and the League of Nations*, Lucknow: The Upper India Publishing House Ltd., 1932.

Ray, R. E. A, *Report on the Dacca Sri Sangha up to 1929*, Calcutta: Bengal Government Press, 1932.

Report of Sir N. Chandavarkar and Mr. Justice Beachcroft on detenus and internees in Bengal; P.P. 1918. (Cmd. 9198).
Report on the trials of Alexander M. Sullivan and Richard Pigott, for seditious liberls on the government, Dublin: printed by Alexander Thom, 1868.
Saaler, Sven and Christopher Szpilman (eds.), Pan-Asianism: A Documentary History, *vol. 1:* 1850–1920, Plymouth: Rowman & Littlefield, 2011.
Samanta, Amiya K. (ed.), *Terrorism in Bengal: A Collection of Documents on Terrorist Activities from 1905 to 1939*, Calcutta: Government of West Bengal, 1995. Vols. 1–6.
Sanyal, Sachindranath, *My Life in Prison*, Shakshi Prakashan, 2012.
Sarkar, Hemanta, *Revolutionaries of Bengal: Their Methods and Ideals*, Calcutta: The Indian Book Club, 1923.
Savarkar, V. D., *The Story of My Transportation for Life*, Bombay: Sadbhakti Publications, 1950.
The Indian War of Independence. London: 1909.
Sedition Committee Report 1918 (Calcutta: Superintendent Government Printing, India, 1918.
Selected Works of Veer Savarkar, vol. 4. Chandigarh: Abhishek Publications, 2007.
Sleeman, W. H., *Ramaseeana, or a vocabulary of the peculiar language used by the Thugs*. Calcutta: G.H. Huttmann, Military Orphan Press, 1836.
Smith, George, *Life of John Wilson: For fifty years philanthropist and scholar in the east*. London: John Murray, 1878.
Summary of the Administration of the Government of India 1910–16, Delhi: Superintendent Government Printing, 1916.
Taylor, Philip Meadows, *Confessions of a Thug*. London: Richard Bentley, 1839.
Waraich, Malwinderjit Singh, and Harinder Singh (eds.), Ghadar Movement Original Documents, *vol. 1:* Lahore Conspiracy Cases I and II, Chandigarh: Unistar Books Pvt. Ltd., 2008.
Wedgwood, Josiah, *Essays and Adventures of a Labour M.P.*, London: George Allen & Unwin Ltd, 1924.
Williams, John Fischer, *Some Aspects of the Covenant of the League of Nations*, London: 1934.
International Change and International Peace, London: Oxford University Press, 1932.
Woodhead, John (Chairman), *Famine Inquiry Commission: Report on Bengal*. Government of India Press, 1945.

Unpublished Dissertations

McClure, Alastair, *Violence, Sovereignty, and the Making of Colonial Criminal Law in India, 1857–1914*. University of Cambridge, 2017. PhD Dissertation.
Smith, Jacob Ramsay, *Imperial Retribution: The Hunt for Nana Sahib and Rebel Leaders in the Aftermath of the Indian 'Mutiny' of 1857*. Queen Mary University of London, 2017. PhD Dissertation.
Winther, Paul, *Chambal River Dacoity: A Study of Banditry in North Central India*. Cornell University, 1972. PhD Dissertation.

Yechury, Akhila, *Empire, Nation and the French Settlements in India, c.1930–1954*, University of Cambridge, 2012. PhD Dissertation.

Books and Articles

Aaronson, Mike et al., *Precision Strike Warfare and International Intervention: Strategic, Ethico-Legal and Decisional Implications*, London: Routledge, 2015.

Agamben, Giorgio, *State of Exception*, trans. Kevin Attell. Chicago: University of Chicago Press, 2005.

Homo Sacer: Sovereign Power and Bare Life, trans. Daniel Heller-Roazen. Stanford, CA: Stanford University Press, 1998.

Akenson, Donald and Amitava Chowdhury (eds.), *Between Dispersion and Belonging: Global Approaches to Diaspora in Practice*, Montreal: McGill-Queen's University Press, 2016.

Alavi, Seema, *The Sepoys and the Company: Tradition and Transition in Northern India 1770–1830*, Delhi: Oxford University Press, 1995.

Almy, Ruth L., '"More Hateful because of Its Hypocrisy": Indians, Britain and Canadian Law in the Komagata Maru Incident of 1914', *Journal of Imperial and Commonwealth History* 46, no. 2 (2018): 304–22.

Amin, Shahid, *Event, Metaphor, Memory: Chauri Chaura, 1922–1992*, New Delhi: Oxford University Press, 1995.

Anand, Anita, *The Patient Assassin: A True Tale of Massacre, Revenge, and India's Quest for Independence*, New York: Scribner, 2019.

Anderson, Benedict, *Under Three Flags: Anarchism and the Anti-Colonial Imagination*, London: Verso, 2005.

Imagined Communities: Reflections on the Origin and Spread of Nationalism, London: Verso, 1983.

Anderson, Clare, 'Transnational Histories of Penal Transportation: Punishment, Labour and Governance in the British Imperial World, 1788–1939', *Australian Historical Studies* 47, no. 3 (2016): 381–97.

Subaltern Lives: Biographies of Colonialism in the Indian Ocean World, 1790–1920, Cambridge: Cambridge University Press, 2012.

'"The Wisdom of the Barbarian": Rebellion, Incarceration, and the Santal Body-Politic', *South Asia: Journal of South Asian Studies* 31, no. 2 (2008): 223–40.

The Indian Uprising of 1857–8: Prisons, Prisoners and Rebellion, London: Anthem Press, 2007.

Legible Bodies: Race, Criminality and Colonialism in South Asia, Oxford: Bloomsbury, 2004.

Andrew, Christopher, *The Defence of the Realm: The Authorized History of MI5*, Toronto: Penguin, 2010.

Appadurai, Arjun, *Fear of Small Numbers: An Essay on the Geography of Anger*, Durham, NC: Duke University Press, 2006.

Arendt, Hannah, *The Origins of Totalitarianism*, New York: Harcourt Brace Jovanovich, 1973.

On Violence. New York: Harcourt, Brace & World, 1970.

Armitage, David, *Civil Wars: A History in Ideas*, New York: Allen Lane, 2017.

Foundations of International Thought, Cambridge: Cambridge University Press, 2013.

Arnold, David, 'Islam, the Mappilas, and Peasant Revolt in Malabar', *The Journal of Peasant Studies*, 9, no. 2 (1982): 255–65.

Arondekar, Anjali, 'Without a Trace: Sexuality and the Colonial Archive', *Journal of the History of Sexuality*, 14, no. ½ (2005): 10–25.

Arora, Saurabh, 'Gatherings of Mobility and Immobility: Itinerant "Criminal Tribes" and Their Containment by the Salvation Army in Colonial South India', *Transfers: Interdisciplinary Journal of Mobility Studies* 4, no. 1 (2014): 8–26.

Ashton, Steven, *British Policy towards the Indian States*, London: Curzon, 1982.

Aslan, Reza, *Beyond Fundamentalism: Confronting Religious Extremism in the Age of Globalization*, New York: Random House, 2010.

Aydin, Cemal, *The Politics of Anti-Westernism in Asia: Visions of World Order in Pan-Islamic and Pan-Asian Thought*, New York: Columbia University Press, 2007.

Bailkin, Jordanna, 'The Boot and the Spleen: When Was Murder Possible in British India?', *Comparative Studies in Society and History* 48, no. 2 (2006): 462–93.

Baker, Keith, *Inventing the French Revolution: Essays on French Political Culture in the Eighteenth Century*, Cambridge: Cambridge University Press, 1990.

Bakhle, Janaki, 'Savarkar (1883–1966), Sedition and Surveillance: The Rule of Law in a Colonial Situation', *Social History* 35, 1 (2010): 51–75.

Banerjee, Prathama, 'Historic Acts? Santal Rebellion and the Temporality of Practice', *Studies in History* 15, no. 2 (1999): 209–46.

Barrier, N. Gerald, *Banned: Controversial Literature and Political Control in British India, 1907–1947*, New Delhi: Manohar, 1976.

Bashford, Alison, *Global Population: History, Geopolitics, and Life on Earth*, New York: Columbia University Press, 2014.

Bashford, Alison and Jane McAdam, 'The Right to Asylum: Britain's 1905 Aliens Act and the Evolution of Refugee Law', *Law and History Review* 32, no. 2 (2014): 309–50.

Bashford, Alison and Catie Gilchrist, 'The Colonial History of the 1905 Aliens Act', *The Journal of Imperial and Commonwealth History* 40, no. 3 (2012): 409–37.

Basu, Subho, *Does Class Matter? Colonial Capital and Workers' Resistance in Bengal, 1890–1937*, New Delhi: Oxford University Press, 2004.

Bates, Crispin et al. (eds.), *Mutiny at the Margins: New Perspectives on the Indian Uprising of 1857*, New Delhi: Sage, 2013–2017. Vols. 1–7.

Bayly, Christopher, *The Birth of the Modern World, 1780–1914: Global Connections and Comparisons*, Malden, MA: Blackwell, 2004.

Empire and Information: Intelligence Gathering and Social Communication in India, 1780–1870, Cambridge: Cambridge University Press, 1996.

Imperial Meridian: The British Empire and the World, 1780–1830, London: Routledge, 1989.

Rulers, Townsmen and Bazaars: North Indian Society in the Age of British Expansion, 1770–1870, Cambridge: Cambridge University Press, 1983.

Bayly, Christopher and Tim Harper, *Forgotten Armies: Britain's Asian Empire and the War with Japan*, London: Penguin Books, 2005.

Bell, Christopher (ed.), *Naval Mutinies of the Twentieth Century: An International Perspective*, New York: Routledge, 2003.

Bender, Jill C., *The 1857 Indian Uprising and the British Empire*, Cambridge: Cambridge University Press, 2016.

Benton, Lauren, *A Search for Sovereignty: Law and Geography in European Empires, 1400–1900*, New York: Cambridge University Press, 2010.

'Colonial Law and Cultural Difference: Jurisdictional Politics and the Formation of the Colonial State', *Comparative Studies in Society and History* 41, 3 (1999): 563–88.

Beyer, Cornclia, *Violent Globalisms: Conflict in Response to Empire*, Aldershot: Ashgate, 2008.

Bhargava, Meena (ed.), *The Decline of the Mughal Empire*, New Delhi: Oxford University Press, 2014.

Bhattacharyya, Amit, *Swadeshi Enterprise in Bengal, 1900–1920*, Calcutta: Mita Bhattacharyya: Distributed by Seagull Bookshop, 1986.

Birla, Ritu, *Stages of Capital: Law, Culture, and Market Governance in Late Colonial India*, Durham, NC: Duke University Press, 2009.

Bix, Herbert P., *Hirohito and the Making of Modern Japan.*,New York: Perennial, HarperCollins, 2001.

Borgonovo, John, 'Review Article: Revolutionary Violence and Irish Historiography', *Irish Historical Studies* 38, no. 150 (2012): 325–31.

Bose, A. C., *Indian Revolutionaries Abroad 1905–1922, in the Background of International Developments*, Patna: Bharati Bawan, 1971.

Bose, Sugata, *His Majesty's Opponent: Subhas Chandra Bose and India's Struggle against Empire*, Cambridge, MA: Harvard University Press, 2011.

Brantlinger, Patrick, *Taming Cannibals: Race and the Victorians*, Ithaca, NY: Cornell University Press, 2011.

Brown, Emily, *Har Dayal: Hindu Revolutionary and Rationalist*, Tucson: University of Arizona Press, 1975.

Brown, Giles, 'The Hindu Conspiracy, 1914–1917', *Pacific Historical Review* XVII (1948): 299–310.

Brown, Mark, *Penal Power and Colonial Rule*, New York: Routledge, 2014.

Brückenhaus, Daniel, *Policing Transnational Protest: Liberal Imperialism and the Surveillance of Anticolonialists in Europe, 1905–1945*, New York: Oxford University Press, 2017.

Bryant, G. J., *The Emergence of British Power in India, 1600–1784: A Grand Strategic Interpretation*, Woodbridge: The Boydell Press, 2013.

Burleigh, Michael, *Blood and Rage: A Cultural History of Terrorism*, London: HarperPress, 2008.

Burton, Antoinette (ed.), *After the Imperial Turn: Thinking with and through the Nation*, Durham, NC: Duke University Press, 2003.

Butler, Judith, *Frames of War: When Is Life Grievable?*, London: Verso, 2009.

Campbell, Gwyn, 'Piracy in the Indian Ocean World: A Survey from Early Times to the Modern Day', *Interventions: International Journal of Postcolonial Studies* 16, no. 6 (2014): 775–94.

An Economic History of Imperial Madagascar, 1750–1895: The Rise and Fall of an Island Empire, Cambridge: Cambridge University Press, 2005.

Campbell, Peter, 'East Meets Left: South Asian Militants and the Social Party of Canada in British Columbia, 1904–1914', *International Journal of Canadian Studies* 20 (1999): 35–65.

Carol, Gluck and Anne Lowenhaupt Tsing (eds.), *Words in Motion: Toward a Global Lexicon*, Durham, NC: Duke University Press, 2009.

Carr, Matthew, *The Infernal Machine: A History of Terrorism*, New York: The New Press, 2006.

Chakrabarty, Dipesh, *Provincializing Europe: Postcolonial Thought and Historical Difference*, Princeton, NJ: Princeton University Press, 2000.

Chaliand, Gérard and Arnaud Blin (eds.), *The History of Terrorism: From Antiquity to Al Qaeda*, Berkeley: University of California Press, 2007.

Chatterjee, Partha, *The Black Hole of Empire: History of a Global Practice of Power*, Princeton, NJ: Princeton University Press, 2012.

The Politics of the Governed: Popular Politics in Most of the World, New York: Columbia University Press, 2004.

The Nation and Its Fragments: Colonial and Postcolonial Histories, Princeton, NJ: Princeton University Press, 1993.

Chatterjee, Ruma, 'Cotton Handloom Manufactures of Bengal, 1870–1921', *Economic and Political Weekly* 22, no. 25 (1987): 988–97.

Choudhury, Deep Kanta Lahiri, *Telegraphic Imperialism: Crisis and Panic in the Indian Empire, c.1830*. Houndmills: Palgrave Macmillan, 2010.

'Sinews of Panic and the Nerves of Empire: The Imagined State's Entanglement with Information Panic, India c. 1800–1912', *Modern Asian Studies* 38, no. 4 (2004): 965–1002.

Clark, Christopher, *The Sleepwalkers: How Europe Went to War in 1914*, New York: HarperCollins, 2013.

Cohn, Bernard, *Colonialism and Its Forms of Knowledge: The British in India*, Princeton, NJ: Princeton University Press, 1996.

An Anthropologist among the Historians and Other Essays, Delhi: Oxford University Press, 1987.

Condos, Mark, *Insecurity State: Punjab and the Making of Colonial Power in British India*, Cambridge: Cambridge University Press, 2017.

'"Fanaticism" and the Politics of Resistance along the North-West Frontier of British India', *Comparative Studies of Society and History* 58, 3 (2016): 717–45.

'License to Kill: The Murderous Outrages Act and the Rule of Law in Colonial India, 1867–1925', *Modern Asian Studies* 50, 2 (2015): 1–39.

Conrad, Sebastian and Dominic Sachsenmaier (eds.), *Competing Visions of World Order: Global Moments and Movements, 1880s–1930s*, New York: Palgrave Macmillan, 2007.

Cook, Hugh, *The Sikh Wars: The British Army in the Punjab, 1845–1849*, London: Leo Cooper, 1975.

Cooper, Frederick, 'Mau Mau and the Discourses of Decolonization', *Journal of African History* 29, no. 2 (1988): 313–20.

Cooper, Randolf G. S., *The Anglo-Maratha Campaigns and the Contest for India: The Struggle for Control of the South Asian Military Economy*, Cambridge: Cambridge University Press, 2003.

Cooter, Roger, *The Cultural Meaning of Popular Science: Phrenology and the Organization of Consent in Nineteenth-Century Britain*, Cambridge: Cambridge University Press, 1984.

Copland, Ian, *The Princes of India in the Endgame of Empire*, Cambridge: Cambridge University Press, 1997.

Curry, J. C., *Tegart of the Indian Police*, Tunbridge Wells, 1960.

Dalrymple, William, *The Return of a King: The Battle for Afghanistan*, London: Bloomsbury, 2013.

The Last Mughal: The Fall of a Dynasty, Delhi, 1857, London: Bloomsbury, 2006.

Datta, V. N. and S. Settar (eds.), *Jallianwala Bagh Massacre*, Delhi: Pragati Publications, 2000.

Davies, Charles E., *The Blood-Red Arab Flag: An Investigation into Qasimi Piracy, 1797–1820*, Exeter: University of Exeter Press, 1997.

Davis, Mike, *Late Victorian Holocausts: El Niño Famines and the Making of the Third World*, London: Verso, 2002.

Deery, Philip, 'The Terminology of Terrorism: Malaya, 1948–52', *Journal of Southeast Asian Studies* 34, 2 (2003): 231–47.

Deflem, Mathieu, *Policing World Society: Historical Foundations of International Police Cooperation*, Oxford: Oxford University Press, 2002.

Devji, Faisal, *The Terrorist in Search of Humanity: Militant Islam and Global Politics*, London: Hurst & Company, 2008.

'Apologetic Modernity', *Modern Intellectual History* 4, no. 1 (2007): 61–76.

Dickens, Charles, *Household Words XII*, 10 November 1855.

Dignan, Don, 'The Hindu Conspiracy in Anglo-American Relations during World War I', *Pacific Historical Review* 40, no. 1 (1979): 57–76.

Dirks, Nicholas, *Castes of Mind: Colonialism and the Making of Modern India*, Princeton, NJ: Princeton University Press, 2001.

Dodge, Toby, *Inventing Iraq: The Failure of Nation Building and a History Denied*, New York: Columbia University Press, 2003.

Draxe, Prabhakar B., 'A Failed Revolt against the Raj: The Rebellion of the Berad, a Criminal Tribe, under the Leadership of Umaji Naik', *Social Change* 35, no. 2 (2005): 127–30.

Egerton, George, *Great Britain and the Creation of the League of Nations*, London: Scholar Press, 1979.

Elam, Daniel, Kama Maclean, and Chris Moffat, (eds.), 'Writing Revolution: Practice, History, Politics' in *South Asia: Journal of South Asian Studies* 39, 3 (2016).

Elden, Stuart, *Terror and Territory: The Spatial Extent of Sovereignty*, Minneapolis: University of Minnesota Press, 2009.

Elkins, Caroline, *Imperial Reckoning: The Untold Story of Britain's Gulag in Kenya*, New York: Henry Holt, 2005.

Elliott, Derek, 'The Politics of Capture in the Eastern Arabian Sea, c. 1700–1750', *International Journal of Maritime History* 25, no. 2 (2013): 187–98.

'The Pirate and the Colonial Project: Kanhoji Angria', *Darkmatter* 5: Special Issue, *Pirates and Piracy* (2009): 80–90.

Esenbel, Selcuk, 'Japan's Global Claim to Asia and the World of Islam: Transnational Nationalism and World Power, 1900–1945', *The American Historical Review* 109, 4 (2004): 1140–70.

Essays in Honour of Prof. S.C. Sarkar. New Delhi: People's Publishing House, 1976.

Evans, Richard, *The Third Reich at War: How the Nazis Led Germany from Conquest to Disaster*, London: Allen Lane, 2008.

The Third Reich in Power, 1933–1939, New York: Penguin, 2005.

The Coming of the Third Reich, London: Allen Lane, 2003.

Fay, Peter Ward, *The Forgotten Army: India's Armed Struggle for Independence, 1942–1945*, Ann Arbor: University of Michigan Press, 1993.

Fenech, Louis E., 'Contested Nationalisms; Negotiated Terrains: The Way Sikhs Remember Udham Singh 'Shahid', (1899–1940)', *Modern Asian Studies* 36, no. 4 (2002): 827–70.

Ferguson, Niall, *Empire: How Britain Made the Modern World*, London: Penguin Books, 2007.

Ferris, John, '"The Internationalism of Islam": The British Perception of a Muslim Menace, 1840–1951', *Intelligence and National Security* 24, no. 1 (2009): 57–77.

Fischer-Tiné, Harald, *Anxieties, Fear and Panic in Colonial Settings: Empires on the Verge of a Nervous Breakdown*, Houndmills: Palgrave, 2017.

Shyamji Krishnavarma: Sanskrit, Sociology and Anti-Imperialism, London: Routledge India, 2014.

'Indian Nationalism and the 'World Forces': Transnational and Diasporic Dimensions of the Indian Freedom Movement on the Eve of the First World War', *Journal of Global History* 3 (2007): 325–44.

Forth, Aidan, *Barbed-Wire Imperialism: Britain's Empire of Camps, 1876–1903*, Berkeley: University of California Press, 2017.

Foucault, Michel, *Security, Territory, Population: Lectures at the Collège de France, 1977–1978*, New York: Palgrave Macmillan, 2009.

Discipline and Punish: The Birth of the Prison, New York: Vintage Books, 1995.

French, Patrick, *Liberty or Death: India's Journey to Independence and Division*, London: Penguin, 2011.

Fuerst, Ilyse R. Morgenstein, *Indian Muslim Minorities and the 1857 Rebellion: Religion, Rebels, and Jihad*, London: I.B. Tauris, 2017.

Gerwath, Robert (ed.), *Twisted Paths: Europe 1914–1945*, Oxford: Oxford University Press, 2008.

Ghandour, Zeina, *A Discourse on Domination in Mandate Palestine: Imperialism, Property, Insurgency*, London: Routledge, 2009.

Ghosh, Anindita, *Power in Print: Popular Publishing and the Politics of Language and Culture in a Colonial Society, 1778–1905*, New Delhi: Oxford University Press, 2006.

Ghosh, Durba, *Gentlemanly Terrorists: Political Violence and the Colonial State in India, 1919–1947*, Cambridge: Cambridge University Press, 2017.

'Gandhi and the Terrorists', *South Asia* 32, no. 3 (2016): 560–76.

Ghosh, Durba and Dane Kennedy (eds.), *Decentring Empire: Britain, India and the Transcolonial World*, New Delhi: Orient Longman Private Ltd., 2006.

Ghosh, Kalyan Kumar, *The Indian National Army; Second Front of the Indian Independence Movement*, Meerut: Meenakshi Prakashan, 1969.

Gildea, Robert, *Empires of the Mind: The Colonial Past and the Politics of the Present*, Cambridge: Cambridge University Press, 2019.

Gong, Gerrit, *The Standard of 'Civilization' in International Society*, Oxford: Clarendon Press, 1984.

Gooptu, Sharmistha and Boria Majumdar (eds.), *Revisiting 1857: Myth, Memory, History*, New Delhi: Lotus Collection, Roli Books, 2007.

Gordon, Leonard, *Bengal: The Nationalist Movement 1876–1940*, New York: Columbia University Press, 1974.

Gorman, Daniel, 'Britain, India, and the United Nations: Colonialism and the Development of International Governance, 1945–1960', *Journal of Global History* 9, 3 (2014): 471–90.

The Emergence of International Society in the 1920s, Cambridge: Cambridge University Press, 2012.

Gopal, Priyamvada, *Insurgent Empire: Anticolonial Resistance and British Dissent*, London: Verso, 2019.

Gould, Stephen Jay, *The Mismeasure of Man*, London: W.W. Norton, 1981.

Gould, William, *Hindu Nationalism and the Language of Politics in Late Colonial India*, New York: Cambridge University Press, 2004.

Gregory, Derek, *The Colonial Present: Afghanistan, Palestine, Iraq*, Malden, MA: Blackwell, 2004.

Grey, Daniel, 'Creating the "Problem Hindu": Sati, Thuggee and Female Infanticide in India, 1800–60', *Gender & History* 25, no. 3 (2013): 498–510.

Guha, Ramachandra, *Gandhi: The Years That Changed the World, 1914–1948*, Toronto: Random House Canada, 2018.

Gandhi before India, London: Penguin Books, 2014.

Guha, Ranajit, *Dominance without Hegemony: History and Power in Colonial India*, Cambridge, MA: Harvard University Press, 1997.

'Not at Home in Empire', *Critical Inquiry* 23, no. 3 (1997): 482–93.

Elementary Aspects of Peasant Insurgency in Colonial India, Delhi: Oxford University Press, 1983.

(ed.), *Subaltern Studies II*, New Delhi: Oxford University Press, 1983.

Gupta, Amit Kumar, 'Defying Death: Nationalist Revolutionism in India, 1897–1938', *Social Scientist* 25, no. 9/10 (1997): 3–27.

Gupta, Ashin Das, *Indian Merchants and the Decline of Suraj, c. 1700–1750*, Wiesbaden: Franz Steiner Verlag, 1979.

Gupta, Manik Lal, *Constitutional Development of India*, New Delhi: Atlantic Publishers & Distributors, 1989.

Hanhimäki, Jussi and Bernhard Blumenau, (eds.), *An International History of Terrorism*, New York: Routledge, 2013.

Hansen, Thomas Blom, *The Saffron Wave: Democracy and Hindu Nationalism in Modern India*, Princeton, NJ: Princeton University Press, 1999.

Harper, Tim, 'Singapore, 1915, and the Birth of the Asian Underground', *Modern Asian Studies* 47, no. 6 (2013): 1782–1811.

Heehs, Peter, *The Lives of Sri Aurobindo*, New York: Columbia University Press, 2008.

Nationalism, Terrorism, Communalism: Essays in Modern Indian History, New Delhi: Oxford University Press, 1998.

'Foreign Influences on Bengali Revolutionary Terrorism, 1902–1908', *Modern Asian Studies* 28, no. 3 (1994): 533–56.

The Bomb in Bengal: The Rise of Revolutionary Terrorism in India, 1900–1910, New Delhi: Oxford University Press, 1993.

Heller-Roazen, Daniel, *The Enemy of All: Piracy and the Law of Nations*, New York: Zone Books, 2009.

Henig, Ruth, *The League of Nations: The Peace Conferences of 1919–1923 and Their Aftermath*, London: Haus Histories, 2010.

Herbert, Auberon, *The Right and Wrong of Compulsion by the State, and Other Essays*, ed. Eric Mack. Indianapolis: Liberty Classics, 1978.

Hinchy, Jessica, 'Obscenity, Moral Contagion and Masculinity: Hijras in Public Space in Colonial North India', *Asian Studies Review* 38, no. 2 (2014): 274–94.

Hobsbawm, Eric, *Age of Extremes: The Short Twentieth Century, 1914–1991*, London: Abacus, 1995.

Hoffman, Bruce, *Inside Terrorism*, London: Victor Gollancz, 1998.

Hoover, Karl, 'The Hindu Conspiracy in California, 1913–1918', *German Studies Review* 8, no. 2 (1985): 245–61.

Hopkins, B. D., 'Jihad on the Frontier: A History of Religious Revolt on the North-West Frontier, 1800–1947', *History Compass* 7, no. 6 (2009): 1459–69.

Hopkirk, Peter, *On Secret Service East of Constantinople: The Plot to Bring Down the British Empire*, London: John Murray, 1994.

Horn, David G., *The Criminal Body: Lombroso and the Anatomy of Deviance*, New York: Routledge, 2003.

Houen, Alex, *Terrorism and Modern Literature: From Joseph Conrad to Ciaran Carson*, Oxford: Oxford University Press, 2002.

Howe, Stephen, *Anticolonialism in British Politics: The Left and the End of Empire, 1918–1964*, Oxford: Oxford University Press, 1983.

Hughes, Michael, 'British Opinion and Russian Terrorism in the 1880s', *European History Quarterly* 41, no. 2 (2011): 255–77.

Huntington, Samuel, *The Clash of Civilizations and the Remaking of World Order*, New York: Touchstone, 1997.

Hussain, Nasser, *The Jurisprudence of Emergency: Colonialism and the Rule of Law*, Ann Arbor: University of Michigan Press, 2003.

Imai, Hissei et al., 'Amok: A Mirror of Time and People. A Historical Review of Literature', *History of Psychiatry* 30, no. 1 (2019): 38–57.

Jackson, Ashley, *Distant Drums: The Role of Colonies in British Imperial Warfare*, Brighton: Sussex Academic Press, 2012.

James, Helen, 'The Assassination of Lord Mayo: The "First" Jihad?', *IJAPS* 5, no. 2 (2009): 1–19.

Jeffery, Keith, *1916: A Global History*, London: Bloomsbury, 2015.
Jeffrey, Robin (ed.), *People, Princes, and Paramount Power: Society and Politics in the Indian Princely States*, Delhi: Oxford University Press, 1978.
Jensen, Joan, 'The "Hindu Conspiracy": A Reassessment' *Pacific Historical Review* 48, no. 1 (1979): 65–83.
Jensen, Richard Bach, *The Battle against Anarchist Terrorism: An International History, 1878–1934*, Cambridge: Cambridge University Press, 2014.
Jivani, Jamil, *Why Young Men: Rage, Race and the Crisis of Identity*, Toronto: HarperCollins, 2018.
Johnson, Robert, 'Command of the Army, Charles Gwynn and Imperial Policing: The British Doctrinal Approach to Internal Security in Palestine 1919–29', *Journal of Imperial and Commonwealth History* 43, no. 4 (2015): 570–89.
Jung, Dietrich, '"Islam as a Problem": Dutch Religious Politics in the East Indies', *Review of Religious Research* 51, no. 3 (2010): 288–301.
Kamra, Sukeshi, 'Law and Radical Rhetoric in British India: The 1897 Trial of Bal Gangadhar Tilak', *South Asia: Journal of South Asian Studies* 39, no. 3 (2016): 546–59.
Kapila, Shruti, 'Race Matters: Orientalism and Religion, India and Beyond c. 1770–1880', *Modern Asian Studies* 41, no. 3 (2007): 471–513.
Kaul, Chandrika, *Reporting the Raj: The British Press and India, c. 1880–1922*, Manchester: Manchester University Press, 2003.
Kaur, Raminder and William Mazzarella (eds.), *Censorship in South Asia: Cultural Regulation from Sedition to Seduction*, Bloomington: Indiana University Press, 2009.
Kenna, Shane, *War in the Shadows: The Irish-American Fenians Who Bombed Victorian Britain*, Newbridge: Merrion Press, 2013.
Khalili, Laleh, *Time in the Shadows: Confinement in Counterinsurgencies*, Stanford, CA: Stanford University Press, 2013.
Khan, Yasmin, 'Performing Peace: Gandhi's Assassination as a Critical Moment in the Consolidation of the Nehruvian State', *Modern Asian Studies* 45, no. 1 (2011): 57–80.
The Great Partition: The Making of India and Pakistan, New Haven, CT: Yale University Press, 2008.
Knepper, Paul, 'The Other Invisible Hand: Jews and Anarchists in London before the First World War', *Jewish History* 22 (2008): 295–315.
Kochi, Tarik, 'The Partisan: Carl Schmitt and Terrorism', *Law and Critique* 17, no. 3 (2006): 267–95.
Kolsky, Elizabeth, 'The Colonial Rule of Law and the Legal Regime of Exception: Frontier "Fanaticism" and State Violence in British India', *The American Historical Review* 120, no. 4 (2015): 1218–46.
Colonial Justice in British India: White Violence and the Rule of Law, Cambridge: Cambridge University Press, 2010.
Kunst, Jonas R., Lisa S. Myhren, and Ivuoma N. Onyeador, 'Simply Insane? Attributing Terrorism to Mental Illness (Versus Ideology) Affects Mental Representations of Race', *Criminal Justice and Behavior* 45, no. 12 (2018): 1888–1902.

Kuracina, William F., 'Sentiments and Patriotism: The Indian National Army, General Elections and the Congress's Appropriation of the INA Legacy', *Modern Asian Studies* 44, no. 4 (2010): 817–56.

Lahiri, Tarapada, *Rashbehari Bose: The Indomitable Revolutionary*, Calcutta: Anushilan Samiti, 1984.

Laidlaw, Zoe, 'Breaking Britannia's Bounds? Law, Settlers, and Space in Britain's Imperial Historiography', *Historical Journal* 55, no. 3 (2012): 807–30.

Lake, Marilyn and Henry Reynolds, *Drawing the Global Colour Line: White Men's Countries and the Challenge of Racial Equality*, Cambridge: Cambridge University Press, 2008.

Langan, Mark, *Neo-Colonialism and the Poverty of 'Development' in Africa*, Cham, Switzerland: Palgrave Macmillan, 2018.

Laushey, David M., *Bengal Terrorism and the Marxist Left: Aspects of Regional Nationalism in India, 1905–1942*, Calcutta: Firma K.L. Mukhopadhyay, 1975.

Laqueur, Walter, *A History of Terrorism*, New Brunswick, NJ: Transaction Publishers, 2001.

The New Terrorism: Fanaticism and the Arms of Mass Destruction, New York: Oxford University Press, 1999.

Laqueur, Walter and Christopher Wall, *The Future of Terrorism: ISIS, Al-Qaeda, and the Alt-Right*, New York: St. Martin's Press, 2018.

Laursen, Ole Birk, 'Anarchist Anti-Imperialism: Guy Aldred and the Indian Revolutionary Movement, 1909–14', *Journal of Imperial and Commonwealth History* 46, no. 2 (2018): 286–303.

Lausey, David M., *Bengal Terrorism and the Marxist Left: Aspects of Regional Nationalism in India, 1905–1942*, Calcutta: Firma K.L. Mukhopadhyay, 1975.

Layton, Simon, 'Hydras and Leviathans in the Indian Ocean World', *International Journal of Maritime History* 25, no. 2 (2013): 213–25.

'The "Moghul's Admiral": Angrian "Piracy" and the Rise of British Bombay', *Journal of Early Modern History* 17 (2013): 75–93.

'Discourses of Piracy in an Age of Revolutions', *Itinerario* 35, no. 2 (2011): 81–97.

The League of Nations in Retrospect: Proceedings of the Symposium, organized by the United Nations Library and the Graduate Institute of International Studies, 6–9 November 1980 (Berlin: Walter de Gruyter, 1983).

Legg, Stephen, 'An International Anomaly?: Sovereignty, the League of Nations and India's Princely Geographies', *Journal of Historical Geography* 43 (2014): 96–110.

(ed.), *Spatiality, Sovereignty and Carl Schmitt: Geographies of the Nomos*, London: Routledge, 2011.

Lindqvist, Sven, *'Exterminate All the Brutes': One Man's Odyssey into the Heart of Darkness and the Origins of European Genocide*, New York: The New Press, 1996.

Littlewood, Roland, *Pathologies of the West: An Anthropology of Mental Illness in Europe and America*, Ithaca, NY: Cornell University Press, 2002.

Lloyd, Tom, 'Thuggee, Marginality and the State Effect in Colonial India, circa 1770–1840', *The Indian Economic and Social History Review* 45, no. 2 (2008): 201–37.

'Acting in the "Theatre of Anarchy": The "Anti-Thug Campaign" and Elaborations of Colonial Rule in Early Nineteenth-Century India', *Edinburgh Papers in South Asian Studies* 19 (2006): 1–50.

Macfie, Alexander Lyon, 'Thuggee: An Orientalist Construction?', *Rethinking History* 12, no. 3 (2008): 383–97.

Maclean, Kama, *A Revolutionary History of Interwar India: Violence, Image, Voice and Text*, London: Hurst & Company, 2015.

Maclean, Kama and Daniel Elam, 'Reading Revolutionaries: Texts, Acts, and Afterlives of Political Action in Late Colonial South Asia', *Postcolonial Studies* 16, no. 2 (2013): 113–23.

Macmillan, Margaret, *Peacemakers: The Paris Conference of 1919 and Its Attempt to End War*, London: John Murray, 2001.

Major, Andrew, 'State and Criminal Tribes in Colonial Punjab: Surveillance, Control and Reclamation of the "Dangerous Classes"', *Modern Asian Studies* 33, no. 3 (1999): 657–88.

Manela, Erez, *The Wilsonian Moment: Self-Determination and the International Origins of Anticolonial Nationalism*, Oxford: Oxford University Press, 2009.

Manjapra, Kris, *Age of Entanglement: German and Indian Intellectuals across Empire*, Cambridge, MA: Harvard University Press, 2014.

'Knowledgeable Internationalism and the Swadeshi Movement, 1903–1921', *Economic & Political Weekly* 47, no. 42 (2012): 53–62.

M.N. Roy: Marxism and Colonial Cosmopolitanism, Delhi: Routledge, 2010.

Marriott, John, *The Other Empire: Metropolis, India and Progress in the Colonial Imagination*, Manchester: Manchester University Press, 2003.

Marshall, P. J., *Bengal: The British Bridgehead: Eastern India, 1740–1828*, New York: Cambridge University Press, 1987.

Matthews, Weldon, *Confronting an Empire, Constructing a Nation: Arab Nationalists and Popular Politics in Mandate Palestine*, London: I.B. Tauris, 2006.

Mawani, Renisa, *Across Oceans of Law: The Komagata Maru and Jurisdiction in the Time of Empire*, Durham, NC: Duke University Press, 2018.

Mayer, Arno, *Wilson vs. Lenin: Political Origins of the New Diplomacy, 1917–1918*, Cleveland, OH: World Publishers Co., 1964.

Mazower, Mark, *Governing the World: The History of an Idea*, London: Allen Lane, 2012.

Mazzetti, Mark, *The Way of the Knife: The CIA, a Secret Army, and a War at the Ends of the Earth*, New York: Penguin Books, 2014.

Mbembe, Achille, 'Necropolitics', *Public Culture* 15, no. 1 (2003): 11–40.

McClintock, Anne, *Imperial Leather: Race, Gender and Sexuality in the Colonial Contest*, New York: Routledge, 1995.

McClure, Alastair, 'Sovereignty, Law and the Politics of Forgiveness in Colonial India, 1858–1903', *Comparative Studies of South Asia, Africa and the Middle East* 38, no. 3 (2018): 385–401.

McMahon, Paul, *British Spies and Irish Rebels: British Intelligence and Ireland, 1916–1945*, Woodbridge: Boydell Press, 2008.

McQuade, Joseph, 'The New Asia of Rash Behari Bose: India, Japan, and the Limits of International, 1912–1945', *Journal of World History* 27, no. 4 (2016): 641–67.

'Political Discourse, Political Violence: Fenians, Nihilists, and the Revolutionaries of Bengal, 1907–1925', *Sikh Formations* 10, no. 1 (2014): 43–55.

Mehta, Uday, *Liberalism and Empire: A Study in Nineteenth Century British Liberal Thought*, Chicago: University of Chicago Press, 1999.

Melchiori, Barbara, *Terrorism in the Late Victorian Novel*, London: Croom Helm, 1985.

Menon, Kalvani Devaki, '"Security", Home, and Belonging in Contemporary India: Old Delhi as a Muslim Place', *Etnofoor* 27, no. 2 (2015): 113–31.

Metcalf, Thomas, *Imperial Connections: India in the Indian Ocean Arena, 1860–1920*, Berkeley: University of California Press, 2007.

Ideologies of the Raj, Cambridge: Cambridge University Press, 1995.

Miller, Martin, *The Foundations of Modern Terrorism*, Cambridge: Cambridge University Press, 2013.

Mishra, Pankaj, *From the Ruins of Empire: The Intellectuals Who Remade Asia*, New York: Farrar, Straus and Giroux, 2012.

Moffat, Chris, 'Bhagat Singh's Corpse', *South Asia: Journal of South Asian Studies* 39, no. 3 (2016): 644–61.

Moyn, Samuel, *The Last Utopia: Human Rights in History*, Cambridge, MA: Belknap Press of Harvard University Press, 2010.

Mufti, Aamir, *Enlightenment in the Colony: The Jewish Question and the Crisis of Postcolonial Culture*, Princeton, NJ: Princeton University Press, 2007.

Mukerjee, Madhusree, *Churchill's Secret War: The British Empire and the Ravaging of India during World War II*, New York: Basic Books, 2010.

Mulvagh, Conor, *Irish Days, Indian Memories: V.V. Giri and Indian Law Students at University College Dublin*, Dublin: Irish Academic Press, 2016.

Muppidi, Himadeep, *The Colonial Signs of International Relations*, New York: Columbia University Press, 2012.

Nair, Janaki, *Mysore Modern: Rethinking the Region under Princely Rule*, Minneapolis: University of Minnesota Press, 2011.

Nakajima, Takeshi, *Bose of Nakamuraya: An Indian Revolutionary in Japan*, New Delhi: Promilla, 2009.

Nietzsche, Friedrich, *On the Genealogy of Morals and Ecce Homo*, New York: Vintage Books, 1989.

ni Fhlathuin, Maire, 'The Campaign against Thugs in the Bengal Press of the 1830s', *Victorian Periodicals Review* 37, no. 2 (2004): 124–40.

Norris, Jacob, *Land of Progress: Palestine in the Age of Colonial Development, 1905–1948*, Oxford: Oxford University Press, 2013.

'Repression and Rebellion: Britain's Response to the Arab Revolt in Palestine of 1936–39', *The Journal of Imperial and Commonwealth History* 36, no. 1 (2008): 25–45.

Northedge, F. S., *The League of Nations*, Leicester: Leicester University Press, 1986.

Oddie, G. A., 'Hook-Swinging and Popular Religion in South India during the Nineteenth Century', *Indian Economic & Social History Review* 23, no. 1 (1986): 93–106.

Odysseos, Louiza and Fabio Petito (eds.), *The International Political Thought of Carl Schmitt: Terror, Liberal War and the Crisis of Global Order*, London: Routledge, 2007.

Omissi, David (ed.), *Indian Voices of the Great War: Soldiers' Letters, 1914–18*, London: Macmillan Press, 1999.

Osha, Atsuti (ed.), *In the Name of the Battle against Piracy: Ideas and Practices in State Monopoly of Maritime Violence in Europe and Asia in the Period of Transition*, Leiden: Brill, 2018.

Osterhammel, Jürgen, *Unfabling the East: The Enlightenment's Encounter with Asia*, Princeton, NJ: Princeton University Press, 2018.

Owen, Nicholas, 'The Soft Heart of the British Empire: Indian Radicals in Edwardian London', *Past & Present* 220, no. 1 (2013): 143–84.

The British Left and India: Metropolitan Anti-imperialism, 1885–1947, Oxford: Oxford University Press, 2008.

'The Cripps Mission of 1942: A Reinterpretation', *The Journal of Imperial and Commonwealth History* 30, no. 1 (2002): 61–98.

Padamsee, Alex, *Representations of Indian Muslims in British Colonial Discourse*, New York: Palgrave Macmillan, 2005.

Pape, Robert A., *Dying to Win: The Strategic Logic of Suicide Terrorism*, New York: Random House Trade Paperbacks, 2006.

Patel, Hitendra, *Khudiram Bose: Revolutionary Extraordinaire*, Delhi: Publications Division Ministry of Information and Broadcasting Government of India, 2008.

Pati, Biswamoy (ed.), *The Great Rebellion of 1857 in India: Exploring Transgressions, Contests and Diversities*, London: Routledge, 2010.

Pati, Budheswar, *India and the First World War*, New Delhi: Atlantic Publishers and Distributors, 1996.

Peckham, Robert (ed.), *Empires of Panic: Epidemics and Colonial Anxieties*, Hong Kong: Hong Kong University Press, 2015.

Pedersen, Susan, *The Guardians: The League of Nations and the Crisis of Empire*, Oxford: Oxford University Press, 2015.

'Back to the League of Nations', *The American Historical Review* 11, no. 4 (2007): 1091–1117.

Peers, Douglas M., *Between Mars and Mammon: Colonial Armies and the Garrison State in Early Nineteenth-Century India*, London: Tauris Academic Studies, 1995.

Pincince, John, 'De-centering Carl Schmitt: The Colonial State of Exception and the Criminalization of the Political in British India, 1905–1920', *Politica Comun* 5 (2014).

Plowman, Matthew Erin, 'Irish Republicans and the Indo-German Conspiracy of World War I', *New Hibernia Review* 7, no. 3 (2003): 80–105.

Popplewell, Richard, *Intelligence and Imperial Defence: British Intelligence and the Defence of the Indian Empire, 1904–1924*, London: Frank Cass, 1995.

Price, John, 'Canada, White Supremacy, and the Twinnings of Empire', *International Journal* 64, no. 4 (2013): 628–38.

Raghavan, Srinath, *India's War: World War II and the Making of Modern South Asia*, New York: Basic Books, 2016.

Raja, Masood Ashraf, 'The Indian Rebellion of 1857 and Mirza Ghalib's Narrative of Survival', *Prose Studies* 31, no. 1 (2009): 40–54.
Ramnath, Maia, *Haj to Utopia: How the Ghadar Movement Charted Global Radicalism and Attempted to Overthrow the British Empire*, Berkeley: University of California Press, 2011.
Ramusack, Barbara, *The Princes of India in the Twilight of Empire: Dissolution of a Patron-Client System, 1914–1939*, Columbus: Ohio State University Press, 1978.
Rangarajan, Padma, 'Thug Life: Confession, Subjectivity, Sovereignty', *ELH* 84, no. 4 (2017): 105–128.
Rapoport, David C., 'Fear and Trembling: Terrorism in Three Religious Traditions', *The American Political Science Review* 78, no. 3 (1984): 658–77.
Read, Anthony, *The World on Fire: 1919 and the Battle with Bolshevism*, New York: W.W. Norton, 2008.
Rediker, Marcus, *Villains of All Nations: Atlantic Piracy in the Golden Age*, Boston: Beacon Press, 2004.
Reinkowski, Maurus and Gregor Thum (eds.), *Helpless Imperialists: Imperial Failure, Fear and Radicalization*, Gottingen: Vandenhoeck and Ruprecht, 2013.
Richard, Anne-Isabelle, 'Competition and Complementarity: Civil Society Networks and the Question of Decentralizing the League of Nations', *Journal of Global History* 7, no. 2 (2012): 233–56.
Risso, Patricia, 'Cross-Cultural Perceptions of Piracy: Maritime Violence in the Western Indian Ocean and Persian Gulf Region during a Long Eighteenth Century', *Journal of World History* 12, no. 2 (2001): 293–319.
Robb, Peter (ed.), *The Concept of Race in South Asia*, Oxford: Oxford University Press, 1995.
Rosenfeld, Jean E., *Terrorism, Identity and Legitimacy: The Four Waves Theory and Political Violence*, New York: Routledge, 2011.
Rosselli, John, 'The Self-Image of Effeteness: Physical Education and Nationalism in Nineteenth-Century Bengal', *Past and Present* 88 (1980): 121–48.
Roque, Ricardo, 'The Razor's Edge: Portuguese Imperial Vulnerability in Colonial Moxico, Angola', *The International Journal of African Historical Studies* 36, no. 1 (2003): 105–24.
Roque, Ricardo and Kim Wagner, *Engaging Colonial Knowledge: Reading European Archives in World History*, Basingstoke: Palgrave Macmillan, 2012.
Roy, Anjali Gera, *Imperialism and Sikh Migration: The Komagata Maru Incident*, Abingdon: Routledge, 2018.
Roy, Parama, *Indian Traffic: Identities in Question in Colonial and Postcolonial India*, Berkeley: University of California Press, 1998.
Said, Edward, *Covering Islam: How the Media and the Experts Determine How We See the Rest of the World*, New York: Vintage Books, 1997.
Orientalism, New York: Vintage Books, 1979.
Sanyal, Shukla, *Revolutionary Pamphlets, Propaganda and Political Culture in Colonial Bengal*, Cambridge: Cambridge University Press, 2014.
Sarkar, Sumit, *The Swadeshi Movement in Bengal, 1903–1908*, New Delhi: People's Publishing House, 1973.

Satia, Priya, 'Drones: A History from the British Middle East', *Humanity: An International Journal of Human Rights, Humanitarianism, and Development* 5, no. 1 (2014): 1–31.

Spies in Arabia: The Great War and the Cultural Foundations of Britain's Covert Empire in the Middle East, Oxford: Oxford University Press, 2008.

Saul, Ben, 'The Legal Response of the League of Nations to Terrorism', *Journal of International Criminal Justice* 4, no. 1 (2006): 78–102.

Savage, John, '"Black Magic" and White Terror: Slave Poisoning and Colonial Society in Early 19th Century Martinique', *Journal of Social History*, 40, no. 3 (2007): 635–62.

Schmid, Alex and Jany de Graaf, *Violence as Communication: Insurgent Terrorism and the Western News Media*, London: Sage, 1982.

Schmitt, Carl, *Legality and Legitimacy*, Durham, NC: Duke University Press, 2004.

The Nomos of the Earth in the International Law of the Jus Publicum Europeaum, New York: Telos, 2003.

Political Theology: Four Chapters on the Concept of Sovereignty, trans. George Schwab. Chicago: University of Chicago Press, 1985.

Scott, James C., *The Art of Not Being Governed: An Anarchist History of Upland Southeast Asia*, New Haven, CT: Yale University Press, 2009.

Weapons of the Weak: Everyday Forms of Peasant Resistance, New Haven, CT: Yale University Press, 1985.

Sen, Amartya, *Poverty and Famines: An Essay on Entitlement and Deprivation*, Oxford: Clarendon Press; New York: Oxford University Press, 1983.

Sen, Satadru, 'Contexts, Representation and the Colonized Convict: Maulana Thanesari in the Andaman Islands', *Crime, History & Societies* 8, no. 2 (2004): 117–39.

Sengupta, Nitish K., *Land of Two Rivers: A History of Bengal from the Mahabharata to Mujib*, New Delhi: Penguin Books India, 2011.

Silvestri, Michael, *Policing 'Bengali Terrorism' in India and the World: Imperial Intelligence and Revolutionary Nationalism, 1905–1939*, New York: Palgrave Macmillan, 2019.

Ireland and India: Nationalism, Empire and Memory, New York: Palgrave Macmillan, 2009.

'The Bomb, *Bhadralok, Bhagavad Gita*, and Dan Breen: Terrorism in Bengal and Its Relation to the European Experience', *Terrorism and Political Violence* 21, no. 1 (2009): 1–27.

'"An Irishman Is Specially Suited to Be a Policeman": Sir Charles Tegart & Revolutionary Terrorism in Bengal', *History Ireland* 8, no. 4(2000): 40–4.

Simpson, A. W. Brian, *Human Rights and the End of Empire: Britain and the Genesis of the European Convention*, New York: Oxford University Press, 2004.

Singh, Dharmit, *Lord Linlithgow in India, 1936–1943*, Jalandhar: ABS Publications, 2005.

Singh, Harkirat, *The INA Trial and the Raj*, New Delhi: Atlantic Publishers and Distributors, 2003.

Singh, Harleen, *The Rani of Jhansi: Gender, History, and Fable in India*, Cambridge: Cambridge University Press, 2014.

Singh, Upinder, *Political Violence in Ancient India*, Cambridge, MA: Harvard University Press, 2017.

Singha, Radhika, 'Punished by Surveillance: Policing "Dangerousness" in Colonial India, 1872–1918', *Modern Asian Studies* 49, no. 2 (2015): 241–69.

'The Great War and a "Proper" Passport for the Colony: Border-Crossing in British India, c.1882–1922', *Indian Economic and Social History Review* 50, no. 3 (2013): 289–315.

A Despotism of Law: Crime and Justice in Early Colonial India, New Delhi: Oxford University Press, 1998.

Sinha, Mrinalini, *Colonial Masculinity: The 'Manly Englishman' and the 'Effeminate Bengali' in the Late Nineteenth Century*, Manchester: Manchester University Press, 1995.

Sloan, Geoff, 'The British State and the Irish Rebellion of 1916: An Intelligence Failure or a Failure of Response?', *Intelligence and National Security* 28, no. 4 (2013): 453–94.

Slomp, Gabriella, *Carl Schmitt and the Politics of Hostility, Violence and Terror*, Basingstoke: Palgrave Macmillan, 2009.

Sluga, Glenda, *Internationalism in the Age of Nationalism*, Philadelphia: University of Pennsylvania Press, 2013.

Sluga, Glenda and Patricia Clavin (eds.), *Internationalisms: A Twentieth-Century History*, Cambridge: Cambridge University Press, 2016.

Sohi, Seema, *Echoes of Mutiny: Race, Surveillance and Indian Anticolonialism in North America*, New York: Oxford University Press, 2014.

'Race, Surveillance, and Indian Anticolonialism in the Transnational Western U.S.-Canadian Borderlands', *The Journal of American History* 49, no. 2 (2011): 420–36.

Stampnitzky, Lisa, *Disciplining Terror: How Experts Invented 'Terrorism'*, Cambridge: Cambridge University Press, 2013.

Stephens, Julia, 'The Phantom Wahhabi: Liberalism and the Muslim Fanatic in Mid-Victorian India', *Modern Asian Studies* 47, no. 1 (2013): 22–52.

Stern, Philip J., *The Company-State: Corporate Sovereignty and the Early Modern Foundation of the British Empire in India*, New York: Oxford University Press, 2011.

Stoler, Ann, *Duress: Imperial Durabilities in Our Times*, Durham, NC: Duke University Press, 2016.

Along the Archival Grain: Epistemic Anxieties and Colonial Commonsense. Princeton, NJ: Princeton University Press, 2009.

'Colonial Archives and the Arts of Governance', *Archival Science* 2 (2002): 87–109.

Stolte, Carolien, '"Enough of the Great Napoleons!": Raja Mahendra Pratap's Pan-Asian Projects (1929–1939)', *Modern Asian Studies* 46, no. 2 (2012): 403–23.

Stolte, Carolien and Harald Fischer-Tiné, 'Imagining Asia in India: Nationalism and Internationalism (ca. 1905–1940)', *Comparative Studies in Society and History* 54, no. 1 (2012): 65–92.

Streets, Heather, *Martial Races: The Military, Race and Masculinity in British Imperial Culture, 1857–1914*, Manchester: Manchester University Press, 2004.

Streets-Salter, Heather, *World War One in Southeast Asia: Colonialism and Anticolonialism in an Era of Global Conflict*, Cambridge: Cambridge University Press, 2017.

'The Local Was Global: The Singapore Mutiny of 1915', *Journal of World History* 24, no. 3 (2013): 539–76.

Studer, Brigitte, *The Transnational World of the Cominternians*, Houndmills: Palgrave Macmillan, 2015.

Subramanian, Lakshmi, *The Sovereign and the Pirate: Ordering Maritime Subjects in India's Western Littoral*, New Delhi: Oxford University Press, 2016.

Suzuki, Hideaki (ed.), *'Abolitions' as a Global Experience*, Singapore: National University of Singapore Press, 2016.

Taussig, Michael, *Mimesis and Alterity: A Particular History of the Senses*, New York: Routledge, 1993.

Thomas, Martin, *Fight or Flight: Britain, France, and Their Roads from Empire*, Oxford: Oxford University Press, 2014.

Violence and Colonial Order: Police, Workers and Protest in the European Colonial Empires, 1918–1940, Cambridge: Cambridge University Press, 2012.

Thompson, E. P., *Whigs and Hunters: The Origin of the Black Act*, London: Allen Lane, 1975.

Thorup, Mikkel, *An Intellectual History of Terror: War, Violence, and the State*, New York: Routledge, 2010.

Thwin, Maitrii Aung, *The Return of the Galon King: History, Law, and Rebellion in Colonial Burma*, Athens: Ohio University Press, 2011.

Tickell, Alex, *Terrorism, Insurgency and Indian-English Literature, 1830–1947*, London: Routledge, 2012.

Torpey, John, *The Invention of the Passport: Surveillance, Citizenship, and the State*, Cambridge: Cambridge University Press, 2000.

Trivedi, Lisa, 'Visually Mapping the "Nation": Swadeshi Politics in Nationalist India, 1920– 1930', *The Journal of African Studies* 62, no. 1 (2003): 11–41.

Untarman, Katherine, *Uncle Sam's Policemen: The Pursuit of Fugitives across Borders*, Cambridge, MA: Harvard University Press, 2015.

Urban, Hugh, *Tantra: Sex, Secrecy, Politics and Power in the Study of Religion*, Berkeley: University of California Press, 2003.

Varma, Pavan, *Ghalib: The Man, The Times*, New Delhi: Penguin Books India, 2008.

Vartavarias, Mesrob, 'Pacification and Patronage in the Maratha Deccan, 1803–1818', *Modern Asian Studies* 50, no. 6 (2016): 1749–91.

Wagner, Kim, *Amritsar 1919: An Empire of Fear and the Making of a Massacre*, New Haven, CT: Yale University Press, 2019.

'Savage Warfare: Violence and the Rule of Colonial Difference in Early British Counterinsurgency', *History Workshop Journal* 85, no. 1 (2018): 217–37.

The Skull of Alum Bheg: The Life and Death of a Rebel of 1857, London: Hurst & Company, 2017.

Rumours and Rebels: A New History of the Indian Uprising of 1857, Oxford: Peter Lang, 2017.

'"Calculated to Strike Terror": The Amritsar Massacre and the Spectacle of Colonial Violence', *Past and Present* 233, no. 1 (2016): 185–225.

'"Thugs and Assassins": "New Terrorism" and the Resurrection of Colonial Knowledge', in Carola Dietze and Claudia Verhoeven (eds.), *The Oxford Handbook of the History of Terrorism*, Oxford: Oxford University Press, 2016.

'"Treading upon Fires": The "Mutiny"-Motif and Colonial Anxieties in British India', *Past & Present* 218, no. 1 (2013): 159–97.

'Confessions of a Skull: Phrenology and Colonial Knowledge in Early Nineteenth-Century India', *History Workshop Journal* 69 (2010): 27–51.

(ed.), *Stranglers & Bandits: A Historical Anthology*, New Delhi: Oxford University Press, 2009.

Thuggee: Banditry and the British in Early Nineteenth-Century India, New York: Palgrave Macmillan, 2007.

Walters, F. P., *A History of the League of Nations*, New York: Oxford University Press, 1952.

Walton, Calder, *Empire of Secrets: British Intelligence, the Cold War and the Twilight of Empire*, London: HarperCollins, 2013.

Williamson, Thomas, 'Communicating Amok in Malaysia', *Identities: Global Studies in Culture and Power* 14 (2007): 341–5.

Wilson, Jon, *The Chaos of Empire: The British Raj and the Conquest of India*, New York: PublicAffairs, 2016.

Wolfers, Alex, 'Born Like Krishna in the Prison House: Revolutionary Asceticism in the Political Ashram of Aurobindo Ghose', *South Asia: Journal of South Asian Studies* 39, no. 3 (2016): 525–45.

van Woerkens, Martine, *The Strangled Traveler: Colonial Imaginings and the Thugs of India*, Chicago: University of Chicago Press, 2002.

von Tunzelmann, Alex, *Indian Summer: The Secret History of the End of an Empire*, New York: Henry Holt, 2007.

Yang, Anand (ed.), *Crime and Criminality in British India*, Tucson: University of Arizona Press, 1985.

Zizek, Slavoj, *On Violence: Six Sideways Reflections*, London: Profile Books, 2009.

Index

CPSIA information can be obtained
at www.ICGtesting.com
Printed in the USA
LVHW081940071120
671042LV00006B/102